MONTROSE

*Sedulo curavi humanas actiones non ridere,
non lugere, neque detestari, sed intelligere.*
—SPINOZA

JOHN BUCHAN

MONTROSE

HODDER AND STOUGHTON
ST. PAUL'S HOUSE, LONDON, E.C.4

First printed . . . 1928
First edition in this form . 1938
Reprinted 1941
Reprinted 1949

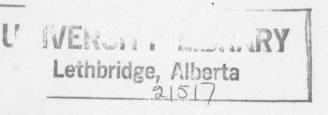
*Made and Printed in Great Britain for Hodder and Stoughton Limited
by Northumberland Press Limited, Gateshead upon Tyne*

FRATRI DILECTISSIMO

W. H. B.

When we were little, wandering boys,
  And every hill was blue and high,
On ballad ways and martial joys
  We fed our fancies, you and I.
With Bruce we crouched in bracken shade,
  With Douglas charged the Paynim foes;
And oft in moorland noons I played
  Colkitto to your grave Montrose.

The obliterating seasons flow—
  They cannot kill our boyish game.
Though creeds may change and kings may go,
  Yet burns undimmed the ancient flame.
While young men in their pride make haste
  The wrong to right, the bond to free,
And plant a garden in the waste,
  Still rides our Scottish chivalry.

Another end had held your dream—
  To die fulfilled of hope and might,
To pass in one swift, rapturous gleam
  From mortal to immortal light.
But through long hours of labouring breath
  You watched the world grow small and far,
And met the constant eyes of Death
  And haply knew how kind they are.

One boon the Fates relenting gave.
  Not where the scented hill-wind blows
From cedar thickets lies your grave,
  Nor 'mid the steep Himálayan snows.
Night calls the stragglers to the nest,
  And at long last 'tis home indeed
For your far-wandering feet to rest
  For ever by the crooks of Tweed.

In perfect honour, perfect truth,
  And gentleness to all mankind,
You trod the golden paths of youth,
  Then left the world and youth behind.
Ah no! 'Tis we who fade and fail—
  And you, from Time's slow torments free,
Shall pass from strength to strength, and scale
  The steeps of immortality.

Dear heart, in that serener air,
  If blessed souls may backward gaze,
Some slender nook of memory spare
  For our old happy moorland days.
I sit alone, and musing fills
  My breast with pain that shall not die,
Till once again o'er greener hills
  We ride together, you and I.

PREFACE

IN SEPTEMBER 1913 I PUBLISHED A SHORT SKETCH OF MON-
trose, which dealt chiefly with his campaigns. The book
went out of print very soon, and it was not reissued, because I cherished the hope of making it the basis of a larger
work, in which the background of seventeenth-century
politics and religion should be more fully portrayed. I also
felt that many of the judgments in the sketch were exaggerated and hasty. During the last fifteen years I have been
collecting material for the understanding of a career which
must rank among the marvels of our history, and of a
mind and character which seem to me in a high degree
worthy of the attention of the modern reader. The manuscript sources have already been diligently explored by
others, and I have been unable to glean from them much
that is new; but I have attempted to supplement them by
a study of the voluminous pamphlet literature of the time.
My aim has been to present a great figure in its appropriate
setting. In a domain, where the dust of controversy has
not yet been laid, I cannot hope to find for my views
universal acceptance, but they have not been reached without an earnest attempt to discover the truth.

J.B.

ELSFIELD MANOR, OXON,
June, 1928.

MONTROSE

(from an engraving by A. Matham, forming the frontispiece to the 1647 Hague translation of Wishart)

CONTENTS

A*

CONTENTS

MAPS

11

ABBREVIATIONS

A. P. S.	*Acts of the Parliaments of Scotland.* 12 vols., 1834-75.
Army of the Covenant	*Papers relating to the Army of the Solemn League and Covenant (1643-47).* 2 vols. (S. H. S.), 1917.
Baillie	*Letters and Journals of the Rev. Robert Baillie.* 3 vols., 1841.
Balfour	*Historical Works (Annales) of Sir James Balfour.* 4 vols., 1824-25.
Burnet, *Mem. of the Hamiltons*	*The Memoirs of James and William, Dukes of Hamilton,* by Gilbert Burnet, 1677.
Calderwood	*History of the Kirk of Scotland (1524-1625),* by David Calderwood (Wodrow Society). 8 vols., 1842-59.
Cal. S. P., Dom.	*Calendar of State Papers, Domestic.*
Clanranald MSS.	The narrative of Alasdair Macdonald's campaign, by a shanachie of Clanranald in the "Black Book of Clanranald." It is translated in Cameron's *Reliquiæ Celticæ,* II., 138-209 (Inverness, 1894), and the Gaelic text has been edited by Joseph Lloyd, with an historical introduction by Professor Eoin McNeill, in *Alasdair Mac Colla* (Dublin, 1914).
Clarendon, *Hist.*	*History of the Rebellion,* by Edward, Earl of Clarendon (ed. Macray), 1888.
Firth	*Cromwell's Army,* by Sir C. H. Firth, 1902.
Forbes Leith	*Memoirs of Scottish Catholics during the Seventeenth and Eighteenth Centuries,* by William Forbes Leith, S.J. 2 vols., 1909.
Gardiner	*History of England,* by S. R. Gardiner. 10 vols., 1886.

13

Gardiner, *Civil War* . . .	*History of the Great Civil War*, by S. R. Gardiner. 4 vols., 1910.
Gordon of Rothiemay	*History of Scots Affairs*, by James Gordon (Spalding Club). 3 vols., 1841.
Gordon of Ruthven . . .	*Britane's Distemper*, by Patrick Gordon (Spalding Club), 1844.
Gordon of Sallagh . . .	Continuation (by Gilbert Gordon of Sallagh) of *A History of the Earldom of Sutherland*, by Sir Robert Gordon of Gordonstoun, 1813.
Guthry	*Memoirs of Henry Guthry, Bishop of Dunkeld*. 2nd edition, Glasgow, 1747.
Gwynne . . .	*Military Memoirs of the Great Civil War*, by John Gwynne (ed. Sir W. Scott), 1822.
Hist. MSS. Comm. . . .	*Reports of the Royal Commission on Historical Manuscripts.*
Lang	*History of Scotland*, by Andrew Lang. 4 vols., 1900-6.
M. & S.	Editorial matter in edition of Wishart by Murdoch and Simpson.
Mem. of M. . . .	*Memorials of Montrose and his Times*, ed. by Mark Napier (Maitland Club). 2 vols., 1848-50.
Monteith	*The History of the Troubles of Great Britain*, etc., by Robert Monteith of Salmonet. Eng. trans., 1738. The French original, *Histoire des Troubles de la Grande Bretagne*, was published in Paris in 1661.
Napier.	*Memoirs of the Marquis of Montrose*, by Mark Napier. 2 vols., 1856.
P.C.R.	*Register of the Privy Council of Scotland.* 2nd series, 8 vols., 1899-1908.
Rothes . . .	*Relation of Proceedings concerning the Affairs of the Kirk of Scotland*, by John, Earl of Rothes (Bannatyne Club), 1830.
Row . .	*History of the Kirk of Scotland (1558-1637)*, by John Row (Wodrow Society), 1842.
Rushworth . . .	*Historical Collections of Private Passages of State*, etc., by John Rushworth. 8 vols., London, 1721.

S.H.R.	*Scottish Historical Review.*
S.H.S.	Scottish History Society.
Spalding	*The History of the Troubles and Memorable Transactions in Scotland and England (1624-45), by John Spalding (Bannatyne Club). 2 vols., 1828.*
Spottiswoode . .	*History of the Church and State of Scotland (203-1625), by John Spottiswoode (Spottiswoode Society). 3 vols., 1851.*
Wardlaw MS. . . .	*Chronicles of the Frasers: the Wardlaw MS., by James Fraser (S. H. S.), 1905.*
Wariston	*Diary of Sir Archibald Johnston of Wariston, Vol. I., 1632-39 (S. H. S.), 1911; Vol. II., 1650-54, 1919.*
Wigton Papers . . .	" Documents from the Archives of the Earls of Wigton, 1520-1650," in *Miscellany of the Maitland Club,* Vol. II., 1840.
Wishart .	*The Memoirs of James, Marquis of Montrose, by the Rev. George Wishart, edited by Alexander Murdoch and H. F. Morland Simpson, 1893. [Wishart's narrative is referred to by its chapters, and when a page is indicated the reference is to the Latin text in this edition.]*

THE EARLY SEVENTEENTH CENTURY

IN A FAMOUS LETTER KEATS HAS EXPOUNDED LIFE UNDER THE similitude of Chambers. There is first the Thoughtless Chamber, when man lives only for sensation; then comes the Chamber of Maiden Thought, when he consciously rejoices in the world of sense, and from this happy illumination acquires insight into the human heart; thence open many doors—" but all dark, all leading to dark passages." The simile applies not only to individual experience, but to the corporate life of peoples. There come epochs when a nation seems to move from the sun into the twilight, when the free ardour of youth is crippled by hesitations, when the eyes turn inward and instinct gives place to questioning.

Such a period commonly follows an age of confidence and exuberant creation. We can see the shadows beginning to lengthen in the early years of Elizabeth's successor, and they do not lift till the garish dawn of the Restoration. It is dangerous to generalize about an epoch, but the first half of the seventeenth century has a character so distinct that it is permissible to separate certain elements in its intellectual atmosphere, which affected the minds of all who dwelt in it, whatever their creeds or parties. Whether we study it in the record of its campaigns and parliaments, or in the careers of its protagonists, or in the books of its great writers, three facts are patent in contrast with its predecessor.

" Is not this world a catholic kind of place? " Carlyle has written. " The Puritan gospel and Shakespeare's plays: such a pair of facts I have rarely seen saved out of one chimerical generation." The greatness of the Elizabethan age was that it was catholic; that is, a number of potent, and usually conflicting, forces were held for a brief season in equilibrium. The Reformation had broken certain seals of thought, but it had not destroyed the integrity of the

17

Church. The Middle Ages, in the monarchy and in much of the law and custom of the people, co-existed with the new learning and the adventurous temper of the Renaissance. England could conquer strange worlds and yet maintain intact her ancient domestic life. The national mood was one of confidence and ardour, so intent upon present duties and enjoyments that it could permit the latent antagonisms to slumber. But in the first decade of the seventeenth century the mutterings in sleep became a restless awaking. The monarchy, when the great figure of Elizabeth passed, was seen to be a mediæval anomaly, and prerogatives hitherto unchallenged were soon a matter of hot debate. The ecclesiastical compromise which created the Anglican Church found many critics, and even those who accepted the fact were at odds about the theory. Sanctions, which had seemed imperishable, began to tilt and crack. The old world was crumbling, and there was no unanimity about the new.

Following upon this loss of harmony in institutions came a change in the national mood, which may be described, perhaps, as a failure of nerve. The forthright enjoying temper of the Elizabethans had gone; the world was no longer so simple and so spacious; the stage had become full of questioning Hamlets. It is a mood familiar to students of classical antiquity, and may be found in high relief during the first centuries of our era. The weakening of the social fabric, and consequently of the protective power of society, increases the strain on the personality. The hopefulness of youth is succeeded by a sad acquiescence, if not by despondency; the eye looks inward; the soul is disillusioned with the world, and seeks refuge elsewhere. It is the *preparatio evangelica*, for it turns the mind to God. In such a mood religion comes to birth, for the worldliness of youth rejoicing to run its course is exchanged for the spirituality of those who find here no continuing city. Life seems no longer a thing to be shaped by man's endeavour, and in every creed, from the predestination of the Calvinist to the mystical Platonism of the scholar, it is conceived as a puppet-play moved by the hand of Omnipotence. Metaphysic has broken into a secure world, and with it have come a sense of sin, a constant dwelling upon death, a haunting consciousness of eternity.

Something of this temper soon became dominant in the land. Robust spirits might reject it and recover the pagan standpoint; wise men might struggle through it to certainty and peace; but the shadow of it was universal, even in the defiance of the pagan. There was everywhere a quickening and intensifying of certain spiritual emotions, a sense of man's littleness and dependence upon the unseen, a movement away from humanism towards mysticism, a clouding of horizons which had once been so bright and clear. The congregations which listened to Donne's analysis of sin and his pictures of the " various and vagabond heart of the sinner " thronged to St. Paul's because the preacher was in tune with their own thoughts. Death was so much with them that they found comfort in envisaging its terrors. There was satisfaction in the belittling of life: " We have a winding-sheet in our mother's womb, which groweth with us from our conception, and we come into the world wound up in that winding-sheet, for we come to seek a grave."[1] The unthinkableness of eternity hag-rode their imagination. " Methusalem with all his hundreds of years was but a mushroom of a night's growth to this Day, and all the four Monarchies with all their thousands of years, and all the powerful Kings and all the beautiful Queens of this world, were but as a bed of flowers, some gathered at six, some at seven, some at eight, all in one morning, in respect of this Day."[2]

A consequence of such a mood was that men believed, as in the days of St. Cyprian, that the youth of the world had gone, and that they were living in its old age. The new science, the new astronomy, assisted the mood by breaking down the old comfortable, concentric universe. " There prevailed in his (Milton's) time an opinion that the world was in its decay, and that we have had the misfortune to be produced in the decrepitude of Nature. It was suspected that the whole creation languished, that neither trees nor animals had the height or bulk of their predecessors, and that everything was daily sinking by gradual diminution."[3] We find the belief in Raleigh: " The long day of mankind draweth fast towards an evening, and the world's tragedy and time are near at an end."[4] " Think not thy time short in this world," wrote Sir Thomas Browne, " since the world itself is not long."[5] It is everywhere in the sermons of the divines. Man is " an aged child, a grey-headed infant," and but a ghost of his own youth.[6] " As the world is the whole frame of the

[1] Donne, *Deaths Duell.*
[2] Donne, *Sermon LXXIII.*
[3] Johnson, *Lives of the Poets: Milton.*
[4] *History of the World.*
[5] *Christian Morals,* 29.
[6] Donne, *Sermon XXII.*

world, God hath put into it a reproof, a rebuke, lest it should seem eternal, which is a sensible decay and age in the whole frame of the world and every piece thereof. The seasons of the year irregular and distempered; the sun fainter and languishing; men less in stature and shorter lived. No addition, but only every year new sorts, new species of worms and flies and sicknesses, which argue more and more putrefaction of which they are engendered."[1] " This is the world's old age; it is declining; albeit it seems a fine and beautiful thing in the eyes of them that know no better, and unto those who are of yesterday and know nothing it looks as if it had been created yesterday, yet the truth is, and a believer knows, it is near the grave."[2] " The world's span-length of time is drawn now to less than half an inch, and to the point of the evening of the day of this old grey-haired world."[3] The result of such a belief was to cheapen the value of human endeavour, to show human greatness as trivial against the vastness of eternity. " Jezebel's dust is not amber, nor Goliath's dust *terra sigillata*, medicinal; nor does the serpent, whose meat they are both, find any better value in Dives dust than in Lazarus."[4] There was but one paramount duty in life, to save the soul. " These are the two great works which we are to do in this world: first to know that this world is not our home, and then to provide us another home whilst we are in this world."[5] " Build your nest upon no tree here," Samuel Rutherford wrote to Lady Kenmure, " for ye see God hath sold the forest to death." These are more than the commonplaces of theology; they are the expression of a temper which, by the year 1630, had become a background to thought, an atmosphere which insensibly coloured every man's outlook.[6]

In an age of uncertainty and change there is inevitably a craving for definition and discipline. Even if this or that law is dubious, Law itself is regarded as more than ever essential; in Hooker's famous panegyric her seat is in the bosom of God, her voice the harmony of the world, and

---

[1] Donne, *Sermon XXXVI*. The same thought will be found in Donne's " First Anniversary," *Poems* (ed. Grierson), I., 237.
[2] Binning, *Sermons*, III., 372.   [3] Samuel Rutherford, *Letters*.
[4] Donne, *Sermon LXXX*.   [5] Ibid., *Sermon LXXII*.
[6] Even to a sporting squire like Charles Cotton, the transience of man's life is linked with the fragility of the solid earth:

" You and I,
By a condition of mortality,
With all this great and more proud world must die."

she is the mother of all peace and joy. To live at all, man must make rules and keep them, and in the prevalent flux he hankers after rigidity. The more doubtful the political outlook the fiercer will be the dogmas which men create and contend for; the more the foundations of the Church are shaken the more high-flying and arbitrary will be the conflicting creeds. It is an old trait of human nature, when in the mist, to be very sure about its road. In such an era a religious faith tends to become a complete philosophy of life, governing also the minutest details of the secular world. Man cries for guidance and authority, and if he rejects one sanction he will invent others more compelling than the old. Having shaken himself loose from history, he tends to an abstract idealism. The English polity had been built up piecemeal by many compromises, but its seventeenth-century critics were apt to forget this, and to devise, like Milton, a brand-new symmetrical structure, unrelated to the past.[1] But Milton had the supreme merit that he always believed in the free and rational soul of man. " He who wisely would restrain the reasonable soul of man within due bounds, must first himself know perfectly how far the territory and dominion extends of just and honest liberty. As little must he offer to bind that which God hath loosened as to loosen that which He hath bound. The ignorance and mistake of this high point hath heaped up one huge half of all the misery that hath been since Adam." The human reason was not commonly valued so high by Milton's contemporaries, and they readily bent themselves before authority—of king or parliament, of bishop, Bible or congregation, or of personal revelation. Differences, which should have been discretionary, were elevated into matters of essential principle, and men were ready to stake body and soul on the finest points of dogma in Church and State.

Happily these troubles of the spirit, so far as England was concerned, befell in a society nicely integrated and fundamentally stable. Men of quick conscience and fine intelligence, who are the shaping spirits in any era, felt their impact, but there were in the land strong stabilizing forces which were for long untouched by them, and which made it certain that change would come by slow degrees. There was not, as on the continent of Europe, a gulf fixed between the nobility and the commonalty; the nobles were no more

[1] See especially Milton's *Of Reformation in England, and the Causes that Hitherto have Hindered it.*

than the topmost class of a great body of gentry which in
the lower ranges came very near to the yeomanry, and
embraced what we know to-day as the middle and professional classes. Even at the summit, the grandees of
Plantagenet and Tudor origin found themselves compelled
to mix with the new creations of James I. A family of
Norman descent would apprentice a younger son to a
trade, and marry a daughter to some new City knight or
young lawyer from the Temple. Boys of ancient houses
sat side by side on the grammar-school benches with the
sons of farmers and tradesmen. The land was organized
locally for defence and administration; an unpaid
magistracy enforced the king's mandates and administered
the new poor law; the ordinary citizen was the only soldier,
the mediæval levy had not yet disappeared, and on the
Marches manorial tenants armed with broadswords still
met the judges of assize. There was little rigidity among
classes, but the intensity of provincial feeling gave immense
power to those local leaders who had a long tradition of
popularity, so that the Lancashire gentry were accustomed
to wear the Stanley livery. Shire, parish, and town were
living organisms, managing their affairs with little outside
interference, and to buttress their honest particularism
there was a mass of hoar-ancient custom and tradition
which gave a man of Gloucestershire a different outlook
from a man of Devon or Kent. England still stood in the
old ways, and in her affection for them lay a vast latent
conservative power. But with this conservatism was joined
a high measure of independence. The progress of enclosures was bringing the yeoman and the tenant-farmer
into greater importance, and if each locality had its special
patriotism, so had each class its own stubborn loyalties. So
far as we can judge, it was on the whole a comfortable
society, full of ancestral jollities, and secure, for in most
parts of England a century had elapsed since the tramp of
armies had echoed in their fields.

North of the Tweed the case was different. Scotland had
for centuries been emptied from vessel to vessel, and civil
war was in the memories of living men. In the Highlands
the clan system still held together a primitive society, but
its Border variant had broken down, and elsewhere no
settled order of life had been developed. The Scottish
nobles had not laid aside their ancient turbulence; whereas
in England the duel was coming into fashion (a step
towards civilization), they still held by bravos and the

" killing affray."[1] All classes were miserably poor; the gentry lived squalidly in their little stone towers, the peasant was half-starved and half-clad, and rural life had few of the English amenities. The land was strewn with the relics of mediævalism, and amid this lumber the spirit of the Knoxian Reformation burned furiously, destroying much that was ill and not a little that was good. In a later chapter we shall consider more closely the condition of Scotland; here it is sufficient to note that the land was far readier for violent change than its southern neighbour. Its conservatism was a thing of private sentiment and passion rather than of fidelity to proved institutions; its history had given it a noble patriotism, but few things to cherish beyond a savage independence, and the cataclysmic breach with the ancient Church had predisposed it to other breaches. At the same time the Union of the Crowns had brought it into close relations with England, its nobility frequented the court, its civil and ecclesiastical policies were affected by Westminster. No overt act, no spiritual mood of England could be without its reactions in the north, and a flame which burned slowly amid the lush meadows and green hedgerows might run like wildfire among the dry heather.

An era of unrest produces a thousand types, but in the long run they range themselves into two parties, for human nature—especially English human nature—tends always to a dualism. It is not easy to find a definition for either Cavalier or Puritan which shall embrace on the one hand Suckling and Traherne, Laud and Clarendon, Rupert and Falkland: on the other Hampden and Barebone, Bunyan and Milton, Ireton and Lilburne. From the one party we may exclude the mere roysterers—Milton's " sons of Belial, flown with insolence and wine "—and from the other the hypocrites and the crack-brains; every great cause has its unworthy camp-followers. The division was not a social one, for the Puritans had many of the old nobility and some of the best of the country gentry in their ranks; and the Cavaliers had the bulk of the peasantry and a share of the trading and professional classes. The two factors in the situation were the crumbling of old things and the needs of substitutes, the questioning and the demand for certainty; the problem was how to define the fundamentals, and where to find authority. Men of the same party answered it in different and often inconsistent ways.

[1] See the case of Lord Sanquhar. Gardiner, II., 131-133.

The stream of the Cavalier temperament was fed by many distant springs. There was the punctilio of honour, the devotion to a master, which made royalists of simple and chivalrous souls: men like Hopton and Capel, Sunderland and Sir Bevil Grenville; men like Sir Edmund Verney, the knight marshal, from whose dying hand the standard dropped at Edgehill, though his creed was not that of the king. There were the lovers of Old England like Clarendon, its old Church, its folk religion, " its old good manners, its old good humour, and its old good nature " —things like to be destroyed by rash hands which could only offer a drab alternative. There were the believers in a central authority, and in the domain of law as against anarchy—liberal thinkers for the most part, and zealous reformers, who stood as firmly as Milton for the freedom of the human spirit, but resisted an iconoclasm which they held to be the path to servitude. Such were Falkland— who has given true conservatism its motto: " When it is not necessary to change, it is necessary not to change " —and Sidney Godolphin, who, like his friend, fell early on the battlefield.[1] There were the opportunists as against the dogmatists, the men who held with Donne that truth is not found by the straight road of an easy revelation, but must be sought by a spiral course, and that, as Cosin put it, " faith is not on this side knowledge, but beyond it." There were the scholars, full of the classical Renaissance; and the Platonists, who were not content to make the Bible the one source of truth or to condemn as carnal what they held to be divine. And there were the poets, who refused to narrow the world which God had made, and, like Herbert and Vaughan and Traherne, found everywhere " bright shoots of everlastingness "; in such men mysticism does not reject humanism, but enfolds and transcends it.

In this medley of types there was infinite room for difference—Laud's theory of church government, for example, was antipathetic to most of the party—but under the pressure of their opponents they found common ground, and a temperament was hardened into a creed. That creed was, shortly, the need of preserving a central

---

[1] Hobbes wrote of him: " I have known clearness of judgment and largeness of fancy; strength of reason and graceful elocution; a courage for the war and fear for the laws: and all eminently in one man." This " fear for the laws " was a Cavalier characteristic too often forgotten.

authority in the kingship. Men who had hotly criticized Charles's policy, who had no love for Laud and his ways, who had sympathized with Hampden and Eliot, found themselves ranged beside country squires who had few ideas beyond ale and foxes. Just as Oxford's treasures of Renaissance plate were melted down to provide current coin for the troops, so far-reaching doctrines were given a partial and popular statement, and philosophies were reduced to formulas and watchwords. In the Middle Ages treason was held the rankest of crimes, because so little was needed to wreck the brittle mechanism of the State. So now, with change and anarchy in the air, lovers of order stood by the one well-sanctioned existing authority —the king.

In the Puritan party we find less variety of type and a simpler temperament, but here also is diversity. The basis was in the first instance religion.[1] The original Puritan was one who desired to purify the Church from all taint of Romanism, and to the end there were Puritans who remained Churchmen. But presently, as the difficulties of the task became apparent, criticism of liturgical forms and of the extravagances of episcopal power hardened with many into an opposition to all hierarchical church government, and the acceptance of the Presbyterian doctrine of the " priesthood of all believers " and the polity of the reformed churches in France, Switzerland, and Scotland. This ecclesiastical preference was extended into secular affairs, and the Puritan added to his creed a passion for civic freedom. There were also the sectaries who had been persecuted since the early days of Elizabeth, and who were distasteful alike to Anglican and Presbyterian—men who were extreme individualists in church matters, and regarded the congregation as the divinely appointed organism.

Puritanism was neither an ecclesiastical system nor a theological creed. Calvinism, with its doctrine of " exclusive salvation," was, at first, the belief of Anglican and Presbyterian alike, and it remained the prevailing creed of the Puritan party as of the bulk of their opponents—rejected only by Laud's Arminian school, and by sects like

---

[1] There was also, of course, an economic basis, but I think that Mr. R. H. Tawney (*Religion and the Rise of Capitalism*, 235) overestimates it, at least so far as concerns the first forty years of the seventeenth century, though what he says is true of post-Restoration nonconformity. The clash was far more one of political and theological theories than of " contradicting economic interests and incompatible conceptions of social expediency."

the Baptists and the Quakers. The most powerful statement of Puritan theology will be found in Anglican divines like Donne; no Scottish Covenanter ever dwelt more terribly upon original sin, the torments of hell, and the awe of eternity.[1] Nor was the Puritan either a very learned and subtle theologian, or a profound expositor of his own ecclesiastical tastes. When a man of Milton's genius embarks upon doctrinal questions[2] he is " in wandering mazes lost," like the evil spirits in *Paradise Lost*, who sat on a hill and debated predestination. For wisdom, breadth of knowledge, and logical acumen, no Puritan champion can vie with Hooker, Chillingworth, John Hales, and Jeremy Taylor—few even reach the standard of Laud.

Puritanism was above all things the result of a profound spiritual experience in the Puritan. It is to John Bunyan and George Fox that we must go if we would learn the strength of the faith. The questioning of the epoch resulted for such men in an overwhelming sense of sin and an overpowering consciousness of God; their knowledge, in Cromwell's famous words, was not " literal and speculative, but inward and transforming the mind to it." Unless we realize this primary fact we cannot explain why so many diverse creeds were ultimately conjoined to form one conquering temperament. Inevitably the faith and the practice narrowed and hardened. Sunday, the day on which Calvin played bowls and John Knox gave supper parties, became the Jewish Sabbath, and the Mosaic law in many of its most irrelevant details was incorporated with the Christian creed. Toleration was impossible for men who saw life as a narrow path through a land shaken by the fires of hell; only kindred communions were tolerated, save by those few sects who, from hard experience, had learned a gentler rule. A limited number inclined to a complete separation of Church and State, but the majority desired a purified State, which would be the ally and the servant of the Church. They rejected the world of sense, for there could be no innocency in what had been corrupted by Adam's sin, and their eyes were fixed austerely upon their own souls. The strength of Puritanism lay in its view of the direct relation of God and man; its weakness in the fact that this relation was narrowly and often shallowly construed. The Puritan became, by his severe abstraction, a dangerous element in society and the

---

[1] See especially *Sermons I., XIII.,* and *LXVI.*
[2] In his *Treatise of Christian Doctrines.*

State, since human institutions are built upon half-truths, opportunisms, and compromises. He was pre-eminently a destructive force, for he was without the historical sense,[1] and sought less to erect and unite than to pull down and separate. Milton's words might be taken as his creed: "By His divorcing command the world first rose out of chaos; nor can be renewed again out of confusion but by the separating of unmeet consorts."[2]

With the Puritans, as with the Cavaliers, many streams from remote wells were in the end canalized into a single channel. The mood of those who accepted the natural world as the gift of God was set against that which saw that world as conceived in sin and shapen in iniquity: the ancient institutions of the realm, which to the mind of the Cavalier should be reformed, but in substance retained, were opposed to a clean page on which men could write what they pleased; the conception of the State as a thing of balances and adjustments was met by a theory of government as an abstract ideal to be determined mainly by the half-understood words of an old book: the free exercise of men's conscience in religion was confronted with a denial of freedom except to those of a certain way of thinking. The truth is that the Puritan was hampered both in civil and ecclesiastical statesmanship by that intense individualism which was also his strength. His creed was not social or readily communicable—

> " . . . a dark lanthorn of the spirit,
> Which none see by but those who bear it."

To him, as to Newman in his youth, the world was narrowed to " two, and two only, supreme and luminously self-evident beings "—himself and his Creator.

If we put the contrast thus, it would seem that generosity and enlightenment were predominantly on the side of the Cavaliers. But it must not be forgotten that, owing to the spiritual atmosphere of the age and the tendency in such a conflict to narrower and yet narrower definition, the common creed of Puritanism did not fairly represent the best men in its ranks. Had Hampden and Falkland ever argued on fundamentals they might well have found themselves in substantial agreement. The difference, as the struggle progressed, came to lie far less in creeds than in the moods behind them, and the Puritan mood, solemn under the

---

[1] The Puritan statesmen were often zealous collectors of precedents, but their legal antiquarianism was not the same thing as a sense of history. [2] *The Doctrine and Discipline of Divorce.*

Almighty's eye, austere, self-centred, unhumorous, unbending, was more formidable and more valuable than their crude apologetics. Its spiritual profundity was as rich a bequest to the future as the saner and sunnier temper of the Cavalier. The difference between the best men of the two parties was a fine one—the exact border-line between the king's prerogative and popular liberties in Church and State; but most great contests in the world's history have been fought on narrow margins. And in practice the narrowness disappeared, and the divergence was glaring. For the Cavalier, with his reasoned doctrine of a central authority based on historical sanctions, had to define that authority as the king, and that king not an ideal monarch, but an actual person then living in Whitehall. The Puritan, who might have dissented reluctantly from the abstract argument, was very ready to differ about Charles.

The conflict which we call the Civil War took place under the shadow which overhung the thought of the first half of the seventeenth century. In that gloom, as we have seen, men were predisposed to define arbitrarily and fly to rigid dogma as to a refuge, for in such a constriction they found peace and strength. Those who maintained the integrity of the spirit, and refused to blindfold their minds, cloistered themselves, or, if they ventured on a life of action, were as a rule Verneys or Falklands, heartsick, distracted, "ingeminating Peace." The effective protagonists were those Cavaliers whose loyalty knew no doubts, and those Puritans who were strong in the confidence of their Lord.

It is the purpose of this book to trace the career of one whose campaigning ground was Scotland, where antagonisms were fiercer and blinder than in the south; one who did not drug his soul with easy loyalties, but faced the problem of his times unflinchingly, and reached conclusions which had to wait for nearly two hundred years till they could be restated with some hope of acceptance; one who, nevertheless, had that single-hearted gift for deeds which usually belongs to the man whose vigour is not impaired by thought. Montrose has been called by Carlyle the noblest of the Cavaliers, yet clearly he was no ordinary Cavalier; for at the start he was a Covenanter and in rebellion against the king—rebellion of which he never saw reason to repent, and to his dying day he remained a convinced Presbyterian.

BOOK I

PREPARATION

CHAPTER I

YOUTH

(1612-36)

> I know the ways of pleasure, the sweet strains,
> The lullings and the relishes of it;
> The propositions of hot blood and brains;
> What mirth and music mean; what love and wit
> Have done these twenty hundred years and more;
> I know the projects of unbridled store:
> My stuff is flesh, not brass; my senses live.
>
> GEORGE HERBERT.

THE HIGHLAND LINE IN THE SCOTTISH MAINLAND, THOUGH variously determined at times by political needs, has been clearly fixed by nature. The main battlement of the hills runs with a north-easterly slant from Argyll through the Lennox, and then turns northward so as to enclose the wide carselands of Tay. Beyond lie the tangled wildernesses stretching with scarcely a break to Cape Wrath; east and south are the Lowlands proper—on the east around Don and Dee and the Forfarshire Esks: on the south around Forth and Clyde, and embracing the hills of Tweed and Galloway. Scotland had thus two Borderlands—the famous line of march with England, and the line, historically less notable but geographically clearer, which separated plain from hill, family from clan, and for centuries some semblance of civilization from its stark opposite. The northern Border may be defined in its more essential part as the southern portion of Dumbarton and Lennox, the shire of Stirling, and the haughs of the Lower Tay. There for centuries the Lowlander looked out from his towns and castles to the blue mountains where lived his ancestral foes. Dwelling on a frontier makes a hardy race, and from this northern Border came famous men and sounding deeds. Drummonds, Murrays, Erskines, and Grahams were its chief families, but most notably the last. What the name of Scott was in the glens of Teviot, the name of Graham was in the valleys of Forth and Earn. Since the thirteenth century they had been the unofficial wardens of the northern marches.

The ancient nobility of Scotland does not show well on the page of history. The records of the great earldoms—Angus, Mar, Moray, Buchan—tell too often an unedifying tale of blood and treason, and, after the day of the Good Lord James, St. Bride of Douglas might have wept for her children. But the family of Graham kept tolerably clean hands, and played an honourable part in the national history. Sir John the Graham was the trusted friend of Wallace, and fell gloriously at Falkirk. His successors fought in the later wars of independence, thrice intermarried with the royal blood, and gave Scotland her first primate. In 1451 the family attained the peerage. The third Lord Graham was made Earl of Montrose, when the short-lived Lindsay dukedom lapsed, and the new earl died with his king in the steel circle at Flodden. A successor fell at Pinkie; another became Chancellor and then Viceroy of Scotland when James the Sixth mounted the English throne. The Viceroy's son, the fourth earl, apart from a famous brawl in the High Street of Edinburgh, lived the quiet life of a county laird till, shortly before his death he, too, was appointed Chancellor. He was a noted sportsman, a great golfer, and a devotee of tobacco. His wife was Lady Margaret Ruthven, a daughter of the tragically-fated house of Gowrie, who bore him six children, and died when her only son was in his sixth year. The family was reasonably rich as the times went, for the home-keeping Earl John had conserved his estate. They owned broad lands in Stirling, Perth, and Angus, and wielded the influence which the chief of a house possesses over its numerous cadets. They had three principal dwellings—the tower of Mugdock in Strathblane; the fine castle of Kincardine in Perthshire, where the Ochils slope to the Earn; and the house of Old Montrose, which Robert Bruce had given to a Graham as the price of Cardross on Clyde.

James Graham, the only son of the fourth earl and Margaret Ruthven, was born in the year 1612, probably in

the month of October[1]—according to tradition, in the town
of Montrose. The piety of opponents has surrounded his
birth with omens; his mother is said, with the hereditary
Ruthven love of necromancy, to have consulted witches,
and his father to have observed to a neighbour that this
child would trouble all Scotland.[2] Like Cromwell, he was
the only boy in a family of girls. Of his five sisters, the
two eldest were married young—Lilias to Sir John Colquhoun of Luss, and Margaret to a wise man of forty, the
first Lord Napier of Merchiston. Their houses were open
to him when he tired of catching trout in the little water of
Ruthven, or wearing out horseshoes on the Ochils, an
occupation to which the extant bills of the Aberuthven
blacksmith testify. There was much in the way of adventure to be had at Rossdhu, Lady Lilias's new dwelling, and
there the boy may have learned, from practising on the roe-
buck and wild goats of Lochlomondside, the skill which
made him in after years a noted marksman.

At the age of twelve Lord Graham was entrusted to a
certain William Forrett, master of arts, to be prepared for
the college of Glasgow. Thither he journeyed with a valet,
two pages in scarlet, a quantity of linen and plate, a selection from his father's library, and his favourite white pony.
He lived in the house of Sir George Elphinstone of Blyths-
wood, the Lord Justice Clerk; it stood near the Townhead,
and may have been one of the old manses of the canons
of the Cathedral. The avenues to learning must have been
gently graded, for he retained a happy memory of those
Glasgow days and of Master Forrett, who in later years
became the tutor of his sons. He seems to have read in
Xenophon and Seneca, and an English translation of Tasso;
but his favourite book, then and long afterwards, was
Raleigh's *History of the World*, the splendid folio of the
first edition.

In the second year of Glasgow study the old earl died,
and Lord Graham posted back to Kincardine, arriving two
days before the end. Thither came the whole race of
Grahams for the funeral ceremonies, which lasted the

[1] In October 1632 he signed a large number of charters, convey-
ances, and other documents, which suggests that in that month he
entered on his twenty-first year, and began, as in these days often
happened, to exercise the rights of a major.
[2] *The Staggering State of Scots Statesmen*, by Sir John Scot of
Scotstarvet, 14. Scotstarvet adds that the infant " is said also to
have eaten a toad whilst he was a sucking child "—a tale told about
the Regent Morton in the previous century.

better part of three weeks. Prodigious quantities of meat
and drink were consumed, for each neighbour and kinsman
brought his contribution in kind—partridges and plovers
from Lord Stormont, moorfowl from Lawers, a great hind
from Glenorchy—the details are still extant, with the values
of woodcock and wild geese, capercailzie and ptarmigan,
meticulously set down. If such mourning had its draw-
backs, at any rate it introduced the new head of the family
to those of his name and race. He did not return to Glasgow (though five years later he showed his affection for the
place by making a donation to the building of the new
college library), and presently was entered at St. Salvator's
College, St. Andrews, of which one of his forbears had been
a founder. Master Forrett brought his possessions from
Glasgow, and the laird of Inchbrakie bestowed these valuable items, the books, in a proper cabinet.

We have ample documents to illustrate his St. Andrews'
days.[1] The university, the oldest and then the most famous
in Scotland, had among its alumni in the first half of the
seventeenth century men so diverse as Montrose and Argyll
and Rothes, Mr. Donald Cargill and Sir George Mackenzie.
His secretary was a Mr. John Lambie, and Mr. Lambie's
accounts reveal the academic life in those days of a gentle-
man-commoner. In sport his tastes were catholic. He
golfed, like James Melville a century before, and paid five
shillings Scots for each golf ball. His rooms at St. Salvator's were hung round with bows, and in his second year
he won the silver medal for archery, which to the end of
his college course he held against all comers. Argyll, who
was some years his senior, had carried off the same trophy.
He was an admirable horseman, and he seems to have
hunted regularly; it is recorded in the accounts that after
a day with hounds his horse was given a pint of ale. He
was fond of hawking, and he went regularly to Cupar races,
handing over, according to the excellent statute of 1621,
his winnings beyond one hundred marks to the local kirk
session for the relief of the poor. His chief friends of his
own order seem to have been Wigton, Lindsay of the
Byres, Kinghorn, Sinclair, Sutherland, and Colville, and he
varied his residence at St. Andrews with visits to his
brother-in-law (the hills of Rossdhu, complains his steward,
wore the boots off his feet), the cadet gentry of his name,
and Cumbernauld, Glamis, Kinnaird, Balcarres, and the
other country-houses of his friends. In October 1628 he

[1] *Mem. of M.*, I., 156-201.

gave a great house-warming at Kincardine, which lasted for three days. In the March following he visited Edinburgh, where he appeared in gilt spurs and a new sword, and was lent the Chancellor's carriage. The picture which has come down to us of the undergraduate is that of a boy happy and well-dowered, popular with all, eager to squeeze the juice from the many fruits of life. Nor was he above youthful disasters. When his sister Dorothea married Sir James Rollo, there was huge feasting in Edinburgh and Fife, and the young earl returned to college only to fall sick. Two doctors were summoned, who charged enormous fees, and prescribed a rest cure—strict diet, and no amusements but cards and chess. The barber shore away his long brown curls, and "James Pett's dochter" attended to the invalid's food. The régime seems high feeding for what was probably an attack of indigestion—trout, pigeons, capons, "drapped eggs," calf's-foot jelly, grouse (out of season), washed down by "liquorice, whey, possets, aleberry, and claret."

From the accounts preserved we can trace something of his progress in learning. He began to study Greek, and continued his reading in the Latin classics, his favourites now being Cæsar and Lucan, in his copies of which he made notes. He can never have been an exact scholar, and it is probable that the wide knowledge of classical literature which he showed later was largely acquired from translations. For it was the day of great translators, and at St. Andrews he had at his service North's *Plutarch*, Philemon Holland's *Livy* and *Suetonius*, Thomas Heywood's *Sallust*, and the *Tacitus* of Sir Henry Savile and Richard Grenewey. Nor did he neglect romances, and he made his first essays in poetry. To this stage may belong the lines ascribed to him by family tradition, in which the ambitious boy writes his own version of a popular contemporary conceit; but he does not end, like the other versions, on a note of pious quietism:

> " I would be high; but that the cedar tree
> Is blustered down whilst smaller shrubs go free.
> I would be low; but that the lowly grass
> Is trampled down by each unworthy ass.
> For to be high, my means they will not doe;
> And to be low my mind it will not bow.
> O Heavens! O Fate! when will you once agree
> To reconcile my means, my mind, and me? "[1]

---

[1] The first four lines, in a different form, are included in the *Compleat Angler*, where they are ascribed to Donne or Sir Henry Wotton. They have also been credited to Henry King and Sir

He had a touch of the bibliophile, for he had his copies
of Buchanan and Barclay's *Argenis* specially bound. To
poor authors he was a modest Mæcenas. The accounts
show a payment of fifty-eight shillings Scots to " ane
Hungarian poet, who made some verses to my lord." He
subscribed for the travels of the fantastical William Lithgow, and was good-humoured enough to read and advise
upon a poem in manuscript by the same hand which bore
the unsavoury title of " The Gushing Tears of Godly
Sorrow."[1]

In those days the business of life crowded fast upon
boyhood. After the university came marriage as the next
step in a gentleman's education. Not far from Old Montrose stood the castle of Kinnaird, where Lord Carnegie[2]
dwelt with six pretty daughters. There Montrose had often
visited, and there he fell in love with Magdalen, the
youngest girl. The match was too desirable for opposition
either from the Carnegies or from the young lord's
guardians, and the children—Montrose was only seventeen
—were married in the parish church of Kinnaird on
November 10, 1629. In the marriage contract Lord
Carnegie bound himself " to entertain and sustain in house
with himself, the said noble earl and Mistress Magdalene
Carnegie, his promised spouse, during the space of three
years next after the said marriage."[3] Accordingly the
young couple remained at Kinnaird for a little over three
years, until Montrose came of age, and there two of their
four sons were born.[4] They were years of quiet study, the
leisurely preparation which is all too rare in youth for the
necessities of manhood; and they were the only season of
peaceful domestic life which Montrose was fated to enjoy.
The famous Jameson portrait, given by Graham of
Morphie as a wedding gift to the young countess, shows
him in those years of meditation, when he was scribbling
his ambitions in his copy of Quintus Curtius. It is a charming head of a boy, with its wide, curious, grey eyes, the
arched, almost fantastic, eyebrows, the delicate mobile lips.

Kenelm Digby. For the variants see Donne's *Poems* (ed. Grierson),
I., 466; II., 269.

[1] It was published in 1640 at the Edinburgh press of R. Bryson.

[2] David Carnegie, created Lord Carnegie of Kinnaird by James I.
in 1616, and Earl of Southesk by Charles I. in 1633.

[3] *Hist. MSS. Comm.*, 2nd Report, 168.

[4] They had five children: John, who died on active service with
his father (see p. 198); James, the second marquis; David, who
died in infancy; Robert; and one daughter, Jean. See Balfour Paul,
The Scots Peerage, VI., 254-255.

Life was to crush out the daintiness and gaiety, armour was
to take the place of lace collar and silken doublet; but one
thing the face of Montrose never lost—it had always an
air of hope, as of one seeking for a far country.

In June 1633 Charles came to Scotland to be crowned.
Such an occasion was well suited for the introduction of
a young nobleman to the court, for in that year Montrose
attained his majority, his father-in-law was high in the royal
favour, and his brother-in-law Napier was one of the four
peers chosen to hold the canopy over the king's head. That
the world expected his presence is shown by his friend
William Lithgow's recommendation of his merits in the
preposterous poem, " Scotland's Welcome to her Native
Son and Sovereign Lord, King Charles." But when mid-
summer came he was on a foreign shore. The reason may
be traced in the scandal connected with his sister's husband,
Sir John Colquhoun, which in the beginning of that year
was the talk of Scotland. The laird of Luss, in company
with a German necromancer of the name of Carlippis, had
fled from his lawful wife, carrying with him his sister-in-
law, the little Lady Katherine, who had for a time been
Montrose's companion in his Glasgow lodgings. The malefactor was outlawed and excommunicated, returning
fourteen years later to be received into grace by Church
and State; the unhappy girl disappears from history. With
such a family horror on his mind, Montrose sought the
anodyne of new scenes and fresh faces.

We know little of his travels. He started probably in
the beginning of 1633, accompanied by his secretary of St.
Andrews days, John Lambie, and young Graham of
Morphie. According to Burnet, his travelling companion
was Basil Fielding, Denbigh's son and Hamilton's brother-
in-law, who flung in his fortunes later with the Puritan
party. He financed his journey by drawing bills on William
Dick of Braid through the latter's " factors " in Paris. The
winter of 1633-34 was spent at Angers, where he no doubt
was a pupil of the famous school of arms. In the old
library at Innerpeffray there is still preserved a French
Bible which he bought on his travels, scribbled throughout
with mottoes which had caught his fancy, such as " Honor
mihi vita potior " and " Non crescunt sine spinis." In
Rome he met Lord Angus, the future Marquis of Douglas,
and others of the Scots nobility, and dined with them at
the English College there. He studied all the while—" as
much of the mathematics as is required of a soldier," wrote

his faithful adherent Thomas Saintserf, "but his great study was to read men and the actions of great men." It is a phrase which aptly describes the attitude of high dedication in which the young man passed his youth. He went gravely about the business of life, and already had made certain of renown, though careless enough of happiness. Long afterwards, to foreign observers like the Cardinal de Retz, he seemed like one of the heroes of Plutarch, and there was something even in his boyish outlook of the high Roman manner. It was at this time that his interests began to move strongly towards the military art. Europe was in the throes of the Thirty Years' War, half its gentry were in arms, the great Gustavus was but two years dead, and in court and college the talk was all of leaguers and campaigns.

The descriptions of his person and habits at this date are familiar; of middle stature and gracefully built, chestnut hair, a clear fresh colour, a high-bridged nose, keen grey eyes; an accomplished horseman, and an adept at every sport which needed a lithe body and a cool head.[1] On his manner all accounts are agreed, and most accounts are critical. He was very stately and ceremonious, even as a young man, in no way prepared to forget that he was a great noble, except among his intimates. To servants and inferiors he was kindly and thoughtful, to equals and superiors a little stiff and hard. Burnet says of him that he was "a young man well learned, who had travelled, but had taken upon him the port of a hero too much."[2] "He was exceedingly constant and loving," a friend wrote, "to those who did adhere to him, and very affable to such as he knew; though his carriage, which indeed was not ordinary, made him seem proud." One is reminded of Sir Walter Raleigh, whose "næve," says Aubrey, "was that he was damnable proud." Adventurous and imaginative youth is rarely free from the fault; its sensitive haughtiness is both defensive armour and a defiance; it believes itself destined for great deeds, and a boyish stateliness is its

[1] See Saintserf, *Relation of the True Funeralls*, 1661, his dedicatory epistle to the second Marquis of Montrose appended to the translation of Marmet's *Entertainments of the Course*, 1658, and the additions (probably by Saintserf) to *Montrose Redivivus*, 1652. A description, different in some respects, is given by Gordon of Ruthven, 76.
[2] *Hist. of his Own Time* (ed. 1724), I., 30. For Clarendon's judicious estimate on similar lines see *Hist. of the Rebellion*, XII., 142.

advertisement to the world of the part it has set itself to play.

Montrose returned home in 1636, in his twenty-fourth year—a figure of intense interest to the Scottish faction-leaders, and of some moment to the king's court. He was altogether too remarkable to please the Marquis of Hamilton, who was the interpreter of Scottish business to the royal ear, and for the first time he came into conflict with one with whom he was to fight many battles. James, third Marquis, and soon to be first Duke, of Hamilton, was not the least futile of the many schemers of his day. A vain, secret being, a diligent tramper of backstairs, and a master of incompetent intrigue, he is throughout his career the sheep in wolf's clothing. He looks at us from the canvas of Vandyck, a martial figure, grasping a baton, but in his face we can detect what Sir Philip Warwick noted—" such a cloud on his countenance that Nature seems to have impressed *aliquid insigne* "—something crack-brained, uncertain and tortuous, a warning that this was no man to ride the ford with. The royal blood in his veins gave him high ambitions, and his fierce old mother, Ann Cunningham of Glencairn, strongly coloured these ambitions, so that he was for ever halting between King and Covenant, dreaming now of winning Scotland for his master, and now of reigning himself in some theocratic millennium. His life was one long pose, but the poses were many and contradictory, and the world came to regard as a knave one who was principally a fool. Burnet, the Hamilton champion, has done his best for his memory, but the verdict of history has been written by Clarendon, who was no ill-wisher to his house. " His natural darkness and reservation in his discourse made him to be thought a wise man, and his having been in command under the King of Sweden, as his continual discourse of battles and fortifications, made him to be thought a soldier. And both these mistakes were the cause that made him to be looked upon as a worse and a more dangerous man than in truth he deserved to be."[1]

When Montrose reached London he appeared at court, and naturally asked Hamilton to be his sponsor, announc-

[1] Clarendon, XI., 262; Burnet, *Mem. of the Hamiltons*; Sir Philip Warwick, *Memoirs of the Reign of King Charles I.,* 1701. The evidence for Hamilton's conduct to Montrose is Heylin's *Life of Laud,* and his *Commentary upon L'Estrange*—a good authority, for Heylin tells us that he had much of his information from Lord Napier, who, more than any other man, was in Montrose's confidence.

ing his wish " to put himself into the king's service."
Hamilton did his best to dissuade him by representing
Charles as the foe of Scottish rights, and then promptly
sought out the king to tell him that Montrose, by reason
of his royal descent, was a danger to the royal interests,
and should be discouraged. The upshot was that the
traveller was received by Charles with marked coldness.
The king spoke a few chilly words, gave him his hand to
kiss, and turned away. It was enough to discourage the
most ardent loyalist, and the rebuff made it certain that
personal affection for his monarch would play no part in
determining the young man's conduct on his return to his
own country.

CHAPTER II

THE STRIFE IN SCOTLAND

(1636-38)

It is bad policy to represent a political system as having no charm
but for robbers and assassins, and no natural origin but in the brains
of fools or madmen, when experience has proved that the great
danger of the system consists in the peculiar fascination it is calculated to exert upon noble and imaginative spirits.

COLERIDGE, *The Friend*.

TO UNDERSTAND THE DECISION WITH WHICH MONTROSE WAS
confronted on his return, we must examine the elements of
the storm which was now gathering to a head in the north,
and to this end cast our eyes back over a tangled century
of Scottish history.

I

The Reformation in Scotland has been often miscon-
ceived as a sudden and universal turning from an old way
of life, and as sudden a birth of Presbytery fully matured
in creed, discipline, and constitution. In reality it was a
slow and halting process, where at the start only one thing
was determined—the breach with Rome; and the positive
structure suffered long delays and hesitations. The mascu-
line genius of Knox was better fitted for action than for
constructive thought; he knew when to defy and when to
yield, for, in F. W. Maitland's phrase, a shrewd worldly

wisdom underlay his Hebraic frenzies; but he was nobly inconsistent, his views passed through baffling permutations, and, in spite of the acumen of his mind, the fabric he reared was neither well planned nor soundly masoned. But on the negative side his work was final. The old building had been razed to the ground, so that in Scotland there was at no time the remotest chance of a counter-Reformation. The faults of the pre-Reformation Scottish Church have doubtless been too darkly painted. In many ways its rule was beneficent, and it was rarely oppressive, but it had little hold upon the mind of a people which, in the Middle Ages, was notably careless about Rome. When Scotland found religion, she found it in a form which made her historic Church seem the flat opposite of the commands of Omnipotence. Moreover, the Renaissance came to her mainly through the Reformation, and, besides the religious impulse, there were stirrings towards democracy and freedom of thought which were satisfied by her new creed. Also there was her ancient dislike of foreign meddling. Rome became a hissing and a reproach, though men might differ hotly about what should take its place. When Knox thundered against the " diabolical," " rotten," and " stinking " ritual which had once been a familiar and comforting part of the people's life, when he declared that the mass was more odious in God's sight than murder, he had the assent of the bulk of the nation. " They think it impossible to lose the way to Heaven," wrote Sir Anthony Weldon of the Scots, " if they can but leave Rome behind them." On the destructive side the work was complete.

We may date the Scottish Reformation from the first " Band " of December 1557, which denounced the abuses of Rome and demanded the introduction of the English Prayer-book; but it was not till the Edinburgh Parliament of 1560 that we see the dawnings of Presbytery. Presbyterianism, as we understand the word to-day, is distinguished by its theory of church government, its ritual, and its creed. In each domain its special principles were slow to establish themselves.

Take the matter of church government. The cardinal doctrine of the priesthood of all believers was no doubt there in germ from the beginning, but at first there was little besides. The Presbyterian belief in the equality of ministers came neither from Calvin nor from Knox; Knox's " superintendents," as diocesan chiefs, were strangely like bishops, and the first reformed Scottish

Church was a limited episcopacy. It was Andrew Melville who introduced the doctrine of ministerial parity, and made bishops an offence not only against the Scriptural conception of the Church, but against the new notion of democracy. " Ye may have bishops here," the minister of Dunfermline told King James, " but ye must remember to make us all equal; make us all bishops, else will ye never content us."[1] The first Book of Discipline of 1561 accepted a hierarchy; the second Book of Discipline twenty years later swept it away. But the battle was not won; its fortunes see-sawed during the reign of James, according as the monarch felt his power, for he had reached the firm conclusion that a hierarchy was a necessary protection for the throne against the potential anarchy of Presbytery. In 1584 came the Black Acts, and a short-lived royal triumph; in 1592 the king was forced to accept a full Presbyterian polity; by 1600 he had won again, and bishops sat in Parliament. His accession to the English throne gave him a new authority, the Melvilles were exiled, and, by means of packed ecclesiastical conventions, which he called General Assemblies, he had the Act of 1592 repealed and episcopacy established by law. But it was no more than a parliamentary episcopacy, scarcely affecting the life of the people, since kirk sessions, presbyteries, and synods continued to meet, and a staunch Presbyterian could write in 1616: " At that time I observed little controversy in religion in the Kirk of Scotland, for though there were bishops, yet they took little upon them."[2] In the early years of the reign of Charles I. the familiar Presbyterian régime was the rule in Scotland, with bishops affixed to it as a meaningless adminicle.

In the same way the General Assembly—that palladium of the new Church—was slow to come to maturity. When it was introduced in 1560, it was a copy of the national synod of the French Church. It was not a gathering of ecclesiastics, but representative of the whole religious life of the people, containing both clergy and laity popularly elected. From the start it possessed a representative authority which was lacking in the Scottish Parliament, and it presently became its rival. In the confused early years of James it wielded great powers and interfered much in secular policy—not without reason, for at the time every political problem had a religious connotation. But after

[1] Row, *History of the Kirk of Scotland* (Wodrow Society), 418.
[2] Blair's *Life* (Wodrow Society), 12.

the king's victory in 1597 its influence declined, and before the end of his life it became an instrument in his hands. Andrew Melville had stated its claims so high that the civil authority could not choose but oppose them. " Thair is twa Kings and twa Kingdoms in Scotland," he had told his master. " Thair is Chryst Jesus the King and his Kingdom the Kirk, whase subject King James the Saxt is, and of whase Kingdom nocht a King nor a Lord nor a heid but a member. And they whom Chryst has callit and commandit to watch over the Kirk and govern his spirituall Kingdom has sufficient power of him and authoritie sa to do." This might seem a reasonable statement of spiritual independence, were it not that the particular Assembly to which James objected had been called to discuss a question of secular politics.

We see, indeed, through the whole period between 1560 and 1638 the hardening and the magnifying of the claims of the new Church in other than legitimate matters of spiritual doctrine and discipline. It was this arrogance that made James and Charles desire a system which would bring the ecclesiastical leaders directly into the body politic, and so make them responsible to their sovereign; the trouble was that the real leaders saw that their power lay in being detached from King and Parliament, the chiefs of an *imperium in imperio*. There is no warrant for this separation to be found in Calvin. A preacher at Nîmes took to overthrowing images and altars, declaring that it was a matter of conscience. " God," said Calvin, " never commands any one to overthrow idols, except every man in his own house, and, in public, those whom He has armed with authority. Let that firebrand show me by what title *he* is lord of the land where he has been burning things."[1] This was also the view of Knox, though he spoke at different times with different voices. He bade his Berwick congregation give due obedience to magistrates, however ungodly, without tumult or sedition, and " not to pretend to defend God's truth and religion, ye being subjects, by violence or sword, but patiently suffering what God shall please be laid on you for constant confession of your faith and belief "; seven years later he was advising the faithful in England that " a prince who erects idolatry . . . must be adjudged to death." But his considered view seems to have been that in a Christian state the last word, even in

[1] Quoted from the *Corpus Reformatorum* (xlvi., 609; xlvii., 409-11) by Lang, *John Knox and the Reformation*, 113.

B*

religion, lay with the civil authority. " The ordering and
reformation of religion doth especially appertain to the
Civil Magistrate. . . . The King taketh upon him to command the Priests."[1] The true father of the doctrine of the
divine right of Presbytery was Andrew Melville, and under
his influence the new presbyter became, in the extravagance
of his claims, but too like the old priest. When ministers,
called to account before the Privy Council for preaching
civil sedition, declared that they could only appear before
a Church court, they were laying down a principle, ancient
indeed, but none the less destructive of civil society. Elizabeth in England saw what was coming, and in 1590
counselled her brother of Scotland: " Let me warn you
that there is risen, both in your realm and mine, a sect of
perilous consequence, such as would have no kings but a
presbytery, and take our place while they enjoy our
privileges, with a shade of God's Word, which none is
judged to follow right without by their censure they be
so deemed."[2] The comparative impotence of the Scottish
Kirk in the early years of Charles I. should not blind us
to the fact that in the minds of some of its ablest divines
there was developing a perilous doctrine of spiritual
despotism.

The question of ritual was also unsettled. The first
reformers in Scotland had no objection to the use of settled
forms in public worship: none of them would have understood the objection of later Covenanting extremists even
to the Lord's Prayer. In 1557 the Second Book of
Edward VI. had been recommended, and was generally
used in churches, till Knox secured its supersession by the
Genevan Book of Common Order. The abhorrence of
prescript prayer came into Scotland from the English
Puritans. Knox disliked many things in the English
Prayer-book, for it was his business to magnify differences
between the old worship and the new, so as to stimulate
Protestant fervour. He objected to kneeling at communion,
because he believed—without historical warrant—that the
first disciples sat, but he told his Berwick congregation that
they might kneel if the magistrates commanded it, and
made it clear that it was not retained for " maintenance
of any superstition," like " the adoration of the Lord's
Supper." Later his attitude stiffened, and he considered
that kneeling at the Lord's table, responses, singing of the

[1] *Works* (ed. Laing), IV., 486, 488, quoted by Lang.
[2] *Letters of Elizabeth and James VI.* (Camden Society), 63.

litany, services on saints' days, and the use of the cross in baptism were " diabolical inventions." But these were personal opinions; he disliked equally the imposition of hands at the ordination of ministers, which has long been a settled Presbyterian usage. The Scottish Kirk was content to have a liturgy, but it wanted its own Genevan version, and had the authorities been wise they might have found a method of reuniting the worship of both sides of the Tweed by some such eirenicon as John Hales dreamed of—a public form of service embracing only those things upon which all Christians were agreed.[1] Scotland was willing to accept a ritual, but it must not be too suggestive of the Roman, and it must be her own and not an imposition from England. The five Articles of Perth, ratified by Parliament in 1621, enjoined kneeling at communion, the private administration of the sacrament to the dying, baptism in private houses, the confirmation of the young, and the keeping of certain church festivals—all English practices and foreign to the Genevan code: Scotland disliked them, but when they became law there was no further trouble, and, since they were not strictly enforced, they might soon have perished from desuetude. James, indeed, seems to have regarded the Perth Articles as the most he was prepared to demand, and to have guaranteed no increase of English innovations.[2] Scotland had, therefore, a legal ritual, which was imperfectly observed[3] because it was out of tune with the spirit of the Kirk, but not overtly opposed, because it had been established by means of her own law. The real strife would begin if the monarch should arbitrarily impose further Anglican forms upon her, for that would call to arms not only the Genevan purism of the Kirk, but the sleepless nationalism of the people.

At the time which we are now considering only one of the Kirk's foundations had been securely built—her dogmatic creed, which was the Calvinism of Knox's Confession of Faith, accepted by the reforming Parliament of 1560. That stood without cavil, though in the interpretation of its articles there was considerable difference of emphasis. For the rest, the Kirk was a nominal episcopacy, but the bishops were impotent, and the discipline was in substance Presbyterian: her General Assembly was in abeyance

[1] See Hales's anonymous *Tract concerning Schisme*. London, 1642.
[2] Hacket, *Life of Archbishop Williams*, 64.
[3] Calderwood, VII., 611.

owing to royal encroachments, but it was an integral and
established part of her, so that at the right moment it could
be revived; she had moved far from the moderate Erastian-
ism of Knox, and had come to regard herself as a self-
governing commonwealth, wholly independent in all things
which by any stretch of language could be called spiritual,
and entitled to interfere even in secular politics; her worship
was in the main according to the Genevan form, but not
universally regular owing to James's ill-obeyed decrees.
She was a living organism, the only institution which commanded the loyalty of the majority of the people, and she
was a national thing—for she was neither Genevan, Gal-
lican, nor Anglican, but Scottish.[1]   Among the mediæval
lumber of Parliament, Lords of the Articles and Privy
Council, the Kirk stood out like a throbbing power-house
among tombs. Whether the land were ill or wisely guided,
the chief part of the guiding must be hers.

II

The ecclesiastical structure is much, but we must look
closer at that more vital thing, the spirit which inspired it.

The essence of the Reformation was simplification. The
great organism of the Catholic Church, with all its intricate
accretions of fifteen centuries, was exchanged for a simple
revelation—God speaking through His Word to the individual conscience. The Bible was its palladium, but the
question presently arose as to how the Bible was to be construed, once the authority of the Church had been rejected.
If the individual soul was the basis of the new creed, so
apparently must be the individual judgment. That way lay
anarchy and anabaptism, and it was necessary, before the
Reformed Church could come into being, to establish some
canon of interpretation, otherwise Protestantism would go
to pieces.   The liberal theologians of the seventeenth
century held that the Bible was subject to the ultimate tests
of conscience and reason. " The authority of man," said

[1] It is too often assumed that Scottish Presbytery was a wholesale
borrowing from Geneva. As a matter of fact, while professing to
follow only the Scriptures, it was highly composite in origin.
" There is evidence of the formative influences of Lambert's Hessian
constitution, of the Swiss, and especially of the Genevan reformation, of the foreign churches of a'Lasco and Pullain in England,
with some slight influence of the Edwardian Church of England
itself, and of close study of the new French ecclesiastical polity."
See Miss J. G. Macgregor, The Scottish Presbyterian Polity: a Study
of its Origins, Edinburgh, 1926; and F. W. Maitland, Cambridge
Modern History, II., c. 16.

Hooker, " is the key which openeth the door of entrance into the knowledge of the Scriptures." To him the Bible was not a cyclopædia of all knowledge and all truth. " Admit this and mark, I beseech you, what follows. God, in delivering Scripture to His church, should claim to have abrogated amongst them the law of nature, which is an infallible knowledge imprinted in the minds of all the children of men, whereby both general principles for directing of human action are comprehended, and conclusions derived from them; upon which conclusions groweth in particular the choice of good and evil in the daily affairs of this life. Admit this, and what shall the Scriptures be but a snare and a torment to weak consciences, filling them with infinite perplexities, scrupulosities, doubts insoluble, and extreme despairs."[1] This was the creed of Laud and Chillingworth, of John Hales and Jeremy Taylor, and from it followed the view that, if human reason were the ultimate guide to interpretation, diversity of opinion was inevitable and indeed essential. But such a foundation was too insecure on which to found a militant church. Calvin took a bolder course. We know that the Bible is God's Word, not because of the authority of an historic church, but because of the revelation of the Holy Spirit. This revelation must be systematized and made explicit by God's servants, so that the wayfaring man may understand. From this it is a short step to the foundation of a church which is the direct medium of the Holy Spirit, and a repository of inspired interpretation. The second edition of Calvin's *Institutes*—he was only thirty when it was published—definitely claims to be the canon of Scripture teaching; from it alone the reader may learn what Scripture means. Already the Bible is in a secondary place, and we are not far from Tertullian's doctrine that the *regula fidei* is not Scripture but the creed of a church.

Calvin was perhaps the most potent intellectual force in the world between St. Thomas Aquinas and Voltaire. Though he rejected in his system whatever the Bible did not warrant, and not, like Luther, only what the Bible expressly forbade, he was in many ways nearer to Catholicism than the German reformer. Like most great men, he was greater than the thing he created. He was a profounder statesman than his followers, and far less of a formalist. He could be so inconsistent as to be accused of heresy :

[1] *Ecclesiastical Polity.* See also Laud's controversy with Fisher, Jeremy Taylor's *Liberty of Prophesying*, and Clarendon on Hales.

he saw the dangers into which his church might drift, and
declared that he had no desire to introduce " the tyranny
that one should be bound, under pain of being held a
heretic, to repeat words dictated by some one else "; a man
to whom Plato was of all philosophers *religiosissimus et
maxime sobrius*, had more affinities with humanism than
is commonly believed. But a law-giver must be dogmatic,
and the founder of a church must narrow his sympathies.
He faced the eternal antinomies of thought—the reign of
law and the freedom of the human spirit—and provided
not a solution but a practical compromise. He begins with
the conceptions of an omnipotent God of infinite purity and
wisdom, of man cradled in iniquity, and of salvation only
through God's grace. The sinner is foreordained—since
God orders all things—alike to sin and to destruction. It
is the omnipotence of God that he stresses, rather than the
fatherhood, for he faces the problem from another angle
than Luther: the triviality of the created and the majesty
of the creator; the eternal damnation of man unless lifted
out of the pit by God's election.

These doctrines and this angle of vision were not new.
Origen and Gregory of Nyssa might preach a milder code,
but they were the orthodox creed of the Fathers of the
Church. Men like Tertullian exulted in contemplating the
tortures of the damned. Unbaptized infants, a span long,
would burn for ever in hell, in spite of the fact that their
creation and death were the direct acts of their Maker.
It was the universal mediæval belief, in spite of the
questioning of a Socinus; it was the common doctrine of all
the Reformers except Zuinglius. "This is the acme of
faith," said Luther, " to believe that He is merciful who
saves so few and who condemns so many; that He is just
who, at His own pleasure, has made us necessarily doomed
to damnation. . . . If by any effort of reason I could conceive how God could be merciful and just who shows so
much anger and iniquity, there would be no need for
faith."[1]   On such a view man's reason and man's moral
sense must alike be discarded as temptations of the devil.

This was the creed of Augustine, stated by him more
passionately and harshly than by any Reformer; from him
Calvin largely derived his dogmas, but he took the doctrine
and discarded Augustine's church. Its central principle,
the inexorableness of law, the impossibility of free will,

[1] *De servo arbitrio*, I., c. 23. For Calvin's view see *Institutes*,
III., c. 21-23, and his tract *De æterna Dei predestinatione*.

has been held by many secular thinkers from Spinoza to Mill, who would have rejected its theological implications. It was the creed of William the Silent and Coligny and Cromwell, of Donne and Milton and Bunyan—men in whom both conscience and intellect were quick. Only by a noble inconsistency and a tacit forgetfulness could it be a worthy rule of life, and this was in fact what happened. Calvin was greater than Calvinism, and the Calvinist was a humaner and a wiser man than his creed. But with all its perversities it put salt and iron into human life. It taught man his frailty and his greatness, and brought him into direct communion with Omnipotence. It preached uncompromisingly the necessity of a choice between two paths; in Bunyan's words the mountain gate " has room for body and soul, but not for body and soul and sin." It taught a deep consciousness of guilt, and a profound sense of the greatness of God, so that they who feared Him were little troubled by earthly fears. Historically its importance lay in its absoluteness, for a religion which becomes a " perhaps " will not stand in the day of battle. It claimed to be truth, the whole truth, when everything else was a conjecture or a lie. " In God's matters," said Samuel Rutherford, " there be not, as in grammar, the positive and comparative degrees; . . . there are not here true, and more true, and most true. Truth is an indivisible line which hath no latitude and cannot admit of splitting."[1] It brigaded men into serried battalions; the free-lance disappeared; Mr. Haughty, in the *Holy War*, who declared " that he had carried himself bravely, not considering who were his foes, or what was the cause in which he was engaged," was duly hanged by the men of Mansoul. A creed which was fighting for its life could not afford to be liberal. " On such subjects, and with common men, latitude of mind means weakness of mind. There is but a certain quantity of spiritual force in any man. Spread it over a broad surface, the stream is shallow and languid."[2]

Calvin's fame rests rather on the church which he created than on the creed which he gave it, for he was a greater legislator than a theologian. It was not in belief alone that safety was to be found, but in belief within a church; in his own words, " Beyond the bosom of the Church no remission of sins is to be hoped for nor any

[1] *The Due Right of Presbyteries*, 1644.
[2] Froude, *Short Studies*, I., 180.

salvation "—a strange return to the ecclesiasticism which
he had rejected. He might have said, in the words of a
recent Vatican decree, " La Chiesa non è un credo; la
Chiesa è un impero, una disciplina." John Knox considered the Genevan Church " the most perfect School of
Christ that ever was on earth since the days of the
Apostles," and this was the view taken by his successors of
the quasi-Genevan edifice which he erected in Scotland.
It was divine, guided and inspired by God, and not to be
judged by human standards. It could not err, though that
fallible thing the human conscience might regard certain
of its actions as immoral.[1] It was a complex legal
machine, for it was not for nothing that Calvin, like Knox
and Donne, was bred to the law, and legal phraseology
became the fashion among the divines.[2] Wielding the most
awful powers and penalties, acting under the most august
sanctions, inspired by a narrow and absolute creed, cun-
ningly articulated so that the whole nation was embodied
under its dominion, the Kirk in Scotland was well able to
speak with its adversaries in the gate.

In principle it was a noble democracy. The Kirk made
no distinction of class; the ministry was not a hierarchy,
but issued from the ranks and could be reduced to them
again; an educated laity therefore became the pre-condition
of an educated ministry. In Scotland, with its decrepit
Parliament, which was no better than a machine for
registering the edicts of other people, the pulpit was the sole
organ by which public opinion could be expressed. Only
by means of it could the masses scrutinize the conduct of
their rulers. It gave expression to the very ancient and
stubborn sense of liberty in the Scottish people, and to their
jealous nationalism. The doctrine of divine right had
never come to birth north of the Tweed; the Scots were
ready to fight for their king, unless they happened to be
fighting against him; the monarchy was a useful institution,
and their own, but it was hedged about with no divinity.
The Reformation had come about through the strife of
sovereign and nobles, and the new clergy, already in opposition to the throne, when they came to quarrel with the
nobles were compelled to throw themselves upon the
people. Scotland had learned from Knox and George

---

[1] See Calvin's Machiavellianism in his *Commentary on Joshua.*
[2] *Cf.* Donne, *Sermons I.* and *XXXIV.*, and the constant use of law
terms like " surety," " cautioner," " dyvours," " bond," " articles,"
and " writs " in Covenanting sermons.

Buchanan[1] that the king derived his power from a contract with the nation, and if that contract were broken might be deposed and slain. The passive obedience which Jeremy Taylor preached in his *Ductor Dubitantium*, and which captured many of the best minds in contemporary England, was a plant which did not flourish on Scottish soil. The claim of Presbytery to authority became yearly more arrogant. There was justice in the complaint of Charles I. : " The nature of presbyterian government is to strike or force the crown from the king's head, for their chief maxim is (and I know it to be true) that all kings must submit to Christ's kingdom, *of which they are the sole governors.*"

But by its very nature the Kirk could not remain a democracy. The theocratic conception is inconsistent with the democratic doctrine of majority rule, for, as Selden pointed out, it is blasphemous to identify the odd man with the Holy Ghost.[2] Buckle has declared that the paradox of seventeenth-century Scotland was that the same people were liberal in politics and illiberal in religion, but the theological narrowness was soon to counteract the political liberalism. Holding the creed they did, the ministers gradually came to rule the nation, and, if it was largely a willing servitude, how could it be otherwise when they possessed such crushing spiritual sanctions? Calvinism, as interpreted by Knox and Andrew Melville, involves a theocracy, and the plain man, out of fear of hell fire, will surrender his conscience and his judgment as absolutely to his minister as any Catholic to his priest. A Kirk so inspired will find itself claiming powers which only supreme genius could wield without disaster, and the atmosphere will not be favourable for the presence of genius. Its leaders are more likely to be of the type which Lord Morley has drawn in Lilburne—" the men whom all revolutions are apt to engender : intractable, narrow, dogmatic, pragmatic, clever hands at syllogism, liberal in uncharitable imputation and malicious construction, honest in their rather questionable way, animated by a rather pharisaic love of self-applause which is in truth not any more meritorious nor less unsafe than vain love of the world's applause; in a word, not without sharp insight into theoretic principle, and thinking quite as little of their own ease as of the ease of others, but without a trace of the instinct for government or a grain of practical common sense."[3]

[1] *De Jure Regni apud Scotos*, 1579.
[2] *Table Talk*: Council.   [3] *Cromwell*, 291.

The prime defect of the Kirk was intolerance. It shared this fault with many other communions, but then no communion, save the Church of Rome, claimed its absolute powers. There was no " liberty of cult " in Elizabeth's Prayer-book, which laid down the only lawful form of worship; and Nowell, Dean of St. Paul's—Izaak Walton's " good old man and honest angler "—could clamour for the death of the Marian bishops as savagely as any Scots reformer. Laud was tolerant enough about creeds, but not about church government. In England only the rare few, like Hales and Falkland and Chillingworth, attained to that true toleration which is based not on indifference but on spiritual humility;[1] only a few asserted with Milton the right of private judgment—" if a man believe things only because his pastor says so, . . . though his belief be true, yet the very truth he holds becomes his heresy."[2]

The question must be viewed in its due historical perspective. The nursing-ground of intolerance is a complete dogmatic certainty about the ordering of the world. To the modern mind, accustomed to think of man as a clot of vivified dust, set on an inconsiderable planet which revolves with an infinity of others in the immensity of space, conscious, too, that human life has relations through countless æons with lower existences, and is kin alike to the brutes and to the stars, it is hard to understand the habit of thought which about everything can pronounce unhesitatingly that here is final truth. Such cosmic assurance requires a simple cosmogony, and this—save in the case of a few advanced thinkers—the seventeenth century possessed. To it the earth and all therein were made purposely by God for man, and man's journey heaven-ward or hell-ward was the essential purpose of creation. It held that a few thousand years earlier the universe had been fabricated out of chaos in six calendar days, that all history antecedent to our era had been a preparation for the coming of Christ, and that, the supreme sacrifice having been accomplished, at any moment the skies might open, and the trumpets sound, and the short story of the earth

<hr />

[1] " He therefore exceedingly detested the tyranny of the Church of Rome more for their imposing uncharitably upon the consciences of other men, than for the errors in their own opinions; and would often say that he would renounce the religion of the Church of England to-morrow if it obliged him to believe that any other Christians should be damned; and that nobody would conclude another man to be damned who did not wish him so." Clarendon on Hales. *Life* (ed. 1759), 27-28.   [2] *Areopagitica.*

be closed. There were mysteries indeed, stupendous mysteries, but, if their content was unplumbed, their limits could be exactly defined. Such a cosmos was both intimate and simple, made according to man's scale and for his uses; it was without blurred lines or shadowy corners, and the mind which accepted it was ready to pronounce upon its problems as upon matters of ascertained fact.

If the nature of the popular cosmogony predisposed men to dogma, so did the quality of the revelation that illumined it. That revelation was absolute; its acceptance gave eternal life, its neglect eternal torment. Toleration is a high virtue, when it springs from humility and is regarded as in itself a religious act; but it is important to remember that in certain mental states it may be a vice, a synonym for spiritual apathy and moral sloth. "What," St. Augustine asked, "can be more deadly to the soul than the liberty of error?" The doctrine of exclusive salvation, honestly held, involves intolerance, and finds its logical consequence in persecution. If a man believes that his heart is desperately wicked, that he is doomed to eternal fires but for the interposition of God's grace, and that to walk in grace it is necessary to observe literally the precepts of the Scriptures without any attempt to rethink them in the light of new conditions—nay, that such an attempt is in God's eye the unpardonable sin—tolerance must be only another name for lukewarmness, and reason only the temptation of the devil. If he is right, all those who differ from him must be wrong, and it is his duty to enforce his faith with fire and sword. What suffering that man can inflict is comparable to the eternal misery of those who embrace false doctrine? This was the creed alike of St. Augustine and St. Thomas Aquinas; it was an integral part of seventeenth-century Protestant theology: in a milder form it will be found in more than one Papal bull of the nineteenth century. Even a liberal thinker like Richard Baxter pronounced toleration to be " soul murder," and in that era only Cromwell in practice, and men like Harrington, Milton, Jeremy Taylor, and Chillingworth in their writings, propounded a gentler doctrine. It is unhappily true that in such an age the best men, in whom religion is a living fire, are apt to be the narrowest. "The only true spirit of tolerance," Coleridge has written, "consists in conscientious toleration of each other's intolerance. Whatever pretends to be more than this, is either the unthinking cant of fashion or the soul-palsying narcotic of

moral and religious indifference."[1]   But before such a
mood can be attained, there must be a critical breaking-
down of the adamantine bulwarks of dogma.   Charles
James Fox was right when he said that " the only foundation for toleration is a degree of scepticism."[2]   Only the
rare few could conceive of a tolerance which was not
indifferentism, but a supreme religious duty.[3]

The Scottish Kirk held the current doctrine in its
extremest form, and for a manual of practice had recourse
to the Bible.   She interpreted it arbitrarily and literally,
forgetting Donne's pregnant saying that " sentences in
Scripture, like hairs in horses' tails, concur in one root of
beauty and strength, but, being plucked out one by one,
serve only for springes and snares."   Finding little warrant
for force in the New Testament, her divines had recourse
to the Old Testament, where they discovered encouraging
precedents in the doings of Elijah and Hezekiah and Josiah.
This constant resort to the Mosaic dispensation encouraged
a stiff and autocratic temper.   Cromwell's famous appeal
—" We should be pitiful . . . and tender towards all
though of different judgments. . . . Love all, tender all,
cherish and countenance all, in all things that are good.
. . . And if the poorest Christian, the most mistaken Christian, shall desire to live peaceably and quietly under you
—I say, if any shall desire but to lead a life of godliness
and honesty, let him be protected "—would have sounded
in their ears like a fearful blasphemy.   Their church was
a theocracy, and that involves both a claim to infallibility
and a meticulous physical discipline applied in the spiritual
sphere.   They held the keys of heaven and hell, and had
power to deliver the erring over to Satan and to anticipate
by exemplary punishment in this world the torments of
the next.[4]

With such a creed there could be no real delimitation
between the spiritual and the secular, between Church and
State.   The right of the Kirk to dominate personal and
family life was soon extended to the duty of interference

---

[1] *The Friend*, I., 123.   [2] Rogers, *Recollections*, 49.
[3] The authorities on this point will be found in Lecky, *Rationalism
in Europe*, c. 4.   See also Harrington, *Political Aphorisms*, and *A
System of Politics*, in his *Works* (ed. Toland, 1700); Milton, *Areopagitica*; Jeremy Taylor, *Liberty of Prophesying*; Chillingworth, *The
Religion of Protestants*; Southey on Bogue's *History of Dissenters*
in *Quarterly Review*, October 1813; Coleridge, *Notes, Theological,
Political, and Miscellaneous*, 319-321; Morley, *Cromwell*, 163-168.
[4] See the notes to Buckle, *History of Civilization*, c. xix.

with civil government. Indeed, the rejection of toleration
and the belief in uniformity led inevitably to a usurpation
of civil power. The Kirk believed, as Catholicism believed,
in a single church, a complete and exclusive system to
which a single separatist was anathema. In her zeal for
uniformity she in no way differed from Laud, though she
preferred another pattern. The secularization of politics
did not fully come about till the toleration of religious
variety had first been established. When the Kirk usurped
powers which seem to us in no way to belong to her
province, she was following the prevailing tendency of the
age. She was true to the mediæval idea of one church,
one rule. Against the universal claim of Rome it was
necessary to establish a counter-universalism. Presbytery
professed, as Rome professed, to be based upon *jus
divinum*, and therefore there could be no limits to its
sovereignty. With Catholic and Anglican it waged truce-
less war, but it drew, like them, from the Middle Ages, and
accepted the same kind of dogmatic sanction. High
Cavalier and high Covenanter talked the same language,
though with different applications, and divine right was the
watchword of both. To each the man who looked upon
the world with a cool secular eye and talked sober reason
was worse than their avowed opponents; he was a heretic
in the fundamentals, the ultimate blasphemer.

The Scottish ministers have fared ill with later historians,
except in the copious literature of their own communion.
The wisest and greatest, Robert Leighton, belongs to a later
date, and soon deserted the manse of Newbattle. They
have been represented as violent and illiterate peasants,
mob-orators rather than divines. As a matter of fact, they
sprang either from the landed gentry and the clergy, or
from well-to-do burgher families. Robert Traill had for
his father a gentleman of the Privy Chamber to Prince
Henry; Robert Blair was the son of an Ayrshire laird, and
his mother was a Mure of Rowallan; James Durham was
an Angus proprietor; Robert Baillie was of the Baillies of
Lamington; Robert Douglas was a son of that George
Douglas who helped Queen Mary to escape from Loch-
leven; James Guthrie was a son of Guthrie of that ilk.
Almost all had received a sound education in the humani-
ties as well as in theology, and some, like Robert Boyd
and Alexander Henderson, Hugh Binning and Samuel
Rutherford, were notable scholars. Among them, too,
were many types of mind and temperament, from the

political shrewdness of Robert Baillie and the quaint
humanity of William Guthrie of Fenwick to the fanatic
hardness of Nevoy and the oriental lusciousness of Samuel
Rutherford.[1]

They preached a creed which, in most of its details, is
now forgotten, and the language of which is fantastic or
ridiculous to our ears. They laid down as the necessary
and universal progress towards salvation a rigid curriculum
of experiences—" exercise," " law-work," " discovery of
interest," " damps," " challenge," " outgate," " assurance."
Well might a later seventeenth-century Scotsman exclaim:
" I doubt it hath occasioned much unnecessary disquiet
to some holy persons that they have not found such a
regular and orderly transaction in their souls as they have
seen described in the books. . . . God hath several ways
of dealing with the souls of men, and it sufficeth if the work
be accomplished whatever the methods have been."[2] But
behind their narrowness and their legal jargon we can see
in many the true exaltation of the saint. Among the
crudities and absurdities of their sermons and biographies
there are passages of apostolic power, visions such as
George Fox records in his journal, which led them to an
ecstasy of praise, moments of deep tenderness towards the
souls of their flocks. They must be judged by their work,
and beyond doubt they gave to the Scottish people a moral
seriousness, a conception of the deeper issues of life, and
an intellectual *ascesis*, gifts which may well atone for their
many infirmities.

Yet there is much to be atoned for, and the immediate
result of their predominance was not less disastrous than
beneficent. " Deliver me, O Lord," was the cry of Archbishop Leighton, " from the errors of wise men, yea, and
of good men."[3] They perverted the Gospel into a thing
of subtle legal conundrums; they made morality difficult
by destroying its rational basis; they took the colour out
of life for their people by condemning the innocencies of
the world with a more than monastic austerity; they
inflamed the superstitions of the country by peopling it
with a fanciful pandemonium. If any one has the patience
to labour through a dozen volumes of their sermons, he
will be aghast at the childishness and irreverence of much

---

[1] *The Commissions of the General Assemblies* (S.H.S.), III.,
Introd.; Howie, *Scots Worthies.*
[2] Scougal, *The Life of God in the Soul of Man*, 65.
[3] *Commentary upon the First Epistle of St. Peter.*

of their teaching. Like an African witch-doctor, they " smelled out " offenders, and they were the principal up-stay of witch-burning. Miracles and portents adorned their path, and natural laws were suspended to point their lessons. They magnified their office till they hedged themselves round with a false divinity. The clouds of their dogmatic terrors darkened the world for their hearers, and condemned weak spirits to religious mania. Their neurotic supernaturalism, which saw judgments and signs in the common incidents of life, weakened in the people the power of rational thought.[1] If they gave manhood and liberty to Scotland, they did much to sap the first and shackle the second. Condemning natural pleasures and affections, they drew a dark pall over the old merry Scottish world, the world of the ballads and the songs, of frolics and mummings and " blithesome bridals," and, since human nature will not be denied, drove men and women to sinister and perverted outlets. In a word, they established over the whole of human life, alike in its public duties and in its most intimate private affairs, a harsh and senseless tyranny, and against them, as the delegates of heaven, there was no appeal. Tougher spirits might emerge unscathed and even fortified, but the frail were warped and demented. Yet it was the strongest thing in Scotland, and presently in all the Lowlands it had made good its sway over every class of the people; *ruere in servitium consules, patres, eques.*

III

To balance the claims of the Kirk there was no strong apparatus of secular government. The so-called Parliament, with its three estates of clergy, tenants-in-chief, and burgesses, delegated its power in the Lords of the Articles, who had the sole right to initiate business, and the selection of whom was controlled by the king. It was neither representative nor free. " The Crown manipulated elections, determined the composition of the committee through which all business must pass before it reached the throne, sternly limited the time allowed for the discussion of the committee's report, forced a long series of measures through the House at a single sitting, and cajoled or threatened opponents."[2] The Privy Council, the equiva-

---

[1] " Away with such rash and bold conceits: the love of God either to causes or persons is not to be measured by these external and outward accidents." Spottiswoode, III., 183.
[2] Rait, *The Parliaments of Scotland*, 62.

lent of the Cabinet, was almost identical with the Lords of
the Articles. The Convention of Royal Burghs was a kind
of minor parliament charged with burgh concerns, and its
existence did much to distract the interest of burgess members from national affairs. In all this mechanism there was
no authority which could act as a makeweight to the growing popular authority of the Kirk, guard the liberties of
Scotland against royal encroachment, or, on behalf of the
nation at large, control the traditional high-handedness of
the nobility.

The Scottish nobles from the fourteenth to the sixteenth
century were probably the most turbulent, rapacious, and
ignorant in Europe. Resolute champions of indefensible
privileges, they resisted all the reforming efforts of their
kings, and were the death of more than one sovereign.
They had not even the merit of patriotism, for often they
were in arms against their own land, and Scottish history
is stored with ugly tales of treason. Their prime foes had
been the king and the church, and they had always cast
longing eyes at the fat abbeys and the rich glebes of their
clerical rivals. The Reformation gave them their chance.
Two-thirds of the church plunder fell into their hands, and
their Protestantism was mainly determined by self-interest.
Knox complained, not without reason, that in all the Lords
of the Congregation there was not one righteous man. A
few became dogmatic enthusiasts, but the majority cared
as little for the difference between priest and minister as
for the Ten Commandments. Nor were they, like many
of the great families of England—like Pembroke in Wilt-
shire, or Stanley in Lancashire, or Beaufort on the West
Marches—magnates who performed useful duties of local
administration. Their mediæval satrapies were antagonistic
to the first principles of a modern state. Knox had
struggled to win from the old church property reasonable
endowments for his new Kirk, but the tithes and the lands
went to the nobles and barons, who were determined not
to disgorge. Their opposition to the Anglicanism of
Charles was largely due to the fact that it involved sooner
or later a redivision of ecclesiastical plunder; they would
vehemently oppose any church except one which they
could starve.

At first sight it would seem that there could be little in
common between a proud Kirk, with a great popular
following, laying down the austerest rule of life, and a
nobility which was irreligious and oppressive, which clung

to wealth which Knox had destined for the Kirk, and of which the Kirk was sorely in need. Indeed it was only the blundering of the king that prevented a breach between the two, with the clergy for once on the royal side. The tithe had become a crying scandal, for the feudal lords, to whom it had passed, could levy it in kind much as they pleased and when they pleased, so that the tenant could not get in his harvest till the lord had taken his toll. In 1625 Charles undertook the work of reform. He removed the judges from the Privy Council, that they might have time for their proper business of the Court of Session, and by the Act of Revocation of 1625 he attempted to recover as much as he could of the old church property for national uses. In the most modern way he appointed a royal commission to work out the details; the teinds were to afford a living wage to the ministers, and the holders of church lands were in future to pay rent to the Crown. Mr. Gardiner calls the measure the "one successful act of Charles's reign," and considers that it "weakened the power of the nobility, and strengthened the prerogative in the only way in which the prerogative deserved to be strengthened . . . by the popularity it gained through carrying into effect a wise and beneficent reform."[1] But no popularity followed. Perhaps the money-getting motive was too clear in the reform, for it was instituted after the English Parliament had refused to grant adequate supplies; perhaps the royal interference with property suggested further revolutionary designs. At any rate the king got no gratitude from the Kirk, and he incurred the deadly displeasure of the aristocracy. The way was prepared for an alliance between the two contraries, who were agreed only in their stubborn conservatism—nobles desperately intent on holding what their fathers had won, and churchmen desperately in earnest about their spiritual prerogatives. It was a very pretty powder-magazine for the inevitable spark.

The time was one of deep poverty for the common people. The bonnet-lairds and the tacksmen, the labourers and shepherds, the petty craftsmen in the villages, even the burghers in the little towns, lived very near the edge of destitution. The rudimentary and wasteful system of agriculture, with its sodden in-fields and its rank out-fields, its wretched grain, its shallow ploughing, placed the farmers at the mercy of an indifferent climate and a poor

[1] *Hist. of England*, VII., 279-280.

soil—for the richer valley bottoms were uncultivable from lack of drainage. Stock was in no better case, for the cattle were stunted and perpetually lean, and the sheep were moving masses of tar and vermin. At the close of each winter the spectre of starvation came very near to man and beast. Idyllic pictures have been drawn of the Covenanting peasant as a stalwart fellow in good homespun clothes and blue bonnet, and of his house as a snug dwelling like an illustration to *The Cotter's Saturday Night*. The truth seems to be that the physique of most was early ruined by poor feeding and incessant toil, that they had small regard for bodily cleanliness, that their clothes were coarse at the best and generally ragged, and that their dwellings resembled a Connemara cabin. Recurrent plagues carried off their thousands, and foul habits and a diet of thin brose and bannocks weakened the survivors. Nasty, brutish, and short was the life of the seventeenth-century Lowlander. Education did something to counterbalance the economic defects, but it is easy to exaggerate the extent of Scottish education at this era. Kirkton, indeed, records that before 1660 " every village had a school, every family almost had a Bible, yea, in most of the country all the children of age could read the Scriptures ";[1] but Kirkton was *laudator temporis acti*, and his testimony is not borne out by parish and burgh records. Knox's great scheme remained largely an unrealized ideal; the report of the commission of 1627 reveals very many parishes in the Lowlands and the Borders without school or schoolmaster; and the remedial Acts of 1633 and 1643 were for the most part a dead letter. The fact that the new religion was based on private Bible-reading was indeed an inducement to literacy, but in the very places where theological interest was keenest we find a surprising proportion unable to write, while Wodrow was told by his father that in his day " the generality by far in the country . . . could not read."[2]

There was no middle-class to act as a force of social persistence and a sober nursery of new civic ideas, like the great bourgeoisie which was the strength of English Puritanism. Scottish commerce was a petty thing; her

---

[1] *History of the Church of Scotland*, 64.
[2] *Report of Parishes in 1627* (Maitland Club); Wodrow, *Life of Professor Wodrow*. At Dalmellington, in Ayrshire, a Covenanting stronghold, the Solemn League and Covenant was subscribed by 222 people, 179 of whom could not write.

noblesse de robe were reactionary manipulators of a reactionary law; her burghers and bonnet-lairds were too
near the peasant; she had no parallel class to the yeomanry
and merchantry of England. If strife came it would be
conducted between king, nobles, and Kirk, with the bulk
of the people obedient under the spiritual narcotics of the
last. There was little hope for that fruitful political dispute which is the basis of a free polity, but for wild and
barren explosions there was an uncomfortable amount of
powder.

IV

The spark came from a blundering king. Charles had
been born in Scotland, and, according to Clarendon, was
" always an immoderate lover of the Scottish nation "; but
he had not his father's knowledge of the national temperament, and he had for his advisers on Scottish affairs men
altogether out of touch with the people. When he came
to Scotland in the summer of 1633 to be crowned, he had
already estranged the nobility by his perfectly just and
reasonable treatment of the tithes question. The visit
revealed the existence of an opposition even in the packed
Scots Parliament, and, since Laud was in his company,
the coronation ceremonies roused suspicion in Presbyterian
breasts. In August of that year Laud became Archbishop
of Canterbury, and entered upon the policy of reclaiming
Scottish barbarism to his ideal of ecclesiastical decency.
A year later the Court of High Commission was established
by royal warrant, and the number of bishops in the Privy
Council was increased to seven. In January 1635 Archbishop Spottiswoode was made Chancellor in succession
to Kinnoull, the first time since the Reformation that the
office had been given to a churchman.

The Scottish hierarchy of the time has been portrayed,
perhaps, in darker colours than it deserves. Spottiswoode
himself, and men like Forbes and Maxwell, Sydserf and
Wedderburn, were liberal in doctrine and exemplary in
private life, and saintliness was the prerogative of neither
party. But the bishops for good and ill were out of tune
with their countrymen; they represented a theological
creed which was in advance of their age, and an ecclesiastical creed which lagged behind it, for they did not
appreciate the passion for spiritual autonomy which had
become part of the national mood.[1] They were impossible

[1] For what can be said in defence of the bishops see W. L.
Mathieson, *Politics and Religion in Scotland*, I., c. x.

as mediators, since the best of them talked a language unintelligible to that age, and the worst of them shared in Laud's perilous hieratic dreams. They might be intellectually tolerant like their leader, but they were ecclesiastically dogmatic. Their sudden rise to political power roused the extreme suspicion of the Kirk, it offended the pride of the nobles, and it stirred the opposition of even the staunchest moderates. " That Churchmen have competency," wrote Montrose's guardian and brother-in-law, Lord Napier, " is agreeable to the law of God and man; but to invest them into great estates and principal offices of the State, is neither convenient for the Church, for the King, nor for the State. . . . Histories witness what troubles have been raised to kings, what tragedies amongst subjects, in all places where Churchmen were great. Our reformed Churches, having reduced religion to the ancient primitive truth and simplicity, ought to beware that corruption enter not into their Church in the same gate."[1]

In the year 1635 the royal blunders multiplied. A temperate protest by Lord Balmerino against certain recent acts came into Spottiswoode's hand, and thence to the king's. It was construed as high treason, and in March 1635 the writer was put on trial, convicted by a majority of one, and condemned to death. He was presently pardoned, but the affair deeply impressed his countrymen; it was the bishops' doing, and it seemed as if the old liberty was now dead in the land. A crisis had been reached when a man like Drummond of Hawthornden, no lover of the Kirk, was forced into vigorous remonstrance, and could advise his sovereign to study Buchanan's *De Jure Regni apud Scotos*.[2] In May a royal warrant authorized a new book of canons to regulate the government of the Church of Scotland, and the book was published in January 1636, prepared by a committee of the Scottish bishops and revised by Laud and Juxon. It re-enacted in substance the Articles of Perth, which had become a dead letter, prohibited extempore prayer, allowed confession, and claimed for the king supreme authority in ecclesiastical causes. More ominous still, it promised a service book, or liturgy, and threatened in advance excommunication against all those who should not accept it. It would be hard to conceive of a more foolish provocation. The book had no authority except the royal *ipse dixit*, and yet many

[1] Napier, I., 104.
[2] Masson, *Drummond of Hawthornden*, 237-241.

of the canons dealt with civil as well as with ecclesiastical law.[1] It challenged not only religious but political liberty.

The promised liturgy appeared in an atmosphere already superheated. In November 1636 Charles wrote to the Privy Council, ordering that the new " Book of Public Service " be used, and that each parish provide itself with two copies before the following Easter. But it was not till 1637 that the book was published. It is probable that the Scottish bishops had little to do with it, for even the most sacerdotal among them hesitated before this monstrous innovation.[2] Laud and his English colleagues took the English Prayer-book, made a few changes which the Scottish hierarchy had suggested, and made many others in the direction of a more exacting ritual. " The book, with the canons which preceded it, had no ecclesiastical sanction, either of all the bishops, or of a General Assembly. The imposition was an act of sheer royal autocratic papacy; the book, being English, insulted Scottish national sentiment; the changes from the English version were deemed to imply a nearer approach to Rome. Protestantism was in danger. The landowners suspected that Charles meant to recover some of their old ecclesiastical estates for the rebuilding of cathedrals and cleaning of churches; and thus, from the ' rascal multitude ' upwards, through every rank and condition of his subjects, he gave intolerable offence, and caused extreme apprehension. He lost three kingdoms and his head, not for a mass, but for a surplice."[3]

The tumult was instant and universal. The devout women of Edinburgh rose in their wrath, and the first attempt to read the new service-book in St. Giles's church was the signal for a riot.[4] The flame ran fast over Scotland, for the offence was grievous; to endure such interference with private worship was to stultify the whole Reformation principle, and to sit quiet under flagrant illegality was to sacrifice the ancient liberties of the realm. Every post to England carried a supplication or remon-

[1] Row, 393.
[2] See for a full study of its antecedents Sprott, *Scottish Liturgies*, Introd., and Hill Burton, *History of Scotland*, c. lxviii.
[3] Lang, III., 25-26.
[4] See the account in Rothes, *Relation of the Affairs of the Kirk*, App.; Gordon of Rothiemay, I., 7-11; Wariston, *Diary*, I., 265; and for the general situation, Baillie, I., and Balfour, II. The king's statement of his case will be found in the *Large Declaration*, 1639.

strance to His Majesty.[1] The Privy Council, divided
between the lay lords and the bishops, was helpless; it
suggested deputations which Charles would not receive, and
meantime it was being flooded with petitions from every
part of the Lowlands. The king's proclamations only made
matters worse, and by October public meetings were being
held everywhere, bishops were being rabbled, and the
pacific Mr. Robert Baillie was writing: " No man may
speak anything in public for the king's part, except he
would have himself marked for a sacrifice to be killed one
day. I think our people possessed with a bloody devill."[2]

On 15th November an important step was taken. With
the sanction of the Lord Advocate, Sir Thomas Hope, the
malcontents organized themselves into a body of commissioners—four committees of nobles, lairds, burgesses, and
ministers, henceforth to be known as the Tables. It was
in substance a provisional government, and behind it was
all Scotland, except the remoter Highlands and Aberdeen.
In opposition to the king stood the solid phalanx of the
Kirk, led by Alexander Henderson of Leuchars, the ablest
statesman among the ministers; the burgesses were unani-
mous on the same side, as were also the lawyers; the lairds
were represented by such names as Stirling of Keir, Hume
of Wedderburn, Douglas of Cavers, Fraser of Philorth,
Mure of Rowallan, and Agnew of Lochnaw; among the
nobles were Sutherland, Cromartie, Ruthven, Eglinton,
Wemyss, Lothian, Home, Loudoun, Lindsay, and Yester.
The peerage and the lesser baronage of Scotland were
united as they had never been before and were never to
be again. Even the Lords of the Council were inclining
to the malcontents, and the bishops had withdrawn from
that uneasy assembly.

At the meeting of petitioners on 15th November the
young Montrose was present. In September leading
ministers had been appointed to secure adherents for the
opposition, and Mr. Robert Murray of Methven was
nominated for Perth and Stirling. Montrose at a later date
named Mr. Murray as " an instrument of bringing me to
their cause."[3] Along with Rothes, Loudoun, and Lindsay
of the Byres he was appointed to the Table of the nobility.

---

[1] Montrose signed the document entitled " Scotland's Supplication
and Complaint against the Book of Common Prayer, the Book of
Canons, and the Prelates," of October 18, 1637. See Dr. Hay
Fleming's paper in *Proceedings of the Society of Antiquaries of
Scotland*, LX., 314-383.   [2] I., 23.   [3] Napier, I., 136.

The unrest could have only one consequence. Traquair, the Treasurer, got no comfort at the royal court; indeed, in a proclamation which he brought back in February 1638, Charles took complete responsibility for the new liturgy, and required all petitioners to disperse on pain of treason and not to reassemble without the Council's consent. On February 22, 1638, when that proclamation was made in Edinburgh, a public protestation was read by Wariston, and one act of war was met by another. On that day Montrose was among the protesting leaders, mounted in boyish enthusiasm on a barrel, so that the prophetic soul of Rothes was moved to observe: " James, you will never be at rest till you are lifted up above the rest in three fathoms of a rope."[1] The Tables decided to revive the Covenant of 1581 against popery, and to add their own grievances, and Alexander Henderson and Wariston drafted the new version. It was an old device, for when the Scottish nobles chose to walk in the path of rebellion it had been their fashion to enter into " ane band." This was, however, to be a legal act, and to make the Almighty a party; in Wariston's word it was " the glorious marriage day of the Kingdom with God."[2] The first part repeated the Covenant of 1581 against Rome; the second part recited the acts of Parliament passed since the Reformation in favour of the Kirk; the third part pledged its signatories to defend their religion against all innovations not sanctioned by Parliament and Assembly, and to " stand to the defence of our dread sovereign the King's Majesty, his person and authority, in the defence and preservation of the foresaid true religion, liberties, and laws of this Kingdom." It was a candid and straightforward document, temperately expressed and accurately directed to the grievances which it was designed to remedy. The claim was to both spiritual and civil freedom, and the formidable sanction behind it was at once ecclesiastical, feudal, and democratic. On the last day of February it was read in Greyfriars' church in Edinburgh, with its solemn appeal that " religion and righteousness may flourish in the land, to the glory of God, the honour of the King, and the peace and comfort of us all." On that and succeeding days it was signed amid scenes of deep popular emotion, and in subsequent months copies were carried far and wide through the land, and even overseas to Scots serving in foreign wars.

[1] Gordon of Rothiemay, I., 33.   [2] *Diary*, I., 322.

On the first day Montrose subscribed his name. According to Baillie he was brought in " by the canniness of Rothes." John Leslie, sixth Earl of Rothes, was an adroit diplomat, and had an old grievance against the Act of Revocation. He was disliked by Charles, and probably returned the dislike. He was little of a precisian in character, for he is described by Clarendon as " very free and amorous, and unrestrained in his discourse by any scruples of religion, which he only put on when the parts he had to act required it, and then no man could appear more conscientiously transported "; nor was he extreme in politics, and Clarendon believed that but for his early death he would have gone over to the king's side.[1] Doubtless Rothes desired to strengthen the movement by the adhesion of the representative of an historic house, who was still an attractive mystery to his countrymen; doubtless Montrose was not insensitive to the persuasive charm of one who was much his elder and was the most generally popular man in Scotland. Talks with Rothes and Mr. Robert Murray, and the fact that the Fife nobles with whom he had spent much of his time during his St. Andrews years were among the promoters of the new Covenant, may have predisposed him to the popular side.

But indeed Montrose required no " canniness " of noble or cleric to help him to a decision. There were those among the protagonists of the Covenant who may have been antipathetic to him—Loudoun, his colleague on the Tables, who had been a Campbell of Lawers and was trusted by no man; Wariston, that strange youth of twenty-seven, a devotee in a lawyer's gown, who would forget time in prayer and be on his knees for fourteen hours at a stretch, and often, as his nephew Burnet tells us, slept but three hours in the twenty-four. But all Scotland was in the bond, except a few Catholic nobles and Aberdeen doctors, and in it were the companions of his youth, and Napier, his most trusted counsellor. The Covenant was legal, pronounced to be so by the Lord Advocate and by the bulk of the judges, and Montrose from his youth was a lover of legality.[2] Further, the main issues were not yet confused. There was no attack upon the king's authority;

---

[1] *History*, I., 171; III., 38; IV., 23, 250. *Cal. S. P., Dom.* (1641-43), 105-107.
[2] Lord President Inglis has also defended its legality in his article, " Montrose and the Covenant of 1638," in *Blackwood's Magazine*, November 1887.

indeed, the royal sovereignty was vehemently asserted. The bishops were unpopular, but there was as yet little of that morbid hatred of the very name of episcopacy which followed later, when dislike of the thing done became detestation of the suspected means. In 1637 Baillie could still write: " Bishops I love;"[1] and there must have been many in Edinburgh to relish the dialectical triumph of the Episcopalian vintner over the Presbyterian shoemaker, recorded by James Howell in his letter to Lord Clifford.[2] The true point of conflict was far greater than any squabble about niceties of church government. It was the right of Scotland to her ancestral liberties, the confinement of prerogative within its legal limits, the keeping of church-men out of civil offices. To a young man nourished on Plutarch and Thucydides and familiar with the current political thought of Europe, to one who at no time in his life could tolerate the ecclesiastic in politics, to a Scotsman who had his full share of the national pride, the cause of the Covenant was the cause of the patriot, the philosopher, and the well-wisher to the king.

That February noon in Greyfriars was one of the most momentous in our history, for it was the first step in a con-flict which did not end till the December day, half a century later, when a king of England became an exile. To Charles it may at first have seemed but another spasm of recal-citrance which would be presently forgotten—a matter less important than the impending judgment of the Exchequer Chamber in the ship-money case. But when the news out of Scotland came, after many days, to the ears of a certain middle-aged Huntingdonshire grazier, who had lately re-moved to Ely, it may have caused deeper reflections. For this grazier, in the intervals of examining the work of God in his soul, had a quick eye for public portents, and he had won so much prestige as the defender of the rights of the fen commoners, that he might hope to be sent to Westminster, should the king call another Parliament.

[1] I., 2.   [2] *Epistolæ Ho-elianæ*, I., 36.

C

CHAPTER III

THE FIRST COVENANT WARS

(1638-39)

As for discontentments, they are in the politic body like to humours in the natural, which are apt to gather a preternatural heat and to inflame. And let no prince measure the danger of them by this, whether they be just or unjust; for that were to imagine people to be too reasonable who do often spurn at their own good : nor yet by this, whether the griefs whereupon they rise be in fact great or small; for they are the most dangerous discontentments where the fear is greater than the feeling. *Dolendi modus, timendi non item.*   BACON.

In 1639 even the most obscure woods began to be penetrated with flashes.   *Memoirs of Colonel Hutchinson.*

I

THE NATIONAL COVENANT WAS BASED UPON SOUND CONSTITU-tional law, but the form of the protest—the " band " borrowed from the Middle Ages—and certain passages in the document were of dubious legality. Especially ominous was the clause which bound the signatories to mutual defence " against all sorts of persons whatsoever," which might be interpreted as including the king. There were many irregularities in the obtaining of signatures, for in certain districts it was " obtruded upon people with threatenings, tearing of clothes, drawing of blood."[1] Moreover, to Charles in Whitehall it might have seemed that there had been already overt acts of revolution. The new Committee of Sixteen, the Tables, had set about organizing a provisional Government. As early as February 1638 steps had been taken to raise a revenue. In March a " voluntary " tax was levied in every shire of one dollar for every thousand merks of free rent; the Covenanting lords subscribed largely, and twenty-five dollars was Montrose's contribution; there were signs that presently the levy would cease to be optional, and that non-Covenanters would be mulcted.[2] It all looked suspiciously like the creation of a war-chest. It was certain, too, that the movement would not remain within the four corners of the Covenant, but was capable of indefinite extension. The country was on fire, and every Sunday the ministers were

---

[1] Gordon of Rothiemay, I., 53-56. Napier, I., 142-144.
[2] Rothes, 72, etc.; Baillie, I., 213.

fanning the flame. Wariston records a sermon in Edinburgh on 1st April, when the preacher, Mr. Rollock, after
reading the Covenant, requested the nobles present—Montrose, Boyd, Loudoun, and Balmerino—to hold up their
hands and swear by the name of the living God: " at the
which instant of rising up, and then of holding up their
hands, there rose sic a yelloch, sic abundance of tears, sic
a heavenly harmony of sighs and sobs, universally through
all the corners of the church, as the like was never seen
nor heard of."[1]   Scotland was in a high-strung and perilous
mood.

The wise course for Charles would have been to withdraw the service book and to give assurance that he would
meddle no more with property and heritable jurisdictions;
in that way he would have driven a wedge between those
unnatural allies, the nobles and the Kirk. But from this
course he was estopped by his passionate desire, fostered
by Laud, to establish a uniform standard of worship
throughout his realm, and the fear that such a concession
would weaken his cause in the quarrel now drawing to a
head with the English Parliament. He would fain have
acted as he did in the ship-money case, and have secured
a condemnation of the Covenant in the law courts, but the
whole Scottish bench and bar believed in its legality.[2] He
had for a moment hopes of organizing a royalist opposition
in Scotland, with the help of the Highland clans and pos-
sibly of Irish troops under Antrim, but he abandoned the
project when he realized that, except for Huntly and the
Gordons, and the doubtful cases of Hamilton, Lanark,
Traquair, and Roxburgh, he had at the moment no Scottish
supporters. Yet the king, who had at times no mean
capacity for judging a situation, arrived at a shrewder
estimate of the Scottish situation than his advisers. If he
was to win his will force must be used, and to collect that
force he must have time. The Privy Council had sent the
Justice Clerk to court to expound the true state of Scotland.
The king was impressed, and summoned Traquair and
Roxburgh to advise him; Spottiswoode, too, and certain of
the Scots bishops; likewise Lord Lorn, who had not signed
the Covenant, and whom Baillie thought the most powerful subject in the kingdom.[3] The outcome of this consulta-
tion was that the Marquis of Hamilton was appointed a

[1] *Diary*, I., 331.
[2] See two letters of Traquair in *Hardwicke Papers*, II., 103-104.
[3] I., 146.

special royal commissioner to Scotland, with authority to treat with the malcontents.

It is clear that Charles was only playing for time, and his unfortunate envoy knew well the futility of his errand. Scotland, as he once told the king, he hated " next to hell," and he had no liking for a task where success and failure would be alike without profit to himself. He arrived in the north on 7th June, to find sullen looks and little of the welcome due to a royal commissioner. He brought with him two proclamations, which promised that the canons and the service book would not be pressed " except in such a fair and legal way as should satisfy all our loving subjects "; one demanded that all copies of the Covenant should be surrendered, which the other did not; he was to use one or other according to his discretion. Traquair and Roxburgh had already warned him that a demand to give up the Covenant would wreck his mission; and, since the tenor of the first proclamation had become known, his diplomacy was prejudiced from the start. He saw Rothes, and the Tables appointed a committee of three ministers and three nobles to confer with him, one of whom was Montrose. Things had moved fast during the previous months. Henderson and Wariston had prepared " articles of peace," which went far beyond the mere matter of the liturgy. The Committee of the Tables asked for the withdrawal of the obnoxious canons and service book, but they also demanded the summoning of a free General Assembly, and, finally, of a Parliament to decide all the questions at issue. The Scottish Church was to shape its own ecclesiastical policy, and a Scottish Parliament was to give such policy the validity of the civil law. It was an honest assertion of a justifiable nationalism.

Hamilton hummed and hawed, promised and withdrew, and finally left Edinburgh in despair. While negotiating with the Covenanters, he had been discussing secretly with his master the possibilities for the use of arms in Scotland —the chance of help from the Highland clans who hated Lorn; the best base to hold, since Edinburgh castle was in Covenanting hands. Charles was adamant on the question of giving up the Covenant; otherwise, he said, he " had no more power than the Duke of Venice," and he intended " not to yield to the demands of those traitors, the Covenanters."[1] With such terms in his instructions no emissary had a chance. The king was negotiating only to

[1] Burnet, *Mem. of the Hamiltons*, 43-59.

gain time, and the duplicity of the monarch was matched
by that of his commissioner. For we know, on Montrose's
evidence, that Hamilton privately told the Covenanters,
" as a kindly Scotsman," that if they took a firm stand
they were likely to win.[1] Then ensued a war of king's proclamations and Covenanting protests. Hamilton fluttered
between London and Scotland, carrying royal concessions
—lavish concessions which meant nothing, since Charles
had already determined to appeal to the arbitrament of
war. In any case they came too late. The king proposed
a new covenant of his own, the chief point of which was
the abjuration of popery; but the Covenanting leaders,
whose detestation of Rome needed no advertisement, not
unnaturally described it as a " mockery of God." Their
aim was now nothing less than the complete suppression
of episcopacy in Scotland. But the General Assembly was
granted, and Hamilton had succeeded in some degree in
sowing suspicion between the nobility and clergy by warning each of the danger to be apprehended from the other.

During the absence of the royal commissioner from
Scotland in July, the Tables made a great effort to win
Aberdeen and the Gordon country to the Covenant's side.
Huntly himself would have none of it. His house might
be perverse and uncertain, but it never lacked a high spirit
and a wild chivalry, and he went his own way contemptuous of Lowland fashions. The Tables sent Colonel Robert
Monro, an old soldier of Gustavus, to ask him to subscribe
the Covenant, promising to give him first place in the command of their forces; but Huntly replied nobly that his
family had risen by the kings of Scotland, and that if the
king were to fall he was resolved to bury his life, honour,
and estate under the rubbish.[2] But something might be
done in the city and its environs, though Knox's disputation
in 1561 with the Aberdeen professors was not an encouraging precedent. Montrose, with three ministers in his suite
—Mr. Alexander Henderson, Mr. David Dickson, and Mr.
Andrew Cant—arrived on 20th July, bearing a letter from
Rothes to his cousin the provost, Patrick Leslie. " Do ye
all the good ye can in that town and in the country about
—ye will not regret it—and attend my Lord Montrose,
who is a noble and true-hearted cavalier."[3] Montrose had
been made a burgess of Aberdeen nine years before, and
he and his retinue were hospitally welcomed. But he
seems to have been in an unbending humour. He declined

[1] Guthry, 40-41.   [2] Gordon of Rothiemay, I., 49.   [3] Napier, I., 148.

the proffered banquet until the authorities submitted to
the Covenant, whereupon the provost and the bailies distributed the wine among the poor.[1] On the Sunday the
three ministers proposed to occupy the city pulpits, but
the Aberdeen clergy were not to be ousted. The mission-
aries were accommodated in a yard attached to the Earl
Marischal's town-house, where his sister, Lady Pitsligo, was
then dwelling. The three preached in turn from a wooden
gallery, and on the Monday repeated the performance,
amid the ribaldry of certain scoffers in an adjoining
building.

Thereafter the envoys proceeded into the neighbouring
villages, where they met with more success.[2] The Aberdeen
ministers presented fourteen " demands," and there followed a wordy warfare of " answers," " replies," and
" duplies," in which the Covenant champions did not get
the best of the argument.[3] Aberdeen declared that it
adhered to the discipline of the reformed Kirk of Scotland,
but refused to condemn episcopacy or admit " the im-
mutability of presbyterial government."[4] It is to be noted
that, in asking for subscriptions to the Covenant, Montrose
drew up and made his colleagues sign an emphatic declaration " that we neither had nor have any intention but of
loyalty to his Majesty, as the Covenant bears."[5] He was
interpreting what he then believed—and the bulk of Scotland with him—to be its spirit. But the incident is piquant
when we remember who were his ministerial companions.
Henderson, the wisest head and the purest character in the
Kirk, was five years later to make the last attempt to hold
him to the Covenant's side, and Dickson and Cant were
to be the central pillars of the theocracy which he sought
to overthrow. Perhaps on that northern journey he may
have found in their hearts that which gave his enthusiasm
pause, and developed those scruples which made Baillie
complain that he was " hard to be guided," and " capri-
cious for his own fancies."[6] He returned to Edinburgh at
the end of July with but little to show for his labours. His
future visits to Aberdeen were to be to better purpose.

[1] Spalding, I., 57.
[2] Guthry, 39. Spalding, I., 59. Gordon of Rothiemay, I., 84-85.
[3] Gordon of Rothiemay, I., 86-95.
[4] Burnet, *Mem. of the Hamiltons*, 86.
[5] Spalding, I., 58.
[6] I., 247.

II

The Assembly which met in Glasgow in November was a legal gathering, sanctioned by the king, and duly presided over by Hamilton, the royal commissioner. The issues between sovereign and people had been narrowed. Charles had surrendered all the earlier objects of strife—the liturgy, the book of canons, and an irresponsible episcopate. It appeared that he was prepared to accept a moderate episcopacy responsible to a General Assembly, the original constitution of the Reformed Kirk in Scotland. But with the people at large the controversy had now gone far beyond the articles of the National Covenant. Episcopacy in any form had become suspect, because it had been made the instrument of an assault upon both civil and religious freedom. To Charles, as to Hamilton, some form of episcopate was an essential corollary of a monarchy. To them it appeared that the control over the Kirk given by bishops appointed by the king was the only safeguard against an anarchical theocracy; to the Scottish people it seemed that so long as this channel for arbitrary government was left unblocked there was no security against further encroachments upon their liberties. The historian may admit that there was reason in both views, but it was certain that the Assembly, the first held for twenty years, would demand the complete removal of the latter menace.

It met on the 21st day of November, in the old Cathedral of Glasgow, one of the few ancient churches in Scotland which had escaped the destroying zeal of the Reformers. Glasgow was then a clean little city of some 12,000 inhabitants, clustered about its college and cathedral above the shining links of the Molendinar burn. The Assembly was a packed one, since the Tables, as appeared during the proceedings, had exercised a rigorous veto over the delegates. Of these there were some 240, 142 being ministers, and 98 laymen, ruling elders appointed by presbyteries. The Privy Council attended, and there were numerous assessors. Hamilton had striven to regulate the body by a proclamation—completely disregarded—against the presence of retainers and the bearing of arms. The nobles and barons appeared each with his usual " tail," and not a few of the clerical members had swords and pistols, ostensibly to defend themselves on the journey against a certain John Macgregor, a bandit who professed a distaste for the Covenant and a liking for the king.[1]

The crowd at the opening was so great that the town guard had the utmost difficulty in opening a way for the members to their seats. The Glasgow populace attended in great numbers, and their behaviour in the kirk shocked the decorous soul of Mr. Robert Baillie. " It is here alone where, I think, we might learn from Canterbury, yea, from the Pope, from the Turks, or pagans, modesty and manners. . . . Our rascals without shame, in great numbers, made such dinn and clamour in the house of the true God, that if they minted to use the like behaviour in my chamber, I could not be content till they were down the stairs."[2] Hamilton sat uneasily on a high chair of state, and below him the Lords of the Privy Council—conspicuous among them the lean aquiline face and the red hair of Lorn, now, by his father's death, Earl of Argyll, and a figure of interest to every man, since he had not declared himself. In front of them was a chair for the Moderator, and a table for the Clerk. Then came a long bench at which were seated the nobles and barons elected by the presbyteries, and at which sat Montrose as an elder, representing his own presbytery of Auchterarder. At the end of the church a platform had been erected for the eldest sons of peers, and in tiers on both sides were the seats of the clerical and burgess members. The " rascal multitude," including many women, occupied the aisles and galleries. It was a strange form of ecclesiastical assembly, for among the black gowns of the ministers were the slashed and laced doublets of the laity, and the gleam of many swords.[3]

Alexander Henderson was unanimously elected Moderator, and Wariston, Clerk. The first step was to verify the commissions of the members, and Hamilton found cause to question the legality of many. His objection to the presence of laymen was without substance, as their admission was in accordance with the letter and spirit of Presbyterianism. With better reason he protested against the method of electing these laymen, and the way in which the Tables had supervised the appointments. A test case was that of Lord Carnegie, Montrose's brother-in-law, who had been nominated by the presbytery of Brechin, but disallowed by the Tables, and Erskine of Dun named in his stead. Montrose had been the chief mover in the

[1] Wariston, I., 399. *Large Declaration*, 232, 385.
[2] I., 124.   [3] Gordon of Rothiemay, I., 157.

matter, and, when Wariston inadvertently read the letter of the Tables, Hamilton seized upon the irregularity. Montrose hotly defended it, and thereby came into conflict not only with Southesk, his father-in-law, but with Mr. David Dickson, who questioned his action. The young man was in a high temper, and in the cause he had chosen was prepared to respect neither kinsman nor cleric.[1]

The Assembly waved aside the royal commissioner's doubts as to its competence and constitution, and proceeded to the business at the back of every member's head—the abolition of episcopacy. The bishops had refused to acknowledge the court or to appear before it, and, when their formal declinature had been handed in, Hamilton decided to dissolve the Assembly. On the morning of 28th November, after recapitulating the king's concessions, he declared the Assembly illegal owing to the method of its election, and " discharged their further proceedings under pain of treason." He was answered in moderate language by Rothes and Henderson, but the latter refused to accept the dissolution. " All that are here know the reasons of the meeting of this Assembly, and, albeit we have acknow-ledged the power of Christian kings for convening of Assemblies, yet that may not derogate from Christ's right; for He has given divine warrants to convoke Assemblies whether magistrates consent or not." Then arose Mr. David Dickson, who said, looking towards Hamilton, " that that nobleman was very much to be commended for his zeal and faithfulness to his master the king, and sticking close by what he thought for his credit and interest; and he craved leave to propose his example for the Assembly's imitation. They had a better master, Christ the King of Kings, to serve, and his credit and honour to look after according to their commission and trust; and therefore he moved that, having this in their eye, they might sit still and do their Master's work faithfully."[2] In this high mood the Assembly saw Hamilton depart. It was a moment which von Ranke has compared to that scene a century and a half later, when the new French National Assembly for the first time withstood the commands of its king.[3]

Before leaving for the south, Hamilton summoned the members of the Privy Council together and counselled them to do their duty by the king. One or two withdrew, declaring that they were on the popular side, and among

[1] Gordon of Rothiemay, I., 152. *Large Declaration*, 240.
[2] Wodrow, *Analecta*, II., 116.   [3] *History of England*, II., 116.

them was Argyll, who, the day before, when Hamilton
dissolved the Assembly, had defended the legality of the
lay element and announced his adhesion to the Covenanting cause.[1] Hamilton wrote to Charles and to Laud
announcing the failure of his mission, and urging the
necessity of speeding on the armed preparations. In his
letter to the king of 27th November he provided his master
with certain character-studies of the Scots nobility. Two
of his comments are worth noting: Argyll " will prove
the dangerousest man in this state "; of the Covenanting
leaders there was " none more vainly foolish than
Montrose."[2]

The Assembly resumed its sittings on the 29th, with
Argyll as the solitary Privy Councillor. It sat till 20th
December, and, says Burnet, " went on at a great rate, now
that there were none to curb them." It pronounced the
last six General Assemblies invalid; condemned the service
book, the book of canons, and the Court of High Commission; annulled the Articles of Perth; declared episcopacy
to be utterly abjured and cast out of the Kirk; established
a press censorship, under the control of Wariston; and,
in a mood of startling enlightenment, prohibited salmon-
fishing on Sundays.[3]

The whole Scottish hierarchy was deposed, and most of
its members excommunicated as well. The bishops had
declined to appear, so there was no defence; the Aberdeen
doctors were not there to raise their voices, which Baillie
thought might have induced a more moderate temper. Undoubtedly there had been much laxness of conduct on the
part of the bishops, and certain scandals; but many of the
charges were absurd, and few were supported by evidence
which would have satisfied a court of law. The fact of
holding episcopal office was held sufficient to afford pre-
sumptive proof of moral delinquencies. Episcopacy and
its ministrants were abolished root and branch, and certain
dubious historical dogmas were affirmed, against which
Baillie, to his honour, protested.[4] He had been impressed
by Hamilton's conduct in the commissioner's chair, and
had wept at his withdrawal; he may be taken as the type
of the moderate Covenanter, who was against episcopacy

---

[1] Gordon of Rothiemay, I., 192. Baillie, I., 144. Burnet, *Mem.
of the Hamiltons*, 106.
[2] *Hardwicke Papers*, II., 113, 121.
[3] Gordon of Rothiemay, II., 162.
[4] Ibid., II., 108 Baillie, I., 177, etc.

as a system, but did not think it necessarily forbidden by the reformed faith. But the ministerial leaders, with the support of the lay members, would be content with no half-hearted condemnation. On the day when the prelates were sentenced, Henderson preached the sermon, long known as " The Bishops' Doom "; but the passage of Scripture selected by the reader may have had an ominous ring in other ears than Mr. Robert Baillie's. " These things I have spoken to you that you should not be offended. They shall put you out of the synagogue; yea, the time cometh that whosoever killeth you will think that he doeth God service."

The Assembly had clearly gone beyond its legal powers. When the king's commissioner dissolved it, under the Act of 1592, it ceased to exist at law. Henderson's act had all the significance which von Ranke has claimed for it; in the words of his most recent biographer, it " spelt revolution."[1] The Assembly claimed to repeal the laws of the land, and it proceeded to carry its edicts into action. The treatment of the bishops was as harsh as it was irregular, but revolutions are not considerate of individual rights. Our judgment of its doings must be based upon the assumption that it was a definite revolt against the king's authority. It sought, indeed, to be a modified revolution. A treasonable sermon by Mr. George Gillespie was condemned by implication by the Moderator; Argyll warned them, and Henderson repeated his warning, against any disrespect to " so good and gracious a prince "; and at the end an address was drawn up to his Majesty, humbly asking him to confirm their acts in the Parliament presently to be summoned. But a revolution is a hard thing to delimit, and it has a fatal habit of producing a reaction in kind. The doings of 1638 were exactly paralleled by the Act Rescissory of 1661, which blotted out twenty-three years of legislation and re-established episcopacy. One form of violence was to be matched by another.

> " The Gods alone
> Remember everlastingly; they strike
> Remorselessly, and ever like for like.
> By their great memories the Gods are known."

Yet to judge the protagonists at Glasgow with the cold-blooded retrospective reason of history is to do grave injustice. The implications of their actions were not present to the minds of the best of the clergy and laity. These

[1] Orr, *Alexander Henderson*, 182.

revolutionaries were still royalists almost to a man. They opposed, not the monarchy, but the dogma of " no bishop, no king," which would impair the royal authority by making it dependent upon a particular ecclesiastical form. Their mark was Laud rather than Charles. Among them were many fanatics of Presbytery, but there were also those who were lukewarm enough towards Presbyterian claims, but enthusiastic for Scottish liberties, and who considered that the people should have the church they wanted. Such men had a well-founded distrust of an episcopate as the gate by which autocracy had often entered the sheepfold. It is to be remembered that few Scots believed in divine right, that the nation had never known an unquestioned monarchy like that of the Tudors in England, and that they had been in the habit of frequently taking up arms to read their kings a lesson. While professing in all honesty their love for Charles, they were prepared to chasten him. They demanded that the nation's liberties should be safe-guarded, and the proof of that would be the grant of the Kirk the nation preferred. On such a policy it was possible to unite for the moment the gross and wary sagacity of Rothes, the young enthusiasm of Montrose, and the profound and subtle ambition of the latest convert, Argyll.

III

To one who studies such portraits as exist of the chief figures in the Scotland of that epoch, there must come a sense of disappointment. Few convey the impression of power which is found among the Puritans and Cavaliers of England. There is Hamilton, self-conscious, arrogant, and puzzled; Lanark, his brother, dark, sullen, and stupid; Huntly, a peacock head surmounting a splendid body; Rothes, heavy-chinned, goggle-eyed, Pickwickian; Glencairn, weak and rustical; old Leven, the eternal bourgeois; the Border earls, but one remove from the Border prickers; Wariston, obstinate and crack-brained; James Guthrie, lean and fanatical. But there are three exceptions. One is the haunting face of Montrose, whose calm eyes do not change from the Jameson portrait of his boyhood to the great Honthorst of his prime. The second is the face of Alexander Henderson, yellow from the fevers of the Leuchars marshes, lined with thought, and burning with a steady fire. The third is that of Archibald, eighth Earl of Argyll. We see him at nineteen, in his marriage clothes, his reddish hair falling over his collar, his grey-blue eyes with ever so slight a cast in them; we see him in his twenty-fourth year, with the air and accoutrements of a soldier; in the Castle Campbell portrait, unfortunately burned in the Inveraray castle fire of 1877, he is in armour, but the face has a scholar's pallor and a curious melancholy; in the familiar Newbattle picture, painted in his late forties, he is in sober black with the skull-cap of a divine on his head, the features are drawn with ill-health and care, the mouth is compressed and secret, the nose is pendulous, and the cast in the eyes has become almost a deformity. But at whatever period we take it, it is a face of power, with intellect in the broad brow, and resolution in the tight lips and heavy chin.[1]

In every national crisis there is some personal antagonism, where the warring creeds seem to be summed up in the persons of two protagonists—Cæsar and Pompey, Pym and Strafford, Fox and Pitt. So were to stand those present allies, Montrose and Argyll, secular types of conflicting temperaments and irreconcilable views. The head of the great house of Campbell was now some thirty-four or thirty-five years of age, eight years the senior of Montrose. He had the widest possessions of any Highland chief except Huntly, and at his back by far the most powerful clan, for he lived close to the Lowlands, and could put 5,000 men into the field. His father, to whom the sobriquet of Gilleasbuig Gruamach—" Gillespie the Sullen "—properly belonged,[2] was an odd character and led an odd life. He was defeated at Glenrinnes in 1594 by the Gordons, but later added to his possessions by subduing the Macdonalds of Islay and Kintyre. But his fortune was not commensurate with his lands, he fell deeply into debt, married a Catholic second wife, joined the Church of Rome, and had to flee the country. He was permitted to return, and lived some ten years in England before his death. His first wife was a daughter of the house of Morton, so his son had in his veins the unaccountable Douglas blood. Like the father, the son had an unhappy childhood, for he lost his mother in his infancy, and during his youth was perpetually at variance with his wandering sire. He had to fight hard during his minority for his rights, and the experience must have made him wary and distrustful, and taught him diplomacy and dissimulation. Charles is said to have assisted him against his vindictive

[1] See Willcock, *The Great Marquess* (Edinburgh, 1903), a careful and temperate biography. [2] Ibid., 6.

parent, and Clarendon reports some dubious gossip about the old man warning the king against his son, " for he is a man of craft, subtlety, and falsehood, and can love no man, and if ever he finds it in his power to do you a mischief, he will be sure to do it."[1]

What is clear is that in his youth he was deeply in debt, and found his great estates less of a boon than an incumbrance. He determined to husband and increase his fortune, and there is record of a curious venture to annex an imaginary island beyond the Hebrides.[2] He took his part in policing the Highlands, and in 1636 brought to justice the outlaw Patrick Macgregor, who is famous in balladry as Gilderoy. With high politics he did not meddle. He defended the laird of Earlston against the Bishop of Galloway, and befriended Samuel Rutherford when brought before the Court of High Commission, but his motive may well have been only friendship to his kinsfolk, the Kenmures. These incidents did not predispose him to love the bishops, and in 1637 he convened a meeting of Rothes, Traquair, and other noblemen, to protest against the " pride and avarice of the prelates seeking to overrule the haill kingdom."[3] But up to 1638 we may regard him as principally occupied with family troubles and the care of his estates, a little suspect by Presbytery as the son of a Catholic and the brother-in-law of Huntly, well regarded by the king in spite of his father's warnings, and with no special predilection towards the Kirk. He was one of the few nobles who, in the summer of 1638, took the king's alternative covenant at the request of Hamilton.

In this mood he attended the Glasgow Assembly. There it would appear that he underwent a profound spiritual experience, and in the theological sense was " converted." It was the habit of Alexander Henderson during the sittings to hold meetings at night for prayer and counsel. " I find," says Wodrow, who must have been repeating a tradition handed down in the ministry, " that their meetings were remarkably countenanced of God, and that the Marquis of Argyll, and several others who sometimes joined in them, dated their conversion, or a knowledge of it, from those times."[4] It was this change of heart, and

---

[1] Willcock, 22. Clarendon, *History*, II., 58. Clarendon is apt to report gossip about Scots affairs which he had no means of verifying.   [2] *Hist. MSS. Comm.*, 6th Report, 631.
[3] Spalding, I., 79.   [4] *Historical Fragments*, 81.

not the discovery that the Covenant was the side of the majority, that determined Argyll's course. He was an acute judge of popular opinion, but it was something more than policy that took him over to the Covenant side. For from that day this man, who in the past had been wholly concerned with his worldly possessions, and had held himself conspicuously aloof from the Kirk, became a religious enthusiast, a fanatic; and no mortal, however consummate an actor, could simulate such enthusiasm as Argyll revealed during the remainder of his troubled life.[1]

In assessing his character we have therefore to start from the fact that in religious matters he was most deeply in earnest, that he had the same proselytizing zeal, and the same complete assurance that the armies of Heaven were on his side, as Wariston and James Guthrie. To this add his Campbell and Douglas ancestry. He had the chief's love of power, and it is possible that, as in Hamilton's case, visions of a crown may have haunted one who boasted that he was the "eighth man from Robert Bruce." Such dreams were common among the higher Scots nobility. His bitter youth had left him suspicious and aloof, without warmth, with few friends and fewer intimates. He could not charm easily; he must win his way by patience, assiduity, and talent; but he learned in time a grace of manner to which even the hostile Clarendon bears witness. He was, so far as can be judged, without any interest in humane letters; his mind was mediæval in its cast, holding firm by law and scholastic divinity. Hence it is vain to look to him for any profound ideal of statecraft. He was essentially a politician, a shrewd judge of character and opinion, able to use both the raw material of fanaticism in the ministers and of gross self-interest in the nobles to further his ends, because he shared the one and wholly understood the other. There was no quicker brain in Britain to probe the possibilities of a situation. Mr. Gardiner thinks him as much superior to Montrose as a statesman as he was inferior in the art of war;[2] and Clarendon, after remarking that Montrose despised him, "as he was too apt to contemn those he did not love," adds that Argyll "wanted nothing but honesty and courage to be a very extraordinary man, having all other good talents in a great degree."[3]

---

[1] See for his personal piety, Wodrow, *Analecta*, I., 22. At Inveraray he always wrote the sermons which his chaplain preached.
[2] *Great Civil War*, I., 126.   [3] *History*, XII., 142.

Honesty and courage are difficult matters upon which
to dogmatize. Argyll was a poor soldier, because he lacked
the power of grasping a tactical or strategical problem—
a gift as specialized as that for poetry or the higher
mathematics—and because he had not the kind of personality which can impress itself upon large bodies of men
under arms. But it is idle to deny courage, even of the
rude physical kind, to a man who time and again risked
his neck, who was prepared to meet an enemy in a duel,
and who went without a tremor to the scaffold. As for
honesty, there is little enough of the high and delicate kind
at any time in the political game, and, if we define it as
scrupulous loyalty to cause and colleague, it was a fruit
which scarcely grew in seventeenth-century Scotland. In
that mad kaleidoscope Argyll had as much of the rare
commodity as most of his contemporaries. His troubles
came primarily from a divided soul—a clear, practical
intellect pulling against an obscurantist creed, the Highland
chief at variance with the Presbyterian statesman, a brain,
mediæval for all its powers, fumbling with the half-understood problems of a new world. With such a one subtlety
will appear as irresolution, perplexity as cowardice, and a
too quick mind will seem to argue a dishonest heart.

Such a man will be a power among fanatics and self-
seekers, for he can read the souls of both. But there will
be one chink in his armour. He will not comprehend so
readily other motives, and, in failing to understand, he will
miscalculate and undervalue. Single-heartedness will not
come within the scope of his capacious understanding.
Sooner or later Argyll was bound to find in Montrose his
stark opposite, by whom he was both puzzled and repelled
—one who, in the common sense of the word, had no personal ambition, who was a civic enthusiast as Wariston
and Guthrie were religious enthusiasts, and who would
force the appeal to that which Argyll hated and feared—
the sword.

IV

Charles had much ado to raise that army which for the
past nine months he had regarded as his ultimate argument. England was apathetic, and a growing proportion
of her people looked askance at episcopacy. There had
been no Parliament for ten years, so there were scanty
supplies. The train-bands were called out, and the nobles
were summoned to perform their feudal duties, but the first

were half-hearted and ill-equipped, and the second was at the best a patchy volunteer service. On paper the king had some 21,000 men—14,000 foot and 2,000 horse, and about 5,000 under Hamilton. The cavalry was under Lord Holland, and the infantry under the Catholic Lord Arundel, neither of whom had much military experience. The plan was an advance to the Border by the main forces, while Hamilton should join hands with Huntly in the north and threaten the Covenanters' rear. Meantime it was hoped that Antrim, with his Irish, would land in Argyll, and Strafford in the Firth of Clyde. Unless the mere threat of an advance brought the Scots to terms, there was little hope in the scheme, for the main army was too weak for an invasion of Scotland, an Irish landing was improbable, and the exchequer was too low to permit of a waiting campaign. With the king went many distinguished figures: Sir Edmund Verney, already in two minds about the merits of the cause; Falkland, whose departure was attended by eulogistic poems from Cowley and Waller; Sir John Suckling, who from his own purse equipped a troop of horse clad in white and scarlet which, by the testimony of his own pasquil, had no stomach for a fight.

The Scots were in a better case. The provident Tables had already created a war-chest by voluntary assessments; their cause was supported by a widespread popular enthusiasm; the troops they could raise were of a more martial stamp than the unwilling English levies, and they had commanders of far higher talent than Holland and Arundel. For, in Spalding's words, " there came out of Germany hame to Scotland ane gentleman of base birth born in Balveny, who had served long and fortunately in the German wars, and called to his name Felt Marshall Leslie, His Excellence."[1] Alexander Leslie, now a man of fifty-seven, had risen high in the service of Gustavus, and at Stralsund had been a match for Wallenstein himself. So great was his professional repute that he was given at once the unquestioned control of the Covenant forces. " We were feared," Baillie wrote, " that emulation among our nobles might have done harm, . . . but such was the wisdom and authority of the old, little, crooked soldier, that all, with ane incredible submission, from the beginning to the end, gave over themselves to be guided by him, as if he had been Great Solyman."[2] With Leslie had come over many Scottish mercenaries of the Dugald Dalgetty

[1] I., 87.   [2] I., 213.

type, who, finding their occupation gone on the Continent, welcomed the chance of turning an honest penny in their native land. Such men, as a rule, cared as little about prayer-books and General Assemblies as they cared for the international quibbles of a German princeling, but they were to provide the Covenant with that which it sorely needed and which England as yet did not possess—a body of experienced and cool-headed professional officers.

The Tables were no laggards in war. Edinburgh castle, which Hamilton had bought from Mar, was surprised and taken; Dumbarton and Dalkeith followed, and soon in the south of Scotland only the castle of Caerlaverock remained hostile. The three Lowland noblemen who were still nominally on the king's side—Traquair, Roxburgh, and Douglas—could do nothing in Clydesdale and Tweeddale. Argyll was given the wardenship of the west, and presently, by his seizure of Hamilton's castle of Brodick and his garrisoning of Kintyre, closed the door by which Antrim and Strafford might have entered, while, with the un-expected assistance of the Camerons, he ravaged Huntly's Badenoch domains. The immediate danger lay in Aberdeen, for Charles's march from the south would be slow. Should Hamilton's 5,000 sail north and join Huntly—now appointed royal lieutenant over all the country between the North Esk and Caithness—the Covenant would have to fight with a conflagration in its rear. Montrose was appointed to deal with the situation, and Leslie, whose formal commission as commander-in-chief was not issued till May 9, 1639,[1] was sent with him to correct the inexperi-ence of this general of twenty-seven.

In January 1639 and the beginning of February Montrose was busy beating up recruits in his own braes of Angus, where he had high words with Southesk, his father-in-law, who had not forgotten the dispute at the Glasgow As-sembly, and, in a sudden fit of royalism, refused the warrant of the Tables.[2] He had summoned the northern Covenanters—the Frasers, Keiths, Crichtons, and Forbeses —to meet him at the little town of Turriff in Aberdeenshire. Huntly heard of the rendezvous, and, resolved to prevent it, marched thither with 2,000 of his clansmen. But

[1] Terry, *Alexander Leslie*, 51.
[2] In the commission to Montrose to be colonel in the shire of Perth, dated May 2, 1639, Atholl is a signatory, and the similar commission for Angus (7th May) is signed, among others, by Lord Carnegie—which shows the political confusion of the time. *Hist. MSS. Comm.*, 2nd Report, 175.

Montrose was to give the first proof of his speed. Getting word of Huntly's intention, he rode through the Grampian passes with 200 horsemen, and was joined at Turriff by 800 men. Huntly, when he arrived, found the churchyard walls lined with muskets, and Montrose and his friends ensconced in the church. He had much the larger force, but he had been forbidden to fight without Hamilton's instructions, so he could only " glare at " his enemies and withdraw to Strathbogie.[1] His orders were not to take the offensive till the king had reached the Border.

But he could fortify Aberdeen, and this it was Montrose's business to prevent. Presently Leslie arrived with the rest of the army, and, with a force of from 3,000 to 4,000 men, Montrose advanced on the city. Huntly, with instructions at all costs to win time, tried to make an arrangement with Montrose, but the latter had his clear instructions from the Tables, and on 30th March he entered Aberdeen. Ever in love with the spectacular side of life, he found a rival colour for the royal scarlet which the young Gordons wore, and decorated his men with knots of blue ribbon. It is curious to note that the Covenant received its famous blue badge from the man who was to prove its chief opponent. The city, deserted by Huntly, had no power of resistance. The Aberdeen doctors fled by sea, and some of the more martial citizens departed to join the king, while the Covenanting chaplains improved the occasion by pointing out in their discourses that upon Aberdeen had fallen the curse of Meroz. Montrose imposed on the city a fine for recusancy, and appointed Kinghorn to the command, while he rode west to look for Huntly.[2]

Now follows a curious tale on which it is hard to form an opinion. Various intermediaries had been busy, and in the first week of April Huntly met Montrose in the latter's camp at Inverurie. Huntly signed a modified version of the Covenant, binding himself " to maintain the King's authority, together with the liberties both of Church and State, Religion and Laws "—probably a version dictated by Montrose himself, whose principles it exactly represented. The Gordons would be allowed to sign the Covenant if they pleased, and the Catholic members of the clan were to be protected so long as they stood by the laws and liberties of Scotland. When Huntly came again to Inverurie, he found the camp full of his hereditary

[1] Spalding, I., 93. Gordon of Rothiemay, II., 212.
[2] Spalding, I., 104, etc. Gordon of Rothiemay, II., 221.

enemies, Frasers, Forbeses, and Crichtons, and sent his
friend Gordon of Straloch to Montrose to warn him that
any attempt to carry him south as prisoner would be hotly
resented by the countryside. Montrose, in reply, declared
that he would stand by Huntly—" but there is this difficulty,
that business here is all transacted by vote and a committee, nor can I get anything done of myself."

Montrose returned to Aberdeen, where he was joined by
other of the Covenanting nobles. A council was held, and
the general was severely chidden for his leniency towards
Huntly. Apparently his command in the field did not carry
any superior authority at the council board, for Huntly
was promptly summoned to attend under a safe conduct,
for which Montrose made himself specially responsible.
The latter had promised more than he could perform, and
the chief of the Gordons found himself in a trap. He was
asked to pay certain expenses, bring in certain prisoners,
become reconciled to Crichton of Frendraught, and naturally refused. He was then told that he must accompany
the Covenanting lords to Edinburgh. He asked if he was
to go as a prisoner or as a free man. Montrose bade him
take his choice, and the marquis replied that he would go
as a volunteer. This is the account of Spalding, who makes
Montrose throughout the leader in the sorry business;
Gordon of Rothiemay, who had reason to know, since he
was Straloch's son, assigns the chief part to Leslie;[1]
Monteith says that Montrose opposed the breaking of the
parole with all his power.[2] Huntly and his heir, Lord
Gordon, were carried to Edinburgh, and his suspicions
proved only too well founded. He refused to subscribe
any other covenant than that which he had taken at
Inverurie, and he and his son were consigned to Edinburgh
castle. According to his fashion, he signalized the event
by a piece of noble declamation. " Whereas you offer me
liberty, I am not so bad a merchant as to buy it with the
loss of my conscience, fidelity, and honour. I have already
given my faith to my Prince, upon whom now this crown
by all laws of nature and nations is justly fallen. . . . I
am in your power, and resolved not to leave that foul title
of traitor as an inheritance upon my posterity. You may

---

[1] Leslie, with most of the foot and artillery, left Aberdeen on
Good Friday, 12th April (Spalding, I., 119), and the interview with
Huntly took place on the 13th. It is possible that Leslie waited a
day or two in Aberdeen before overtaking his army.
[2] *History of the Troubles*, 47.

take my head from my shoulders, but not my heart from my Sovereign."[1]

It is the judgment of Mr. Gardiner that in all this affair Montrose " played but a mean and shabby part," that it was " the only mean action of his life." But the thing is too intricate for such a summary judgment. Montrose was clearly, in matters of policy, only one vote among many, and, moreover, he was in all major matters subordinate to Leslie.[2] Huntly's treatment was probably by Leslie's order, whether or not he was present at the final meeting in Aberdeen, and it is significant that in England it was attributed to him.[3] Moreover, it is by no means clear that Huntly, in spite of his rhetoric, was an unwilling captive. Why did he open negotiations with Montrose? Why did he sign a covenant at Inverurie? He did not want a Covenant army ravaging his lands, while he waited for instructions from Hamilton which never came. What honour was there in being the royal lieutenant when he was under a superior officer who sent neither troops nor commands? He was in an impossible position, and may have welcomed a simple way out of it; otherwise, knowing how many of the foes of his house were assembled at Aberdeen, he would scarcely have put his head into the lion's mouth. It is to be noted that he was no sooner safe in Edinburgh castle than Charles wrote to Hamilton describing him as " feeble and false."[4] It is only on some such supposition that we can explain Montrose's conduct. Had the facts been as Spalding relates them, one so scrupulous of the point of honour would assuredly have laid down his commission. Lord Gordon shared Huntly's captivity, and he was soon to be Montrose's closest friend; it is hard to believe that a flagrant wrong done to the father could so soon have been forgotten by the son. But it is certain that Huntly himself was aggrieved, and never forgave Montrose; it may be because Montrose was a witness of his weakness and humiliation. " He could never be gained to join cordially with him, nor to swallow that indignity, . . . whence it came to pass that such as were equally enemies to both . . . in the end prevailed so far as to ruinate and destroy both of them, and the king by a consequent."[5]

[1] *The Marquis of Huntly, his Reply*, etc. (printed by Robert Young, the King's Printer for Scotland. 1640).
[2] Gordon of Rothiemay, II., 205.   [3] *Cal. S. P., Dom.* (1639), 39.
[4] *Hist. MSS. Comm.*, 11th Report, App. VI., 102.
[5] Gordon of Rothiemay, II., 238.

On the day that Montrose reached Aberdeen Charles entered York. On 7th April he issued a proclamation to his rebellious subjects in Scotland, inviting them to come in and be punished. It was a blunder which he repaired by a later proclamation of 7th May, in which he announced that he would give his people all just satisfaction in Parliament as soon as the present troubles subsided, that he would not permit the Scots to invade England, but that he did not propose to invade Scotland, " if all civil and temporal obedience was shown him." This last clause seemed to open a way to negotiation. But Leslie, on whose head a price of £500 had been set,[1] took no risks; he mustered his army on the links of Leith, and before the end of the month was encamped at Dunglass, on his way to the Border. Meantime, on May Day, Hamilton had arrived in the Forth with nineteen ships of war and 5,000 men, to find the approaches to Edinburgh strongly fortified, and both shores of the firth in arms. His mother, the terrible old dowager-countess, arrived from the west with pistols in her holsters and the resolve to shoot her son if he set foot on Scottish soil. The king's commissioner proved as futile in war as in diplomacy. He contented himself with landing his men on the islands of the firth, paying secret visits to Covenanting lords, and writing melancholy letters to his master.

But up in the north the Gordons and certain local barons —Ogilvies, Urquharts, and Setons—had taken matters into their own hands. In a one-sided engagement, called the Trot of Turriff, they drove out a small Covenanting garrison under the Master of Forbes, and marched on Aberdeen, which they occupied on the 15th of May. Meantime Huntly's second son, Lord Aboyne, had made his way to Charles at Newcastle, and had offered his sword to the royal side. He was sent back to Hamilton for troops, but Hamilton gave him nothing but a few field-pieces and the services of a certain Colonel Gun, who had fought in the German wars. There was a chance now for a real diversion, but Hamilton did not take it; he sent two of his three regiments to the king, and himself remained snugly in the Forth.

Montrose was in Edinburgh on 18th May when he got word of the doings in the north. Hastily collecting a force of some 4,000, he reached Aberdeen on the 25th, to find that the barons had marched westward to get Highland

[1] *Cal. S. P., Dom.* (1639), 81.

support, and that the young Earl Marischal had occupied
the city. Some of his colleagues pressed him to make an
example of the place, but he summarily declined.[1] The
next day was Sunday, and while the officers were in church
the soldiers made short work of any dog that had been
decked in scorn with the blue ribbon of the Covenant.
They also came to blows with the fisher-folk over sundry
essays in salmon-poaching, forgetful of the sound resolution of the Glasgow Assembly.[2] But beyond a fine of
10,000 merks levied by the visitors, Aberdeen suffered
little.

On the 30th of May Montrose marched into the Gordon
country and laid siege to the castle of Gight. But two
days later he had news which changed his plans. He heard
that Aboyne, with a large force, was on the sea, and he
assumed that Hamilton was with him. At all costs he
must keep his communications open, so after a day's rest
in Aberdeen he hastened south. On the 5th of June
Aboyne arrived, with Tullibardine and Glencairn, two
field-pieces, and Colonel Gun. His brother, Lord Lewis
Gordon, who had attained the mature age of thirteen,[3]
rode into the city with 1,000 of his clan, and so aroused
the spirit of the burghers that by the 14th of June Aboyne
had 4,000 men at his back.

Montrose had joined Marischal,[4] the head of the house
of Keith, at Stonehaven, and when word came of Aboyne's
landing, he went north to meet him. Aboyne's following
showed the inclination, common to all Highland levies, to
melt mysteriously away, but he had 600 Gordon cavalry,
and he had the citizen forces of the twice-captured Aberdeen, who could expect little mercy if the war went against
them. He had a strong position, for the Dee was in flood,
and the narrow bridge might be held by resolute men
against great odds. Had all the officers been of the stamp
of Colonel Johnston, the provost's son and a professional
soldier, it would have gone ill with Montrose. The muskets
at the bridge-head bit fiercely into the Covenant ranks, the
spirit of the townspeople was high, and the fighting of the

---

[1] Baillie, I., 205.   [2] Spalding, I., 141.
[3] It was a war of youth, for Aboyne was nineteen, and Marischal
twenty-three
[4] Marischal had an odd career. As we shall see, he was a signatory to the Cumbernauld Bond, but afterwards became a Covenanter,
and was with Argyll at Fyvie, where his brother was killed. He
opposed Montrose after Inverlochy, but later became an Engager,
and was out in Pluscardine's rising

first day, 18th June, left the defences intact. But in the
night Montrose brought up his heavier cannon from Dunnottar, and at daybreak feinted with his cavalry, sending
them upstream towards an impossible ford. Gun fell into
the trap, and drew off the Gordon horse to follow them,
and in their absence the Covenanters made a general
attack. Gun, having made nothing of his ride, fell into
a panic, which communicated itself to the rest. The
Gordons fled, with the unwilling Aboyne, to their own
country, and the citizens, deprived of their allies, broke
at last.

So ended Montrose's first serious essay at command in
the field. Marischal and others of his colleagues would
have burned and pillaged the city, but Montrose pled for
a respite,[1] and, fortunately for Aberdeen, events had taken
place in the south which made the truce a peace. While
Leslie was at Dunglass, the king sent scouting parties across
the Border, so the Scots moved to Duns Law, a strong
strategic position. That remarkable camp, where good
provender was abundant, and the sound of prayer and
psalm rose morning and evening, and at each captain's
tent-door flew a banner with the legend " For Christ's
Crown and Covenant," and the Lowland peasants stared,
open-mouthed, at Argyll's plaided and kilted Highlanders,
may be read of in the vivid pages of Baillie.[2] The spirit
of the troops, says that chronicler, was " sweet, meek,
humble, yet strong and vehement." The same could not
have been said of the royal army, which was ill-fed, ill-
paid, ill-guided, and sorely troubled by a species of vermin
which they called " Covenanters." Both sides had their
doubts and troubles, and the time was ripe for negotiation,
since Charles could not defeat Leslie, and Leslie at the
moment did not desire to defeat Charles. A conference
was arranged, and ultimately Charles assented to the
principle that General Assemblies should deal with ecclesiastical questions and Parliament with civil, and that a free
General Assembly and a free Parliament should be convened for the coming August. The king made a good
impression upon the sensitive Baillie, who had been impressed by Hamilton the previous November; he thought
him " one of the most just, reasonable, sweet persons they
had ever seen." On this understanding it was agreed to
disband both armies, and the Covenanters seem to have

---

[1] Gordon of Rothiemay, II., 281. Guthry, 57. Baillie, I., 222.
[2] I., 211, etc.

been so strangely confident that they had found a lasting basis of peace, that they prepared to send Leslie with a Scottish army to the help of the Elector Palatine. Yet the main point was evaded. The Covenanters held by the findings of the Glasgow Assembly, with its abolition of episcopacy and its excommunication of the bishops; the king might consent to a free General Assembly, but he would never consent to its decrees if, as it was certain to do, it reaffirmed the doings at Glasgow.[1]

That hollow treaty, variously called the Pacification of Berwick and the Pacification of Birks, was signed on the 18th of June. Montrose, when the news of it arrived, imposed a further fine upon Aberdeen, released his prisoners, and dismissed his men to their homes. A few days later he himself left with Marischal—" to post to Duns," says Baillie, " to have their part in the joy, as well they did deserve, in the common peace; where they were made most welcome both to their comrades and their king."[2] He had won his first battle and proved his gift for war; but as he journeyed southward he can have had little of the joy of victory in his heart. The affair with Huntly, and his experience of the mediæval temper of Huntly's enemies, must have taught him how remote was his point of view from that of the colleagues whom fate had given him. He was no professional soldier like Leslie, but a perplexed and patriotic statesman, and by now he must have begun to realize how precarious was the future of the loyalty and the liberty which were the twin principles of his life. To Baillie he seemed a " generous and noble youth," whose discretion was too great. There were soon to be harsher words used about that discretion.

---

[1] See, for the details of the terms, Burnet, *Mem. of the Hamiltons*, 140, etc., Lang, III., 62, etc.
[2] I., 223.

CHAPTER IV

MONTROSE AND ARGYLL

(1639-42)

> If my name were liable to fear,
> I do not know the man I should avoid
> So soon as that spare Cassius. He reads much:
> He is a great observer, and he looks
> Quite through the deeds of men; he loves no plays,
> As thou dost, Antony; he hears no music;
> Seldom he smiles, and smiles in such a sort
> As if he mocked himself, and scorned his spirit
> That could be moved to smile at any thing.
> Such men as he be never at heart's ease.
>
> *Julius Cæsar.*

I

THE HOLLOWNESS OF THE SETTLEMENT BETWEEN KING AND Covenant was soon to be revealed. On 1st July proclamation of the coming Assembly was made in Edinburgh, and to the consternation of the people the prelates were summoned to attend. Legally, Charles was in the right; if the hierarchy was formally to be abolished, it had the right to be present and to defend itself; but to the Covenanters it seemed to prove that the king had not accepted the policy of the Glasgow Assembly, and was determined to find some way of perpetuating the episcopate. In this the popular instinct was partly correct. Charles, with England in view, was not prepared to assent to the wholesale condemnation of episcopal principles which the majority in Scotland desired.[1] But if the king was unwilling to abide by the understanding of the treaty which he must have known was in the mind of the Covenant leaders, these leaders had already broken its letter. They did not dissolve the Tables, or disband the army, or dispense with Leslie, or return the stores and ordnance to Edinburgh castle, which was now in Ruthven's hands. Riots broke out in the Edinburgh streets on 3rd July, and Traquair, Kinnoull, and Aboyne were roughly handled by the mob. Loudoun was sent to Berwick to apologize, but the king, not unnaturally, demanded more —the presence of fourteen of the Covenant leaders to dis-

---

[1] See the instructions to Hamilton, Burnet, *Mem. of the Hamiltons*, 149, etc.

cuss the situation. Some of them, like Argyll, refused; others were forbidden by their colleagues to attend;[1] five stalwarts only were permitted to go—Montrose, Loudoun, Lothian, Rothes, and Dunfermline—accompanied by Mr. Alexander Henderson, who had not been bidden. The discussion was a fiasco. Rothes quarrelled with the king, and warned him that, if bishops were not abolished in Scotland, the Scots would join with the Puritans in attacking them in England. Charles, deeply offended, gave up his intention of attending the forthcoming Assembly in person, and on 3rd August returned to London.

But this farcical conference had a profound effect on one man. He who embarks on the tide of a popular revolution is carried insensibly in a direction and at a speed which he has not foreseen, and it demands a scrupulous moral and intellectual integrity to keep true to his first purpose. Montrose had found himself in full agreement with the National Covenant, but the boisterous flood which now bore him along was very different from the even and disciplined stream for which he had hoped. He had opposed churchmen in politics, but the governance of Scotland was now slipping into the hands of the Kirk; he had condemned the king's breaches of law and constitution, but in this respect the Covenant looked as if it would soon be as flagrant a sinner; on behalf of the commons of Scotland he had fought the power of nobles like Hamilton and Huntly, but there were others in his own faction with the same ambitions. Above all, he had made a central and inviolable sovereignty the foundation of his creed, and he saw this sovereignty dissolving in confusion. To this period, when his doubts first became insistent, we may perhaps assign these verses:

> " Can little beasts with lions roar,
>   And little birds with eagles soar?
>   Can shallow streams command the seas,
>   And little ants the humming bees?
>   No, no—no, no—it is not meet
>   The head should stoop unto the feet."

Already his path had begun to diverge ever so little from the broad road of the Covenant. The divergence was slight, and to the world he still seemed to be marching in its company, but the angle must widen, for he was aiming at a different goal.

In those July days at Berwick Montrose had his first true

[1] Guthry, 61. Balfour, II., 341.

meeting with the king. Charles was no longer the formal
and distant monarch who, under Hamilton's influence, had
received coldly his boyish offer of service. He was a man
in deep distress, who had just been successfully defied by
his subjects—a king without an army or a war-chest, who
had insults for his daily bread, and no counsellor who was
not a broken reed. That singular character is one of the
paradoxes, but not one of the enigmas, of history, for its
weakness and strength are abundantly plain. His mild but
immovable fanaticism, his lack of any quick sense of
realities, his love of wooden intrigues, his defect in
candour, his inability to read human nature, his incapacity
to decide swiftly and act boldly—they are as patent as his
piety, his fortitude, and his fidelity to what he held to be
right. But he had in the highest degree the charm of his
race, and could cast a glamour over the most diverse minds.
It was those who knew him best who were most under his
spell, so that Clarendon could describe him as " the
worthiest gentleman, the best master, the best friend, the
best husband, the best father, and the best Christian," and
Sir Philip Warwick could write: " When I think of dying,
it is one of my comforts that, when I part from the dunghill of this world, I shall meet King Charles."[1]

In Montrose, the sight of his king in straits which were
not kingly may have awakened a chivalrous loyalty to the
person of his sovereign. Moreover, since he was not
cognizant of Charles's secret dealings with Hamilton and
Traquair, he must have considered that the king had thus
far kept his part of the bargain better than the Covenanters,
and had granted all that the National Covenant demanded.
Burnet will have it that he " was much wrought upon, and
gave His Majesty full assurance of his duty in time coming,
and upon that entered in a correspondence with the king,"[2]
but this story of a sudden conversion was probably
Covenanting gossip of a later date, when the breach had
widened and it was necessary to find some easy explanation.[3] Montrose was still a Covenanter, and resolute to
complete the work which had been begun on that spring
morning in Greyfriars the year before; but he had come
to think somewhat less well of his colleagues, and,
after the meeting at Berwick, somewhat better of his
sovereign.

[1] Clarendon, *History*, XI., c. 243. Warwick, *Memoirs of the
Reign of King Charles I.*, 331.
[2] *Mem. of the Hamiltons*, 149.   [3] Guthry, 65.

The General Assembly met in Edinburgh in the east kirk of St. Giles on 12th August, with Traquair as the royal commissioner and Mr. David Dickson of Irvine as Moderator. The previous Assembly at Glasgow was not officially mentioned, but all its work was re-enacted " at a gallop."[1] Episcopacy was abolished in Scotland, and the terms used, in spite of Traquair's advice, were made as offensive as possible to the king; episcopal government and the power of churchmen were held not only " unlawful to this Kirk," but " contrary to the Word of God."[2] The *Large Declaration*, the statement of the king's case, written by Dr. Balcanquhal, the Dean of Durham, was condemned in violent language, and the Privy Council was prayed to order that the National Covenant should be signed by every dweller in Scotland, " of what rank or quality soever in time coming." This piece of intolerant coercion was presented by a committee, which had Montrose and Alexander Henderson among its members,[3] and duly embodied in an Act of Council. Traquair, as royal commissioner, assented to the various proceedings, and the session closed in an atmosphere of unwonted peace. To old and staunch Presbyterians, who had fought for the Kirk as Andrew Melville conceived it, it seemed that the day of miracles had come, and a certain Mr. John Wemyss, an aged minister, speaking with difficulty, " for tears trickling down along his grey hairs, like drops of rain or dew upon the top of the tender grass," spoke a moving *nunc dimittis*. " I do remember when the Kirk of Scotland had a beautiful face. I remember since there was a great power and life accompanying the ordinances of God, and a wonderful work of operation upon the hearts of the people. This my eyes did see—a fearful defection after procured by our sins. And no more did I wish before my eyes were closed but to have seen such a beautiful day, and that under the conduct and favour of our King's Majesty."[4]

The Parliament, which met on 31st August, was a very different gathering. A more momentous Parliament had never sat in Scotland, for until it ratified the acts of the Assembly these had no legal validity, and the Kirk had no security. The first difficulty that arose was constitutional. One of the estates, the clergy, had dissolved itself, since the bishops had fled the country. In choosing the

---

[1] Gordon of Rothiemay, III., 63. [2] Ibid., III., 47. Guthry, 62.
[3] Gordon of Rothiemay, III., 57.
[4] Peterkin, *Records of the Kirk*, 251.

Lords of the Articles, it had been the custom for the nobles
to elect the representatives of the church, and the bishops
to elect the representatives of the nobles, while both
together chose the representatives of the lairds and
burgesses, while the king added eight nominees of his own.
By means of the bishops the Crown could in this way
ensure a majority. Charles desired to fill the vacancy left
by the bishops by fourteen ministers chosen by the Crown,
or, in the alternative, by fourteen laymen;[1] but the
ministers suspected a trap, and the nobility were jealous
of the ministers, so this scheme fell to the ground. Under
protest from Argyll a temporary arrangement was come
to. Traquair himself chose the nobles,[2] who in turn chose
the lesser barons and burgesses. This provisional Committee of the Articles set to work, and its reach was long.
It ratified the acts of the recent Assembly, and proceeded
to remodel the constitution of Scotland. It whittled away
the royal prerogative, by transferring the control of the
Mint and the appointment of great officers of state to
Parliament, and, by one vote, passed Argyll's motion that
each estate, nobles, barons, and burgesses, should elect its
own lords.[3]

To this sudden essay in parliamentary government
Montrose was opposed, and there were many other
doubters in the Covenant ranks. It must be clearly understood that Argyll's proposal, for all its modern sound, was
not an early stirring of democratic ideals. The common
people of Scotland had no say in the government of the
country, and were to have none for many a year, except
through the General Assembly. It was a provision aimed
directly against the royal prerogative, and, considering the
recent use made of that prerogative, it had its justification.
But such a change was not a reassertion of ancient liberties,
but a wholly new departure, and so violent an innovation
roused suspicion. The new régime would throw the
government of Scotland into the hands of him who was
the most adroit electioneer, and in this connection all men's
thoughts turned to Argyll. It altered, but it did not
seriously liberalize, the basis of representation. Moreover,
it was a demand which struck at the whole conception of
monarchy as then existing. At one stroke it reduced the
king to a cypher in matters in which hitherto he had

---

[1] Burnet, *Mem. of the Hamiltons*, 150.
[2] Huntly, released from Edinburgh castle, was one.
[3] Gordon of Rothiemay, III., 66. *A. P. S.*, V., 252, etc., 303.

been all-powerful. To Montrose it seemed to weaken sovereignty, the central sanction of law, without putting a reasonable equivalent in its place, for, if the king had his faults, a legislature of factious lairds and nobles was not without them. Further, it had no finality. If the king assented, he would be pressed to greater concessions, and the foundations of order would crumble. This was also the doubt of Mr. Robert Baillie. "Whatever the Prince grants, I fear we press more than he can grant; and when we are fully satisfied, it is likely England will begin where we have left off."

It was the turning-point of Montrose's political career. His enthusiasm for the National Covenant had made him an active member of the late Assembly, as an elder from Auchterarder, and he had supported the compulsory signature of that Covenant—an extreme step for one of his beliefs. At the moment he had no quarrel with the Kirk. He was prepared to accept every act of the Assembly, even its wholesale condemnation of episcopacy as hostile to God's Word. Two months later, when the king summoned him to London, he asked to be excused, after consulting with the Covenant leaders, on the ground that at such a time his going to court would be misconstrued—conduct which Wariston lauded as "noble."[1] To the clerical side of the movement he was still profoundly sympathetic. But the proposed constitutional revolution made him pause, and presently sent him into opposition, for of the two sections in his party he distrusted the nobles more than the ministers. Six years later he put his position before his countrymen. "Members of the said Parliament, some of them having far designs unknown to us, others of them having found the sweetness of government, were pleased to refuse the ratification of the acts of Assembly with the abjuration of episcopacy and the Court of High Commission introduced by the prelates, unless they had the whole alleged liberty due to the subject; which was in fact intrenching upon authority, and the total abrogation of his Majesty's royal prerogative; whereby the king's commissioner was constrained to rise and discharge the Parliament."[2] Men began to whisper that the young Covenant general had been seduced by the royal blandishments at Berwick, and a paper with the words "*Invictus armis*

[1] Napier, I., 228-229.
[2] "Montrose's Defence and Remonstrance," 1645. *Mem. of M.*, I., 215.

verbis vincitur " was presently found pinned to his chamber door.[1]

Traquair, who had been severely censured by Charles for his conduct as commissioner to the Assembly, refused, on the king's instructions, to accept the decisions of Parliament. The ostensible ground, in which Montrose ingenuously believed, was the attack on the prerogative; the true reason was the ratification of the Assembly's abolition of episcopacy. With England in view, Charles could scarcely be expected to assent to the condemnation of episcopacy as " unlawful," though he might admit it to be contrary to the constitution of the Kirk; he clung to his intention to restore the bishops at some later date, and therefore would not assent to the act rescinding the old acts which had established them.[2] On 14th November Parliament, after it had protested against the illegality of the proceeding, was prorogued till the following June.[3] On the part of Charles it was a grave blunder, for the people of Scotland were not slow to grasp the true explanation. He could have found some support for the defence of the prerogative; he could even have mustered to his side tender consciences like that of Mr. Robert Baillie, who was not prepared to condemn episcopacy as in itself unlawful;[4] with these points, if honestly stated, he might have driven a wedge into the Covenant party. As it was, a conviction that the king was playing fast and loose with them on the main question of the episcopate, and dislike of the egregious Traquair, rallied the doubters for the moment. Napier, the typical moderate, sat on the committee which represented the prorogued Parliament. As for Montrose, we have seen his refusal to go to court in December, and we find him a signatory, along with Loudoun and Leslie, of a letter addressed to the King of France, representing to Louis the " candour and ingenuity " of the Covenanters towards their king.[5]

[1] Guthry, 65. I see no reason for Lord Stanhope's suspicion of this story, in his *Historical Essays*, 131.

[2] See the king's letter to Traquair in Burnet, *Mem. of the Hamiltons*, 158-159.

[3] Rait, *The Parliaments of Scotland*, 63.

[4] See Baillie's letter to Loudoun, *Letters and Journals*, I., 181.

[5] Rushworth, III., 1,120. *Cal. S. P., Dom.* (1640), 19-20. For the other negotiations of the Covenanters with France at this date, see Gardiner, IX., 91, etc. One curious result was the raising of a regiment of 2,000 Scots under Irvine, Argyll's half-brother, which, in 1643, fought under Condé at Thionville. See Montereul (Montreuil), *Corr.*, II., 604. The negotiations with France must have been

II

With the abortive Parliament of 1639 went one of the last embankments of the old régime, and henceforth the tide of revolution runs fast. Parliament had been prorogued that the king might muster his forces, and the Covenanters did not let the grass grow under their feet in a similar duty. It was clear that the Covenant could only be defended on the field of battle. Through the early months of 1640 levies were being raised and drilled throughout the Lowlands, and on 17th April Leslie was given his commission as commander-in-chief.[1] In the same month Charles in England, in desperation for supplies, summoned the Short Parliament, but no supplies were forthcoming, and in three weeks he dissolved it. The Covenanters were much heartened thereby, for it was plain that England in the coming war was not behind the king. By the end of the summer Leslie had under him some 22,000 foot and 3,000 horse, and by freewill offerings, and offerings not so free, a considerable war-chest had been created. Charles could only scrape together less than half these numbers of ill-disciplined and reluctant recruits, and after trying every device, legal and illegal, he was still lamentably short of money. Strafford had come over from Ireland to advise his master, and on Strafford's counsel the Short Parliament had been summoned. But Strafford misread the temper of England no less than Charles, and his plan of using an Irish army in Scotland (which, misunderstood by Vane, was to be damning evidence against him at his trial) was not accepted. With a starved and slender force, and lacking the goodwill of the country which formed his base, the king went out to war against what was virtually a united nation in arms.

The prorogued Parliament of Scotland was due to meet on 2nd June. Charles, by a proclamation in May, prorogued it for a further month, but the proclamation was disregarded. There was some technical informality about it, which the acute Covenanting lawyers were not slow to seize upon.[2] But the Parliament which met was clearly unconstitutional, for there was no royal commissioner; it

begun before Huntly's imprisonment in Edinburgh castle, for he mentions them as one of the arguments used to persuade him. See pamphlet cited on pp. 84-85.

[1] *A. P. S.*, V., 285.

[2] Burnet, *Mem. of the Hamiltons*, 167. Rait, *The Parliaments of Scotland*, 65-66.

constituted itself a Parliament by its own act, and appointed Lord Burleigh its president; but it still maintained a show of loyalty, declaring that it acted by his Majesty's " tacit consent " and " presumed allowance," and that it was only " receiving and making use of that benefit which his Majesty, in his justice and goodness, had publicly granted to us and never recalled." It was the fiction which the Long Parliament in England was presently to adopt and maintain for seven feverish years. The true state of the case was summed up in a phrase which was probably Argyll's, " to do the less was more lawful than to do the greater ";[1] the alternative to holding an unauthorized Parliament was to depose the king. Having embarked upon this bold course, the new Parliament did not lag. It ratified all the acts of the previous Assembly, created free parliamentary committees in place of the old Committee of the Articles, organized the military preparations against the king, and passed a triennial act. In five weeks it had accomplished a huge body of legislation, which must have been carefully prepared beforehand, and thereafter it prorogued itself till the following November.

Revolution had thus been openly declared, for by no ingenuity of argument could these proceedings be defended as constitutional. Montrose opposed them to the utmost of his power, but his was the only voice;[2] since war was declared against the sovereign there was less need to be scrupulous about minor prerogatives. But his opposition made him a marked man. A Committee of the Estates was appointed with dictatorial powers to act as a Government while Parliament was not sitting, and to this body, which was virtually a Committee of Public Safety, and consisted of " about forty members, from earls to tailors and saddlers,"[3] Montrose was appointed, no doubt with the intention of paralysing his opposition. There was no alternative before him but to accept. He still held the greater part of the Covenant creed; he was in favour of the coming war, believing that it was necessary to open the king's eyes to the anti-episcopal resolution of Scotland; had he resigned he would have been impotent, and must either have fled to the king, like Airlie, or, like Huntly, hidden himself in northern fastnesses. The moment had

[1] Napier, I., 234, 236.

[2] Wariston to Hepburn of Humbie, Napier, I., 236.

[3] The Committee included at least three men of Montrose's views, Napier, Wigton, and Stirling of Keir.

not yet come for the final breach. Argyll was not a member of the Committee; that lover of secret power was happier pulling the wires behind the scenes. Besides, he had much business in the west, on the watch for Strafford's army. His countrymen did not attribute his abstention to modesty. " All saw he was *major potestas*, and, though not formally a member, yet all knew that it was his influence that gave being, life, and motion to these new-modelled governors; and not a few thought that this *juncto* was his invention."[1]

The first care of the Covenanting lords, as in the former war, was to prevent trouble in their rear. Angus, the Gordon country, and the Atholl domains in Perthshire were something less than lukewarm for the Covenant, and to Argyll was given the congenial task of taking order not only with the enemies of true religion, but with the ancestral foes of his house. For this commission of the Committee of Estates Montrose must share the responsibility, and his name was the first appended. He realized the need in war of safeguarding the country behind an army, and he recognized that gentler means than a commission of " fire and sword " would scarcely suffice. Argyll was authorized to pursue the clans " until he should either bring them to their bounden duty, and give assurance of the same by pledges or otherwise, or else to the utter subduing and rooting them out of the country."[2]

He was not slack in the execution of his warrant. With 5,000 of his clan he left Inveraray on 18th June, entrapped Atholl by a ruse similar to that employed by Montrose's army with Huntly a year before,[3] and presently arrived in the lowlands of Angus, where the Campbells were regarded with the same detestation and fear as was felt elsewhere for Antrim's Irishry. Airlie was in England with the king, and his son, Lord Ogilvy, was persuaded by Montrose to surrender Airlie castle for " the use of the public."[4] Montrose accordingly wrote to Argyll saying that his presence in Angus was needless, but Argyll was not minded to take instructions from Montrose when an ancient enemy was at his mercy. He burned the " bonnie house o' Airlie," and the other Ogilvy dwelling of Forthar in Glenisla; and from the latter Lady Ogilvy was driven, so the story goes, in circumstances of extreme barbarity. He then carried fire and sword into Lochaber, and com-

[1] Gordon of Rothiemay, III., 182.
[2] *A. P. S.*, V., 398.
[3] Guthry, 75. Spalding, I., 271
[4] Napier, I., 245.

pleted his commission to the satisfaction of the Estates.[1] In it all he had behaved like the ordinary feudal baron with grievances to avenge. This zealot of the Kirk had conducted a Highland campaign according to the most ruthless traditions of the past, and had thereby compiled against himself a reckoning which Highland memories were not likely to forget.

In July Montrose marched south with his contingent to join Leslie's army, which now lay in camp near the town of Duns. He had with him the Stirling and Strathearn levies—2,500 men, says Napier, 1,600 the English spies reported. In the camp the breach with Argyll widened. Argyll accused him of undue lenity in his recent work in Angus, and of needless delay in moving his regiments; but he was absolved from blame by Leslie and the other members of the Committee. But his distrust of Argyll promptly received a full justification. The Committee of Estates was too large and heterogeneous to be an effective instrument in time of war, and proposals were being privately made to narrow it. This was common sense, but the actual scheme took an ominous form. There were already stories abroad that in his recent northern foray Argyll's soldiers had declared that they were not King Stewart's but King Campbell's men, and a Gaelic song was made of which a verse ran: "I gave Argyll the praise, because all men say it is truth, for he will take gear from the Lowland men, and he will take the Crown perforce, and he will cry king at Whitsunday."[2] The throne, as we have seen, was never far from the imagination of the great Scots nobles who had the blood of Bruce in their veins.

---

[1] Argyll was granted an act of indemnity for his conduct by Parliament in November 1641, when the king was present (*A. P. S.*, V. 399). The comprehensive list of offences indemnified, which included " all manner of burnings and the putting of persons to torture and death," sheds some light upon his doings. At his trial in 1661 he denied ordering the burning of Forthar, but his instructions to his lieutenant are extant (Gardiner, IX., 167, *n.* 3. *Hist. MSS. Comm.*, 6th Report, 616). Sir James Balfour (II., 380-381) says that the expedition was conducted with an exact discipline, but there may be disciplined barbarism. For the treatment of Lady Ogilvy, the chief authority is Gordon of Rothiemay (III., 165), who, however, gets his dates into confusion. In this kind of war many atrocities must occur, and many more will be invented. The popular mind, as shown in the ballad of *The Bonnie House o' Airlie*, had no doubts on the subject. For Montrose's behaviour, see Lord Ogilvy's answer to interrogatories, and the libel against Montrose in 1641. *Mem. of M.*, I., 264, etc.: 328, etc.

[2] *Mem. of M.*, II., 477.

But that was for the future; for the moment the proposals were more modest—that one man, Argyll, should be made responsible for the country north of Forth, and two men for the country south of it. Montrose protested, and had the draft commission for the north altered, so that beside Argyll's appeared his own name, with Mar, Cassilis, and others.[1]

But, alarmed by the incident, he posted back to Edinburgh, where he met his old college friend, Lord Lindsay of the Byres, and heard of a scheme to make " a particular man " dictator of all Scotland, after the Roman fashion. The man, in view of Lindsay's antecedents, could only be Argyll. To check this intrigue, before returning to the army, Montrose summoned a meeting of his friends at Lord Wigton's house of Cumbernauld, near Glasgow, and signed an agreement to resist " the particular and indirect practising of a few." The Cumbernauld Bond bound the signatories to uphold the letter and spirit of the National Covenant " to the hazard of our lives, fortunes, and estates," and concluded with words not usually found in Scottish " bands," for they swore to adhere to each other " so far as may consist with the good and weal of the public."[2] Among others, Marischal, Wigton, Kinghorn, Home, Boyd, Atholl, Mar, Seaforth, and Almond (Leslie's second in command) appended their names. None, except Montrose, were men of power; they were the moderates, the Girondins, of the revolution, and of little moment compared to the " lawless resolutes " who opposed them.

Though the Bond was kept secret, the general antagonism to Argyll's project was known, and this was sufficient for the moment to defeat it. Montrose returned to the army at Duns, and Leslie prepared for the invasion of England —the ostensible purpose being merely to present to the king a petition praying that the recent acts of Assembly and Parliament be ratified. The armed petitioners at once took the offensive. On 20th August, the day on which Charles left London to assume the command of his army with Strafford as his lieutenant-general, Leslie crossed the Tweed at Coldstream, by the very ford which Scott makes Marmion ride on the eve of Flodden. His Lowlanders were in hodden-grey with blue caps, and each, in the ancient Scottish fashion, bore oatmeal in a haversack. The

[1] Montrose's own account at his trial in May 1641. Napier, I., 255.
[2] The Bond was burned, but Napier discovered a transcript in the handwriting of Sir James Balfour. Napier, I., 269-270.

Highland contingent were scantily clad, and carried broad-swords and bows and arrows.[1] The colours of the foot had the motto " Covenant for Relligion, Crowne, and Country."[2] " We are sadder and graver than ordinary soldiers," Lothian wrote, " only we are well provided of pipers." They had fiddlers, too, but these were " intolerably given to drink."[3] By a curious fate the privilege of leading the van fell by lot to Montrose. Tweed was in high flood, so he first forded it alone on foot, and then returned to encourage his men.[4]

The campaign was short and inglorious. Conway, at Newcastle, had a force far inferior to Leslie's in both numbers and quality, and he was an indifferent general. " I am teaching cart-horses to manage," he wrote, " and making men that are fit for Bedlam and Bridewell to keep the Ten Commandments, so that General Lesley and I keep two schools: he has scholars that profess to serve God, and he is instructing them how they may safely do injury and all impiety; mine to the utmost of their power never kept any law of God or the king, and they are to be made fit to make others keep them."[5] " I fear," he wrote also, " unpaid soldiers more than I do the Scots, and the devil to boot."[6] He had cause for his forebodings. Leslie marched without opposition to the ford of Newburn, four miles above Newcastle, the crossing of which would not only give him command of the Tyne, but enable him to attack Newcastle on the unfortified side. There Conway attempted a stand, but on 28th August he was blown out of his position by the Scottish guns. His cavalry fled to Durham, while his foot fell back on Newcastle, which next morning surrendered. It was, Clarendon wrote, " the most shameful and confounding flight that was ever heard of." A battle, which played a major part in our constitutional history, and which was to Charles what Bouvines was to King John, was won in an afternoon with a loss of a dozen to the victors and sixty to the vanquished. Charles fell back on York; he could not do otherwise, for he had no force which could have withstood Leslie for an hour.

The Covenanters' occupation of Newcastle, with the surrounding district, gave them a powerful lever in sub-

[1] Cal. S. P., Dom. (1640), 615. [2] Gordon of Rothiemay, III., 261.
[3] Earls of Ancrum and Lothian, I., 103, etc.
[4] One of them was drowned. Napier, I., 271. Terry, Alexander Leslie, 108.   [5] Cal. S. P., Dom. (1640), 268.   [6] Ibid., 548.

sequent negotiations, for they controlled the supply of coal to London, and thereby £50,000 of the king's revenue.[1] They behaved discreetly, for they had no desire to antagonize the English people. The first problem was that of subsistence, and Charles consented to their raising a daily levy from the four neighbouring counties. Negotiations began at Ripon, and were presently transferred to London, but it was not till August 7, 1641, that the dispute, mainly financial, was finally settled. Meantime his difficulties forced Charles to call a Parliament, and on November 3, 1640, as a direct result of the Scottish invasion, the Long Parliament assembled. Already many communications had passed between the English malcontents and the Covenanters, beginning with Lord Savile's assurance, with its forged signatures, in June 1640, when Leslie's army was mustering. Now, with London as the venue of discussion, Covenanters like Henderson and Wariston were brought into close touch with Pym and the Puritan leaders, and we find the idea first mooted of the forcible introduction of Presbytery into England. Wariston had suggested something like it to Savile in June 1640, and Henderson, in London, came to believe that the one hope of safeguarding Presbytery in Scotland was by securing its establishment south of the Tweed. The Scottish commissioners were instructed to table, as one of their propositions, " a desire for unity in religion and uniformity in Church government as a special means of conserving the peace between the two countries," and they found much support in Parliament. The London " root and branch " petition for the abolition of episcopacy was presented to Parliament on 11th December, and others flowed in from the shires. Parliament for the moment rejected the Scottish plan, but the Scottish commissioners continued to hope. The papers drafted at that time by Henderson on the subject contain the policy which, two years later, bore fruit in the Solemn League and Covenant. " Nothing so powerful to divide the hearts of people as division in religion; nothing so strong to unite the hearts of people as unity in religion; and the greater zeal in different religions the greater division, but the more zeal in one religion the more firm union. In the paradise of Nature the diversity of flowers and herbs is pleasant and useful, but in the paradise of the Church different and contrary religions are unpleasant and hurtful."[2]

[1] *Cal. S. P., Dom.* (1640), 116.
[2] *Arguments given in by the Commissioners of Scotland unto the*

That was one omen for those who had eyes to read it; the Scots, who had at the moment the vantage, were suggesting a higher price for peace than the bills of expenses which Leslie was patiently presenting. Another was the swift movement in Parliament to exact retribution from those who, like Strafford and Laud, were commonly held to be the pillars of monarchical policy. There was a third —most fateful of all; for the Huntingdonshire grazier, who had been so active in defending the rights of the fen commoners, was now at Westminster. On a certain November day, at the opening of the session, a young courtier, Sir Philip Warwick, very proud of his fine clothes, found a member speaking in the House whom he did not know, a gentleman in a plain suit made by a bad country tailor, his linen not very clean, and a speck of blood on his little band. " His stature was of a good size, his sword stuck close to his side, his countenance swollen and reddish, his voice sharp and untunable, and his eloquence full of fervour."[1] This was he of whom John Maidston, his servant and no flatterer, wrote that " a larger soul hath seldom dwelt in a house of clay." Oliver Cromwell had set his foot upon the road which was to lead him to the mastery of England.

III

Montrose may have hoped to find a solution of his doubts in swift action in the field, but the easy victory of Newburn brought no comfort. Of his part in that campaign we know nothing, except that in his opponents' eyes he was one of the Covenanting leaders, and that Strafford hastened to report from Darlington to the king the false rumour that he had been killed by Wilmot.[2] A man of active temper and complete honesty, if he cannot see his way plain, is apt to make a sorry business of waiting. Perplexities thickened about the path of the undecided Montrose. He saw clearly the necessity of asserting and safeguarding the central authority, the king's, if Scotland was to be saved from anarchy, and he saw no less clearly the direction of Argyll's thoughts; but he still believed that the Covenanters as a whole were willing to listen to moderate counsels, and that if he bided his time he might yet lead his countrymen into reasonable ways. After the

Lords of the Treaty, 1641. See also Baillie, I., 269, 274, 275, 287, 305, etc. [1] *Memoirs of the Reign of King Charles I.*, 247-248. [2] *Cal. S. P., Dom.* (1640), 649.

fiasco of Newburn and the ready capitulation of Newcastle, he may have argued that Scotland had sufficiently vindicated her rights against Charles, and that the time was ripe for insisting that the royal rights in turn should be safeguarded. He did not know how closely the interests of the Covenant were linked with Pym and his followers in the English Parliament, whose maxim it was rapidly becoming that the king could do no right. Nor did he realize the direction of the thoughts of the Scottish commissioners and their grandiose scheme for imposing Presbytery on England. He looked about for like-minded associates, and found few. He was not a simple-souled royalist like Airlie, who saw the problem as a plain choice between honour and dishonour, or a mediæval satrap like Huntly, who thought in terms of family pride and ancestral enmities. He had a philosophy of politics, which we shall presently consider, and he explored the nobility of Scotland to see if he could find others, besides Napier, who subscribed to it. So he became zealous in discussing public affairs, and thereby played into Argyll's hand.

Suspicion of him had grown among the Covenanting leaders, and he was closely watched. From Newcastle he wrote to the king a simple protestation of loyalty, and the letter came to the knowledge of the Committee—picked up by accident, says Burnet; disclosed by spies in the royal bedchamber, says Wishart. He was accused of " having intelligence with the enemy," and made the unanswerable reply that the king, against whose person and authority any aspersion was made treason by the articles of war, could not be " the enemy."[1] In Baillie's report of the incident he is spoken of as one " whose pride long ago was intolerable and meaning very doubtful." November found Montrose back in Scotland, summoned to explain the Cumbernauld Bond, the contents of which had come to Argyll's ear through hints dropped by Lord Boyd on his deathbed. The Committee of Estates called before them the signatories, who acknowledged and justified their action. Some of the ministers demanded the death of the accused, but these were too powerful to receive more than censure, since some of them commanded regiments, and all were territorial magnates. " They consulted to patch up the business after a declaration under their hands that they intended nothing against the public, together with a

[1] Baillie, I., 262. Burnet, *Mem. of the Hamiltons*, 228. Guthry, 87-88. Wishart, c. i. Napier, I., 271-273.

surrendering of the bond, which the Committee, having gotten, caused it to be burned."[1] The breach between Montrose and his former allies had become very wide. He returned to the army, and his indignation made his tongue run loose. In January 1641 he told Colonel Cochrane, in the presence of old Leslie, that he could prove that certain leaders in Scotland were scheming to depose the king, and he left no doubt in the mind of his embarrassed hearers that he referred to Argyll.[2]

In the beginning of 1641 it would appear that Montrose and his few friends decided upon a policy. They must induce the king to come to Scotland and satisfy every reasonable Covenanting demand; that done, he would be able, with the country behind him, to resist the follies of fanatical preachers, to check the aggression of selfish nobles, and above all to curb the ambition of Argyll, whose treason they would be in a position to prove. In a letter to Charles, written in the early months of the year, Montrose offered wise advice to his sovereign.

" Your ancient and native kingdom of Scotland is in a mighty distemper. It is incumbent on your Majesty to find out the disease, remove the cause, and apply convenient remedies. The disease in my opinion is contagious, and may infect the rest of your Majesty's dominions. It is a falling sickness, for they are like to fall from you, and from the obedience due to you, if, by removing the cause, and application of wholesome remedies, it be not speedily prevented. The cause is a fear and apprehension, not without some reason, of changes in religion, and that superstitious worship shall be brought in upon it, and therewith all their laws infringed and their liberties invaded. Free them, sir, from this fear, as you are free from any such thoughts; and undoubtedly you shall thereby settle the State in a firm obedience to your Majesty in all time coming. They have no other end but to preserve their religion in purity, and their liberties entire. That they intend the overthrow of monarchial government is a calumny. They are capable of no other, for many and great reasons; and ere they will admit another than your Majesty, and after you your son and nearest of your posterity, to sit upon your throne, many thousands of them will spend their dearest blood. You are not like a tree lately planted, which oweth a fall to the first wind. Your ancestors have governed theirs, without interruption of race, two thousand years or thereabouts, and taken such root as it can never be plucked up by any but yourselves. If any others shall entertain such treasonable thoughts, which I do not believe, certainly they will prove as vain as they are wicked.

" The remedy of this dangerous disease consisteth only in your Majesty's presence for a space in that kingdom. It is easy to you in person to settle their troubles, and to disperse these mists of apprehension and mistaking—impossible to any other. If you send

---

[1] Guthry, 90. Spalding, I., 376.　　　　[2] Napier, I., 276-277.

down a commissioner, whatever he be, he shall neither give nor get contentment, but shall render the disease incurable. The success of your Majesty's affairs, the security of your authority, the peace and happiness of your subjects, depend upon your personal presence. The disease is of that kind which is much helped by conceit[1] and the presence of the physician. Now is the proper time and the critical days. For the people love change, and expect from it much good—a new heaven and a new earth; but, being disappointed, are as desirous of a re-change to the former estate.

" Satisfy them, sir, in point of religion and liberties, when you come here, in a loving and free manner; that they may see your Majesty had never any other purpose, and doth not intend the least prejudice to either. For religious subjects, and such as enjoy their lawful liberties, obey better and love more than the godless and the servile, who do all out of base fear, which begets hate. Any difference that may arise upon the Acts passed in the last Parliament, your Majesy's presence, and the advice and endeavour of your faithful servants will easily accommodate. Let your Majesty be pleased to express your favour and care of your subjects' weal by giving way to any just notion of theirs for relief of the burdens these late troubles have laid on them, and by granting what else may tend to their good; which your Majesty may do with assurance that therein is included your own.

" Suffer them not to meddle or dispute of your power. It is an instrument never subjects yet handled well. Let not your authority receive any diminution of that which the law of God and Nature and the fundamental laws of the country alloweth; for then it shall grow contemptible: and weak and miserable is the people whose prince hath not power sufficient to punish oppression and to maintain peace and justice.

" On the other side, aim not at absoluteness. It endangers your estate and stirs up trouble. The people of the western parts of the world could never endure it any long time, and they of Scotland less than any. Hearken not to Rehoboam's counsellors. They are flatterers, and therefore cannot be friends; they will follow your fortune, and love not your person. Pretend what they will, their hasty ambition and avarice make them persuade an absolute government that the exercise of the same (may be put) on them, and then they know how to get wealth . . .[2]

" Practise, sir, the temperate government. It fitteth the humour and disposition of the nation best. It is most strong, most powerful, most desirable of any. It gladdeth the heart of your subjects, and then they erect a throne there for you to reign. *Firmissimum imperium quo obedientes gaudent.* Let your last act there be the settling the offices of State upon men of known integrity and sufficiency. Take them not upon credit and other men's recommendation; they prefer men for their own ends and with respect to themselves. Neither yet take them at a hazard, but upon your own knowledge, which fully reacheth to a great many more than will fill those few places. Let them not be such as are obliged to others than yourself for their preferment; not factious nor popular; neither such as are much hated; for these are not able to serve you well, and the others are not willing if it be prejudice to those upon whom they depend. They who are preferred and obliged to your Majesty will study to behave them well and dutifully in their places,

---

[1] Imagination.   [2] Gap of two lines in MS.

if it were for no other reason yet for this, that they make not your Majesty ashamed of your choice.

" So shall your Majesty secure your authority for the present, and settle it for the future time. Your journey shall be prosperous, your return glorious. You shall be followed with the blessings of your people, and with that contentment which a virtuous deed reflecteth upon the mind of the doer. And more true and solid shall your glory be than if you had conquered nations and subdued a people.

> " . . . pax una triumphis
> Innumeris potior."[1]

This sagacious letter might be elaborately annotated from contemporary history. There was no sentence in it which future events were not to justify abundantly, save that optimism about Scottish opinion which was to prove to Montrose a deceptive light. What could Argyll offer on the other side? It would be a mistake to take too seriously the gossip about his monarchical ambitions. The chief of the Campbells was far too shrewd a man to let a glittering dream divert him from a practicable purpose. His aim was to be dictator of Scotland, and his abilities were adequate to the task. Had he had military genius, he might well have played in Scotland the part of Cromwell, and wholly upturned the old foundations of sovereignty. But what had he to put in its place? Another autocracy without the sanctions of the old. He had made the cumbrous mediæval Parliament a more efficient and representative thing, but this reform merely strengthened the hands of the new oligarchy. He was sworn to the creed of intolerant Presbyterian domination in its extremest form. Above all, he was the clan chief, who supported his friends and did not forgive his enemies. To Montrose the alternative was unthinkable, for it would bring to Scotland not peace but a naked sword. He himself, in his young enthusiasm for the national religion and liberties, had been led into courses which were alien to his beliefs. He had assented to the constraint of private consciences, when he approved of the compulsory signature of the Covenant; he had given his approval to feudal barbarities when he signed Argyll's commission for the subjection of the North. But his eyes were now opened, and he hastened to draw aside from that perilous road.

Montrose was an ingenuous conspirator, for in his eagerness to discover like-mindedness and make converts he talked freely to the wrong people. At Scone, during a visit

---

[1] Napier, I., 311-313.

to Lord Stormont, he heard from Atholl, Stewart of Grand-
tully, and John Stewart of Ladywell, the commissary of
Dunkeld, reports of treasonable speeches made by Argyll
during the Perthshire expedition of the previous year. He
spoke of them to his friend, Mr. Robert Murray, the
minister of Methven, who mentioned them to Mr. John
Graham, the minister of Auchterarder, who repeated the
story to the Auchterarder presbytery, whence it came to
the ear of Argyll. Graham and Murray were asked for
their authority, and they named Montrose, who accepted
responsibility and in turn cited his evidence. His witnesses,
he said, were Lindsay of the Byres, Cassilis, Mar, and
Stewart of Ladywell. The witnesses were summoned before
the Committee of Estates, and proved unsatisfactory.
Lindsay remembered the conversation, but said that he had
not named Argyll. Ladywell stood by his words, signed
a written statement, and was thereupon, on 31st May, sent
to Edinburgh castle.

There something happened. Either Ladywell's nerve
broke down, or he was worked on by friends of Argyll,
like Balmerino; for next day he saw Argyll, recanted the
charges against him, and declared that he had forged them
out of malice. He did more, for he confessed that he had
been privy to discussions between Montrose, Napier, his
nephew Sir George Stirling of Keir, and Keir's brother-in-
law, Archibald Stewart of Blackhall, and that, acting on
their instructions, he had sent a report of Argyll's treason
to the king. The messenger who carried it was a certain
Walter Stewart of the Traquair family, and on the return
journey he was captured by the Committee. Among the
papers found on him was a short note from the king to
Montrose about his coming to Scotland, to which no
exception could be taken, and certain papers written in a
strange jargon, which was in all likelihood the product of
Stewart's own half-witted fancy, but which to the Committee had an ugly look of a secret cypher. Stewart was
ready with a confused but dark-sounding interpretation,
and on this document Montrose, Napier, Stirling, and
Stewart of Blackhall were arrested and confined in separate
rooms in the castle.[1]

It is not likely that Ladywell's first story was true.
Argyll was too cautious a man to speak rashly on such
matters in uncertain company; if he talked of the deposition of kings, it is probable that it was as an abstract pro-

[1] Napier, I., 295, etc. Guthry, 92, etc. Spalding, II., 47, etc.

position of kings in general. Nor did he show the desire of the rest of the Committee for the summary punishment of Ladywell—which would have been natural if Ladywell had been an inconvenient witness whom it was politic to silence. We know from Guthry, a hostile witness, that he consulted the Lord Advocate to see if a more lenient sentence could not be imposed.[1] The wretched man was duly convicted under the old Scottish statute of "leasing-making,"[2] and publicly beheaded in Edinburgh on 28th July.

Meantime there was the far graver business of Montrose. Argyll could afford to neglect the wild gossip of the commissary of Dunkeld, but it was another matter to have responsible Scottish nobles, with influence in the army, negotiating behind his back with the king. Napier was offered release as a favour, but declined to accept it; he declared that if any one was guilty he was, and he would not be separated from his companions. Montrose refused to answer any question before the Committee, and demanded a public trial by his peers. Traquair angrily denied any complicity with his preposterous kinsman, Walter Stewart. The king wrote on 12th June to Argyll to clear himself; his letter to Montrose was "fit for me to write, both for the matter, and the person to whom it is written;"[3] he had made no promise to any one as to the distribution of offices; he was coming to Scotland for no other purpose than to settle the affairs of the kingdom "according to the articles of the treaty." This might seem sufficient to clear Montrose, but his opponents, having got him under duress, did not intend to let him readily go. His house was broken into and his papers ransacked, but nothing more dangerous to the peace of the realm could be found than a paper justifying the Cumbernauld Bond, and "some letters from ladies to him in his younger years, flowered with Arcadian compliments."[4] On 27th July he was brought before Parliament, and declared that he had nothing to confess or to defend. "Truth doth not seek corners, it needeth no favour." He awaited their lordships'

[1] Guthry, 94.

[2] Acts of 1584, cap. 134; and of 1585, cap. 10. The punishment was reduced by 6 Geo. IV., cap. 47, and abolished by 7 Will. IV., cap. 5. According to Baillie it had never been put in force before (I., 381-382). These were the Acts under which Mr. Oldbuck, in *The Antiquary*, threatened vengeance against Mrs. Macleuchar, the proprietrix of the Queensferry diligence.

[3] Napier, I., 314-315.

[4] Guthry, 112.

questions or commands. " My resolution is to carry along
with me fidelity and honour to the grave."[1] They could
make nothing of such a man, and sent him back to prison.
He was brought again before Parliament on 6th August,
and a third time on 14th August.[2] On the evening of the
latter day the king arrived in Edinburgh.

Charles's determination to come to Scotland, so puzzling
to Clarendon, was due to the belief that he had still a
powerful following in that kingdom, which needed only to
be heartened by his presence. But a few days in Edinburgh
were sufficient to disillusion him. With Lennox and
Hamilton as his companions he recovered neither popularity nor authority. He had come north largely in the hope
of securing part of Leslie's army for use in the struggle
which he saw to be imminent in England, and for this he
was prepared to pay a high price. He paid the price, but
he did not secure his end, for Leslie's army was disbanded.
Non-Covenanting nobles like Lennox, Hamilton, Morton,
and Roxburgh were compelled to take the Covenant.
Hamilton, always, as Charles said, " very active in his own
preservation," made his peace with Argyll. Henderson
became the royal chaplain, and the king was obliged to
listen to many sermons and attend endless services conducted under the austerest Presbyterian forms. He was
prepared to ratify the Acts of the unconstitutional Parliament of 1640, but he was not permitted. These Acts, he
was curtly informed, were already valid, and he was
instructed merely to sanction their proclamation.[3] Parliament demanded, and he granted, a control over the executive and judiciary far more complete than anything claimed
by the English Parliament at Westminster.[4] Its triennial
meeting was guaranteed, independent of the royal assent.
Loudoun was nominated Chancellor; for Treasurer, the
king's suggestions first of Morton and then of Almond were
vetoed, and the office was put into commission. There was
no proposal of the Covenanters, however drastic, to which
the king did not assent. In return he received much lip
loyalty and many fine speeches, but no general popularity
or confidence. As was his fatal habit, he had been too late
in his concessions, and what, if voluntarily given, might
once have re-established his power, now, taken by force,
left only distrust and contempt.

[1] Napier, I., 346.   [2] Balfour, III., 38.
[3] Rait, *The Parliaments of Scotland*, 68, etc.
[4] Balfour, III., 65.

Meanwhile, what of Montrose, now fast in prison? Was he to go the way of Strafford? There was an ominous sentence used by Argyll at the opening of Parliament in his reply to the speech from the Throne, when he spoke of the State as a ship in distress and the need of casting out " some of the naughtiest baggage to lighten her."[1] The old statute against " leasing-making " might be used as a weapon against nobler game than the humble commissary of Dunkeld. On 15th September Sir Patrick Wemyss wrote to Ormonde that the king had promised Montrose not to leave Scotland till he was brought to trial, " for, if he leave him, all the world will not save his life."[2] On 28th August the four prisoners were called before Parliament, when the king nodded friendlily to Napier,[3] but their case was postponed. It would have been highly inconvenient to Argyll and Hamilton to have Montrose at this juncture pleading his cause before his peers.

Back again in the castle, Montrose was in a state of miserable anxiety and impotence. He heard of the new Act making the choice of Ministers dependent upon the will of Parliament—a piece of constitutionalism which, lacking the machinery and safeguards of modern government, was simply a premium set upon faction and sectarian tyranny. He heard of the decision that no one who had shown himself active on the king's side should be eligible for office. He must have exclaimed with Perth: " If this be what you call liberty, God give me the old slavery again."[4] He heard that among the nobles there were many who, whatever their past attitude, now saw with alarm the road which Argyll was taking. His one hope was Charles. He alone, if he clearly understood the situation, had the power of making it clear to Parliament and checking this drift towards oligarchy. Twice he wrote from prison praying for an interview with the king, that he might reveal matters " which not only concerned his honour in a high degree, but also the standing or falling of his crown."[5] These matters could only have been Hamilton's previous duplicity and Argyll's present ambitions. The third time he put his cards on the table, and on 11th October offered to prove a clear case of treachery to the commonwealth. Charles was impressed, and prepared to lay the business before the Chancellor and others of the Privy Council.

But in the meantime there had begun the curious per-

formance known to history as the " Incident "—a thing
as obscure in its origins as the Popish Plot. For some
weeks there had been a mysterious influx of armed men
into the capital, against which Loudoun, on 5th October,
had warned Parliament.[1] We know that Hamilton and
Argyll had 5,000 of their friends, and in the other faction
Lord Ker, Roxburgh's son, had 600 Borderers. On the
evening of 11th October, the day on which Montrose's third
letter was received, Hamilton went to the king in the garden
of Holyrood, complained of being traduced, and asked permission to leave the court.[2] Next day Charles told this
story to Parliament, but on that morning Hamilton, Argyll,
and Lanark had retired to the Hamilton house of Kinneil,
near Bo'ness. Their story was that they had learned
through Leslie that there was a plot against their lives.[3]
For a day or two king and Parliament faced each other
in a strange mood, the former protesting with tears against
the insult done to his honour, the latter in complete be-
wilderment. A Committee of the Estates investigated the
business, and Montrose's correspondence with the king was
laid before them; but no definite conclusion was reached,
and the truth must remain one of the secrets of history.

Charles was clearly innocent; so was Montrose, who at
the time was close in prison. No doubt there were nobles,
such as Ker and Crawford, with bands of retainers at their
heels, who would gladly have taken the old Scots way of
settling matters with their enemies. There were others,
such as Carnwath, who made no secret of their view that
there were now three kings in Scotland, and that two of
them could be dispensed with. But the study of the confused evidence leaves a strong impression that the whole
affair was a trick, a device of Hamilton's and Argyll's to
escape from the difficulties in which Montrose's third letter
might have placed them. Argyll was a master of elec-
tioneering ingenuities, and he knew that the suspicion of
being in peril is a supreme asset to a leader. The impression abides, too, that there was an *agent provocateur* at
work behind the scenes, and this may well have been
William Murray, a gentleman of the king's bedchamber,
the son of the minister of Dysart and the nephew of
Montrose's friend, the minister of Methven. Beginning as
the king's whipping-boy, he was to finish his career as Earl

---

[1] Balfour, III., 90. [2] Ibid., III., 95.
[3] Leslie, however, declared afterwards that he had considered it
" a foolish business." *Cal. S. P., Dom.* (1641-43), 137, etc.

of Dysart, and the father-in-law of Lauderdale. By general consent he was one of the most degraded characters of the age, and he was already suspect of meddling with the king's letters; it is at least possible that the Incident was mainly his work, a bogus conspiracy staged to give Hamilton the chance of discrediting his opponents.[1]

On 28th October, while the Incident was at its height, the king was playing golf at Leith, when a letter was put into his hands. It contained the news of the outbreak of the Irish rebellion. In a week the atmosphere in both England and Scotland had become tense and ominous, fear of popery spread like a flame, and the king's enemies had no need to create suspicion, for suspicion rose like a mist from every corner of the land. Charles could not linger in the north. On 18th November, at eight o'clock in the morning, he rode south, leaving for ever the country which he had so loved and misgoverned. He departed with a lavish shower of honours. Henderson was made dean of the Chapel Royal at Holyrood, Wariston was knighted, Loudoun and Leslie[2] became earls, and Argyll was made a marquis.[3] The day before the king left, Montrose and his friends were released on probation, and in March 1642 the case against them was finally closed. The four gentlemen, who had been five months in prison without trial, were informed that they owed their escape only to the clemency of Argyll. Montrose had engaged, ingenuously

[1] This is Mr. Lang's view, III., 99. The depositions taken at the inquiry may be read in *Hist. MSS. Comm.*, 4th Report, 163-170. See also Balfour, III., 94-137. In the first edition of Clarendon's *History* (Oxford, 1702-4), Montrose is accused of offering to the king, at a private interview, to make away with Hamilton and Argyll (see Macray's ed., IV., c. 20). This story was repeated by most historians, though discredited by Hume on general grounds. The passage, so inconsistent with Clarendon's general view of Montrose, seems to have been some rough notes for his *Life*, which somehow became mixed up with the *History*, based perhaps, as Mr. Gardiner suggests, on the confusion of Montrose and Crawford. In an appendix to the new edition of Clarendon, collated with the original MSS. in the Bodleian, and published in 1826, a revised version of the story is given which exonerates Montrose. This Clarendon perhaps intended to replace the faulty passage. See Napier, I., 359-363. Gardiner, X., 26. For William Murray, see Guthry, 117, Clarendon, IV., 15, *n*.

[2] Apparently the new Earl of Leven gave the king an undertaking that he would not in the future serve against him. See Terry, *Alexander Leslie*, 158 *n*.

[3] Gordon of Ruthven (*Britane's Distemper*, 57) says that there was an ancient prophecy that a red-haired and squinting Argyll would be the last earl and that the marquisate was accepted to avert the curse.

and amateurishly, in the difficult game of subterranean
Scottish politics, and had taken a heavy fall. The new
marquis could afford to be generous to an antagonist
whom, in the business of plots and counterplots, he had so
signally outplayed.

CHAPTER V

THE RUBICON

(1642-44)

In all questions of wide and deep interest it is scarcely less than
a fatal necessity that the best cause should be the worst defended;
the consequence of which is, the temporary victory of the false and
the superficial, and its establishment in the chair of learned as well
as popular opinion. The cause is in the instinct of the mind to aim
at the highest in the first instance—and hence with imperfect means,
and in the absence of all the main conditions of its attainment.
  COLERIDGE, *Notes, Theological, Political, and Miscellaneous.*

I

DURING THESE YEARS OF INEFFECTUAL POLITICS, MONTROSE,
in his long journeys and in quiet hours of retreat at Kincardine, was steadfastly endeavouring to clarify his own
mind. Some time between the autumn of 1640 and the
summer of 1641 he set down his views on the principles
of government in a letter to a " noble sir," who may have
been Lord Napier or Drummond of Hawthornden. The
paper was found by Mark Napier in a small quarto in the
handwriting of Robert Wodrow, and is among the manu-
scripts in the National Library of Scotland.[1] It is one
of those confessions of faith by which, at all periods in
history, sorely perplexed men have striven to ease their
souls. The seventeenth century saw no more searching
political treatise, for it reveals a capacity for abstract
thought rare at any time in a man of action, and especially
rare in an era when, as soon as the lists were set, half-truths
were vested with the authority of Sinai.
  He begins by laying down a doctrine of Sovereign
Power. If a land is to be stably governed there must be
some unquestioned centre of authority which he calls

---

[1] It is printed in Napier, I., 280-289 and *Mem. of M.*, II., 43-53.

Sovereignty, " a power over the people, above which power there is none on earth." It is limited indeed—by the laws of God and nature, the laws of nations, and the fundamental laws of the country; but these limitations are moral, religious, and constitutional, and inherent in its very being; it cannot be limited by division among competing authorities. Springing ultimately from a free people, it may in practice be delegated to a king, as in Britain; a council of nobles, as in Venice; or the estates of the people, as in ancient Rome. It " cannot subsist in a body composed of individuities "; if it is " divided amongst several bodies there is no government, as if there were many kings in one kingdom there should be none at all."

Montrose holds no brief for monarchy, except in so far as it is the form of sovereignty which has been accepted by the British people. He proceeds to analyse the nature of kingship. It is strong when it is temperate and recognizes its moral and constitutional limitations. " It is weak . . . when it is extended beyond the laws whereby it is bounded; which could never be at any time endured by the people of the western part of the world, and by those of Scotland as little as any." But the ills flowing from undue restraint are not less than the ills which spring from undue extension. No section of the people can seize a part of sovereignty, for, if sovereignty be divided, there follows anarchy, " the oppression and tyranny of subjects, the most fierce, insatiable, and insufferable tyranny in the world." He desires free and frequent parliaments and stern dealing with any law-breaking king; but he insists that, when sovereignty has been granted on conditions, it must be inviolable so long as these conditions are observed. Parliaments are guardians of the subjects' liberties, but not less of the delegated rights of the sovereign king.

He passes to the menaces to sovereignty—and therefore the causes of anarchy—and he finds them in " the ambitious designs of rule in great men, veiled under the specious pretext of religion and the subjects' liberties, seconded with the arguments and false positions of seditious precedence : first, that the king is ordained for the people, and the end is more noble than the means; second, that the constituter is superior to the constituent; third, that the king and people are two contraries, like the two scales of a balance—when the one goes up the other goes down; fourth, that the prince's prerogative and the people's privilege are incompatible; fifth, that what power is taken from the king is added to the Estates of the people." On this text he preaches an acute sermon. The two first points, as he explains them, do not mean that he holds that there is any absolutism in a free monarchy, but that, the choice of monarchy having been made by the people, such monarchy, which is their own creation, must be reasonably exalted, since in its exaltation lies their security. With the fear of the encroachments of the nobility and the Kirk in his mind, he appeals to the commons of Scotland:

" And you, ye meaner people of Scotland—who are not capable of a Republic, for many grave reasons—why are you induced by specious pretexts, to your own heavy prejudice and detriment, to be the instruments of others' ambition? Do you not hear, when the monarchial government is shaken, the great ones strive for the garland with *your* blood and *your* fortune? Whereby you gain nothing; but, instead of a race of kings who have governed you for two thousand years with peace and justice, and have preserved your liberties against all domineering nations, shall purchase to yourselves vultures and tigers to reign over your posterity; and yourselves shall endure all these miseries, massacres, and proscriptions of the Triumvirate of Rome—(till) the kingdom fall again into the hands of One, who of necessity must, and for reasons of State will, tyrannize over you. For kingdoms acquired by blood and violence are by the same means retained."[1]

It is the old profound lesson of history, eternally taught and eternally forgotten. After anarchy comes the dictator; the successors of the Gracchi are the Cæsars; the fury of the French Revolution is stamped out by Napoleon; the confusion of a Russia emancipated from her old masters is imperfectly disciplined by a harsher tyranny. In the England of that moment the " One " of whom he prophesied was already walking about in his sober country clothes and great buff boots. Montrose, it is to be noted, preaches the organic nature of the State to the common people, but to the Kirk and the nobility he addresses a different argument. He only warns them that their ambition will fail—the preachers, that the nobles will use them for their own interest, " as a cunning tennis-player lets a ball go to the wall where it cannot stay, that he may take it at the bound with more ease "; the nobles, that, like Æsop's dog, they will lose the substance for the shadow in the well. It would seem that he had made up his mind that the Kirk and the aristocracy were no longer amenable to reason.

[1] There is an even more remarkable forecast of Cromwell in Drummond of Hawthornden's " Address to the Noblemen, Barons, etc.," of May 2, 1639. *Works* (1711), vii.

We must be on our guard against reading into this philosophy of politics more than Montrose intended. If he saw beyond his age, he was also the child of that age. Much in his creed is not new. Fortescue in the fifteenth century had laid down the doctrine of constitutional monarchy. " The King of England cannot alter nor change the Lawes of the Realme at his pleasure; for why, he governeth his people by power, not only royall but politique." The Tudor monarchs had established the principle of an indivisible sovereignty by suppressing local immunities and crushing all rival authorities. But Montrose shows in many respects a startling originality, especially as contrasted with the writers of his own political party. He does not, like James I., identify sovereignty with monarchy;[1] he is willing to accept any form of government, provided it fulfils the requirements which are indispensable in all governments. Unlike his friend Drummond of Hawthornden, he has none of the contemporary belief in Divine Right, and he is no advocate of passive obedience.[2] He is primarily a realist, and he is curiously free from mediæval ideas on monarchy or on religion. His central principle may deduce from Bodin, but its application was based upon his personal observation of Scots affairs.

To orientate his political creed in relation to his age would require a treatise. Many philosophers of diverse schools, like Hobbes and Milton, accepted his doctrine of sovereignty. Montrose did not go into the metaphysics of political origins, the question which has agitated thinkers from Aristotle to Rousseau, whether the title to rule be natural or conventional. He would have accepted Hooker's view that sovereignty should be founded on consent, and while agreeing with Milton that sovereignty is from the people, he would have shrunk from Milton's addendum that the popular liberty of decision is only to be respected so long as the people accept a particular creed.[3] In the realism of his method of thought he has affinities with Hobbes, but not in his conclusion: he has much in com-

---

[1] *Works* (1616), 193. *Cf.* the broadmindedness of the *Scots Confession* of 1560, Article XXIV., Dunlop, *Collection of Confessions*, II., 90.

[2] Drummond's view will be found in his *Irene* (*Works*, 163). Professor Masson, in his *Drummond of Hawthornden*, 346, etc., fails to distinguish the completely different points of view of the two friends. If Montrose had any mentor in his political philosophy, it was Lord Napier. See *Mem. of M.*, I., 70.

[3] See Milton, *A Ready and Easy Way to establish a Free Government*. The doctrine of the popular origin of sovereignty had become

mon with Samuel Rutherford, whose *Lex Rex*, published
in 1644, lays down the thesis that sovereignty comes from
the people, who may, in time of extreme necessity, resume
this power, and nothing in common with Sir George Mackenzie, whose reply to Buchanan's *De Jure Regni*[1] is a
proof of the extravagant lengths to which a Scot could
go in defending the alien dogma of Divine Right. His
doctrine of sovereignty is at the opposite pole from that
of Strafford, who believed that the security of a nation
depended in emergencies upon an executive authority above
and outside the ordinary law, an inalienable and overriding
prerogative—a view which in one form is a truism to-day,
but which in the seventeenth century, if generally accepted,
would have put an end to popular liberties.

But Montrose is not a metaphysician. He is a student
of history and an observer of facts. His inquiry is a
practical one—how to stave off anarchy, and the maxims
which he offers have their direct contemporary applications. He is modern in his doctrine of the organic unity
of the State, but in two matters he is very clearly of his age.

The first is his attitude towards parliamentary government. " It is curious to observe," says Coleridge of the
early seventeenth century, " that the thinner the realm was
(the less both in wealth and influence, and the less they
were diffused) the greater was the division of power."[2]
In the constitution of that age there was no clear determination of function between the executive, the judiciary,
and the legislature. " The ' rule of law,' which the power
of the state existed to enforce, worked through no
specialized machinery, the organization was still fluid, only
here and there hardening into conventions. . . . The conception of an exclusive sovereignty, inherent in any one
branch of the Constitution, was still far distant."[3] In strict
theory, the true sovereign was the law fundamental, the
" law of the land," which was regarded as beyond the reach
of legislative change. Magna Charta had been a solemn
embodiment of one portion of that law. In 1604 the

a commonplace in France, both among the Huguenots and their
opponents. Cf. *Vindiciæ contra Tyrannos*.—" Regis nomen non
hereditatem, proprietatem, usumfructuum, sed functionem et pro-
curationem sonat." The close connection of Scotland and France
popularized this view, but it was also deep in Scottish history. *Cf.*
John Major, *Hist. of Greater Britain* (S.H.S.), 213, etc.
[1] *Works*, II., 472.
[2] *Notes, Theological, Political, and Miscellaneous*, 206
[3] Feiling, *History of the Tory Party, 1640-1714.* 33.

Speaker of the House of Commons divided the laws into
(1) the Common law, not mutable; (2) the Positive law, to
be altered by the occasion of the times; (3) customs and
usages which have time's approbation. The distinction
appears in Sir Walter Raleigh's *Prerogative of Parliaments*;
Sir Edward Coke maintained that the function of king and
parliament was not *jus dare* but *jus dicere*—to declare
the law; in 1659 Nicholas Bacon told Richard Cromwell's
Parliament that, as regarded bicameral government, " long
usage hath so settled it, as Acts of Parliament cannot alter
it." The doctrine of the legislative supremacy of Parliament was still in the womb of time.[1]

Montrose held firmly to this conception of a law im-
mutable and fundamental; it was the code to which both
he and Charles appealed at their trials, and it moulded his
view of sovereignty. With this adamantine sanction in the
background, which no other power could change, he was
compelled to think of a constitution as a thing of delicate
balances, of authority as a commodity scrupulously
weighed out and studiously limited, and of a central
delegated sovereignty as inhering in a monarch rather than
in any Parliament. National health, he maintained,
depended, like bodily health, upon each member playing
its own part without encroachment. The monarchy seemed
to him the most vital part of a nicely adjusted mechanism,
since upon its proper functioning the working of all other
parts specially depended. He places the emphasis on the
Crown, though he gives it no autocracy. He could not
foresee that this delicate adjustment would end in stagna-
tion, and that in a later age it would be necessary to
aggrandize the power of one part in order to make the
wheels revolve. It was difficult for any thinker of his time
to accept the legislative sovereignty of Parliament, to which
the Long Parliament tried to feel its way—the notion of
the " law fundamental " forbade it; but it was doubly
difficult for Montrose. For the Parliament which he knew
was the Scots Parliament, with its bad traditions of
incompetence and servility. It may be that Argyll had a
vision of parliamentary government denied to his contemporaries, but it was a vision, for a sober survey of the
facts seemed to render it impossible. A wise and impartial
king might hold the balance between conflicting interests,
but the Scots Parliament, swung alternately between Kirk

[1] For the " law fundamental," see C. H. McIlwain, *The High
Court of Parliament*, 1910.

and nobles, would, if unfettered, produce only despotism or anarchy.

The second matter in which Montrose is a man of his time, is his attitude towards what we call democracy. He believed that from the whole nation came the sanction of sovereignty, but he was not a democrat in the modern sense, for the common people in his day were scarcely conscious of political rights, and asked rather to be wisely protected than to be endowed with ill-understood duties. But, both in his theory and in his practice, he was more democratic than most of his generation. He held that the laws were the only safeguard of the plain man, the true monarch of which the king was but the creature. He saw that any disturbance of the equipoise in the distribution of public duties would not add to popular liberties, but, by increasing confusion, would augment the power of this or that oligarchical faction. He held—and what student of the period will dissent?—that the contemporary commons of Scotland were " more incapable of sovereignty than any other known." The people, as a political force, did not come within the imagination of seventeenth-century Britain. " They care not what Government they live under," said Haselrig, " so as they may plough and go to market."[1] The proletariat was as meaningless a thing to Cromwell and Vane as it was to Strafford and Clarendon, and the creed of the Leveller was as hateful to the Puritan as to the Cavalier. Indeed it may be said that the silent masses had more to gain from king than from Parliament, for it was the Crown which, in Star Chamber and Council, did its best to check enclosure, protect tenant right, and maintain wages. Montrose, with his doctrine of the organic unity of the State, and his constant appeal to the " mean people," came nearer democracy, it may be argued, than most of his contemporaries.[2]

The purpose of human government is to give to the citizen a free, a secure, and an ordered life. The means of effecting this purpose will vary from age to age and from nation to nation, but one essential will always remain —an effective central power " to unite and incorporate the members into one body politic that, with joint endeavour and abilities, they may the better advance the common good," and this central power must spring from the good-

[1] Burton, *Diary*, III., 257.
[2] There is an interesting study of Montrose's political philosophy by Archdeacon Cunningham, *S.H.R.*, July 1917.

will of the people at large. Montrose found it in a constitutional monarchy such as he conceived it. " He who keeps watch and ward for freedom," Coleridge has written, " has to guard against two enemies, the despotism of the few and the despotism of the many."[1] The second peril in Montrose's day had not arisen, but the first was an ever-present menace, whether it took the form of an aristocratic or an ecclesiastical junta. The truth of his doctrine is not affected by the fact that Britain found a solution by other methods than those which he foreshadowed. The hope of a popular monarchy shipwrecked on the character of Charles, and a religious quarrel in which civil politics were fatally compromised. If Montrose did not foresee either modern parliamentaryism or modern democracy, he foresaw the principle which alone gives them value. They are but means to an end, and to-day, when parliamentary government has lost much of its glamour, and criticism is revealing as mere expedients certain democratic dogmas which once seemed eternal truths, we are being driven back again to the fundamentals.

Open Burke anywhere. " I see no other way for the preservation of a decent attention to public interest in the representatives, but the interposition of the body of the people itself, whenever it shall appear, by some flagrant and notorious act, by some capital innovation, that the representatives are going to overleap the fences of the law, and to introduce an arbitrary power."[2] It is Montrose's defence, first for signing the National Covenant, and then for taking up arms against the Covenanters. " Here it says to an encroaching prerogative, ' Your sceptre has its length, you cannot add a hair to your head or a gem to your crown but what an eternal law has given to it! ' Here it says to an overweening peerage, ' Your pride finds banks that it cannot overflow.' Here to a tumultuous and giddy people, ' There is a bed to the raging sea.' "[3] It is Montrose's conception of constitutional law. Or again, " If civil society be the offspring of convention, that convention must be its law. That convention must limit and modify all the descriptions of constitutions which are formed under it. Every sort of legislative, judicial, or executive power are its creatures. They can have no being in any other state

[1] *The Friend*, I., 94.
[2] *Thoughts on the Causes of the Present Discontents.*
[3] *Speech in the House of Commons on Constitutional Reform*, May 7, 1782.

of things; and how can any man claim, under the convention of civil society, rights which do not so much as suppose its existence—rights which are absolutely repugnant to it."[1]   It is Montrose's case against the encroachments of the Kirk.   He saw that in a stable government the supreme power, while it must be delegated, cannot be made divisible.   The Kirk was willing enough to accept the doctrine of popular sovereignty, but it did not grasp the inevitable conclusion—that the people cannot entrust this power to two conflicting authorities which may both claim to represent them.   Church and State cannot rule conjointly over the same sphere and under the same sanctions. Montrose took the historical as opposed to the metaphysical view of human institutions, and, moreover, in his practical interpretation he curiously anticipated the modern attitude.   He could have little part in an age when most men believed that kings and churches and aristocracies were mystically ordained of God.

From his first entry into public life Montrose was at variance with the bulk of the Scottish nobility, but it seems certain that he began with a real enthusiasm for the Kirk, of which he was a ruling elder.   So long as it stood for spiritual freedom he was its fervent champion, and this championship, as we have seen, led him occasionally into courses which were contrary to his political creed.   He had a reverence for godliness, and from such a man as Alexander Henderson he differed with profound reluctance. His personal religion was the Calvinism of his age, but he had reached it, not by the rigid schedule of grim " experiences " laid down by the Scottish divines, but by the gentler Platonic method, whereby God reveals Himself insensibly through the riches of His world, and piety crowns like a flower the natural growth of mind and soul.[2]   He had the latitude of Hales or Chillingworth about inessentials, and his creed was that of the great saying of Symmachus: " Uno itinere non potest pervenire ad tam grande secretum."   His condemnation was reserved for those who

[1] *Reflections on the Revolution in France.*
[2] In the accounts of the undergraduate Montrose for 1628 there is an item, " For Mr. William Struther's ' Meditations.' "   Struther, who had been tutor to Montrose's cousin, Lord Wigton, published two " centuries " of " Christian Observations and Reflections " in 1628 and 1629, and his teaching must have influenced Montrose's youth.   Robert Baillie thought him " the most eloquent and gracious preacher that ever yet lived in Scotland."

forgot the spirit in the letter and made religion a thing
of scholastic subtleties. His affinities were with men like
the Cambridge Platonists, whose Calvinism was mellowed
and warmed by the love of humanity and of all things true
and beautiful. He would have agreed with Whichcote that
Christ is *magister vitæ non scholæ*, and that he is " the best
Christian whose heart beats with the truest pulse towards
heaven, not he whose head spinneth out the finest cob-
webs." He had Whichcote's stalwart respect for the freedom of the mind. When later he criticized the teaching of
the Scottish divines, it was on the ground of their narrow
legalism and their spiritual pride.[1]

The event which compelled his final breach with the Kirk
was its growing alliance, under Henderson's leadership,
with the Parliamentary party in England, of which the price
was to be the establishment of Presbytery south of the
Tweed. The policy, which culminated in the Solemn
League and Covenant, is capable of defence from the point
of view of the perplexed Scottish divines. The Kirk held
that Presbytery was a *jus divinum*, and it had the mediæval
belief in religious uniformity as the foundation of political
unity. It had suffered grievously from prelatical encroachments, and the impetus for such encroachments had come
from England; its liberties could only be safeguarded if
England were brought to its own way of thinking. Moreover, the Counter-Reformation was making huge strides
on the continent of Europe, and it could be resisted only if
there were the closest unity among all the reformed
Churches; and this seemed to involve the abolition of
Anglican anomalies and the reshaping of English Protestantism according to the universal Protestant pattern.

[1] *Cf.* John Smith of Cambridge: " I doubt sometimes some of
our dogmata and notions about Justification may puff us up in far
higher and goodlier conceits of ourselves than God hath of us; and
that we profanely make the unspotted righteousness of Christ to
serve only as a covering wherein to wrap up our foul deformities
and filthy vices; and when we have done, think ourselves in as good
credit and repute with God as we are with ourselves; and that we
are become heaven's darlings as much as we are our own. . . . God
respects not a bold, confident, and audacious faith that is big with
nothing but its own presumptions. . . . It is not all our strong
dreams of being in favour with heaven, it is not a pertinacious
imagination of our name being enrolled in the book of life, or of
the debt-books of heaven being crossed, or of Christ being ours,
or of the washing away of our sins in His blood . . . it is not, I
say, a pertinacious imagination of any of these that can make us the
better."—*Discourse of Legal and Evangelical Righteousness*, chs. iv.
and v.

A man like Henderson was too wise to believe that he could force Presbytery upon an unwilling England. "We do not presume," he wrote, "to propose the government of the Church of Scotland as a pattern for the Church of England, we do only represent in all modesty these few considerations according to the trust committed to us." The change must come willingly from within, and he believed that the greater part of the Anglican Church desired it.[1] He was misled by his English correspondents; he did not—he could not—realize that the great bulk of the English people disliked Laud and the Anglican extremists, but were attached to a moderate episcopacy, that the Presbyterian majority in Parliament was not the English nation, that English Presbyterianism was very different from Scottish, and that even among the declared opponents of the king and the bishops there were many stalwart Erastians of the Selden type, who would not suffer an ecclesiastical discipline uncontrolled by the civil law. Had Henderson had this knowledge, it is certain that one who sought above all things the unity and peace of the two peoples would have refrained from a policy which was to be the fruitful mother of strife. But there were few ministers with Henderson's sagacity. To most, the bringing of England into conformity with their own communion was a direct command of God, and they devoted themselves to the task with a fanatic missionary zeal. The new Covenant became a mystical compact with the Almighty, its acceptance the test of holiness, its rejection or breach a certain proof of damnation. It was to be attended by "the voice of harpers harping with their harps, which shall fill the whole island with melody and mirth." Civil statesmanship disappears in such a mood, and all that remains is a frantic theocracy.[2] The Kirk, whose spiritual rights had been threatened by Charles, was now, in the enthusiasm

[1] See Orr, *Alexander Henderson*, 287, 312, etc.
[2] This misunderstanding of England's attitude led to an extreme bitterness between the two peoples, the very result which Henderson hoped that the Solemn League would prevent. Compare, for example, Mr. John McClelland: "Englishmen shall be made spectacles to all nations for a broken covenant. . . . If all England were as one man united in judgment and assertion, and if it had a wall round about reaching to the sun, and if it had as many armies as it has men, and every soldier had the strength of Goliath, and if their navies could cover the ocean, and if there were none to peep out or move the tongue against them, yet I dare not doubt their destruction when the Lord hath sworn by His life that He will avenge the breach of covenant." Howie, *Scots Worthies* (1838), I., 200.

of a regained independence, proposing to encroach upon the sphere of secular government.

To Montrose, with his modern conception of the State, both Kirk and nobles seemed to be marching the straight road to anarchy. The National Covenant had been an assertion of unquestioned civil and religious liberties, a united nation, with a reverent acknowledgment of their Maker, recalling their king to the true doctrine of kingship. But, in the Solemn League now preparing, the Kirk had gone far beyond her lawful sphere. He knew the people of England, and realized that the acceptance by the English Parliament of Henderson's scheme could only be a price paid for alliance in rebellion. His way and the Kirk's had come to a sharp parting. The king, in spite of former blunders, was now constitutionally in the right, and if war came it was for Montrose, and for all lovers of law and liberty, to support the central power against anarchic usurpation. If he erred in his view of Charles's character and aims, the error was justifiable, for in the past three years the king had appeared to yield all that the National Covenant had demanded, and to have assented to that historic constitutionalism which Argyll and the Kirk were now denying by word and deed.

The alternative, as Montrose saw it, was a theocracy on a feudal basis, an omnipotent Kirk and a free license to a corrupt and turbulent aristocracy, provided that aristocracy remained orthodox. How would the " mean people " of Scotland fare under such a régime? *Quicquid delirant reges, plectuntur Achivi.* He looked around, and saw the wretchedness of their condition. Throughout all his writings and declarations there rings a note of pity for the common folk, who had to bear the brunt of their rulers' folly. " Ye have oppressed the poor, and violently perverted judgment and justice "—so ran his last tremendous indictment. Public morals were at a low ebb;[1] nor was there any revival of true spiritual life, such as had at other times attended a season of religious wars. The hungry sheep were fed with windy politics. Let us take one witness, the celebrated Mr. Robert Law, a stout Covenanter who was ejected from his church in 1662 after the Restoration. " From the year 1652," he writes, " to the year 1660,

---

[1] See, for Berwick and the Lothians, a letter of an English soldier in Scotland (Sept. 1650), quoted by Lang, III., 204 ; for godly Fife, the evidence of Robert Baillie and the St. Andrews Kirk Session (ibid., III., 102)

there was great good done by the preaching of the Gospel
in the west of Scotland, more than was observed to have
been for twenty or thirty years before; a great many
brought in to Christ Jesus by the saving work of conversion, which was occasioned through ministers preaching
nothing all that time but the Gospel, and had left off to
preach up parliaments, armies, leagues, resolutions, and
remonstrances."[1] The use of the Lord's Prayer was condemned by some zealots as being too much of a " set
form."[2] Private meetings for devotion were discouraged
as savouring of schism—a strange policy for a church
which owned Livingstone and Samuel Rutherford. Religion
was in danger of ceasing to be a quickening spirit, and of
becoming a *hortus siccus* of withered pedantries. Of the
Kirk now dominant in Scotland, Cromwell, before Dunbar,
had certain truths to proclaim. " By your hard and subtle
words," he told the ministers, " you have begotten prejudice
in those who do too much in matters of conscience—
wherein every soul has to answer for itself to God—depend
upon you. Your own guilt is too much for you to bear.
. . . Is it therefore infallibly agreeable to the Word of
God, all that you say? I beseech you in the bowels of
Christ, think it possible that you may be mistaken. There
may be a Covenant made with Death and Hell."[3]

As his path became clearer before him, Montrose, after
his fashion at a crisis in his life, was moved to one of his
rare exercises in verse. He had much leisure during these
months, and spent it at his house of Kincardine with his
wife and his sons, of whom the eldest was now a boy of
twelve. Thither came a pleasant company of neighbours
and kinsfolk, Napiers, Erskines, and Stirlings, and the old
hall by the Ruthven Water heard for the last time the sound
of young voices and children's play. At this period he
must have written the lyric by which his name is best
known in our literature. It is a love song, but it is
addressed to the eyebrows of no mortal Sylvia. In his
youth ladies had written him verses, but his marriage was
the one romance of his life, and, in spite of the jealous
inquisition of the Kirk, no affair of gallantry was ever
linked with his name. In his ballad the ardour of the
patriot is joined to the passion of the lover in singing of his
mistress, Scotland, and what he will do for her if she trusts

---

[1] *Memorials* (ed. by C. Kirkpatrick Sharpe, 1812), 7.
[2] Gordon of Rothiemay, III., 250.
[3] Cromwell's *Letters and Speeches* (ed. Lomas), II., 78-79.

him. It breathes the same spirit as his " Discourse of Sovereignty," a hatred of sectarian war, a plea for the unity which had long fled from his distracted land. Almost every metaphor is drawn from the language of contemporary politics, but that language is warmed and coloured by a passion of loyalty—to an ideal rather than to a person, for with Montrose, in Plato's words, the quest of truth did not lack the warmth of desire.

> " My dear and only love, I pray
>   That little world of thee
> Be governed by no other sway
>   Than purest monarchy ;
> For if confusion have a part,
>   Which virtuous souls abhor,
> And hold a Synod in thine heart,
>   I'll never love thee more.
>
> As Alexander I will reign,
>   And I will reign alone ;
> My thoughts did evermore disdain
>   A rival on my throne.
> He either fears his fate too much,
>   Or his deserts are small,
> That dares not put it to the touch,
>   To win or lose it all.
>
> . . . .
>
> And in the Empire of thine heart
>   Where I should solely be,
> If others do pretend a part
>   Or dare to vie with me,
> Or if Committees thou erect,
>   And go on such a score,
> I'll laugh and sing at thy neglect,
>   And never love thee more.
>
> But if thou wilt prove faithful then,
>   And constant of thy word,
> I'll make thee glorious by my pen,
>   And famous by my sword ;
> I'll serve thee in such noble ways
>   Was never heard before ;
> I'll crown and deck thee all with bays,
>   And love thee more and more."[1]

[1] The texts of this famous song vary considerably. There is no copy extant in Montrose's handwriting. It was first published and attributed to Montrose in Watson's *Choice Collection of Scots Poems*, 1711, apparently from an earlier broadside (*Mem. of M.*, II., 467). Its authenticity has never been questioned, and indeed some of the phrases are to be found in Montrose's correspondence with Prince Rupert (*Mem. of M.*, II., 465). I agree with Mark Napier that the piece is a political and not a love poem, though Lord Stanhope thought otherwise (*Historical Essays*, 172). Lord Stanhope puts the date of its composition as 1648, and Lady Violet Greville as after his wife's death (*Montrose*, 82), but internal evidence seems to suggest 1642, the last season of quiet before the storm broke. A

This is the song of a man who has at last found assurance, the confession of a soul which has a vision of a noble purpose, and holds no risk too high in its attainment.

II

Montrose was soon to be called to witness to his faith. Charles returned to London from Scotland in November 1641, to be confronted with the Grand Remonstrance, which demanded a government responsible to Parliament, and the summoning of an assembly of divines to settle the religious problem. On January 4, 1642, he was guilty of a supreme blunder when, on his queen's advice, he attempted to enter the Commons and arrest the Five Members. Six days later he left London, to which he was not destined to return till he returned to die. The last hope of a peaceful settlement had gone, and both sides began the raising of armies—the Parliament by ordinances, and the king by commissions of array. On 23rd April Sir John Hotham shut the gates of Hull in Charles's face, and civil war began. On 22nd August the royal standard was set up at Nottingham, and in that month and from that place the king wrote to Montrose:

" I send Will Murray to Scotland to inform my friends of the state of my affairs, and to require both their advice and assistance. You are one whom I have found most faithful, and in whom I repose greatest trust. Therefore I address him chiefly to you. You may credit him in what he shall say, both in relation to my business and to your own; and you must be content with words until I be able to act. I will say no more but that I am your loving friend . . ."[1]

It would have been well for Charles had he trusted Montrose in Scots affairs. But Hamilton, as we know from Clarendon, had given him assurances that " he would at least keep that people from doing anything that might seem to countenance the carriage of the Parliament," and it was to Hamilton that Murray went. In the previous November the king had appealed to the Scottish Privy Council for help in dealing with the Irish rebellion. The Council responded by an energetic levy of troops, the first batch of which went to Ulster in February 1642, and sent

large number of verses, many of them indifferent, are printed by Napier, I. App *Mem. of M.*, II., 470-475. Montrose's full poetical works will be found in the appendix to the second volume of Napier's *Montrose and the Covenanters*, Lady Violet Greville's *Montrose*, c. 4, Eyre-Todd's *Scottish Poetry of the Seventeenth Century* (Glasgow, 1895), and Professor Rait's edition of *Montrose and Marvell* (London, 1901).   [1] Napier, II., 372.

E

Lothian and Lindsay to London to attempt to mediate
between king and Parliament. Scotland found herself
courted diligently by both sides, and returned evasive
answers. A special meeting of the Council was held in
May 1642, when Montrose and his friends endeavoured
to induce it to stand to its many pledges and refrain from
assisting the Parliament with arms. The presence of the
royalist nobles in Edinburgh raised the usual cry of a
design against the lives of the Covenanting leaders, the
gentry and clergy of Fife flocked to the capital as a bodyguard for the menaced statesmen, and the Privy Council
was confirmed in its cautious detachment.[1]

But this detachment could not be kept up for ever. In
July the General Assembly met in St. Andrews, when king
and Parliament renewed their solicitations to the body
which especially represented the opinion of Scotland. The
English Puritans did not ask for a definite alliance, but
they declared their detestation of the English episcopacy,
and their earnest desire for " an advancement of the true
religion and such a reformation of the Church as should
be made agreeable to God's Word." This gave the
Assembly its cue; " agreeable to God's Word " must mean
Presbyterianism; so it petitioned the king to labour for
" blessed unity in religion, and uniformity of Church
government "—in other words, the establishment of Presbytery in England. Argyll was in command at St.
Andrews, and ruled the Assembly as he ruled the Scottish
Parliament. When Murray arrived in the early autumn,
he found Hamilton living in Argyll's company, and
negotiating a marriage between his eldest daughter and
Lord Lorn. The Assembly's appeal brought a reply in
September, for the English Parliament voted unanimously
that the present government of the Church of England must
be abolished, and that the national Church must be reconstructed with the aid of an assembly of divines. This
seemed to grant to the Kirk what it had been seeking—the
end of the hated episcopacy, and Presbytery established
from Devon to Caithness. Small wonder that it leaned to
the Parliament's side, and that the Scottish people, whom
it controlled, had the same bias.

Meantime Edgehill had been fought, and in November
the Parliament applied to Scotland for aid. Charles replied
with a defence of his policy, and Hamilton, roused out of
his dreams by the sudden crisis, and anxious at least to

[1] Baillie, II., 43.

save his country from naked rebellion, persuaded the Privy
Council to publish the royal declaration.   But Argyll
insisted that the English Parliament's appeal should also
be published. and there was the usual game of petition and
counter-petition, in which Argyll won.   That of Traquair
and Hamilton asked no more than that Scotland should
do nothing to commit itself to the path of disloyalty and
civil war.[1]   That such a policy should have been
vehemently opposed both by the Assembly and the Estates
shows how Scottish opinion had hardened against the king.

It was high time that Charles should know the facts—
that from Scotland would come no aid for his cause, but
only augmentation to his enemies—for he could learn
nothing from the vain and obtuse Hamilton.   An effort
had been made to draw Montrose again into the Covenant
camp. He had no following among either nobles or people,
but his opponents appreciated the strength of his character
and his talents for war, and he was offered, if he would
join them, the lieutenant-generalship of the army, and, says
Wishart, " quæcunque alia quæ suæ forent potestatis."[2]
The offer must have come from Argyll, who had the wits
to recognize ability, who desired to have on his side a
military genius which he did not himself possess and which
he may well have believed to be superior to old Leven's,
and who must have noted Montrose's sincere attachment
to Presbytery and the reluctance with which he differed
from the Kirk. If Hamilton was privy to it, it can only
have been because he desired to compromise one whom
he hated, for his shallow mind still held to the belief that
he could keep Scotland out of the war.   The incident forced
Montrose to be up and doing.   The royal cause at the
moment was not unprosperous in the field.   In spite of the
check at Turnham Green, Charles had consolidated his
position in the Oxford district, Newcastle was firm in Yorkshire, and Hopton had cleared the south-west.   The way
to London might soon be open unless the Scots army took
the royalists in flank from the north.   The peril from Scotland must at once be made known to the king.

In February 1643 Montrose, with Ogilvy and Aboyne,
crossed the Border.   The Court was at Oxford, whither
Ogilvy and Aboyne repaired, but Montrose, hearing at
Newcastle that the queen was arriving from Holland, went
to meet her at Bridlington Bay.   A year before she had
gone to the Hague to sell the crown jewels for munitions

[1] Burnet, *Mem. of the Hamiltons*, 206.   [2] Wishart, c. 2.

of war, and had now returned with stores and money, to be greeted in her bedroom by the round shot of the Parliament fleet. Montrose urged an immediate grant of a royal warrant to authorize a loyal rising in Scotland. He believed that if Charles struck the first blow the opposition might be overawed, or at any rate crippled. Henrietta was too sea-sick and flustered to listen, and told him that she would discuss the matter at York. But to York had posted Hamilton and Traquair with their smooth words, and the distracted lady followed the path of least resistance. Montrose was dismissed as an alarmist, and Hamilton's optimism prevailed.[1]

He had not long to wait for his vindication. Loudoun, Henderson, and Wariston had gone as a commission to the king at Oxford, to mediate for peace on the basis of Presbyterian uniformity in England, and there Henderson argued the question of episcopacy with no less a person than Jeremy Taylor.[2] The commission asked for a Parliament that summer, though under the grant of triennial parliaments the next did not fall due till June 1644, and this request Charles refused. But Argyll had business on hand which could not wait, and on his own account he arranged for the summoning of a Convention of Estates on June 22, 1643. Here was an act of rebellion as final as Sir John Hotham's, but Hamilton persuaded the king to ignore the breach of prerogative and sanction the meeting, which he himself attended, to watch, as he said, the royal interests.[3] He had just been made a duke, to encourage his slack-lipped loyalty.

Montrose did not attend the Convention. For him and his friends the final parting had come. During the spring of 1643 Argyll's offer had been renewed. He would be given high military command, and his debts, mainly incurred in legal expenses, would be paid if he would join the dominant party. The story reached the ears of the queen, and in a letter of 31st May she offered him arms from Denmark and assured him of her confidence, though she had heard that he had " struck up an alliance with certain persons that might well create apprehension in my mind."[4] In the early days of June Montrose was in the north with Airlie, Huntly, and Marischal, attempting to

[1] Wishart, c. 3. Burnet, *Mem. of the Hamiltons*, 212.
[2] Orr, *Alexander Henderson*, 294-295.
[3] Rait, *The Parliaments of Scotland*, 156.
[4] Napier, II., 380. *Mem. of M.*, II., 77.

form a coalition—an attempt frustrated by the lightheaded-
ness of the latter two. This visit seems to have alarmed
Argyll, for he made one last desperate bid for Montrose's
support. If others were blind to the powers of this young
man of thirty, the dictator of Scotland knew capacity
when he met it. He was aware that Montrose had been
snubbed by the queen, and he hoped to catch him on the
rebound. Montrose had not bluntly refused his overtures,
but had hinted that certain scruples stood in his way. To
solve them, the Moderator of the Kirk, Alexander Henderson, was dispatched to interview the doubter.

One day in the middle of June he met Montrose in a
meadow on the banks of the Forth near Stirling. It was
a curious meeting, the embarrassed Sir James Rollo,[1]
brother-in-law of both Montrose and Argyll, acting as
Henderson's second, and Lord Napier, Lord Ogilvy, and
Stirling of Keir being present as witnesses. The Moderator
frankly avowed that the Covenanters were about to send
an army to England in support of the Parliament, and
repeated the old offer. " Nothing was more earnestly
desired than that he should join with his peers and the
other estates of the realm; it would bring joy to all, and
not only profit, but also honour to himself. His example
would at once bring over the few, if there were any, who
respected the empty shadow of royalty. As for himself,
his most hearty thanks would be due to God if He would
deign to make him the minister and mediator of so great
a work."[2] Montrose asked Rollo if Henderson had authority to make the offer. Rollo said he had, but Henderson
said no, but believed that the Convention would substan-
tiate his promises. This gave Montrose the chance to avoid
a direct refusal. He replied that in these circumstances he
must ask for time to consider, and took a friendly leave
of the man in all Scotland from whom he was most loth
to differ. They never met again. Three years later, after
he had seen Montrose's splendour and decline, as well as
the failure of his own hopes, Henderson died. His last
words were : " I am near the end of my race, hasting home,

---

[1] Sir James Rollo, or Rollock, was the eldest son of the laird of
Duncrub, who was made a peer by Charles II. in 1651. He married
first Montrose's sister Dorothea, and secondly Argyll's half-sister
Lady Mary Campbell. He was present at Inverlochy, and fled in
Argyll's boat. He was among the company at Montrose's funeral
in 1661. His brother, Sir William, was Montrose's faithful companion till he was executed at Glasgow after Philiphaugh.
[2] Wishart, c. 2. Baillie, II., 74. Guthry, 130.

and there was never a schoolboy more desirous to have the play than I am to have leave of this world."

Before the Convention in June, Charles, in a declaration to the people of Scotland, had stated his case against the English Parliament, and had solemnly protested his loyalty to the rights recently assured to the Scottish nation. He was not believed. The war in Ireland had ceased, and the Kirk dreaded that an army might thereby be freed for the defence or restoration of episcopacy. Moreover, Lord Antrim, whose incompetence rivalled Hamilton's in every field of action, had got himself captured in Ulster, along with a budget of letters from Nithsdale, Aboyne, and others. There seemed a risk of a popish invasion. Scotland was to be overrun by Irish kerns, Charles was to join hands with Nithsdale on the Solway, Macdonalds and Macleans were to harass the Campbells, and Huntly and Montrose were to fire the north. Montrose's recent visit to Aberdeen seemed to give authority to the tale.[1] Moreover, things were going ill with the English Parliament. In June John Hampden had fallen on Chalgrove Field, and Fairfax had been defeated in Yorkshire at Adwalton Moor; in the south-west Hopton had cleared Devon, and in July scattered Waller's forces at Landsdown and Roundway Down, while Bristol, the second port of the kingdom, was about to fall to Prince Rupert. To Baillie it seemed that " for the present the Parliament side is running down the brae." But the Covenanters had gone too far to draw back : the triumph of the king meant in their eyes summary vengeance on those who had intrigued with his enemies.

Formerly the English Parliament had asked chiefly for a deputation of divines, but in August commissioners from the English House, among them the younger Vane,[2] arrived to ask for an army. The General Assembly met on 2nd August in a small room in the east kirk of St. Giles, and to Convention and Assembly was presented the English demand. The request for 11,000 troops was complied with, Lanark using the royal seal for a warrant which levied war against its owner, and the price of this support,

[1] Baillie, II., 74.

[2] " He who contributed most to it, and who in truth was the principal contriver of it, and the man by whom the Committee in Scotland was entirely and stupidly governed, Sir Harry Vane the younger, was not afterwards known to abhor the Covenant and the Presbyterians more than he was at that very time known to do, and laughed at them as much as he ever did afterwards." Clarendon, VII., 266.

a new bond to bind still closer the two countries, was drafted by Wariston and Henderson. This document, the Solemn League and Covenant, was accepted by the Estates, and ratified at Westminster by what was left of the English House, being thereafter solemnly subscribed in St. Margaret's Church on September 25, 1643. On 13th October it was sworn by the Estates and the Assembly, and later by the Scottish people in the parish kirks. It was signed by English Parliamentarians, because it was the price of the sorely needed Scottish help. It was extensively signed in Scotland, because the authorities saw to it that those who did not sign should suffer in person and estate.[1]

The Kirk had seized the chance to realize its dream of uniformity, but the dream came through the gates of horn, and was to vanish ere morning. In return Kirk and nobility had involved their land in a course of hypocrisy and dishonour. They wished both to have their cake and eat it; in the Solemn League and Covenant, of which the price was armed rebellion, they vowed also to " preserve and defend the king's majesty's person and authority." They had broken a plain contract with the king; was it any defence to say that they feared lest Charles at some future date might break his contract with them? Montrose, the day before his death, put the point to his inquisitors. " When the king had granted you all your desires, and you were every one sitting under his vine and under his fig-tree, that then you should have taken a party in England by the hand, and entered into a league and covenant with them against the king, was the thing I judged it my duty to oppose to the yondmost."[2] It was not as if the Scots were republicans or shared the advanced constitutional views of certain of the Parliamentarians. They were almost to a man confused and sentimental royalists, and they had been granted every liberty which they had asked for. The verdict of history must be that for the sake of an ecclesiastical whimsy the bulk of the nation chose the path of civic dishonour. The question was not of the relative wisdom of monarchist or Parliamentarian doctrines, but of Scotland forswearing a creed, which she avowedly and sincerely held, for the bribe of a futile dream.

To Montrose the way was clear. To him it seemed that towards Scotland the king had behaved, though tardily, with justice and generosity, and had been rewarded by

[1] The text of the Solemn League is in *A. P. S.*, VI., 42, and Burnet, *Mem. of the Hamiltons*, 238.   [2] See p. 320, *infra*.

flagrant bad faith. Apart from the matter of personal honour, he believed that the path which the Covenant had chosen led only to anarchy and an ultimate tyranny. Every article of his political philosophy was at stake. The one hope seemed to lie in Charles's success. He set off at once for the south, and reached Oxford some time in August. The king had gone to the siege of Gloucester, and Montrose found that he could do nothing with the queen. Her trust in Hamilton was unshaken, and on 28th August she wrote to him reaffirming her confidence.[1] He then sought the king at Gloucester, but the courtiers persuaded Charles that the young man was an alarmist, and that the scheme he proposed was moonshine. Meantime the Solemn League and Covenant had been ratified, Leven was mustering his men, and every day the chance of forestalling him grew more slender. In an agony of anxiety Montrose pled and expostulated.

But as the autumn passed and the king returned to Oxford to winter, the letters of Hamilton and Lanark took a new tone. They confessed that the game was up, that they had been deceived, that Leven was on the eve of marching. Charles sent for Montrose at last and listened to his plan, and Antrim, who had escaped from captivity, was at hand to promise support. In December the Hamiltons came to Oxford to brazen it out, and found their conduct the subject of a commission of inquiry. There could be no question of the verdict. Montrose and Aboyne, Nithsdale, Kinnoull,[2] and Ogilvy were there to testify to a long course of double-dealing, supineness, and folly, which was only saved from being flat treason by the mental confusion of those who pursued it. Hamilton was arrested and sent a prisoner to Pendennis castle in Cornwall; Lanark escaped—first to London, where he shared the bed and board of Mr. Robert Baillie, and then to the Covenant army. At long last the king turned to the only man who could give him hope.

Montrose abode with the court at Oxford during the bitter early months of 1644,[3] and elaborated his plans. It seemed a desperate remedy. The only project he could

[1] Burnet, *Mem. of the Hamiltons*, 241.
[2] This was the second earl, who died at Whitehall, October 5, 1644. His son George, the third earl, joined Montrose after Tippermuir, and was a loyal adherent of his cause till his death in Orkney in the autumn of 1649. For the fourth earl, see note on p. 308.
[3] When Leven crossed the Tweed, on January 19, 1644, the ice was so thick that the baggage carts could pass over on it.

offer was to " raise Scotland for the king "; but it seemed as if Scotland had effectively risen for the king's opponents. Leven's blue-bonnets were over the Border, and the whole line of the Marches was controlled by the Covenanters. They held every city and town in Scotland; Parliament and General Assembly alike were their creatures; the revenue of the country was in their hands; the greater part of the nobles had joined their standard. A year ago there had been a chance; now it seemed the wildest of wild ventures. If the Scottish people were tired of their taskmasters they had given no sign of it, and the supposed loyalists, with a few shining exceptions, had proved the most brittle of reeds. Except for Kinnoull, Ogilvy, and Aboyne, Montrose seemed to have no following even among the royalists of his own class. Huntly disliked him, Crawford was jealous of him, Traquair feared him; the nondescripts, like Carnwath, Morton, Southesk, Nithsdale, Roxburgh, and Home, were disinclined to obey a youth.

But in that strange Oxford, where the colleges had become courts or barracks, and trenches were at the back of Wadham and across St. Giles's, and Rupert and his horse swung over Magdalen Bridge of a morning to raid in the Chilterns—an Oxford of junketing and brawling, hymns and drinking songs, fiery hearts and anxious minds,[1] there were men like Endymion Porter and Digby, men in the inner circle of the royal councils, in whom the grave purpose of the young Scottish earl commanded respect. Among so much that was self-seeking and half-hearted, his ardour was like a sea-wind in a stifling room. They had the wit to recognize that a certain kind of spirit may win against any odds. Hyde, too, was probably his friend. The future Lord Clarendon detested Scotland and all things connected with her, but he loved an honest man and a stout heart; and we know from a letter of Evelyn to Pepys that " the brave Montrosse " was one of the portraits in his private cabinet at Cornbury.[2] In any case it was no season for prudence, for Newcastle was in desperate straits in the north. " I will not," said Montrose, " distrust God's assistance in a righteous cause, and if it shall please your Majesty to lay your commands upon me for this purpose, your affairs will at any rate be in no worse case than they are at present, even if I should not succeed."

[1] For Oxford during the Civil War see the brilliant account in Mallet, *History of the University of Oxford*, II., c. 18.

[2] Vernon Watney, *Cornbury*, 231. Clarendon notes especially his modesty. *History*, XII., 16.

E*

He asked for little help. Antrim was to raise troops in Ireland and the Isles, and land them in the west of Scotland to keep Argyll occupied in his own country. A body of horse from Newcastle's army would assist him to cut his way through the Lowlands to the Highland line. The King of Denmark might lend some German cavalry, and by hook or by crook a sufficient store of arms and ammunition must be transported to the north.[1] Charles consented, and Antrim was dispatched to Ulster with instructions to land 2,000 troops in Argyll by April 1, 1644.[2] Montrose was offered the commission of viceroy and captain-general of the royal forces in Scotland, but very wisely he declined; the title was bestowed on the king's nephew, Prince Maurice, and Montrose was content to be known as his lieutenant-general. He knew something of the jealous temper of the northern forces, and he had no desire to wreck his expedition on an empty name.[3]

The six years of waiting were ended. The fates had cleared the stage, and the waverer had an issue of his perplexities. Words were to give place to deeds; the narrow streets of Edinburgh and the heavy air of conventions and assemblies to the clean winds and the wide spaces of the hills. He had before him a straight path of duty, and little it troubled him that it ran into dark shadows. Once more he had recaptured his boyish ardour, and there was no happier man in the world than Montrose when, on that March morning, with the ash buds black in St. John's gardens, he rode north out of Oxford to win a kingdom.

[1] Montrose's proposal to use foreign troops was natural at a time when half the fighting in Europe was done by mercenaries. A far more flagrant case was the employment of Dutch and Hessian troops against the Highlanders in 1745. The use of Catholic Irish was a more doubtful affair, in view of the recent Irish rebellion, but the troops actually used were chiefly expatriated Macdonalds.

[2] The agreement between Montrose and Antrim, in Montrose's handwriting, is still extant in the possession of the Antrim family. In it Antrim is styled " His Majesty's General of the Isles and Highlands of Scotland," and he undertakes to raise troops before 1st April from the Isles, as well as from Ireland. It is dated 28th January, and Montrose is called the king's lieutenant-general, three days before his commission was issued. The agreement is witnessed by Digby and Sir Robert Spottiswoode.

[3] The commission as lieutenant-general is dated Feb. 1, 1644. There is a commission extant, dated Feb. 13, appointing him captain-general, and styling him marquis (*Hist. MSS. Comm.*, 2nd Report, 172), but this does not seem to have been acted on, though it is superscribed by the king, for there was a separate warrant for the marquisate, dated May 6, 1644, and the commission as captain-general was issued a year later, May 4, 1645.

BOOK II

ACTION

CHAPTER VI

THE CURTAIN RISES

(*March* 1644-*August* 1644)

Worcester. I will unclasp a secret book,
And to your quick-conceiving discontents
I'll read you matter deep and dangerous,
As full of peril and adventurous spirit
As to o'er-walk a current roaring loud
On the unsteadfast footing of a spear.
    Hotspur. If he fall in, good night!—or sink or swim!—
Send danger from the east unto the west,
So honour cross it from the north to south,
And let them grapple.

                              First Part of King Henry IV.

ST. THERESA, WHEN SHE SET OUT AS A CHILD TO CONVERT
the Moors, was engaged on a mission scarcely less hopeful
than that which Montrose had now set himself. It seemed
the wildest of gambles against impossible odds. In the
true knight-errant fashion Charles had given him a sword
engraved with the arms of the flower of his race, Prince
Henry,[1] but he could give him little more. Montrose was
to raise Scotland for the king, but where was he to find an
army? The best of the semi-professional levies were with
Leven in the north of England. The soldiers of fortune
from the German wars were already for the most part
under Leven's banner. He could get nothing from the
towns and villages of the Lowlands, for, whatever the feel-

---

[1] It was for long the property of the Gartmore family, till it was
purchased by John Ballantyne and presented to Sir Walter Scott,
who lent it to his cousin, the knight marshal, to wear at the visit of
George IV. to Scotland. It is now in the Abbotsford armoury.
See Lockhart, II., 395; V. 190.

ing of the people, the Kirk and the Estates had a firm control of the machinery of enlistment. As for the nobles,
the most powerful were Covenanters, and even if it had
been otherwise, were far too jealous and self-centred to
follow a young man of no higher rank than their own in
a cause which was, at the best, forlorn. Did he hope that
his words of wisdom, his far-sighted political doctrines,
would carry conviction to a backward peasantry, harassed
by temporal want on the one side and the fear of eternal
punishment on the other? Besides, he proposed to bring
Antrim's Irishry to his aid, and Antrim's Irishry, though
most of them were Scots, seemed to the Lowlands so many
emissaries of the Pope and the devil. With such allies he
would not attract a single doubting Presbyterian to his
standard.

As in most great adventures, there was no solid hope
save in the soul of the adventurer. In a desperate case the
man who risks most is usually the wisest, and Montrose
staked everything on the speed and gallantry of his spirit.
It seems impossible that at this period he can have intended
to raise the Highlands. He relied on his kinsmen in Perth
and Angus, and he had some hope of the Gordons. It was
the gentry of the northern lowlands—Grahams, Drummonds, Erskines, Stirlings, and Ogilvies—in whom he
trusted, if he trusted in any one besides himself, and not
in the clans of the hills. Probably at the time he knew
very little about the Highlands, and his experience in the
Bishops' War cannot have prepossessed him in favour of
the desultory bands who accompanied Huntly's lowland
levies to battle. Had he known more he would not have
been greatly encouraged. Argyll, poor soldier as he was,
had worked his will with Morvern and Badenoch, Atholl
and Lochaber. Nor were there any of the ordinary politics
in the hills. The chiefs were royalists only in as much
as they were not Covenanters. He might indeed count on
the assistance, could he reach them, of all those who hated
the name of Campbell—Clan Chattan, Clan Donald, the
Macleans, the Stuarts, and the Camerons. But Seaforth
and his Mackenzies would never fight on the same side as
a Macdonald, and, if he enlisted the Gordons, he might
look to find the Grants in the other camp.

If Montrose's venture was desperate in purpose, it was
no less desperate in the lack of a base. He was to fling
himself into the midst of a hostile country to improvise
an army. Nothing could be looked for from the king

except the royal commission. Even had Charles been that
ideal monarch which certain royalists created out of their
fancy, he could have done little to help his champion. As
it was, he passed from blunder to blunder, enraging by
his obtuseness and duplicity both friend and foe. The man
who fought for a Stuart must be content to wage war
without reserves. His life and his reputation alike must be
in his own keeping.

Crawford, Reay, Nithsdale, Ogilvy, and Aboyne accompanied Montrose as he rode out from Oxford, on his way
to Newcastle's camp. The two first presently turned off
with a squadron of horse towards Shrewsbury. Arrived
at York, Montrose found that Newcastle was at Durham,
so he sent on Colonel Cochrane to acquaint him with the
king's commission and his need of men and money. The
reply came that at Durham there was little of either, and
the king's lieutenant-general, on March 15th, proceeded
thither to reason with the royalist commander. Already
the news of his coming north had sent Argyll post-haste
into Scotland, whither, Montrose wrote to Sir Robert
Spottiswoode at Oxford, " we intend to make all possible
dispatch to follow him at his heels, in whatever posture we
can."[1] Newcastle, the great potentate of the north-east,
now a marquis and after the Restoration to be a duke, was
a man of sumptuous and scholarly tastes, a devout loyalist,
and brave and scrupulous in all the relations of life. He
was the idol of his second wife, but in her praise of his
gentility, " which hath something in it of grandeur,"[2] we
can detect the source of his failure. He was too fine for
the rough task before him—the complete dilettante, who,
in Clarendon's words, " the articles of action no sooner
over, returned to his delightful company, music, and the
softer pleasures."[3] As a soldier he was neither fortunate
nor skilful, for he had no experience of war.

On 19th January Leven, with 18,000 foot and more than
3,000 horse, had crossed Tweed. He halted for three weeks
before the town of Newcastle, and then on 28th February
the bulk of his army, assisted by the prayers of Mr. Robert
Baillie in far-away London, forded Tyne. By 2nd March
he was across the Wear, and two days later entered Sunderland. Newcastle, who had only 5,000 foot and 3,000 horse,

---

[1] Napier, II., 391. Spottiswoode was an Oxford man, of Exeter
College, as was also Hamilton. Mallet, *Hist. of Univ. of Oxford*,
I., 253.
[2] *Life of the Duke of Newcastle*, 1667. [3] *History*, VIII., 85.

was opportunely strengthened by the arrival of Sir Charles
Lucas, made a feeble demonstration against him, and then
fell back on Durham. Leven followed, but finding his
commissariat difficult in that devastated country, remained
in the district between Tyne and Wear, and decided to lay
siege to the positions which guarded the mouth of the
former river. The marquis, when Montrose arrived, was
in the worst of spirits. The town of Newcastle still held
out, but Leven was at its gates, and Manchester and Fairfax were closing up on him from the south. Even as
against the Scots he was outnumbered, and he might soon
be caught between two formidable fires. He was in no
condition to spare a silver piece or a man.

Nevertheless, as a great nobleman, he honoured the
king's commission and did his best. A hundred ill-mounted
troopers and two small brass cannon were the most the
perplexed commander could spare Montrose for the conquest of Scotland. He called out for him, however, the
militia of Cumberland and Westmoreland, and sundry local
gentlemen were willing to join his standard. Another disappointment was in store, for Carnwath, who happened to
be in Newcastle's camp, refused to accept from Montrose's
hand the royal commission as lieutenant of Clydesdale. It
was a foretaste of the spirit of even the loyal among the
Scots nobles. There was a curious wildness in the Carnwath family, conspicuous even in a wild age. At the head
of a troop of horse rode a certain Mrs. Pierson, who passed
as Carnwath's daughter, and whose commission was made
out in the name of Captain Francis Dalziel. Her cornet
carried a black banner, which displayed on a sable field
a naked man hanging from a gibbet, under the motto " I
dare."[1]

Montrose's coming stirred the Marquis of Newcastle to
action. Leven, at the mouth of the Tyne, was cut off from
his base and his heavy guns at Sunderland. Here was a
chance for a bold stroke, so on 23rd March he advanced
to Chester-le-street, and next day took up position at Hilton
north of the Wear, a few miles from Sunderland, with
Leven on a hill to the east. But even Montrose's influence
could not put speed into Newcastle's languid soul. There

---

[1] Napier, II., 393. Deposition of Major John Erskine, *Hist. MSS.
Comm.*, 2nd Report, 174. Carnwath is best known as the man
who seized Charles's bridle at Naseby when he was about to charge
at the head of his Guards, an incident to which Clarendon attributes
the loss of the battle.

was an artillery duel and some fighting between advanced troops, but on the 25th Newcastle suddenly drew off towards Durham, and Leven was enabled to inflict considerable damage on his rear. Presently the news of Fairfax's approach caused the marquis to hasten south to York.

With Newcastle's campaign Montrose had no concern, for his business lay north of the Border. He marched towards Carlisle with 200 horse, mostly gentlemen who had served in the foreign wars; Crawford of the fierce counsels, Nithsdale, Ogilvy, and Aboyne were with him, and Captain Francis Dalziel with her grisly banner.[1] The Cumberland and Westmoreland men, 800 foot and three troops of horse, joined him on the road, and on 13th April he led a force of some 1,300 men across the Border. But he had not forded Annan before trouble began. Most of the English militia, worked upon by the emissaries of Sir Richard Graham,[2] deserted, and the loss was not atoned for by the accession of Lord Herries with a small following. With his little force of a few hundreds Montrose reached Dumfries, and occupied the town without opposition. The provost, one John Corsane,[3] welcomed him gladly, and in consequence had five years' trouble with the Estates and the Kirk.

It was at once apparent that nothing could be done in the southern Lowlands. The Maxwells and Johnstones of the Dumfries neighbourhood were in no mood to rise, and their heads—Nithsdale and Hartfell—were jealous of the new commander. Annandale, Morton, Roxburgh, and Traquair, though nominally royalists, refused, like Carnwath, the king's commissions of lieutenancy, by means of which Montrose had hoped to organize a formidable

[1] Wishart, c. III. Depositions of Major John Erskine and Major James Leslie. *Hist. MSS. Comm.*, 2nd Report, 174.

[2] Graham had been an attendant of Buckingham, and had accompanied Buckingham and Charles to Spain on their visit in 1623 to see the Infanta. Montrose, according to Wishart, had once esteemed him, but he was a noted trimmer, and did espionage work for the Parliament. Having been raised " from the dunghill," he founded the families of Esk and Netherby. Wishart, c. iv.; M. & S. 51.

[3] Spalding (II., 391) says that the provost was Sir James Maxwell, and that he was executed for his surrender of the town the following July; he is followed by Lang and by McDowall (*Hist. of Dumfries*, 410). But it is clear from the town records that Corsane was provost, and his subsequent troubles will be found in the Acts of Parliament and the minutes of the Dumfries Presbytery. See *Mercurius Aulicus*, May 4, 1644, and Mr. James Barbour's paper in the *Proceedings of the Dumfries and Galloway Antiquarian Society*. The Maxwell who was hanged was a Maxwell of Munches.

opposition.[1] Farther east Lothian was hot for the Parliament, and the " bauld Buccleuch," a young man of eighteen, was commanding—with no particular credit to himself—a regiment under Leven. The peasantry of Dumfries were under the thumb of the ministers and of fickle noblemen like Glencairn. Montrose issued a declaration, headed by the device which appears on the first page of this volume, explaining that he was now in arms for the king on the same principle as he had once been in arms for the Covenant—" for the defence and maintenance of the true Protestant religion, his Majesty's just and sacred authority, the fundamental laws and privileges of Parliament, the peace and freedom of the oppressed and enthralled subject." " Knew I not perfectly," he added, " his Majesty's intentions to be such, and so real as is already expressed, I should never have embarked myself at all in his service. Nor, did I but see the least appearance of his Majesty's change from these resolutions or any of them, I should never continue longer my faithful endeavour in it."[2] His case was unanswerable; he stood in the direct tradition of the National Covenant and of the spirit of the Glasgow Assembly. But he was speaking a tongue which the burghers of Dumfries, and for that matter the Scottish people, did not understand. " It was not," in Mr. Gardiner's words, " for the restoration of a dead past that he drew the sword. He stood up for that which was, in some sort, the hope of the future."[3] And the language of the future is always strange to contemporary ears.

Montrose lingered on, waiting for news of Antrim's men, from which it would appear that Galloway, as well as Argyll, was their objective. But no news came and his hopes sank, for Antrim had always been uncertain as the wind. He received, however, a message of another kind —from his niece, Lady Stirling of Keir—inviting him, on behalf of the commander, Lord Sinclair, to take possession of the castle of Stirling and the town of Perth. Sinclair and his second in command, Sir James Turner,[4] were probably sincere in their offer, but it was fortunate for Montrose that he did not attempt to accept it. For the Covenant had got wind of the intention of the pair, and, while Montrose was reading his niece's letter, Callander, with Sinclair

[1] See Montrose's instructions to Lord Ogilvy. Napier, II., 406-409.
[2] *Mem. of M.*, II., 146-147.
[3] *Civil War*, II., 132.
[4] See Turner, *Memoirs* (1829), 35. Turner was the original of Dugald Dalgetty.

and Turner in tow, was marching south. Callander, who had once been Almond and a party to the Cumbernauld Bond, presently occupied Dumfries, while Montrose and his handful recrossed the Esk. They barely escaped, and had to leave some of their guns in Annandale.[1] Meanwhile two events had befallen the royalist leader. He had received his patent of marquis from the king, and had been excommunicated by the Kirk in Edinburgh. The latter honour was also conferred at the same time upon Huntly, who had just been conducting an aimless and confused rising in the north, and was now hiding from Argyll in Strathnaver.[2]

There was no course open to Montrose except to wait for Scottish news on English soil, while he kept Callander and his 7,000 levies busy on the western Marches, and to strike a blow, if occasion offered, on behalf of the hard-pressed Marquis of Newcastle. He had no illusions about either that general or the royalist troops in the north of England. He had seen the quality of the Cumberland and Westmoreland militia, most of the gentry were watching the omens, and the Percy's spur was cold in Northumbria. The centre of the war was shifting into Yorkshire, but Montrose's duty was to keep close to Scotland, and his task was only desultory Border fighting. It was sufficient, however, to inspire acute anxiety in the breast of Mr. Robert Baillie and the Covenant leaders.

If Newcastle was to be retained and the position of its marquis improved at York, a blow must be struck forthwith in the north. The town of Morpeth was strongly held by a Covenanting garrison under Somerville of Drum (afterwards the tenth Lord Somerville), and on 10th May Montrose marched against it, assisted by Colonel Clavering, and with Crawford as his intractable colleague. He attempted to carry the place by assault, was repulsed, and then, after bringing up six guns from Newcastle, breached its defence and entered it on 29th May. The air was full of wild rumours, and to a certain Captain John MacCulloch, who parleyed with him, Montrose gave a romantic account of a great disaster to Leven at York, and of the success of the royalists in Scotland.[3] The garrison was

---

[1] *Papers relating to the Army of the Solemn League and Covenant* (S.H.S.), II., 317. These guns were "yrne," and not Newcastle's brass pieces: they must have been part of the armoury captured by Montrose in Dumfries.   [2] Gordon of Ruthven, 50.

[3] Napier, II., 399-402 Spalding, II., 379. *Memorie of the Somervilles* (1819), II., 306, etc. Terry, *Alexander Leslie*, 285.

disarmed and dismissed, and after the surrender Montrose
entertained the governor to dinner. He then recaptured
the fort at South Shields which Leven had taken on 20th
March, and attacked Sunderland, where he was checked
by the energy of its seamen and the cavalry sent by Leven
from York.[1] The Covenanting general was in difficulties,
for so long as he had the Marquis of Newcastle to deal
with he could do little against Montrose. His only hope
was Callander, who was making his leisurely way from
the western Border.[2] Montrose was collecting provisions
from the Alnwick neighbourhood and succeeding in getting
them into the beleaguered Newcastle, when at the end of
June he received a peremptory summons to join Prince
Rupert, who was marching through Lancashire to the relief
of York.

Rupert did not wait for Montrose. He relieved York
indeed, but before he and Montrose met the king's arms
had suffered their first crushing disaster. On 2nd July,
about five in the afternoon, he engaged the Parliament
forces at Marston Moor, and discovered that new thing in
England—the shock of Cromwell's horse. The Huntingdonshire grazier, turned parliamentarian, had made himself
also a great soldier, and had hammered into being an army
to suit his purpose. On that fierce day David Leslie also
wrought famously, and disputes as to the true architect
of victory did not improve relations between Scots and
English.[3] The king's army was scattered, Newcastle fled
overseas, and Rupert, lamenting the loss in action of his
white dog which Puritans believed to be his familiar spirit,[4]
rode with some 6,000 troops into the western hills. Two
days after the battle Montrose found him in an inn at Richmond. "Give me a thousand of your horse," he said,
"and I will cut my way into the heart of Scotland." But
Rupert had nothing to give; on the contrary, he stood much
in need of Montrose's scanty recruits. So with a sad heart
the new marquis rode by Brough and Appleby to Carlisle
to indite his report to the king. The western Marches were
now safer for him, since Callander had gone east to
Newcastle.

Four months had passed and nothing had been done.
Ogilvy and Sir William Rollo had journeyed secretly into
Scotland, and had returned with ill news. The land lay

   [1] Whitelocke, I., 270.   Cal. S. P., Dom. (1644), 242.
   [2] Baillie, II., 196.   [3] Terry, Alexander Leslie, 235 n., 256, etc
   [4] Vicars, God's Ark, 277.

quiet under the Covenant, and Antrim's levies seemed to have vanished into the mist. The nobles, headed by Traquair, were tumbling over each other in their anxiety to swear fealty to Argyll. There seemed nothing to be done except to surrender the royal commission, and to wait abroad for a happier time. So his friends advised, and Montrose made a pretence of acquiescing. He set out for Oxford with the rest, having taken Ogilvy (and later Aboyne) into his confidence. A little way from Carlisle he slipped behind, but as his servants and baggage went on it was presumed that he was following. Had he continued, he would have shared in the capture of the whole party by Fairfax at Ribble bridge.[1]

He had resolved on the craziest of ventures. He would break through the Covenant cordon in the Lowlands, and win to his own country. There, at any rate, were loyal hearts, and something might be devised to turn the tide. He chose as his companions the lame Sir William Rollo and an officer, Colonel Sibbald, who had fought under him in the Bishops' War. They wore the dress of Leven's troopers, while Montrose followed behind as their groom, riding one ill-conditioned beast and leading another.

It was a dangerous road to travel. The country was strewn with broken men and patrolled by Covenant horse, and a gentleman in those days was not easily disguised. At first all went smoothly. Passing through the woods of Netherby, they learned that Sir Richard Graham had joined the Covenant, and in its interests had constituted himself Warden of the Marches. His servant, from whom they had the news, spoke freely, as if to Leven's troopers. A little farther on they fell in with a Scot, one of Newcastle's soldiers, who disregarded the troopers but paid great attention to their groom, hailing him by his proper title. Montrose tried to deny it, but the man exclaimed, " What, do I not know my Lord Marquis of Montrose well enough? But go your way, and God be with you! " A gold piece rewarded the untimely well-wisher.

The journey must have grown hourly more anxious till the Forth was passed. " It may be thought," wrote Patrick Gordon, " that God Almighty sent His good angel to lead the way, for he went, as if a cloud environed him, through

---

[1] The chief prisoners taken were Lord Ogilvy, Sir John Innes, and Montrose's natural brother, Harry Graham. When Newcastle fell in the following October, Lords Crawford, Reay, and Maxwell, and Wishart, Montrose's biographer, were among the captives.

all his enemies."[1] We do not know the road they travelled
—whether by Annandale and the springs of Tweed and
Clyde, or up Eskdale and thence over the Tweedside range
to the Lothians. The safest route was probably by the belt
of bleak moorland which runs north by Carnwath almost
to the Highland hills. Riding chiefly by night, the party
made good progress. On the fourth day they came to the
Montrose lands in Stirling and Strathearn, but they did not
draw rein till they reached the house of Tullibelton,
between Perth and Dunkeld. Here lived Patrick Graham
of Inchbrakie, he who had seen to the ordering of Montrose's little library at St. Andrews, and here was safe shelter
for the traveller while he spied out the land and looked
about for a following.

It was the hour of portents. Airy armies were seen to
contend on a hill in Banff; in Buchan the sun shone clear
at midnight, and a kirk was filled with a choir of unearthly
music; a cannon shot echoed over the whole kingdom to
warn men that an invader was landing in the west.[2] But
the true portent came in humbler form. The curtain rises,
and the first act of the great drama reveals a forlorn little
party late on an August evening knocking at the door of
a woodland tower above the shining reaches of Tay. The
king's lieutenant-general makes a very modest entrance on
the scene. Two followers, four sorry horses, little money
and no baggage seem a slender outfit for the conquest of
a kingdom; but in six months he had Scotland at his feet.

[1] Gordon of Ruthven, 71.
[2] Ibid., 62-63. Forbes Leith, *Memoirs of Scottish Catholics*, I., 288.

CHAPTER VII

TIPPERMUIR

(*September* 1644)

Hotspur. " The purpose you meditate is dangerous; the friends
you have named uncertain; the time itself unsorted; and your whole
plot too light for the counterpoise of so great an opposition! " Say
you so, say you so? . . . By the Lord, our plot is a good plot as
ever was laid; our friends true and constant: a good plot, good
friends, and full of expectation; an excellent plot, very good friends.
What a frosty-spirited rogue is this!

First Part of King Henry IV.

I

FOR SIX DAYS THE KING'S LIEUTENANT LAY CLOSE IN HIDING
while his comrades scoured the country for news. Tullibelton was too near the lowland town of Perth, and its laird
too noted a loyalist for his guest to run needless risks, and
Montrose spent most of his time among the woods and
hills, sleeping at night in hunters' bothies, and soothing his
soul with the lights and colours of a Scottish autumn. The
scouts returned with a melancholy tale. Huntly had failed
ruinously in the north, and the Gordons were leaderless
and divided, while the influence of their uncle, Argyll, was
driving Huntly's sons to the Covenant camp. Some of the
Graham and Drummond kinsmen even, with the alternative
of prison and fines before them, were in arms for the
Estates. There were rumours of Covenant levies in Aberdeenshire, and in the west Argyll had his clan in arms.
Montrose in his despondency may well have wondered at
this strange activity. The tide of war had rolled over the
Border, and with Scotland in so iron a grip such precau-
tions must have seemed odd to one who knew the econo-
mical spirit of his opponents.

He was soon to learn the reason, and at the same time
to recognize his opportunity. The incident is best told in
the words of Patrick Gordon, who had the story from
Montrose's own lips:

" As he was one day in Methven Wood, staying for the night,
because there was no safe travelling by day, he became transported
with sadness, grief, and pity to see his native country thus brought
into miserable bondage and slavery through the turbulent and blind
zeal of some preachers, and now persecuted by the unlawful and
ambitious ends of some of the nobility; and so far had they already
prevailed that the event was much to be feared, and for good patriots

ever to be lamented. And, therefore, in a deep grief and unwonted
ravishment, he besought the Divine Majesty, with watery eyes and
a sorrowful heart, that His justly kindled indignation might be appeased and His mercy extended, the curse removed, and that it
might please Him to make him a humble instrument therein, to His
Holy and Divine Majesty's greater glory. . . . While he was in this
thought, lifting up his eyes he beheld a man coming the way to
St. Johnstoune (Perth), with a fiery cross in his hand, and, hastily
stepping towards him, he inquired what the matter meant. The
messenger told him that Coll Mac Gillespick—for so was Alexander
Macdonald called by the Highlanders—was entered in Atholl with
a great army of Irishes, and threatened to burn the whole country
if they did not arise with him against the Covenant, and he was sent
to advertise St. Johnstoune, that all the country might be raised to
resist him."[1]

Antrim's levies had come out of the mist at last.

Presently Montrose received a letter from Alasdair Macdonald himself, directed to the king's lieutenant-general at
Carlisle. The messenger who carried it asked directions
from Inchbrakie, who took the dispatch and promised to
deliver it. In the letter Macdonald announced his arrival
and begged for instructions. If Montrose needed help, no
less did the Irish commander.

Alasdair Macdonald was of the ancient stock of Dunyveg
in Islay, the son of Macdonald of Colonsay, commonly
called Coll Keitach, or " Coll who can fight with either
hand." The name, corrupted into Colkitto, was transferred
by the Lowlanders (like the Gruamach appellation in the
case of Argyll) from the father to the son. Sorley Boy
Macdonald, the father of the first Earl of Antrim, had been
his father's great-uncle. The Macdonnells of Antrim were
near blood-relations of Alasdair's own people of Islay and
Kintyre, and the Campbell oppression of the latter clan
had left bitter memories on both sides of the North
Channel. Alasdair was a man of herculean strength and
proven courage, self-indulgent and somewhat inclined to
drunkenness; obtuse and incapable of framing or understanding any complex strategy : " no sojer," wrote Sir
James Turner, " though stout enough."[2] But he was a
born leader of men, and so impressed Leven in Ireland
that he did his best to reconcile him to Argyll, and sent
him to Scotland for the purpose. But the chief of the
Campbells treated the Irish commander with contempt, and
Alasdair returned to Ulster with all his hereditary grievances inflamed, and burning for revenge.[3]

Antrim, whom Clarendon thought a man " of excessive

[1] Gordon of Ruthven, 71-72.   [2] *Memoirs*, 45.
[3] Gordon of Ruthven, 64.

pride and vanity, and of a marvellously weak and narrow understanding," had been conspicuous for his large promise and meagre performance. The clan of Macdonnell had a hard life under the fruitless escapades of their chief; " we are worn spectre-thin," sang their bard, " by the earl's oft frequenting of the wave."[1] But now at last he was to influence the course of history. After many difficulties he raised, by the end of June 1644, 1,600 recruits among the exiled Macdonalds and Macleans, and he invited Alasdair to lead them against the ancestral foe. Early in July the invaders landed in Ardnamurchan, an old territory of the Macdonalds, and proceeded to exact vengeance on the unfortunate Campbell settlers. The king's quarrel was forgotten in a more intimate and personal strife. Alasdair ravaged the peninsula with fire and sword, and seized as a base the castle of Mingary on Loch Sunart, and the keep of Lochaline, which still stands where the little river Aline enters its sea-loch. He sent messengers throughout the West Highlands to summon the clans to help him in his task. But there was no response; Macdonalds and Macleans, Macleods and Macneils, were alike silent; the hand of Clan Diarmaid lay too heavy on the mainland and the isles.

Soon his position became desperate, for Argyll was raising an army of pursuit; so he swept back to his base, only to find that all his ships had been destroyed. Alasdair, whatever his defects as a general, was a bold fighting man; his only hope was the Gordons, and he resolved to bid for their support though it meant marching across the breadth of Scotland. Accordingly he led his forces through Morvern and round by the head of Loch Eil to the Lochaber glens, the western fringe of Huntly's country. Here he had his second piece of ill tidings. Huntly's revolt was over, and the Gordons had made their peace with the Covenant. There was nothing for it but to try the more northern clans, and his next venture was Kintail. But the Mackenzies, little though they loved the Campbells, had a long memory of Macdonald misdeeds, and their chief, Seaforth, warned off the intruders.

Headed back on all sides, Alasdair decided that the boldest course was the safest. He marched south again to Badenoch and the head waters of Spey, and himself issued a summons, calling upon the clans to rise in the name of the king and Huntly. This brought him some 500

[1] *Scottish Gaelic Studies*, I., 115.

recruits, most of them Gordons; but he could get no nearer to the heart of that powerful clan, for the Grants, Forbeses, and Frasers blocked the road down Spey, and a thousand of Seaforth's Mackenzies lent their aid. Alasdair now seemed in a fair way for destruction. The Campbells intercepted his retreat to the sea, and Argyll was hot-foot on his track. Seaforth cut him off from the north and east, the new Badenoch levies were mutinous and distrustful, and south lay the unfriendly Lowlands, and clans like the Stewarts of Atholl who would never serve under an alien tartan. He had proved that whoever might band the Highlands into an army, it would not be a man of Highland blood. Hence his despairing letter to the king's lieutenant-general asking for help and instructions. He can scarcely have hoped for much from his appeal, for Carlisle was far from Badenoch and he had the enemy on every side.

Montrose sent back an answer, bidding Alasdair be of good heart and meet him at Blair. It must have seemed a hard saying to a man who believed that his correspondent was still at Carlisle, but he obeyed, and, guided by a Clanranald man,[1] one Donald the Fair, who had seen service in the German wars, he marched into the braes of Atholl. The local clans resented his intrusion, the fiery cross was sent round, and there was every likelihood of a desperate conflict between two forces who alike detested the Covenant and followed the king. The Irish were stout fellows in hard condition, but they were uncouthly dressed, wild-eyed from long travel, and, after their custom, attended by a mob of half-starved women and children. The Atholl clans, living on the edge of the Lowlands, may well have looked askance at such outlandish warriors. Moreover, Alasdair's men were Catholics, and the Reformation in some sort had come to Atholl, as had tales of Irish barbarities in the recent rebellion. The Earl of Atholl was a minor, and the pressure of Argyll kept the leaderless clan quiet, in spite of long memories of Campbell reivings and burnings. Donald Robertson, the Tutor of Struan, seems to have joined Alasdair at once,[2] but the Robertsons as a clan held aloof; and when the Irish had taken the castle of Blair, they were faced by angry and watchful levies, waiting for the word to make an end of them.

The situation was saved by a hairbreadth. Montrose, accompanied by Patrick Graham, the younger, of Inch-

[1] Forbes Leith, I., 291.　　　　[2] Spalding, II., 261.

brakie—Black Pate, the countryside called him—set out
to walk the twenty miles of hill between Blair and Tullibelton to keep the tryst. He had acquired from Inchbrakie
a Highland dress—the trews, a short coat, and a plaid for
the shoulders; he wore a blue bonnet with a bunch of oats
as a badge, and he carried a broadsword and a Highland
buckler. Thus accoutred, he entered suddenly upon the
scene in the true manner of romance. Alasdair and his
ragged troops were waiting hourly upon battle, when
across the moor, between the hostile camps, they saw two
figures advancing. Black Pate was known to every Atholl
man, and there were many who had seen Montrose. Loud
shouts of welcome apprised the Ulsterman that here was
no bonnet-laird, but when he heard that it was indeed the
king's lieutenant he could scarcely credit the news. He
believed him to be still on the road from Carlisle, and he
had looked for cavalry, an imposing bodyguard, and a
figure more like his own swashbuckling self than this slim
young man with the quiet face and the searching grey eyes.
In a moment all quarrels were forgotten. Montrose
revealed his commission, and Alasdair gladly took service
under him, thankful to be out of a plight which for weeks
had looked hopeless. The Atholl clans were carried off
their feet by the grace and confidence of their new leader,
and the Stewarts and Robertsons brought to his side those
broadswords which an hour before had been dedicated to
cutting Ulster throats. Montrose slept the night at the
house of Lude, and next morning unfurled the royal
standard on a green knoll above the Tilt. The king's
lieutenant had got him an army.

II

We pause, on the eve of Montrose's campaign, to consider the conditions under which, in that era, battles were
fought. Some knowledge of the methods of war in the
fifth decade of the seventeenth century is necessary if we
are to understand the magnitude of Montrose's achievement and the causes of his success.

It was an age when, in both Scotland and England,
relatively to the population, surprisingly large numbers of
men were called to arms, but only a small proportion was
brought into action.[1] Difficulties of transport, when roads

---

[1] In the summer of 1642 Essex was supposed to have 24,000 foot
and 5,000 horse, but at Edgehill he numbered only some 13,000. In
April 1643 he started nominally with 16,000 foot and 3,000 horse:

were few and bad; an imperfect intelligence system; the necessity of masking fortresses and protecting communications; pay chronically in arrears; the absence of a strong central authority on either side, and the dissipation of effort in divergent operations; the lack of any adequate provision for recruiting losses—such were the main reasons why the opposing strengths were so slow in forcing a decisive issue. Success must fall to the man who could best overcome or disregard these handicaps, who could move his troops fast and far, who had early news of his enemy's plans, who had no civil problems to perplex him, whose levies had an inducement to fight other than their pay, and who could concentrate all his powers on a single purpose.

Infantry were still held in less esteem than cavalry. A foot regiment consisted of musketeers and pikemen in the proportion of two of the former to one of the latter.[1] The pikemen wore iron corselets and head-pieces, and carried pike and sword, and their chief business was, as at Marston Moor, to repel a cavalry charge. They were heavy troops, and for rapid work the musketeer, who had no body armour, was coming into favour. The musket of the period was still, for the most part, the old matchlock, which required an elaborate rest. It fired a bullet which weighed about an ounce and a quarter, took a long time to load and discharge, and had a range not exceeding 400 yards. It demanded a great deal of match, and in the enemy's neighbourhood it was necessary to keep the match lighted, so that the troops were at the mercy of the weather.[2] The defects of the matchlock were bringing the flintlock into fashion, and in the Parliament armies the latter was employed for cavalry carbines and pistols and for special companies detailed to guard the artillery. The flintlock was primarily a sportsman's weapon, and must have been used by many private citizens when the regular army weapon was the matchlock. There were certainly flintlocks in the Scottish cavalry in 1644.[3] An infantry regi-

in July he had actually only 6,000 foot and 2,500 horse. Firth, *Cromwell's Army*, 23.

[1] In the Scottish army in 1644 as 3 to 2. *Memorie of the Somervilles*, II., 307.

[2] As at the battle of Preston. Turner, *Memoirs*, 59. *Cf.* also the position at Kilsyth and Dunbar. Firth, *op. cit.*, 84.

[3] In Argyll's troop, *A. P. S.*, VI., i., 65; see *Army of the Covenant* (S.H.S.), I., xlvii. In 1668 Lord Atholl complained of his instructions to arm the Perthshire militia with matchlocks, on the ground that his men were " altogether unacquainted with the use of any

ment being composed of musketeers interspersed with pikemen, its efficiency depended upon an exact discipline which could combine the movements of both arms. Only then could it hope, like the regiments of Maitland and Lindsay at Marston Moor, to beat back a charge of horse.

The infantry formation was conditioned by the time which a musketeer required to load and fire, for it was the custom for the first rank to discharge their pieces and then fall to the rear to reload. The ordinary formation at this time was six deep, but in an emergency the files might be reduced to three, to prevent outflanking or to obtain a broader front of fire. At first only one rank fired at a time, till Gustavus Adolphus introduced the fashion of three ranks firing simultaneously, the first kneeling, the second stooping, and the third standing upright. But armies are conservative things, and, in spite of the lesson of Leipsic, it was not till Cromwell's New Model that the method became the accepted practice in Britain. Montrose used it, being in this, as in other things, a reformer.

Infantry tactics were elaborate. Since distinctive uniforms were unknown, it was necessary to have badges,[1] and watchwords or "field signs." These being settled, an action usually began by sending out a body of musketeers, called a "forlorn hope," who fired and fell back. When the main bodies came into touch the musketeers delivered a couple of volleys, and then the pikemen charged. This was for a pitched battle; in lesser engagements there might be something like open order, the troops taking shelter in ditches and behind hedges, as at Worcester.[2] Such cover was eagerly sought by the foot, for it was the best preventive of a cavalry charge. The ordinary soldier marched slowly, for he carried a monstrous weight—at least double the forty pounds of to-day, and in the case of the pikemen far more. The longest day's march of the New Model during 1645-46 seems to have been thirteen miles.[3]

The mounted arm was then at the height of its fame, and the current view was that in a well-equipped army the horse should in numbers be not less than half the foot. In England the old heavy cavalry were becoming obsolete, and their place taken by harquebusiers, who carried sword,

---

other gunnes but fyrelocks, and wherewith they are weill provydit." *P.C.R.*, June 4, 1668.
[1] The Parliament army had orange scarves at Edgehill, green branches at Newbury, and white badges in their hats at Marston Moor. [2] Firth, *op. cit.*, 99.
[3] Sprigge, *Anglia Rediviva*, cited by Firth, *op. cit.*, 107-108.

pistols, and carbine, and by lightly armed dragoons, who were to all intents mounted infantry. They wore a light steel casque, a light cuirass, or often only a padded buff coat. Scotland stood to the old ways, and still armed her horse with four pistols, a carbine, and a lance.[1] The light horse did the outpost work of the army, reconnoitred, seized bridges and passes in an advance, and covered a retirement. In action a cavalry charge was at first made slowly, at a trot rather than a gallop, and trusted largely to the volley from the saddle. The old formation was five deep; this Gustavus reduced to three, and his example was beginning to be followed in England, as also his instructions to cavalry to reserve their fire, to charge at top speed, and to charge home. Rupert owed much of his early success to adopting the Swedish plan, and Montrose followed suit.[2] Rupert also insisted upon cavalry taking the offensive, and both he and Cromwell anticipated the later shock tactics.[3] The charge was always made in close order, knee to knee. The Scottish cavalry had no Rupert to make tactical experiments, and had to wait for reform till David Leslie copied the methods of the New Model.

The field gun employed varied from the culverin, which fired a ball of nearly twenty pounds, had an extreme range of about 2,000 paces, and needed eight horses to move it, down to the little three-pounder.[4] Loading a heavy piece was a cumbrous and perilous business, since the powder was usually carried loosely in a barrel. Scotland began by having a powerful artillery train, for Leven had learned from Gustavus the scientific use of that arm. His master of ordnance, Sir Alexander Hamilton (" dear Sandy " to his countrymen), had an ingenious turn, and in 1644 had invented a new kind of light twelve-pounder, which a single horse could carry.[5] Though the New Model siege train was one of the chief factors in bringing the Civil War in England to an end, it cannot be said that cannon played a decisive part in the field, except at Langport in 1645. In Scotland, after her great effort in equipping Leven, it would seem that the zest for artillery was relaxed, and at Preston the Scots had not a single gun of any kind—" dear Sandy being grown old and doated, and giving no fitting orders

---

[1] Firth, 114. *Army of the Covenant*, I., xcvii. Baillie, II., 440. *Cal. S. P., Dom.* (1640), 616. [2] *e.g.* at Auldearn. See p. 213, *infra*. [3] Firth, 134-142. [4] Ibid., Appendix H. [5] Terry, *Alexander Leslie*, 178, etc. *Army of the Covenant*, I., lxxxvii., etc. Firth, *op. cit.*, 157.

for these things."[1] Yet the mere possession of field-guns, however antiquated and badly handled, was a conspicuous asset against a Highland force. The Highlander detested the " musket's mother " as something outside the decent order of things, and needed much persuasion before he would face cannon.[2]

The army's intelligence was in the hands of the scout-master-general, but whatever the energy of this officer, he had in Lowland and English scouts material not comparable to that afforded by the Highland clans, to whom the most daring espionage was the breath of life. . . . Every regiment dressed as its commander ordained, but red was coming in fast; in Scotland the usual wear was probably hodden-grey, except for the officers and the cavalry.[3] . . . The common soldier's food was bread and cheese, except in garrison; the articles of war enjoined payment for all supplies commandeered, but the pay-chest was often empty. . . . Discipline was provided for by elaborate military codes, such as the one which Leven promulgated in 1644, which, in addition to much that was sensible and humane, enjoined the formation of a kirk-session in every regiment.[4] Religion was amply provided for in the armies of both king and Parliament, but Baillie laments that in 1644 it was hard to get enough ministers.[5] The army chap-lain of these days was a useful person, and his duties were secular as well as sacred, for he was the historian of a campaign and the seventeenth-century substitute for the war correspondent.[6]

Such is a rough sketch of the constitution of the regular armies of Scotland and England in the year 1644. The pick of the Scottish regulars were with Leven, who in January had taken across the Border twenty-one regiments of foot, nine troops of horse, a regiment of dragoons, and an artillery train.[7] What Montrose had to meet was the Scottish second-line army, the home-defence force, raised and equipped like the first line, but a little ruder, clumsier,

---

[1] Turner, *Memoirs*, 59.
[2] Especially if " grenadoes " (*i.e.* shells) were fired, as at the siege of Blackness in 1651: " They swear they will never fight more against guns that shoot twice, meaning in two cracks—the mortar and the shell." Douglas, *Cromwell's Scotch Campaigns*, 168 n.
[3] *Army of the Covenant*, I., xciii., etc.
[4] Ibid., I., xcviii., etc.   [5] I., 213.
[6] *e.g.* Case and Byfield with Essex; Ashe and Goode with Man-chester; Bowles and Hugh Peters with Fairfax and Cromwell; Wishart with Montrose; and Thomas Gumble with Monk.
[7] Rushworth, V., 604.

less disciplined. His own command was meagre and
shabby in the extreme. Alasdair had about 1,100 men
divided into three regiments—men who might be called
regular soldiers, inured to discipline, and seasoned by hard
campaigns. They had firearms, for the most part ancient
matchlocks, an occasional claymore, and a variety of pikes
and cudgels. The Badenoch men, mainly Gordons and
Keppoch Macdonalds,[1] numbered perhaps 300, and the
Atholl clans provided another 800; both, at their own
request, were commanded by young Inchbrakie. Of this
total of 2,200, nearly half—the Highland contingent—were
most inadequately armed. Some of the gentry may have
carried flintlocks, there were a good many claymores, but
the weapons of most were clubs and bows and arrows.
These Highland warriors presented the same picture as the
Highland contingent in Leven's army of 1641—lean, red-
shanked mountaineers, plaided, armed with sword and
bow, such deadly marksmen that with the latter they could
kill a running deer.[2] Nor was the lack of firearms all;
ammunition was so scarce that only one round could be
provided for such weapons as they possessed. There was
no artillery of any kind, and not a plack in the treasury.
The cavalry was limited to three horses, perhaps the unfortunate beasts which had carried Montrose and his
friends from Carlisle—skin and bone, says Wishart,
" omnino strigosos et emaciatos."

Yet, in the then condition of Scotland, there was in that
ragged levy the makings of a most formidable force. If
it could find a leader and loyally follow him, it might
gravely perplex the home-defence army, for it had none
of its faults. The Highlander, accustomed to full meals
of meat from the chase, was physically far superior to the
bannock-fed Lowland peasant or the apprentice from the
foul vennels of the little cities. He was swift where they
were slow, cunning where they were simple, adroit where
they were blundering, daring when they were supine. A
Highland army could pursue a strict military purpose, for
it had no civil preoccupations to compel the holding of
town or fortress.[3] Living on the country, it could do without pay-chests and transport wagons. It had no communications to be cut; its base could not be taken, for its base
was the inviolable hills. Under a general who understood

[1] Spalding, II., 261.   [2] Terry, *Alexander Leslie*, 153.
[3] On the fatal lure of fortresses in the Civil War see Sir John
Meldrum's testimony. *Cal. S. P., Dom.* (1644-45), 91.

its peculiar virtues, it might be to the second line of the
Covenant as a rapier to a ploughshare.

III

It was the true opening of Montrose's military career,
and he seems to have undergone a change of spirit. He
was now thirty-two years of age, and, as men went in his
era, might be held to have left his youth behind him.
Hitherto we have seen him perplexed and tormented, walking delicately and a little sadly in the difficult ways of conscience. He goes steadfastly on the path of duty, but with
head bowed. To his contemporaries he must have seemed
something of a dreamer and a doctrinaire, with nothing of
that large impulsive power which carries men perforce to
do its will. He had a good repute as a soldier, but that
repute was largely academic. In the Bishops' War he had
shown no special gift except speed, and in the Border
campaigning, earlier in the year 1644, he had fought with
weapons which snapped in his hand. But now some seal
is broken in him. Conscious of high talents for command,
he sees an army spring up miraculously at his call, and he
has the wit to perceive in that motley force the germ of
a new kind of war. His spirit is suddenly enlarged, and
he recaptures his youth and his humanity. Something goes
out from him which kindles the ardour of Ulsterman and
Highlander alike, and which makes Alasdair follow obedi-
ently a man the processes of whose mind are utterly beyond
his ken. He discovers a boyish zest for adventure and the
desperate chance. He indulges in a boy's whimsies—the
dress which captures the fancy, the proud word that stirs
the heart. He strides at the head of his men, daring the
wildest cateran to outvie in hardihood this intimate of
scholars, this familiar of courts and senates, the king's
lieutenant-general.

Apparently he sent formal warning to Argyll, as befitted
the holder of the royal commission to the king's principal
antagonist.[1] If a blow was to be struck it must be prompt,
for the Council was arming fast against Alasdair, though
as yet Edinburgh had no news of Montrose. Lord Elcho
was at Perth with a large force drawn from the burghers
of the second city of Scotland, men from Fife and the
Perthshire lowlands, and the mounted gentry of the neighbourhood. Lord Burleigh had another army at Aberdeen,
with the young Gordons serving under him; while from the

[1] *Mem. of M.*, II., 147.

west Argyll was leading his formidable clan to avenge the smoking homesteads of Morvern and Ardnamurchan. To

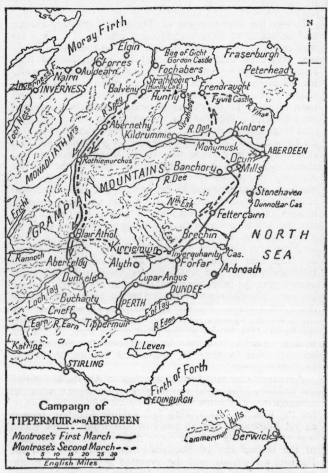

Campaign of
TIPPERMUIR AND ABERDEEN
Montrose's First March ——
Montrose's Second March – – –
0 5 10 15 20 25 30
English Miles

wait in Atholl was to starve, to retreat farther into the hills was to court disaster. Montrose had no supplies, no ammunition, no means of increasing his force except by victory.

On the 30th day of August he left Blair and marched west up the Tummel valley in blue autumn weather. He did not take the shortest road to Perth, for Argyll was coming from the west, and it would be well by fetching a circuit to get news of him before engaging Elcho. Also he had hopes of collecting allies in Strathearn. Rounding Loch Tummel, the army crossed the hills by the eastern side of Schiehallion to Aberfeldy. At Castle Menzies, whose laird was an ally of Argyll, they encountered a slight opposition, and burned a hut or two and some corn in sheaf. Late that night they crossed Tay, and put the river between them and the hostile Menzieses. Next morning at dawn Black Pate led the Atholl men forward as an advance guard, and the army marched with Highland speed across Strathbran, and by the Sma' Glen to the Almond. There at the Hill of Buchanty they fell in with an unexpected reinforcement. Lord Kilpont, the eldest son of the seventh Earl of Menteith; David Drummond, the Master of Maderty; and Sir John Drummond, a younger son of the second Earl of Perth, had raised 500 bowmen at the order of the Estates to oppose Alasdair's invasion. The leaders were kin to Montrose—young Maderty was his brother-in-law—and when they learned who was advancing their purpose changed. They gladly joined the royal general, and brought him a welcome accession of stalwart peasants, who, living on the border-line between Highlands and Lowlands, had some of the virtues of both. The force crossed the ridge to Strathearn, and spent the night on the moor of Fowlis.

It was now Sunday, the 1st of September. Elcho had something under 7,000 infantry, the levies of Fife and the Scottish midlands; 700 horse, composed of the local lairds and their following; and nine pieces of artillery, light pieces firing at the most a five-pound ball.[1] He had ample munitions of war, and his troops were fortified by the Sabbath morning exhortations of an array of ministers. " To give them their due," says Wishart, " they performed their part stoutly at the expense of their lungs, promising them in the name of God Almighty an easy and bloodless victory. Nay, one of them, Frederick Carmichael[2] . . . did not hesitate to declare in his discourse, ' If ever God spoke certain truth out of my mouth, in His name I promise you

---

[1] Wishart says 6,000 foot, while 8,000 is the figure given by one of Alasdair's Irish officers. Carte, *Ormonde Papers*, I., 73.
[2] Minister of Markinch in Fife.

F

to-day a certain victory.' "[1] With Elcho were many of
the neighbouring Covenanting gentry, including Lord
Murray of Gask,[2] and some who were not Covenanters, like
Lord Drummond, Perth's eldest son; and he had the assistance of at least one experienced professional soldier, Sir
James Scott of Rossie, who had just come from serving
under the flag of Venice. Small wonder that the Covenant
forces were in good heart. They had seen something of
the Highlander in the Bishops' War, and thought little of
his prowess. They knew that Alasdair's troops were in rags
—as one of the ministers described them, " naked, weapon-
less, ammunitionless, cannonless men." The view of the
leaders was that of Elspeth's ballad in *The Antiquary*:

> " My horse shall ride through ranks sae rude
>   As through the moorland fern ;
>   Then ne'er let the gentle Norman blude
>   Grow cauld for Highland kerne."

Besides, they outnumbered the enemy by nearly three to
one. So, very early in the day, Elcho with his army
marched three miles westward to Tippermuir, accompanied
by a host of Perth citizens who were not unwilling to see
a surprising judgment fall upon their ancient foes. He took
up a good position in open ground, where his cavalry, his
most formidable arm, had room to manœuvre. His battle-
cry was " Jesus and no quarter! "[3]

Montrose had at the most 2,700 men, all of them foot-
soldiers, for his cavalry, as we have seen, was confined to
the three lean horses from Carlisle. His artillery consisted
of Kilpont's bowmen. The most grievous lack was ammunition, for the Irish, who alone had guns, had but one
round apiece. On Tippermuir, however, there were plenty
of stones, and with these as missile weapons he bade the
rest arm themselves. He put the three regiments of Irish
under Alasdair in the centre of his little force, and Kilpont
with his bowmen on the left, while he himself, carrying
targe and pike, took command of the Atholl men on the
right flank. Elcho's dispositions were not unskilful. He
commanded the right wing, Murray of Gask the centre,

¹ Wishart, ch. v.
² Wishart anticipates and calls him " Earl of Tullibardine." He
succeeded his father as fourth earl four days after the battle.
Military History of Perthshire, I., 252.
³ *A True Relation of the Happy Successes of His Majesty's Forces
in Scotland under the conduct of the Lord James, Marquis of Montrose*, etc., 1644. Copies of this rare pamphlet are in the Bodleian
and the National Library of Scotland.

and Sir James Scott the left, opposite Montrose. The 700 horse, equally divided between the two wings, were under Lord Drummond.

Montrose, faced with so great a numerical superiority, had at all costs to avoid outflanking. So he abandoned the ordinary six-rank formation, and drew up his men in a long line only three deep. He saw further the danger from Drummond's cavalry unless he scattered the enemy foot out of hand by striking at its heart. He knew something of the temper of the unwilling Lowland levies—men drawn from the counter and the plough-tail to a work for which they had no stomach. To such the wild charge of the clans would be a new experience. Then, true to his duty as a constitutional commander, he sent the Master of Maderty with a flag of truce to inform Elcho that he was acting under the royal commission, that he wished above all things to avoid shedding Scottish blood, and to summon him to remember his due and lawful allegiance; in any case, let there be a truce so that the Sabbath should not be profaned. Elcho replied that he had " made choice of the Lord's day for doing the Lord's will "; he had no mind for a truce which would give the doomed royalists a chance to slip away. Moreover, he made the envoy prisoner and dispatched him to Perth in the custody of two Forfar lairds, who told him genially that he would be hanged when the fight was over. The Covenanters were to show throughout their struggle with Montrose a strange reluctance to accept the etiquette of civilized warfare.

The battle began with a skirmish. As the two forces approached within cannon shot, Drummond sent forward a mounted squadron, in order to entice Montrose into one of those frontal attacks to which an undisciplined army is prone. It was Elcho's one glimmer of tactical wisdom. But Montrose was ready. He had adopted the method used by Gustavus at Leipsic by which all three ranks fired at once, though the weapons of the third rank were only stones; and the first volley sent Drummond's troopers flying and halted Elcho's advance. Then he gave the order for a general charge. From behind the smoke came the fierce kerns of Ulster and Badenoch, with pike and claymore and Lochaber axe. The nine guns were submerged by the torrent. Elcho's centre crumpled like paper, and in a few minutes was racing back on the road to Perth. The cavalry could do nothing in the face of such fury and speed. On the Covenant left alone was there any serious

resistance, where on rising ground stood Scott, the wary
professional soldier, with the best of the Fife levies. But
Montrose presently won the ridge, and Scott fled with the
rest. The plain was strewn with lathered horses and pant-
ing foot.[1]

Then followed a grim business. Scarcely a dozen men
fell in the battle, but nearly 2,000, according to Wishart,
died in the rout, and the Irish officer, whose story has come
down to us, declares that a man might have walked to Perth
on the dead.[2] Some perished from the swords of Montrose, some from sheer fatigue—for the pursuit lasted till
nine in the evening of a hot autumn day—and we are told
that ten of the Perth burgesses succumbed unwounded to
their unusual exertions. Presently the enemy was at the
gates of Perth, and the city surrendered without a word.
Cannon, arms, supplies, tents, colours, drums, baggage, all
became the spoil of the victors. Montrose held his wild
forces in a stiff discipline. He refused to allow the
captured guns to be turned on the fugitives, and he permitted no violence of any kind within the walls. He contented himself with fining the burghers £50 sterling,
which went to Alasdair, who was in desperate straits for money,
with compelling the Covenanting sheriff-clerk to copy out
a summons to the local lairds, and with levying a large
contribution of cloth to amend the " looped and win-
dowed " raggedness of his army.

For three days Montrose tarried in Perth. He took up
his quarters in the town, in the house of one Margaret
Donaldson, and sent to Kinnaird for his old tutor, William
Forrett, to act as his secretary, and for his two elder sons,
Lord Graham and Lord James. Like Cromwell, he had
the ministers to dinner, and one of them, Mr. George Haliburton, was afterwards taken to task by the Presbytery for
saying grace at his table.[3] The news of the victory carried

[1] The first-hand evidence for Tippermuir will be found in the
depositions before the Committee of Estates, *Mem. of M.*, II., 149,
etc.; *Hist. MSS. Comm.*, 2nd Report, 174; and in the Irish officer's
narrative in Carte, *op. cit.* There are accounts in Wishart, Spalding,
and Gordon of Ruthven. See also Gardiner, *Civil War*, II., 139-142,
and *Military Hist. of Perthshire*, I., 251-252. There seems to be no
warrant for Baillie's charge of treachery against Lord Drummond
(II., 233). Second-class mounted troops were useless against a Highland charge.
[2] Wishart's figure must be exaggerated. Baillie, who loved horrors,
mentions only " some hundreds of the honest burgesses of Fife " as
slain in the flight. II., 233.
[3] For Montrose's stay in Perth, see the depositions in *Mem. of*

consternation to the Covenant leaders in London, who had written off Montrose for good, and caused them heart-searching as to whether the judgment was due to the sins of Assembly, Parliament, army, or people.[1] It drew off some of the Scots troops from Newcastle,[2] but it did not give Montrose the recruits he had hoped for, Lord Dupplin being the only man of note who arrived at his camp.[3] The Atholl and Badenoch men, according to their custom, made off to their homes to secrete their booty, and his force was soon reduced to little more than Alasdair's Irishry. There were other armies waiting to be met, and one of them, Argyll's, was approaching rapidly from the west. Montrose decided that his force was not sufficient to oppose Argyll, and at that time he was probably not aware of the existence of Burleigh at Aberdeen. His immediate aim was to collect recruits in his own country of Angus, and, if possible, capture Dundee.[4] On the 4th of September he left Perth and, crossing the Tay, reached the neighbourhood of Coupar-Angus. On the 10th Lothian, with Argyll's van-guard of horse, entered the city, and the following day at long last came Argyll himself.

On the night of the 6th the camp was stirred by a tragedy. Young Lord Kilpont shared a tent with one of his lieutenants, James Stewart of Ardvoirlich, whose castle still stands among the birch woods on the south shore of Loch Earn. A quarrel arose in the small hours, and Stewart stabbed Kilpont to the heart, killed two sentries, and with his son and some friends escaped to the Covenan-ters. Argyll three months later procured him a pardon from the Estates,[5] who, on 12th September, to give further proof of their partiality for assassination, offered a reward of some £1,600 sterling to any one who would slay Mon-trose and exhibit his head to them in Edinburgh.[6] The

---

M., II., 149, etc., *Chronicles of Perth* (Maitland Club), 39, and the *MS. Register of the Presbytery of Perth.* For Mr. Haliburton and other perplexed ministers, see *The Diocese and Presbytery of Dun-keld,* I., 84, etc. One of the most perplexed was Montrose's old friend and mentor, Mr. Robert Murray of Methven. The minister of Tippermuir was censured for giving Montrose a cup of water when he called at the manse on the morning of the battle.

[1] Baillie, II., 228.   [2] Ibid., II., 226.   [3] See note on p. 136.

[4] Mr. Gardiner assumes that Montrose left Perth with the intention of engaging Burleigh at Aberdeen; but Wishart says clearly (ch. vi.) that he did not get news of Burleigh's army till he was in Angus.

[5] *A. P. S.*, VI., i., 359.

[6] *Mem. of M.*, II., 163. This barbarous practice was not confined to one side, for in 1639 Charles set a price upon the heads of

murderer was also to have a free pardon for any crimes he might have been unfortunate enough to commit in the past. Mr. Gardiner dryly points out the inconsistency of this course. "The favourable reception given by Argyll to the supposed murderer was a sign that all who joined in a Highland rising might be assassinated with impunity as far as the Covenanting authorities were concerned. It is seldom indeed that a civilized community metes out to a less civilized one the measure by which it judges itself. When Argyll desolated the Highland glens with fire and sword, he was but inflicting due punishment upon barbarians. When Montrose gathered the Highlanders to the slaughter of the burghers and the farmers of the Lowlands, he placed himself outside the pale of civilized warfare."[1] The natural presumption from Argyll's reception of Stewart is that Stewart had been endeavouring to anticipate the wishes of the Estates, and had tried to persuade Kilpont, who had refused. For such a view there is no evidence, and it is intrinsically unlikely. Kilpont would have offered barren soil for any such proposal, and this Stewart must be assumed to have known. It is more probable that the account given in Stewart's official pardon is the true one. He had proposed to desert, and Kilpont, divining his intention, tried to prevent him and was slain. Or, if we like, we can take the family tradition referred to by Scott in his *Legend of Montrose*, that Stewart had challenged Alasdair, and that afterwards, in their cups, Kilpont and Stewart had words which ended in the fatal blow. The Estates have so many deeds of violence on their shoulders that the historian is glad to relieve them of one.

Alexander Leslie and Alexander Hamilton, but only £500 apiece. *Cal. S. P., Dom.* (1639), 81.   [1] *Civil War*, II., 142-143.

CHAPTER VIII

ABERDEEN AND FYVIE

(*September-December* 1644)

There is dross, alloy, and embasement in all human tempers; and he flieth without wings who thinks to find Ophir or pure metal in any. For perfection is not, like light, centred in any one body; but, like the dispersed seminalities of vegetables at the creation, scattered through the whole mass of the earth, no place producing all, and almost all some. So that 'tis well if a perfect man may be made out of many men, and, to the perfect eye of God, even out of mankind. . . .

If generous honesty, valour, and plain dealing be the cognizance of thy family, or characteristic of thy country, hold fast such inclination. . . . Fall not into transforming degeneration. . . . Be not an alien in thine own nation; bring not Orontes into Tiber.

SIR THOMAS BROWNE.

I

DUNDEE PROVED BEYOND MONTROSE'S POWERS. IT WAS TOO well garrisoned for 1,500 men to take, and the guns captured at Tippermuir were no siege pieces. He moved accordingly to the upper waters of the Esks in the hope of enlisting some of the loyal gentlemen of Angus. Here he had definite word of Burleigh's army at Aberdeen, which determined his next step. The Angus recruits came in slowly. Lord Airlie indeed appeared, the father of Lord Ogilvy who had been captured at Ribble Bridge. No Ogilvy was ever anything but a king's man, and two of his sons, Sir Thomas and Sir David, accompanied their father. With the Gordons Montrose fared no better than had Alasdair Macdonald. Huntly was still lurking among the bogs of Strathnaver; Aboyne, the second son, was fighting for the king in the garrison at Carlisle; and Lord Gordon, the heir, and his younger brother, Lord Lewis, were with Burleigh at Aberdeen. The clan, however, was not wholly unrepresented in the royal army. Nathaniel Gordon had been with Huntly in his rising, and now rode joyfully to join the king's lieutenant. He was an intrepid and seasoned soldier, but as rash as any subaltern of Alasdair's. It is a pity that no romancer has made him the subject of a tale, for his career, both early and late, offers rich material. Before he took part in politics, brigandage, kidnapping, piracy, and the baiting of Mr. Andrew Cant had been

among the simple diversions of his life.[1] He brought thirty
horsemen with him, and Airlie had forty-five, so the little
army was no longer without cavalry.

Montrose left his second son, Lord James, in his house
of Old Montrose to continue his schooling, and then, keeping to the skirts of the hills, reached the Dee valley by the
pass known as the Cryne's Cross Mounth.[2] The river was
crossed about midway between Banchory and the Mills of
Drum, and Crathes—the stately castle of the Burnets of
Leys, which lay on the north bank—was peacefully occupied. Sir Thomas Burnet was that rare combination, a
friend of Huntly's and a staunch Covenanter; he hospitably
entertained the royal lieutenant and his staff, and offered
him a sum of money, which was refused. The following
day, the 12th of September, the army advanced down the
river to within two miles of the town of Aberdeen, where
they found Burleigh awaiting them. Montrose had chosen
his route to avoid the strongly fortified bridge of Dee, and
in the hope of effecting a surprise; but the Covenanters had
had ample warning, and had taken up a good position on
the slopes of a hill. A lane, the present Hardgate, ran
downwards from their centre, and around the foot of it
were houses and gardens, which were strongly held. Burleigh had in all some 2,000 foot and 500 cavalry,[3] and he
possessed heavier artillery than the little pieces captured
at Tippermuir. His cavalry seem to have been chiefly the
Forbes, Fraser, and Crichton gentry, and eighteen horse
under the separate command of Lord Lewis Gordon. His
infantry were the usual Covenant levies, including a proportion of Aberdeen townspeople, and the remnants of
Elcho's Fife regiment.[4] Montrose had 1,500 foot and some
70 horsemen. It was his business to beat his opponent as
soon as possible, for Argyll, with a formidable army, was
lumbering in his wake, and Fabian tactics would land him
between two fires.

On the morning of the 13th, according to his custom,
he sent an envoy to the magistrates of the city summoning
them to surrender, advising them at any rate to send the
women and children to a place of safety, and warning them
that those who stayed could expect no quarter. The

---

[1] He was of the Gordons of Ardlogie. For his earlier doings, see
Spalding, *passim*.   [2] See Fraser, *Old Deeside Road*, 75.
[3] Wishart, ch. vi. Guthry says 2,500 foot; Gordon of Ruthven
gives him 3,000 foot and 600 horse.
[4] The second-line regiment. The first-line Fife regiment, commanded by Dunfermline, was with Leven in England.

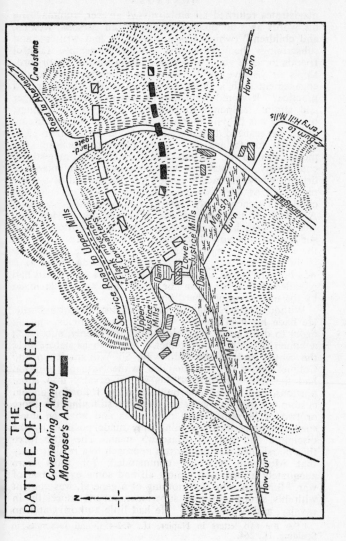

THE
BATTLE OF ABERDEEN

Covenanting Army ▢
Montrose's Army ◼

N ←——|——|

Road to Aberdeen · Crabstone

How Burn

Road to Ferry Hill Mills

Hard-gate

Service Road to Upper Mills

Flank movement of Covenanters

Marsh

Justice Mills

Lower Justice Mills

Dam

Upper Justice Mills

Dam

Dam

Marsh

How Burn

F*

magistrates returned an embarrassed answer, summarizing his words as "no quarter except to old persons, women, and children" (which was not what he had written), and subscribing themselves first "your lordship's faithful friends to serve you," and then altering this to "your lordship's as ye love us."[1] Why did Montrose preface this engagement with a threat so foreign to his character and practice? It would seem that he was in a mood of anger and strain. Kilpont's murder had outraged his feelings; his force was heavily outnumbered and needed encouragement; he realized that his affairs stood on a razor edge, and that his failure now would mean destruction. His mood was to be further embittered. The magistrates courteously entertained his messenger and made a drummer-boy who accompanied him the present of a silver piece, but as the two returned under a flag of truce the child was treacherously shot by one of the Fife soldiers. A breach of the laws of war always revolted Montrose, and this breach was especially cruel and wanton. In a sudden fury he vowed to make the enemy pay dearly for the misdeed, and promised Alasdair the sack of the city if the day was won. Such a promise was as unjust as it was barbarous and unwise. It was not the city which had offended, but levies from the south that were little loved by the townsmen of Aberdeen.

Without further delay he deployed his forces for battle. He bade his men plunder the adjacent cornfields, and, in order to distinguish themselves from the enemy, stick each a bunch of oats in his bonnet. The Irish as before held the centre, and on the right wing Sir William Rollo and Colonel James Hay commanded, while Nathaniel Gordon had the left. He divided his scanty cavalry into equal portions, and placed one on each wing, following an old custom of the Thirty Years' War by stiffening the score or two of horsemen with musketeers and bowmen interspersed among them—a thing only made possible by the discipline and skill of Alasdair's men. The little force thus marshalled was the nearest approach to a regular army that Montrose had yet commanded, for most were adequately armed, and almost all had some experience of war. Burleigh, who was nothing of a general, was content with his strong position, superior numbers, especially in cavalry, and heavier guns. He had little authority and no

---

[1] See the two letters in Napier, II., 452-453, and facsimiles in Spalding, II., 264.

plan of battle, and his lieutenants followed their own devices.

The action began with an attack on the houses and gardens which protected the Covenant centre. Alasdair had little difficulty in driving the enemy out of these and advancing up the slope. Lord Lewis Gordon charged with his eighteen horsemen on Montrose's right wing—a mad boy's escapade in the old cavalry style, discharging their pistols and retiring at the caracole. He made no impression, and Lord Fraser and Crichton of Frendraught[1] followed vainly in the same manner; they knew nothing of the meaning of shock tactics, and sporadic and half-hearted assaults of this kind were easy to repulse. The rest of the cavalry on the Covenant's left wing had apparently no orders, but sat staring at the battle.

Presently, however, the meaning of this manœuvre was plain. It was a diversion against Montrose's right to cover a dangerous attack upon his left. Following a mill road which was out of sight of the combatants, 100 Covenant horse and 400 foot worked their way to a position a little in the rear of Montrose's left flank. A bold attack there might have decided the battle, but the assault was delivered half-heartedly, and Nathaniel Gordon, with his little body of horse and musketeers, was able to hold it until Sir William Rollo's detachment was brought up from the right wing. With this accession of strength Gordon delivered a counter-attack, drove off the Covenant cavalry, and cut to pieces the Covenant foot.

But the denudation of the royalist right did not escape the eye of Sir William Forbes of Craigievar, who commanded on Burleigh's left. There were now no horsemen there to stiffen the defence, and with his cavalry he charged forthwith on that weakened wing—no futile demonstration like Lord Lewis Gordon's, but a charge to be pushed home in the manner of Rupert or Cromwell. Ordinary foot soldiers would have broken, but not Alasdair's Irish. With perfect coolness they opened their ranks and let Forbes's troopers thunder through; then, facing round, they pursued

---

[1] Frendraught was the son of the grim hero of the ballad *The Fire of Frendraught* (Child., No. 194), and was born about 1620. He was with Montrose in his last campaign, and assisted him to escape after Carbisdale. The story of his suicide after that battle, given by the old peerage writers and accepted by the *Dictionary of National Biography*, is without foundation. He lived till 1664 or 1665. See Napier, II., App. VI., and Balfour Paul, *The Scots Peerage*, IV., 129-130.

them with volleys. Saddles emptied fast, and the cavalry became a flying rout. Rollo returned from the now secure left wing, and completed Forbes's destruction.

It was the turning-point of the fight, which had now lasted for several hours. Montrose, who had darted from place to place, reinforcing and heartening his men, called for a general advance. The Irish responded with enthusiasm, the whole army swept forward, and the Covenant centre broke and fled. The ground between the battlefield and the city walls became a shambles, and Alasdair's men, mindful of Montrose's promise before the fight, broke into the streets in pursuit. Patrick Gordon says that the victors lost but seven men and the vanquished a thousand, which is manifestly absurd; but beyond doubt the flying Covenanters were cut down without quarter, and stripped before the fatal blow, that their clothes might not be soiled with their blood. In the streets unarmed citizens were butchered, women were violated and slain or carried into captivity, and death did not spare the very old and the very young. For three terrible days the orgy lasted. Montrose had returned to his camp, and the miserable business continued unchecked, though Donald Farquharson, true to his character for gentleness and mercy, endeavoured to plead for the unhappy city.[1] The mischief was done, and Montrose's record had received its darkest stain.[2]

What is the truth about the sack of Aberdeen? On the nature and magnitude of the atrocities it is hard to dogmatize. The damning evidence is that of the royalist Spalding,[3] and it is explicit not only as to the giving of no quarter to men, but as to the slaughter of women. Alexander Jaffray, who served with the Covenant cavalry and fled as fast as his horse would carry him, says that " about seven or eight score men, besides women and children, were killed."[4] He may have spoken from hearsay, but the burgh records of Aberdeen record the slaughter of all found on the streets, " old and young," and it is fair to assume that both sexes are included. There can be no ground for disbelief in the melancholy fact. As to the extent of the killing, one may be more sceptical; looting there was on a colossal scale, and no quarter was given to Covenanters in arms, but the slaughter of citizens was

[1] Gordon of Ruthven, 111.
[2] The evidence for the battle is chiefly in Gordon of Ruthven, 81-84. Wishart's account (ch. vi.) is unintelligible.
[3] II., 265, etc.　　　　　　　　[4] *Diary* (Aberdeen, 1856), 50.

probably less than 200. Spalding, though his list does not profess to be exhaustive, enumerates only 118. Baillie, not likely to minimize the misdeeds of his opponents, puts the number of slain at seven score,[1] and in another passage his words are: " A great many Aberdeen men were killed, and the town ill plundered."[2] This evidence scarcely suggests a general massacre. Moreover, the Cromwellian Richard Franck, visiting Aberdeen in 1657, had heard of a great battle there, but clearly of no atrocities, for he seizes the occasion for a panegyric on Montrose's " incomparable conduct."[3]

But on Spalding's evidence we must regard the main charge as proven: Montrose, faithlessly faithful to his rash promise to Alasdair, permitted the plunder of the city, the killing of men in cold blood to the number of over a hundred, and of some women, and the carrying off of other women as spoil by the Ulstermen. Among the female prisoners in Selkirk gaol after Philiphaugh are found names like Dunbar, Anderson, Forbes, Lamond, Young, Simson, Tait, Watson, Walker, Park, and Stuart[4]—it may be, some of the unfortunates who were now compelled to follow Alasdair's drum. On Saturday the 14th Montrose entered the city with Airlie, Dupplin, and others, and slept the night there, busied with trying to call his troops to order. But they had got out of hand, and when the march sounded on Monday morning many of the Irish were still at their evil work. When he saw the wretched townsfolk fruitlessly mounting his own whimsy of oats in their bonnets to save their lives, his heart may well have misgiven him.[5] On that day he learned his lesson, and for the remainder of his campaigns he held his men in a grip of iron. Henceforth when he captured a town there might be looting, but there was no murder or outrage.

The sack of Aberdeen was not only a crime, it was a fatal error. This was no Covenanting city, and the majority of those who perished inside its walls had been forced into the fight—as Spalding says, " harllit out sore against their wills to fight against the king's lieutenant." Montrose had spoiled his chance of getting recruits for the king among the burghers of Deeside. All over Scotland, too, the tale, zealously disseminated by the Covenanters, and

---

[1] II., 234.   [2] II., 262.   [3] *Northern Memoirs* (ed. 1821), 226.
[4] *A. P. S.*, VI., i., 492.
[5] Spalding, II., 265-267. This seems to be the occasion referred to in the pamphlet, *A True Declaration*, etc. Bodleian, 40, L., 73.

no doubt wildly embroidered, must have deterred moderate men from casting in their lot with one whose methods seemed more like a Tilly or a Wallenstein than a kindly Scot.

II

On Monday, the 16th of September, Montrose left the city and marched to Kintore on the Don. From there he sent a dispatch[1] to the king by the hand of Sir William Rollo. On the 19th the heavy-footed Argyll entered Aberdeen and proceeded to exact contributions from the surviving citizens. Soon the news of the battle reached Edinburgh, and the Estates were gravely disquieted. Argyll might be a pillar of the Kirk, but he was very slow in bringing malefactors to book; he complained that his army was too small, so requisitions were promptly sent to Leven. Yet Argyll had at least 2,500 foot from the western levies, and Lothian, his master of horse, had 1,500 cavalry.[2] Montrose continued up Strathdon to Kildrummie, whence he sent Nathaniel Gordon to Strathbogie (Huntly castle) and the Bog of Gight (Gordon castle) in a desperate appeal to the Gordons. But the clan was dumb. It would not stir without Huntly's word, and Huntly, jealous of a royal commission which interfered with his own lieutenancy of the north, and not forgetful of his treatment by Montrose in the first Bishops' War, refused to give it.

The place was growing unhealthy for a loyalist with Argyll a day's march off, so Montrose withdrew by way of Strathavon and Tomintoul to the vicinity of Rothie-murchus, that ancient pile on Loch-an-Eilean, of which Shaws and Mackintoshes and Grants have been successive masters. Somewhere on the road he buried the cannon which he had captured at Aberdeen.[3] The Grants and the

---

[1] This dispatch, dated 14th September, is referred to in the dispatch sent after Inverlochy. Rollo, on his return, fell into the hands of the Covenanters, and, according to Wishart (ch. xviii.), was released by Argyll on the understanding that he would assassinate Montrose. There is no evidence to verify or disprove the story.

[2] Spalding (II., 270) says that Argyll had Lawers's regiment of foot and Dalhousie's regiment of horse, but he seems to be anticipating. Lawers's regiment, which was part of Callander's force in England, does not seem to have been against Montrose till Auldearn, or Dalhousie's till Philiphaugh. See *Army of the Covenant*, I., Introd.

[3] Mr. Gardiner says that the guns were buried at Rothiemurchus (*Civil War*, II., 149); Wishart says simply *in palustri quodam* (ch. vi., 374); Gordon of Ruthven gives the locality as between Strathdon and Strathavon. According to Wishart, Huntly dug them up and

other Speyside families showed some inclination to dispute the way, so Montrose turned down the river to Abernethy, which brought him within twenty miles of Argyll, now at the Bog of Gight, and his 4,000 men. Presently he turned south again and made for the head of Spey and the Badenoch country, for he had been compelled to change his plans. Alasdair insisted on departing for the west on an expedition of his own, to raise recruits among the Clan Donald and to see to the security of his castles of Mingary and Lochaline. This left Montrose with no more than 500 men, and compelled a revision of his strategy. For the present he must content himself with troubling the soul of his enemies.

In Badenoch he fell seriously ill; it was rumoured in the south that he was dead, and from a hundred pulpits the Almighty was publicly thanked for espousing the Covenanters' quarrel. The illness lasted for several days, and seems to have been a fever caused by excessive fatigue.[1] By the 4th of October he was on the move again and heading for Atholl. Now began what Baillie calls a " strange coursing," Montrose leading the dance, and Argyll, some seven or eight days behind, footing it heavily from Spey to Tay and from Tay to Don. Alasdair with his female following had left him, and the king's lieutenant travelled light. He passed into Angus, and, clinging as before to the flanks of the hills, crossed the Dee at his old ford on the 17th of October. Now he sanctioned for the first time the burning of the lands of Covenanting lairds, like the Frasers and the Crichtons, in retaliation for the fire and sword which Argyll had carried to every one suspected of loyalism. By the 21st he was in Strathbogie, busy once more with fruitless appeals to the Gordons. Here he had word of Argyll's approach, reinforced by fourteen troops of horse under Marischal, the result of the appeal of the Estates to Leven. Accordingly he turned east into the bleak uplands of Buchan, and on the 24th was at Fyvie on the Ythan. He thought that Argyll was scarcely yet across the Grampians, when in reality he was almost within musket-shot. For once his intelligence failed him, and the king's lieutenant was caught napping.

appropriated them after Philiphaugh, so the *cache* was probably nearer the Gordon centre than Rothiemurchus.
[1] Monteith, 176. This remarkable author, who became secretary to Cardinal de Retz and a canon of Nôtre Dame, must have met Montrose later in Paris, and often records details which he probably had from him in conversation.

Fyvie, an old seat of the Earls of Dunfermline, had by this date become more of a seventeenth-century dwelling-house than a baronial keep. On three sides lay bogs with a few strips of hard ground too narrow for the approach of an army. On the eastern side was a low ridge of hills, which—a rare thing in that countryside—was thickly wooded on one flank. Montrose cannot have had more than 800 foot,[1] and at the moment of the surprise 150 mounted Gordons whom he had recruited in Strathbogie deserted his standard, leaving him with only 50 horse. Argyll outnumbered him by at least five to one, and he dared not meet him on the level; to defend Fyvie was to be caught in a trap; his only hope lay in the strong defensive position afforded by the hill-face broken with ditches and dry-stone walls, and the good cover in the adjacent scrub. He was desperately short of ammunition, and melted down the pewter vessels of the castle to make bullets; for powder he could only look to the pouches of the enemy.

Argyll, believing that at last he had driven his nimble foe into a blind alley, and strong in the consciousness of a force many times as large, attacked the position with—for him—considerable spirit. At last the omens were propitious, for he had heard of the Gordon desertions. A regiment of foot advanced up the little hill and carried some of the dykes and trenches, difficult places from which to eject well-armed men. Montrose saw that the only hope lay in cold steel. He called to a young Ulsterman, Magnus O'Cahan,[2] whom Alasdair had left behind him, and bade him drive the enemy from the slopes. A gallant handful of Irish charged with pikes and broadswords, drove back the Covenanters and made prize of many bags of powder for their famished muskets. It is recorded that one of them, looking at the booty, cried: " We must have at them again; these stingy hucksters have left us no

---

[1] Wishart says 1,500, apparently forgetting that Alasdair and his Irish were absent. Montrose had scarcely increased his non-Irish infantry since Aberdeen.

[2] His name is also spelt O'Kean, O'Cathan, O'Kyan, and Mac-Gahan. The *Clanranald MSS.* calls him " Magnus, son of the Giolla Dubh MacCathan." He was Antrim's foster-brother, and commanded one of Alasdair's three Irish regiments. The O'Cahans were one of the native Irish septs who became attached to the Mac-donnells. He was captured at Philiphaugh, and hanged in Edinburgh without a trial. See p. 257. I have followed Wishart's account, but Gordon of Ruthven (91) gives the exploit to Donald Farquharson, who was Huntly's bailiff of Strathavon.

bullets." Then came a charge of Lothian's horse on the flank. Montrose had his men well in cover, and, had the enemy been drawn in sufficiently deep, there might have been an end of Lothian's 500. But the excitement of the Atholl men brought about a premature volley, the battle was joined too soon, and the Covenant cavalry were easily routed by the charge of Montrose's 50 mounted men supported by his musketeers. After that followed some half-hearted skirmishing, in which Lord Marischal's brother was slain on the Covenant side, and then Argyll withdrew and put the Ythan between himself and his enemy.[1]

But Fyvie was no place to tarry in, since 800 men cannot for ever defy an army. Under cover of darkness Montrose slipped away, and was presently heard of in Strathbogie. Here he hoped for news of Alasdair and his western men, but no news came. His aim is clear; he had still expectations from the Gordons, and was loth to leave their country. This Argyll knew well, and he, too, followed to Strathbogie, keeping up a show of attacks which were easily repulsed. But the Campbell chief was engaged on work more suited to his genius than fighting, and busied himself with making overtures to Montrose's Lowland officers.[2] Since Alasdair went, Montrose had more officers than rank and file, and these Angus and Perthshire and Aberdeen gentry, half-hearted about the campaign and timid about their estates, appeared to be fruitful soil. He did not ask them to betray their cause; he only offered, of his generosity, free passes to any who wished to go home, asking no payment in return. It was a subtle plan, and it largely succeeded. Sibbald, a companion on the ride from Carlisle, left, and the seeds were sown of further discontent.[3] A council of war was called, and it was resolved to retreat into the hills. The royalists marched by moorland roads to Speyside, and at Balveny, on the west bank

[1] I have followed Gordon of Ruthven's story rather than Wishart's: Patrick Gordon describes the country as if he knew it, and he gives only one day to the fighting; more likely than Wishart's " plures dies," for Montrose could not afford to make too long a business of it.

[2] He seems also to have attempted O'Cahan's Irish. Forbes Leith, I., 298.

[3] Forbes of Craigievar appears to have broken parole and fled to Argyll. He was accompanied by Nathaniel Gordon. Spalding, II., 286. There is here a wild story of intrigue and adventure lost to us, for Nathaniel Gordon was always loyal. He may have bluffed his way into the Covenant favour, as Bishop Guthry suggests, in order to get in touch with Lord Gordon.

of the Fiddich, out of reach of Argyll's horse, took stock
of their position.   Argyll, avoiding the mountains, went
south by an easier road, and lay with his army in the
neighbourhood of Dunkeld.

At Balveny matters came to a crisis.   The Lowland
gentlemen had no love for a campaign in midwinter, conducted at Montrose's incredible speed, and offering little
hope of finality.   They feared for their lands and families,
now at the mercy of the Covenant.   Moreover, Highland
and Lowland are ill to mix, and they may well have disliked
their associates.   Montrose accordingly proposed a descent
on the Lowlands, the plan which he had always had in
view, for his aim was to relieve the king by drawing back
Leven's army from England.   So far his victories had
availed nothing to that purpose, for Newcastle had fallen
on 19th October, and Tynemouth on the 27th.   Leven was
now in Scotland, his army was in winter quarters, and a
descent upon the Border would gravely embarrass the
Parliament plan of campaign.   But the scheme found little
favour.   The Lowlanders argued that success in hill warfare was no warrant for victory against regulars in a settled
and hostile country, and the Highlanders had grievances
of their own to avenge, which they thought of far greater
moment than any royal necessities. Men like Dupplin (now
Earl of Kinnoull), Colonel Hay, and Sir James Drummond,
slipped away to make a temporary peace with the Covenant.   Almost alone of the gentry old Airlie and his gallant
sons refused to leave.   They, like Montrose, fought not for
safety or revenge, but for an ideal of statesmanship.

III

It was now far on in November.   In the levels the heavy
rains told of the beginning of winter, the high tops were
whitening with snow, the bogs were morasses, the streams
were red with flood, and the days were short and dark.
Argyll was at Dunkeld, busy with attempts on the loyalty
of Atholl, and he must have believed that no general in his
senses would continue the war in such inclement weather.
Indeed he had already sent his cavalry, his chief arm, into
winter quarters.   Montrose resolved to disappoint his expectations, and led his handful of troops through the Badenoch passes for a descent on Dunkeld.   His route was by
Dalnaspidal and Dalwhinnie to Blair, and in a single night
he covered twenty-four miles.   But long ere he could reach
the Tay Argyll had news of him, and wisely decided that

he could not face him with foot alone, even though the odds were four to one, and that he at any rate would end the campaign. He fell back on Perth, dismissed his Campbells to their homes, and himself posted with Lothian to Edinburgh, where he surrendered his commission as general-in-chief into the hands of the Estates. He complained that he had not been supported—" whether through envy or emulation, or negligence or inability ";[1] but it is hard to see what more he could have needed in the way of foot, horse, or guns; neither Kirk nor Council could give him a genius for war. His reception was a little chilly;[2] his services were formally approved, but it was dryly observed that the approbation was the greater because he had shed so little blood. The question was who should succeed him. Lothian and Callander brusquely declined the thankless post, and the Estates fell back upon a professional soldier, William Baillie of Letham, one of the best of Leven's generals in England.

At Blair Montrose met Alasdair returning out of the western mists. The meeting changed his plans. He may have thought of winter quarters, like his opponents, but that would be a difficult business, since they must be in the desert and hungry hills, and at the best a fruitless one, since precious months would be lost. But now he had the Ulstermen again under his command, and with them a formidable levy of the western clans. Alasdair had been no laggard. Clan Donald had not forgotten Argyll's commission of fire and sword in 1640, and Clan Gillian had long scores to settle with the secular enemy of their name. Five hundred Macdonalds—of Glengarry, Keppoch, Clanranald, and the Isles—had flocked to his standard. None of the resounding names which, forty-five years later, were to muster under another Graham, were lacking. There were Macleans from Morvern and Mull, Stewarts from Appin, Farquharsons from Braemar, and the eastern Camerons of Lochaber. John of Moidart, the Captain of Clanranald, brought his fierce spirit and devoted following to Montrose's side. There was young Æneas of Glengarry, with his three uncles, and Donald Glas of Keppoch, and the chiefs of the fierce septs of Glen Nevis and Glencoe.[3] The middle Highlands, for the first time since Harlaw, were united, but it was not in the king's cause. The hatred of every clansman was directed not at the Covenant, but at

[1] Baillie, II., 262.   [2] Spalding, II., 287.
[3] See for this gathering of the clans the *Clanranald MSS*.

the house of Diarmaid. Now was the time to avenge ancient wrongs, and to break the pride of a chief who had boasted that no mortal foe could enter his borders. The hour had come when the fray must be carried to Lorn.

Montrose had that supreme virtue in a commander which recognizes facts. He could not maintain his army without war, and to Lowland war they would not listen. If he looked for their help in the future he must steel their valour and rivet their loyalty by fresh successes. In return for their assistance in the king's quarrel they must have the help of the king's lieutenant in their own. Again, a blow at the Campbells in their own country would put fear into the heart of the Covenant, and shatter Argyll's not too robust nerve. It was a wild venture, an unheard-of thing to scour the hills when decent soldiers were warm in camp, and even the shepherds and the hunters lay snug in their bothies; but in its audacity lay its merit, for wild ventures have their psychological value in war. In a sense, too, it had always been Montrose's second line of strategy, for we have seen him writing to Sir Robert Spottiswoode from York: " We intend to make all possible dispatch to follow him (Argyll) at his heels in whatever posture we can."[1] He had the wit to see that a deadly thrust might be delivered in a region far from the main front of the campaign. There may have been a further reason. The Estates had confiscated his lands and taken captive his friends. Wishart, his chaplain to be, and Lord Ogilvy, his dearest comrade, were in the Edinburgh Tolbooth; his kinsfolk, when hands could be laid on them, had been consigned to squalid prisons. A blow at the arch-enemy would be some little solace to a heart which was only too prone to the human affections.

[1] See p. 141.

CHAPTER IX

INVERLOCHY

(*December* 1644-*February* 1645)

Through the land of my fathers the Campbells have come,
The flames of their foray enveloped my home;
Broad Keppoch in ruin is left to deplore,
And my country is waste from the hill to the shore.
Be it so! By St. Mary, there's comfort in store!

Though the braes of Lochaber a desert be made,
And Glen Roy may be lost to the plough and the spade,
Though the bones of my kindred, unhonoured, unurned,
Mark the desolate path where the Campbells have burned—
Be it so! From that foray they never returned.

IAN LOM MACDONALD.
(*Mark Napier's translation.*)

IN SEVENTEENTH-CENTURY SCOTLAND CLAN CAMPBELL STOOD
by itself as a separate race, almost a separate state, whose
politics were determined by the whim of its ruling prince.
Built upon the ruins of many little septs, it excelled in
numbers and wealth every other Highland clan; indeed, if
we except the Gordons, it surpassed in importance all the
rest put together. It was near enough to the Lowlands to
have shared in such civilization as was going, including
the new theology. Craftsmen had been brought to Inveraray from the Ayr and Renfrew burghs, schools had been
established, and of a Sunday the townsfolk could listen to
notable preachers of the Word. On the other hand, its
territory was a compact block, well guarded on all sides
from its neighbours, so that it enjoyed the peace and confidence of a separate people. With its immense sea-coast
its doors were open to the wider world, and the Campbell
gentry acquired at foreign universities and in foreign wars
a training which few landward gentlemen could boast;
while Flemish velvets and the silks and wines of France
came more readily and cheaply to its little towns than to
the burghers of Perth or Edinburgh. The country, though
less fertile than the Lowlands, was a champaign compared
to Lochaber or Kintail. Thousands of black cattle
flourished on its juicy hill pastures, and farms and shielings
were thick along the pleasant glens that sloped to Loch
Fyne and Loch Awe. In the town of Inveraray the clan
had its natural capital, and from Inveraray ran the Lowland road through Cowal and Dumbarton for such as pre-

ferred a land journey. Compared with other clans, the
Campbells were prosperous and civilized; they did not live
from hand to mouth like the rest, nor did each winter find
them at the brink of starvation; yet they still retained the
martial spirit of the Gael, and could put into the field the
most formidable of Highland levies. Accordingly, by their
neighbours they were both detested and feared. They had
eaten up the little peoples of Benderloch and Morvern, and
their long arm was stretching north and east into Lochaber
and Strathtay. Every Maclean and Stewart who could see
the hills of Lorn from his doorstep had uneasy thoughts
about his own barren acres. The Campbells had a knack
of winning by bow and spear, and then holding for all
time by seal and parchment.

Not without reason Argyll boasted that his land was
impregnable, for strategically it had every advantage. On
the eastern side, where it looked to the Lowlands, there
were the castles of Roseneath and Dunoon to keep ward,
and deep sea-lochs to check the invader. Besides, the
Lowlands and Argyll were always at peace. South and
west lay the sea, and the Campbells had what little navy
existed at the time in Scotland. The Macleans in Mull
were too small and broken to take the offensive, and in any
case it was a long way from the coast at Knapdale to the
heart at Inveraray. North and east lay a land of high
mountains and difficult passes, where no man could travel
save by permission of the sovereign lord. Moreover, the
Campbells of Lochow and Glenorchy had flung their
tentacles over Breadalbane, and held the marches around
the headwaters of Tay. There might be a raid of Macgregors or Maclarens on the east, or a foray from Appin
on Loch Etive side, but not even the king and his army
could get much beyond the gates. "It is a far cry to
Lochow," so ran the Campbell owercome, and it was a
farther cry to Inveraray.

Montrose, when he assented to Alasdair's wishes, resolved
to strike straight at the enemy's heart. He would wage
war not in the outskirts, but in the citadel. From Blair
there was little choice of roads. To go due west by Rannoch and the springs of Etive would mean a march among
friendly clans, but a few score Campbells could hold the
narrows of Loch Etive or the Pass of Brander against the
strongest army. The Lowland road by Dumbarton and
Loch Lomond was out of the question, for it meant a
dangerous proximity to the Covenanting westlands and the

difficult pass of Glencroe. But midway through Breadalbane ran a possible route, among wild glens and trackless
bogs, which at this winter season would be deep in snow.
This was the old raiding road out of Lorn, and Argyll
flattered himself that his clan alone had the keys of it.[1]
But with Montrose were men who had made many a midnight foray into the Campbell domain, and who knew every
corrie and moss as well as any son of Diarmaid. A Glencoe man, Angus MacAlain Dubh, was the chief guide, and
he promised Montrose that his army should live well on
the country, " if tight houses, fat cattle, and clear water
will suffice."[2] Accordingly, with Airlie and the Ogilvys and
his eldest boy, Lord Graham, as his Lowland staff, the
king's lieutenant ordered the march to the west. The army
travelled in three divisions: the Ulstermen under Alasdair
in three regiments, commanded respectively by James Macdonnell, Ranald Og Macdonnell, and Magnus O'Cahan;
the western clans, Macdonalds, Camerons, Stewarts, and
Macleans, under John of Moidart, Captain of Clanranald;
the Atholl, Badenoch, and Aberdeenshire contingents, and
the small Lowland force under the king's lieutenant himself. Montrose had now some 3,000 troops,[3] drawn from
every corner of Scotland. There were men from Orkney,
from Uist, and from Skye; from the whole Highland mainland between Knoydart and Braemar; from Kintyre; from
Angus and Moray and Buchan; from the villages of Forth,
Earn, and Tay; even from Lothian, Galloway, and the
distant Borders.

Montrose left Blair on or about the 11th day of
December. The road was at first the same as that taken
in the march to Tippermuir. The lands of the small and
uncertain clan of Menzies were traversed, and the laird
of Weem taken prisoner. Then westward by both shores
of Loch Tay swept the advance, where the Macdougal
settlers from Lorn suffered, till the confines of Breadalbane
were reached and a country that owned Campbell sway.[4]
Up Glen Dochart[5] they went, following much the same

---

[1] The difficulty of the road lay not in precipitous gullies, such as
Montrose found later in Lochaber, but in its bogs, which in the then
undrained condition of the valleys were a most serious obstacle.
[2] *Clanranald MSS.* [3] Gordon of Ruthven, 94.
[4] Father Macbreck's letter in Forbes Leith, I., 302. The laird was
Sir Robert Campbell of Glenorchy, a strong Covenanter, but his
brother Patrick, of Edinample, was with Montrose.
[5] On this point Mr. Gardiner's map (*Civil War*, II., 151) is wrong.
He makes Montrose go up Glen Lochay from Loch Tay, which is

road as the present railway line to Oban, past Crianlarich
and Tyndrum, and into the glens of Orchy. John of
Moidart, with the western men, was sent on in advance,
and did not rejoin the army till Kilmartin Glassary, far
down in Argyll; his business was to collect food, and he
brought in a thousand head of cattle. In Glen Dochart
Montrose was joined by the local septs, the Macnabs and
the Macgregors, and it was by a ruse of the former wily
and resourceful clan that the difficult narrows of Loch
Dochart were passed, and the island castle was surrendered.[1] A Catholic priest was the meteorologist of the
army, and he had promised them that the weather would
hold, since the wind blew from the east; he proved right,
for there was neither rain nor snow to hinder their speed.[2]

It was partly a raid of vengeance, and behind them rose
the flames of burning roof-trees. Presently Loch Awe lay
before them under the leaden winter sky, and soon the little
fortalices of the lochside lairds smoked to heaven. All
fighting men who resisted were slain or driven to the high
hills, every cot and clachan was set alight, and droves of
maddened cattle attested the richness of the land and the
profit of the invaders. It was Highland warfare of the old
barbarous type, no worse and no better than that which
Argyll had already carried to Lochaber and Badenoch and
the braes of Angus.[3]

Argyll was well served by his scouts, and to him at
Edinburgh word was soon brought of Montrose's march
to Breadalbane. He must have thought it a crazy venture.
Now at last was his enemy delivered into his hands. No
mortal army could cross the winter passes, even if it had the
key, and the men of Glenorchy would wipe out the starv-

against the authorities, and in any case would have meant a considerable circuit and the crossing of a high and difficult pass.
    [1] Forbes Leith, I., 308-309. Gordon of Ruthven, 97.
    [2] Forbes Leith, I., 308.
    [3] There is no record of any violence done to women and children.
Gordon of Ruthven (98) says that " although, out of a generous
and merciful disposition he (Montrose) would have spared the
people, yet the Clan Donald, wheresoever they found any that was
able to carry arms, did without mercy dispatch them." But, as
there was little resistance, I doubt if there was much slaying (see
Forbes Leith, I., 309), and I do not believe in the story that John
of Moidart in his fury killed 895 men " without battle or skirmish."
The only witness for this is the *Clanranald MSS.*, and the Clanranald
chronicler tells his tale in the high heroic manner of an Irish saga,
and is always carpeting the ground with dead. Father Macbreck
says that the business was chiefly house burning " in just reprisals
of war," and that even in this the humbler folk were spared.

ing remnants at their leisure. Full of confidence he posted across Scotland to Inveraray. There he found that all was quiet. Rumours of a foray in Lorn were indeed rife, but the burghers of Inveraray, strong in their generations of peace, had no fear for themselves. Argyll saw to the defences of his castle, and called a great gathering of his clansmen to provide reinforcements, if such should be needed, for the Glenorchy and Breadalbane men, who by that time had assuredly made an end of Montrose.

Suddenly came the thunderbolt. Wild-eyed shepherds rushed into the streets with the cry that the Macdonalds were upon them. Quickly the tale grew. Montrose was not in Breadalbane or on the fringes of Lorn; he was at Loch Awe—nay, he was in the heart of Argyll itself. The chief waited no longer. He found a fishing-boat and, the wind being right, fled down Loch Fyne to the shelter of his castle of Roseneath. The same breeze that filled his sails brought the sound of Alasdair's pipes, and he was scarcely under way ere the van of the invaders came down Glen Shira. The miracle had happened, and the impregnable fortress had fallen. " We see," commented Mr. Robert Baillie piously, but obscurely, " there is no strength or refuge on earth against the Lord."[1]

Then began the harrying of Clan Campbell. Leaderless and unprepared, they made small resistance to Montrose's lean and battle-worn warriors. Macleans and Macdonalds, Stewarts and Camerons, satiated their ancient grudges with the plunder of Inveraray. The kerns thawed their frozen limbs at the warmth of blazing steadings, and appeased their hunger at the expense of the bakers and vintners and fleshers of the burgh. Never had the broken men of Lochaber and the Isles fared so nobly. For some happy weeks they ran riot in what for them was a land of milk and honey; while the townsmen, crouching in cellars and thickets, or safe behind the castle gates, wondered how long it would be before their chief returned to avenge them. There seems to have been no special barbarity about the treatment of Inveraray. Here and there a refractory Campbell may have been dirked, but Alasdair's men sought victuals and cattle rather than blood.

Meantime word had gone from the exile at Roseneath to the Estates in Edinburgh. William Baillie of Letham, the new commander-in-chief, was a natural son of Sir William Baillie of Lamington; an old soldier of Gustavus,

[1] II., 263.

he had done good service at Marston Moor and at the
siege of Newcastle, and he brought to Scotland some of
the best of Leven's infantry, which he increased by local
levies. He took up the task unwillingly, and his distaste

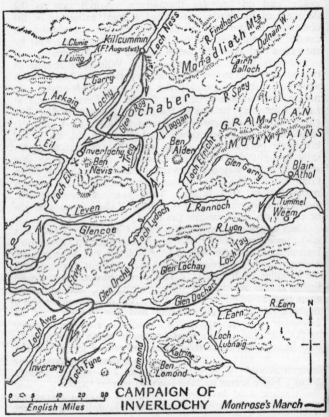

CAMPAIGN OF
INVERLOCHY

English Miles

Montrose's March ——

was not lessened by the behaviour of Argyll, who required
that he should take instructions from him. Baillie refused,
and, says he in his "Vindication," "My lord seemed to
be displeased, and expressed himself so unto some, that
if he lived he should remember it, wherein his lordship

indeed hath superabundantly been as good as his word."[1]
He was instructed by the Estates to repair to Roseneath
and consult with Argyll on the best way of crushing
Montrose. But at Roseneath he found the exile in a
difficult humour. There must be no stranger general in
the Campbell fastness. It was for the chief, and for the
chief alone, to avenge the wrongs of his clan. Accordingly,
the Estates ordered Baillie to transfer to Argyll sixteen
companies of foot, representing the flower of the Scottish
militia. Baillie himself was sent to Perth, and was presently given Sir John Hurry (who had been a royalist a year
before and was to be a royalist again) as his second in
command and master of horse.[2] He was bidden keep in
touch with the Covenanting garrison that had been left in
Aberdeen and with Seaforth's northern army in Inverness.
Argyll, at Roseneath, had had a fall from his horse which
incapacitated him from leading his troops in person, so he
sent hastily to the army in Ireland to summon back his
kinsman, Sir Duncan Campbell of Auchinbreck, the best
soldier that the clan could boast.[3] It looked as if the king's
lieutenant had walked into a final trap. He would be
caught between Argyll and Seaforth, and if he tried to
escape to the right Baillie and Hurry would await him. It
seemed the certainty on which Argyll loved to stake. His
view was that of the general's ministerial cousin, Mr.
Robert Baillie: "If we get not the life of these worms
chirted out of them, the reproach will stick on us for ever."

Midwinter that year was open and mild; the sun shone
brightly on Christmas Day. Had it been otherwise, Clan
Campbell, driven out of house and home, must have been
all but annihilated, and Montrose would never have led his
men safely out of Argyll. About the middle of January
he gave the order for the march.[4] He had as yet no news
of Argyll's preparations, but he must have realized that the

[1] The " Vindication " is printed in Robert Baillie's *Letters and
Journals*, II., 416-419. [2] *A. P. S.*, V., 182.
[3] " A stout sojer," says Robert Baillie, " but a very vitious man."
II., 263.
[4] Wishart (ch. viii.) says that Montrose left Lorn on the 28th or
29th of January. But he was at Kilcumin, on Loch Ness, on 31st
January; and, as a bond was signed there, he must have arrived
by at least the 30th. From Lorn to Kilcumin was four or five days'
march even for Montrose. Further, we know from Balfour
(*Annales*, III., 256) that the Estates heard by 18th January that
Montrose had left Lorn and was in Glen Urquhart. This may have
been a false report, but it is probable that the royalists began to
leave about the middle of the month, and that the rearguard had
gone by the 26th at latest.

avenger would not be slow on his track. His immediate intention was to come to an account with Seaforth, who not only barred him from the Gordon country, but was chiefly responsible for the opposition of the Moray and Speyside gentry, and the powerful clan of Mackenzie. He had guides who promised to show him an easy way out of Lorn into Lochaber, whence the road ran straight by the Great Glen to Inverness. Laden with miscellaneous plunder, and cumbered no doubt with *spreaghs* of cattle, the army passed the north end of Loch Awe, where Alasdair is said to have rescued certain kinsmen from the dungeons of " a strong castle."[1] In the Pass of Brander legend says that an old woman with a scythe opposed the advance and killed a soldier, and that Montrose intervened to save her life.[2] Arrived at the shore of Loch Etive, the bulk of the army turned west towards the narrows at Connel. The shorter road by Glen Etive, King's House, and the Moor of Rannoch, was no route for a heavily-laden force in midwinter, but a detachment may, as tradition avers, have followed the steep brink of the loch to Glen Etive, and there crossed the *beallach* by the old drove road to Appin.

The march from Loch Awe had been in the teeth of a violent south-west gale, but at Connel a windless calm fell upon the sea. It was the weather for crossing, but there were no boats, the land behind them was a provisionless desert, and the great Campbell keep of Dunstaffnage lay menacingly on their flank. The situation was saved by Campbell of Ardchattan—a Macdonald on his mother's side—who undertook to supply ferry-boats on condition that his lands were unmolested. By means of these, in two days of bright sunshine, the army crossed Loch Etive, the horses swimming alongside. The first camp in Benderloch was made memorable by the shipwreck of an armed sloop sent by Argyll to harass the flank of the march; it and its brass guns became the prize of the royalists. Also 150 young men of the Appin Stewarts arrived as recruits. Montrose hurried north through Appin, and was welcomed by the MacIans of Glencoe. Once again the weather broke, this time in a thunderstorm and a deluge of rain, and the roaring Cona seemed to offer an impassable barrier.

[1] Innischonain or Kilchurn. Father Macbreck says " his father and two brothers." Forbes Leith, I., 323.
[2] A legend told me by the late Captain T. A. Nelson of Achnacloich.

But boats were somehow found, the river was crossed at its mouth, the sky cleared, and the advance continued—either by Glencoe, Loch Treig and Glen Spean, or by Loch Leven and Mamore. The king's lieutenant was safe in Lochaber.[1]

Montrose halted one night at Inverlochy, but no more. He had Seaforth in front of him, and Argyll behind, and dared not tarry. By the evening of Wednesday the 29th of January, he was at Kilcumin, at the head of Loch Ness, in a none too friendly country. The weather continued to be mild and dry for the season of the year. Most of the Atholl men and the bulk of Clanranald had left him, after their custom, to deposit their booty. No more than 1,500 remained—Alasdair's Irish, a few hundred Macdonalds, Stewarts, Macleans, and Camerons, and sufficient horse to mount the Lowland gentry and provide an escort for the standard.

At Kilcumin Montrose had definite news of Seaforth. He was thirty miles off at Inverness with 5,000 men—Frasers, Mackenzies, and regulars from the Inverness garrison; a disorderly multitude, says Wishart, for, apart from the old soldiers of the garrison, it was " a mere rabble of new levies, peasants, drovers, shopmen, servants, and camp-followers."[2] Montrose was preparing to make short work of Seaforth, when he received graver tidings. Ian Lom Macdonald,[3] the bard of Keppoch, arrived by the hill-road from Glen Roy to tell of Argyll at his heels. The Campbells were less than thirty miles behind at Inverlochy, 3,000 men-at-arms eager to avenge the shame of Lorn. They were burning and harrying Glen Spean and Glen Roy and the Lochaber braes, and their object was to take Montrose in rear what time Seaforth should hold him in front.

[1] The details are mostly taken from Father Macbreck, who, since the Irish were of his own communion, had special sources of information. Forbes Leith, I., 308-319. [2] Ch. viii.
[3] Napier, II., 480. Guthry (178) gives the name of the messenger as Alan Macildowie of Lochaber, as does the MS. history of Gordon of Buthlaw. Alan Macildowie is also the second-sighted man (" ane old fox ") who warned Argyll before Inverlochy that " there would be a battle lost there by them that came first to such battle." (Gordon of Ruthven, 100.) To Father Macbreck he is the aged " Lord of Lochaber," who brought in the western Camerons to Montrose after Inverlochy. Forbes Leith, I., 323. The sixteenth chief of Lochiel, Alein MacDhonh'uill Dubh (whose grandson Ewen was then in Argyll's charge), was a very old man who had been protected by Argyll, and his politics were undecided. He may have sent Ian Lom to Montrose. He is called Alan MacCoilduy in the *Memoirs of Locheill*.

At Kilcumin Montrose had prepared a bond to which all the chiefs set their names. Such bonds and manifestos were favourite devices of the king's lieutenant. They were his Covenants, the only means by which he could advertise to the world the principles for which he fought. The signatories swore to fight to the death for their sovereign and his legitimate authority against the " present perverse and infamous faction of desperate rebels now in fury against him," and never to swerve from their oath as they " would be reputed famous men."[1] The little army had need of all the heartening it could get, for its plight seemed hopeless. Fifteen hundred very weary men were caught between two forces of 5,000 and 3,000. There was no way of escape to west or east, for the one would lead them to a bare sea-coast, and the other into the arms of Baillie's foot. Of the two hostile forces Seaforth's burghers were the less formidable. Montrose knew well that the fighting spirit of Clan Diarmaid was equal to any in the Highlands, and, now that they were commanded by a skilled soldier and infuriated by the burning of their homes, he could not hope to fight them at long odds. But it is the duty of a good general, when he is confronted by two urgent perils, to meet the greater first. Montrose resolved to fight the Campbells, but to fight them in his own way.

Early on the morning of Friday, the 31st of January, began that flank march which is one of the great exploits in the history of British arms.[2] The little river Tarff flows north from the Monadliath mountains to Loch Ness. Up its rocky course went Montrose, and the royal army disappeared into the hills. Scouts of Argyll or Seaforth who traversed the Great Glen on that day must have reported no enemy. From Tarff Montrose crossed the pass to Glen Turritt, and following it downward reached Glen Roy. Pushing on through the night, he came to the bridge of

---

[1] The original is in the Montrose charter-chest. See *Hist. MSS. Comm.*, 2nd Report, 176. *Mem. of M.*, II., 172.

[2] The ordinary route, given by Napier and others, is by the pass of Corrieyairack, down the sources of the Spey, and thence into Glen Roy. But such a route would have taken Montrose too far to the east and over unnecessarily high ground. Dr. Morland Simpson, basing his view on the *Clanranald MSS.*, has suggested a much more probable way—namely, up the Tarff, crossing above Cullachy; then parallel to the canal till the Calder burn was reached above Aberchalder Lodge; then ascending the burn and turning due south up the Alt-nan-Larach till the headwaters of the Turritt were reached; then south-west into Glen Roy along the " Parallel Roads." Pryce, *The Great Marquis of Montrose*, 240 n.

Roy, where that stream enters the Spean, on the morning of Saturday the 1st of February.

The weather on the high hills was deathly cold, and the march had been through a hyperborean hell. The upper glens were choked with snowdrifts, ravines had to be threaded where avalanches and cornices of ice overhung the adventurers, the rocks were glazed, and impassable save for Highland brogues. Passes were crossed so narrow and steep that a dozen men could have held an army at bay. But there were no patrols of Argyll among those inhospitable wastes; the only enemies were cold and hunger and the uttermost fatigue. The army had neither food nor fire. Now and then in a patch of wood a hind or roedeer may have been found, and its blood lapped and its uncooked flesh devoured by the fortunate discoverers. The rations for gentle and simple alike were oatmeal and water. As they struggled along at the pace of a deerstalker, Montrose walked by his men, shaming them to endurance by the spectacle of his own courage.

From Roy Bridge to Inverlochy is some thirteen miles. But to take Argyll by surprise a circuit was necessary, and Montrose followed the northern slopes of the wild tangle of mountains, the highest in Britain, that surround Ben Nevis.[1] He crossed the Spean at a ford below the present house of Corriechoille, and seems to have met a foraying party of Argyll's and stopped their mouths for ever.[2] Hugging the skirts of the hills, he went by Kilchonate and Leanachan, and before darkness fell was at the base of Meall-an-t'suidhe. In the ruddy gloaming of the February day the vanguard saw beneath and before them the tower of Inverlochy scowling by the sea waves, and not a mile off the men of Clan Diarmaid making ready their evening meal. They had been within sight during the day of that spot, Mucomir, on the north bank of the Spean, where

---

[1] Highland tradition in general credits Montrose with descending on Argyll by way of Glen Nevis. To do this it would be necessary to march to the head of Loch Treig, and then up Glen Treig and so into Glen Nevis, or, alternately, by way of the Learg-nan-Leacan. This would mean a very long journey for very tired men, accompanied by horses; an unnecessary toil, for Argyll would expect Montrose by the main road which descended the Lochy, and would be equally taken by surprise by a flank march along the northern skirts of Ben Nevis. Montrose had excellent guides in the Camerons and Macdonalds. This would seem to be also the view of Gardiner, Lang, and Morland Simpson. See Dr. Cameron Miller's paper, " Montrose in Lochaber, 1645 " (Fort William, 1910).

[2] *Clanranald MSS.*

another Graham was to review the assembled clans on the eve of Killiecrankie.[1]

Shots were exchanged with the enemy pickets, but no effort was made to advance. The surprise had been achieved; it need not be prematurely disclosed. Montrose waited quietly in the gathering dusk till, by eight o'clock, the rest of his famished column had arrived. There, supperless and cold, they passed the night, lighting no fires, and keeping up a desultory skirmishing with the Campbell outposts. The moon was full, and the dark masses of both armies were visible to each other. Argyll thought the force he saw only a contingent of Highland raiders under Keppoch or some petty chief. As Montrose watched the strip of moonlit loch between him and the dark hills of Loch Eil, he saw lights moving towards a little vessel which swung at anchor. Argyll had been persuaded by the Campbell chiefs to retire to his lymphad and take no part in the coming battle. There was little reason why he should, and charges of cowardice are foolish. Auchinbreck, not he, was in command; he was not by physique a useful fighting man, and he was still suffering from a damaged shoulder; he was the chief pillar of the Covenant in Scotland, and the head of a great clan; for him to risk his life, sword in hand, against desperate men was against every counsel of prudence and common sense. Alan McIldowie's prophecy, too, may have influenced his clan in their determination to keep him out of action. His companions on the galley were Sir James Rollo, Wauchope of Niddrie, an Edinburgh bailie, and a minister, Mr. Mungo Law, whom we may take to have been the travelling committee which the Estates were accustomed to send out to fortify their generals.[2]

At dawn on Candlemas Day, the 2nd of February, his ears were greeted by an unwelcome note. It was no bagpipes such as Keppoch might use, but trumpets of war, and the salute they sounded was that reserved for the royal standard. Then came the fierce Cameron pibroch, " Sons of dogs, come and I will give you flesh." The king's lieutenant, who two days before was for certain at Loch Ness, had by some craft of darkness taken wings and flown his army over the winter hills. There was no alternative but to fight. Till Montrose was beaten the Campbells could

    [1] *Grameid* (S.H.S.), 120. *Memoirs of Locheill*, 234.
    [2] Guthry, 178. Baillie, II., 263. Gordon of Ruthven, 100. Baillie and Gordon take the charitable view of Argyll's action.

neither march forward to join Seaforth nor backward to their own land.

Auchinbreck drew up his forces with the fighting men of Clan Campbell in the centre, and the Lowland regiments borrowed from Baillie on each wing. A stiffening of Highlanders was added to the flanks, and behind the main battle was a strong Highland reserve with two field-pieces. Montrose placed the Irish on his wings—the right under Alasdair, and the left under O'Cahan; he himself led the centre, which was composed of the Atholl, Appin, and Glencoe men and the Camerons; Clanranald and Glengarry had the second line, and there was a mixed Highland and Ulster reserve. Sir Thomas Ogilvy commanded the little troop of horse which had managed to make its way with the infantry over the terrible hills. This was the one advantage Montrose possessed; otherwise he had an army inferior in numbers by at least a thousand, weary with travel and on the brink of starvation, having had scarcely a mouthful for forty-eight hours. He himself and Lord Airlie had no breakfast except a little raw oatmeal mixed with cold water, which they ate with their dirks.[1]

Before battle the Catholics in his ranks knelt in prayer, while their priests signed their arms with the cross.[2] The action began with the charge of Alasdair and O'Cahan against the enemy wings; they reserved their fire till, in Patrick Gordon's words, " they gave it in their breath." The firing of famished men with ancient muskets may have been wild, but in a second they were come, as Montrose wrote, " to push of pike and dint of sword." The Lowlanders made no stand; in spite of the experience of many of them with Leven, a Highland charge was a new and awful thing to them, and they speedily broke and fled. This left the centre with naked flanks, and down upon it came Montrose. It was forced back on its second line, which, instead of opening ranks to receive it and so constituting a new battle-front, itself wavered and cracked. Inverlochy was won by strategy. Of tactics there was little, and that little was as rudimentary as at Tippermuir. The Campbell clansmen, outflanked and unsupported, did indeed make a valiant stand; " stout and gallant men," says Wishart, " worthy of a better chief and a juster cause." They knew that they could expect no mercy from their hereditary foes, to whom they had shown none, and they were not forgetful of the honourable traditions of their name.

[1] Gordon of Ruthven, 100.   [2] Forbes Leith, I., 321.

But in time they also broke. Some rushed into the loch
and tried in vain to reach the galley of their chief, now
fleeing to safety; some fled to the tower of Inverlochy,
where they presently surrendered. Most scattered along
the shore, and on that blue February noon there was a
fierce slaughter from the mouth of Nevis down to the
narrows of Loch Leven. The Lowlanders were given
quarter, but, in spite of all his efforts, Montrose could win
no mercy for the luckless Campbells. The green Diarmaid
tartan was a badge of death that day. The western
Camerons, hitherto dubious allies of Argyll, now came over
to the royal cause and joined in the pursuit.[1] On the
royalist side only four perished,[2] but one of them was Sir
Thomas Ogilvy, who died shortly after the battle. On the
Covenant side the slain almost equalled the whole of
Montrose's army. At least fifteen hundred fell in the flight,
and among them were the veteran Auchinbreck, and forty
of the Campbell barons.[3] Well might Keppoch's bard
exult fiercely over the issue:

" Though the bones of my kindred, unhonoured, unurned,
  Mark the desolate path where the Campbells have burned—
  Be it so! From that foray they never returned."[4]

Inverlochy was in one respect a decisive victory, for it
destroyed the clan power of Argyll. From its terrible toll
the Campbells as a fighting force never recovered. Alasdair's policy was justified, and the Macdonalds were amply
avenged; the heather, as the phrase went, was above the
gale at last.[5] To Montrose at the moment it seemed even
more. He thought that with the galley of Lorn fell also
the blue flag of the Covenant. He wrote straightway to
the king, giving him a full account of the fight, and ending
on a high note of confidence:

" The more your Majesty grants, the more will be asked; and I
have too much reason to know that they will not rest satisfied with

---

[1] Forbes Leith, I., 323. Mackenzie, *History of the Camerons*, 92,
etc.
  [2] So say Montrose and Wishart. The *Clanranald MSS.* says eight.
  [3] Fifteen hundred is Montrose's figure in his dispatch to the king;
so also Guthry; Patrick Gordon gives 1,700. The *Clanranald MSS.*
says that every Campbell was killed or made prisoner. Balmerino,
at the next meeting of the General Assembly, had the audacity to
claim that Argyll had only lost 30 men. Guthry, 180. The authorities for the battle are: Montrose's dispatch (*Mem. of M.*, II., 175);
Gordon of Ruthven, 100-102; Guthry, 178-179; Wishart, ch. viii.;
Carte, *Ormonde Papers*, I., 76; Forbes Leith, I., 320-323; Baillie,
II., 263.   [4] The whole poem is in Napier, II., 483.
  [5] The heather is the Macdonald badge; the gale, or bog myrtle,
the Campbell.

less than making your Majesty a King of straw. . . . Forgive me, sacred sovereign, to tell your Majesty that, in my poor opinion it is unworthy of a King to treat with rebel subjects while they have a sword in their hands. And though God forbid I should stint your Majesty's mercy, yet I must declare the horror I am in when I think of a treaty, while your Majesty and they are in the field with two armies, unless they disband, and submit themselves entirely to your Majesty's goodness and pardon.

" As to the state of affairs in this kingdom, the bearer will fully inform your Majesty that, through God's blessing, I am in the fairest hopes of reducing this kingdom to your Majesty's obedience. And if the measures I have concocted with your other loyal subjects fail me not, which they hardly can, I doubt not before the end of this summer I shall be able to come to your Majesty's assistance with a brave army, which, backed with the justice of your Majesty's cause, will make the rebels in England, as well as in Scotland, feel the just rewards of rebellion. Only give me leave, after I have reduced this country to your Majesty's obedience, and conquered from Dan to Beersheba, to say to your Majesty then, as David's general said to his master, ' Come thou thyself, lest this country be called by my name.' "[1]

CHAPTER X

THE RETREAT FROM DUNDEE

(*February-April*, 1645)

I mean to proceed bridle in hand; for if the bubble bursts, and Madrid falls, we shall have a run for it.   SIR JOHN MOORE,
                                                                Dec. 6, 1808.

IT WAS NOT TILL MARCH THAT CHARLES RECEIVED TIDINGS of Inverlochy. By that time he had already rejected the proposals of the Treaty of Uxbridge, one of which was that Montrose should be exempted from the act of oblivion, and the news of Argyll's disaster gave him hopes of a diversion in the north. He wrote to Montrose telling him that he was sending him 500 horse under Sir Philip Musgrave, and announcing that he himself with his army would make his way to Scotland with all possible dispatch. It was a scheme of Digby's which Cromwell was soon to frustrate. Steadily since Marston Moor antagonism had been growing between the new great English soldier and

[1] Napier, II., 484, etc. *Mem. of M.*, II., 175, etc. This famous dispatch was first printed as an appendix to Welwood's *Memoirs*, 1699, and was said to be derived from a MS. copy in the handwriting of the Duke of Richmond. It is referred to in Wodrow, *Analecta*, IV., 301.

the older generals of the Parliament. In especial Cromwell hated the Scots and the Presbyterians, and all who had art or part in the Solemn League and Covenant. " Against these " (the Scots), wrote Manchester in November 1644, " his animosity was such, as he told me, in the way they now carried themselves, pressing for their discipline, he could as soon draw his sword against them as against any in the king's army."[1] Robert Baillie now christened him the " darling of the sectaries," and had hopes of getting the firebrand removed from the army.[2] But the firebrand prevailed. On February 15, 1644, his New Model was constituted—twelve regiments of foot, eleven regiments of horse, 1,000 dragoons—a total of 22,000 picked men under a new training, who were destined to be the undoing both of the Covenant and the king.

Inverlochy had an important effect on Leven at Carlisle, since it increased his reluctance to move south, as Parliament demanded, while Montrose was at large north of the Border. To the Estates in Edinburgh it brought disappointment and panic. Argyll arrived ten days after the battle, with his arm in a sling, to be publicly thanked for his services. Baillie and Hurry were exhorted to fresh efforts, and further calls were made upon Leven. On the 11th of February James Graham, sometime Earl of Montrose, was declared a traitor and his life and estates forfeited.[3] The Kirk, not to be outdone in martial zeal, renewed the excommunication of the preceding spring, and proposed, since it was so hard to lay hold of the chief malefactor, to make a beginning with those in its power. Did not Crawford and Ogilvy and Wishart lie fast in the Tolbooth? Mr. David Dickson, Mr. Robert Blair, Mr. Andrew Cant, Mr. James Guthrie, and Mr. Patrick Gillespie attended as a deputation from the General Assembly to urge their immediate execution. Parliament commended the " zeal and piety " of the clergy, but hinted that, with Montrose victorious in the field, it would be as well to wait a little before making an end of his hostages. It contented itself with, for no apparent reason, outlawing Carnwath, and declaring " whosoever shall kill him to have done good service to his country."[4]

After resting a few days at Inverlochy, Montrose marched northward again. The right course, had it been

[1] Terry, *Alexander Leslie*, 344.   [2] II., 245.
[3] *A. P. S.*, VI., i. 313, etc.
[4] Guthry, 180-181. Balfour, III., 268, 270, 282.

possible, would have been an immediate descent upon the capital. But for Lowland warfare he needed cavalry, and cavalry could not be manufactured in Lochaber. To get them he must go where alone in the north they could be had—among the Gordon gentry. He found that the opposition had melted away. Having no war-chest, he was compelled to provide for his forces by fines and requisitions from the Covenanting lairds, and when these were not forthcoming there was burning and pillage.[1] Inverness was too strongly garrisoned to take, so Montrose passed it by, having no nervousness about fortresses in his rear. On Friday, the 19th, he entered Elgin without sign of Seaforth or any other opponent. The Mackenzies had disappeared into the fastnesses of Kintail. At Elgin, to his joy, he found that recruits began to come in. The first was the laird of Grant with 300 men, and at a plundering of the houses of certain Covenanting absentees the new convert showed himself highly assiduous.[2]

Presently came a far more welcome ally. Nathaniel Gordon's politic desertion had been fruitful; he rode over from the Bog of Gight, bringing with him no less a person than Huntly's heir, now weary of the ways of his uncle Argyll.[3] Lord Gordon was accompanied by his brother, Lord Lewis, whom we have already seen twice arrayed against Montrose at Aberdeen, first with Aboyne and then with Burleigh. He was still in his teens, a fiery and perverse young man, of undoubted gallantry, but of an excitable and fantastic mind. With the Gordons, as an earnest of Gordon support, came 200 well-mounted troopers, a sight to gladden Montrose's eyes, for cavalry could alone make possible that Lowland campaign on which he had set his heart. Lord Gordon was more than a comrade in arms; he was to prove, for the short span of life that remained to him, Montrose's tenderest and truest friend. Last of all came Seaforth to make his peace; he had never been much of a Covenanter, but Mackenzie and Macdonald could not easily mix. Montrose received him joyfully, and dispatched him to hold his own countryside for the king.

[1] He issued a recruiting proclamation under his commission of royal lieutenant, requiring all between the ages of sixteen and sixty " to repair to his standard under the pain of burning and slaying." Napier, II., 491.

[2] Spalding, II., 300. The laird of Grant had a royalist wife, a niece of Huntly's, who " as a sweet, charming nightingale, did never cease powerfully to agent the justice of the king's cause with her husband." Gordon of Ruthven, 85   [3] Spalding, II., 298.

At Elgin, and at the Bog of Gight, which was the next halt-ing-place of the royal army, the bond prepared at Kilcumin received further signatures. It is odd to read in the docu-ment, which is still preserved in the Montrose charter-chest, the names of Grant and Seaforth beside the scrawls of Alasdair and Clanranald, and to remember that, when the latter signed, the former were the foes against whom the bond was aimed.

Montrose had now a compact force of 2,000 foot and about 200 horse. The backbone of his infantry was still Alasdair's Irish, who may have numbered a thousand men. The Lochaber and Badenoch clans had gone home with their booty after Inverlochy, and the rest were Stewarts and Robertsons, the remnant of the Atholl levies, the 300 Grants, and small contingents from Moray, Nairn, and the Gordons. The cavalry, with the exception of the few who had been with Ogilvy, were wholly Gordon. Montrose may well have believed himself strong enough, what with the hope of further Gordon aid and the certainty of more recruits from Atholl, to meet Baillie on equal terms south of the Tay.

At Gight he suffered a sore bereavement. His eldest boy, Lord Graham, now in his fifteenth year, had been his father's companion ever since William Forrett had brought him to Perth after Tippermuir. The swift marches over the winter hills had worn him out, and his life was part of the price paid for that miraculous descent on Inverlochy. He died in the early days of March, and was buried in the neighbouring kirk of Bellie. Shortly after, old Lord Airlie fell dangerously sick, and was sent to Huntly's castle of Strathbogie, with a guard of several hundred men, which the royal army could ill afford. Montrose had to lock up his grief in his heart, for there was no time to spare for sorrowing. He marched east, and by the 9th of March was close upon Aberdeen. There had been much plundering of the little towns and the lands of Covenanting lairds, but no shedding of blood. Aberdeen had been evacuated by Covenant troops; a deputation of its burgesses met him at Turriff; and, remembering with regret his last visit, he undertook that his Irish should not come within eight miles of the city.

There, however, grave misfortune befell the royal army. Nathaniel Gordon, with eighty cavaliers, rode into Aber-deen from the camp at Kintore on a friendly errand of amusement. Word was sent by certain local Covenanters

to Sir John Hurry, who was in the Mearns with his
Covenant cavalry. This soldier of fortune, who at Oxford
had given Rupert that warning of the Parliamentary convoy
at Thame, which led to the battle of Chalgrove Field and
John Hampden's death, had the military virtue of speed.
With a detachment of Balcarres's horse, Hurry made a dash
on the city in the evening. Such royalists as he found in
the street were promptly cut down, most of the horses were
driven off, and among the dead was Donald Farquharson,
the bailie of Strathavon and the chief member of the great
family of Braemar. It was an irreparable loss, for he had
been one of the best of Montrose's lieutenants. " One of
the noblest captains among all the Highlandmen of Scotland," wrote Spalding,[1] and Patrick Gordon is eloquent on
his virtues. " He was beloved of all sorts of people, and
could not be otherwise, for he was of such a harmless and
innocent carriage that there was none alive whom he could
hate; he was never seen to be angry, nor knew he what
that unruly passion meant, and yet he gave proof of as
much true courage as any man could have; he was so far
from pride and vainglory that he was all men's companion,
not out of silly simplicity, but out of a gentle and mild
freedom, in a nature which did always dispose him to a
joyful alacrity, for his conversation, even in the saddest
and most desperate times, was ever jocund and cheerful."[2]
Hurry made off as fast as he had come, and on his way
back took prisoner the new Lord Graham, who was with
his tutor at Montrose, and sent him to Edinburgh. The
king's lieutenant waited in Aberdeen to bury the dead
Farquharson, at whose funeral Alasdair behaved with
almost complete propriety;[3] and then on Monday, the 18th
of March, began his southward journey.

There was burning in the Mearns and the braes of
Angus, now a laird's house, now a manse, and, as the parish
records show, there was a general upsetting of life and a
fleeing of Covenanters to strong places. It was done under
strict discipline, and unauthorized practitioners were
hanged.[4] On 21st March the town of Stonehaven was
burned, and the outbuildings of Dunnottar castle. Marischal, who, like so many Scots nobles, blew hot and cold

---

[1] II., 304.   [2] Gordon of Ruthven, 110.
[3] " He was much respected and well entertained for his love and
favour which he showed in not doing wrong, nor suffering much
wrong to be done, except one or two remarkable Covenanters which
was plundered." Spalding, II., 305.   [4] Fraser Papers (S.H.S.), 61.

in turn, was for the present by way of being a Covenanter, and in the company of sixteen ministers watched from its impregnable keep the destruction of his lands, finding what comfort he could in the consolation of Mr. Andrew Cant that the smoke of his barns was " a sweet-smelling incense in the nostrils of the Lord." By the end of March Montrose was at Fettercairn, with Hurry and his 600 horse only six miles off. There he all but made an end of Hurry. That general, confident in his cavalry, came out to battle near Halkerton castle, and, believing from his scouts' reports that only 200 horse were opposed to him, charged them gaily. But behind the horse Montrose had concealed his best musketeers in a glen of a burn, and Hurry was received with a fire which emptied his saddles and put his cavalry in confusion. Then the royalist horse turned and charged, and Hurry fled incontinent across the South Esk, never drawing rein till he had covered the twenty-four miles between him and Dundee. Next day the royalists occupied Brechin, which was plundered, and the town of Montrose, which was spared by the general for the sake of old times.

Here he heard of the advance of a more considerable opponent than Hurry. Baillie, with 3,000 seasoned infantry, was blocking the road to the south. Veteran troops had been recalled from Ireland, and Leven had given up some of his best regulars.[1] Montrose hastened to meet him, and found him in the neighbourhood of Coupar-Angus. But Baillie was a cautious commander, and he respected his enemy. He was determined to fight only on the most favourable ground, and he knew that Fabian tactics were the likeliest to wear out an army which had no base, no reserves, and no coherence save in the personal influence of its leader. The river Isla ran between the two forces, and Montrose dared not try to wrest the passage in the face of superior strength. So in the true cavalier fashion he sent Baillie a challenge, offering to cross and fight him, if the passage were permitted, or to let him cross unhindered if he preferred the other bank. Baillie wisely replied that he would fight at his own pleasure, and not to suit his adversary's convenience.

Seeing that it was hopeless to wait longer, Montrose

[1] It is not clear what regiments Baillie had drawn from Leven, but it is probable that there had already come north, or from Ireland, the foot regiments of Cassilis (Kyle and Carrick), Crawford-Lindsay (Fife), Loudoun, Lanark, Lawers, Glencairn, Lauderdale (Midlothian), and Balcarres's regiment of horse. The units are hard to trace in the *A. P. S.*, and Balfour.

devised a new plan. He struck camp and marched west to Dunkeld, with the intention of descending on the Lowlands by another road. At Dunkeld he could cross the Tay in safety, and after that he had a straight path to the Forth. Baillie could not keep up with him, and retired south—on his way to Fife, it was reported. Now was the chance for that avalanche from the hills which would sweep the Covenanting Lowlands, and gather up with it all the disaffected and anti-Covenant elements which Montrose believed to be plentiful in the south of Scotland. Baillie had obviously gone off to hold the bridges and fords of Forth, and it would be strange if Highlanders, with less ground to cover, could not get there before him.

But at Dunkeld Montrose was to be reminded of the nature of the Highland army which he led. Once more his forces began to melt away. The Atholl men slipped back to their homes, and so did the recent levies from the north of the Grampians. The Gordon cavalry, led by Lord Lewis, began to grumble, and, though they did not desert yet awhile, he knew that he could not long count on their assistance.[1] Presently his strength had shrunk so gravely that any attempt on the Lowlands was out of the question.

Something must be done if only to keep his remnant together. Twenty-four miles off lay the town of Dundee, the chief base of the Covenant in Angus. To read Dundee a lesson might be a profitable employment, till he saw his way more clearly. Moreover, his soldiers were short of every kind of supply. Their clothes scarcely held together, and they were shod for the most part with sandals made of the raw hides of looted cattle.[2] He had now no infantry but Alasdair's Irish. Of them he sent the weaker half on to Brechin with the baggage, and with 600 foot and 150 horse left Dunkeld at midnight on the 3rd of April. By ten o'clock next morning he was under the walls of Dundee.[3]

---

[1] Wishart (ch. ix.) implies that Lord Lewis Gordon deserted before Dundee. Gordon of Ruthven (115) denies this, and in W. Gordon's *History of the Illustrious Family of Gordon* (II., 453), Lord Lewis's presence at Dundee is asserted on the authority of an eyewitness. This seems the better view, for the Gordons would take the easiest road home, which lay through Angus, and would not miss the chance of a sack. See Gardiner, *Civil War*, II., 218 n.

[2] Forbes Leith, I., 325.

[3] Wishart makes it clear that Montrose left Dunkeld shortly *before midnight* on 3rd April. Gardiner (*Civil War*, II., 219) says he left *before dawn* on the 3rd. The march was twenty-four miles, and the speed was evidently considered remarkable, but, on Gardiner's ac-

Dundee in the year 1645 was a little town with a big kirk and a market-place in the centre, from which radiated the four main streets. It had a volunteer garrison and substantial walls, and inside the walled area at the north-west corner was a mound called the Corbie Hill, long since levelled, on which guns had been mounted. Montrose sent a trumpeter, one John Gordon, a servant of the laird of Rothiemay, to summon the magistrates to surrender, but the reply tarried, and the assault was begun before it could be written, so the envoy was committed to the Tolbooth.[1] Dundee was a strong place, but the walls were being mended in the north-west angle, and there the royalists soon made a breach. The guns on the Corbie Hill were captured and turned against the town, the defenders of the West Port and the Nethergait Port were taken in the rear, and presently the church and the market-place were in the invaders' hands. Several houses were set on fire, but pillage rather than burning was the order of the day. The booths of the merchants were turned inside out, and the plenishing of many a well-doing citizen took to the streets on Highland backs.[2] Stores of ale and wine were discovered, and soon many of the assailants, who had marched all night without a halt, were in that state of bodily and mental ease which Wishart describes as " vino paululum incalescentes."[3]

It was now late afternoon, and, as Montrose stood on the Corbie Hill watching the ongoings in the town, his scouts brought him startling news. Baillie and Hurry had not crossed the Tay on their way to Fife. With 3,000 foot and 800 horse they were now within a mile of the West Port of Dundee. It was as parlous a position as any commander ever stood in, and his colonels gave counsels of despair. Some urged him to leave his half-drunken troops to their fate and save himself, on the plea that another army could be found, but not a second Montrose. Others, of a more heroic temper, cried out that all was lost but honour, and were for dying in a desperate charge. Only Montrose kept his head. He was resolved to escape, not alone, but with his army—a decision which shows the flawless courage of the man. Somehow or other—how,

count, there would be nothing remarkable in doing twenty-four miles in thirty hours.

[1] He was tried and found guilty, but Napier (II., 496 *n*.) concludes too hastily that he was put to death. The *Register of the Committee of Estates* shows that he was alive in Edinburgh on 13th June.

[2] *A. P. S.*, VI., i., 519.   [3] Ch. ix., 385.

Heaven only knows—he beat off his men from their plunder: a feat, says Mr. Gardiner, " beyond the power of any other commander in Europe." Four hundred of his foot he sent on in front, and behind them he kept 200 of his best musketeers, as a support to the horse in case of a stand. Last, as rearguard, went his 150 cavalry. As the

Campaign of
DUNDEE AND AULDEARN

March of Montrose before
the taking of Dundee
March of Montrose after
the taking of Dundee

0   5   10   15   20
English Miles

royalists rode out of the Seagait and the East Port, Baillie entered at the West Port, and Hurry's van was within a gunshot of Montrose's rear.

Night had now fallen, the clear night of a northern April, but the Covenanters were confident of their prey. Hurry followed hard on Montrose as he marched east along the sea-coast. A few miles from Dundee he tried to charge, but the picked musketeers among the royalist horse were

too much for him, and their fire beat off his 800 troopers.
He fell back, while the king's lieutenant pushed on in the
direction of Arbroath. The shock of peril had sobered the
Irish, and they marched like heroes. Meanwhile Baillie
had conceived a better plan. He knew that Montrose must
break westward for the hills as soon as possible, not only
for safety, but to pick up the men he had sent on to await
him at Brechin. He observed, too, that his enemy was
marching along the arc of a circle, and he resolved himself
to take the chord. He had made arrangements for guard-
ing the nearest hill passes, and he hurried north-east
towards Arbroath to hem his enemy between his troops and
the sea.

It was precisely the strategy that Montrose had anticipated. At midnight he turned sharp in his tracks, marched
south-west to Panbride, and then north by Carmyllie,
Guthrie, and Melgund, and so quietly slipped round Baillie
in the dark. By daybreak he was at Careston castle, a
Carnegie house on the South Esk, with the friendly hills
in sight and at hand. Here he had news from Brechin
that the men who were to meet him there had already been
given the alarm, and had betaken themselves to the mountains. He halted for a little to give his weary troops a
breathing-space. In the past thirty-six hours they had
marched fifty or sixty miles, fought several engagements,
drunk quantities of liquor, and sacked a town. When the
halt was sounded nearly every man dropped to the ground
and slept like the dead.

Meanwhile Baillie at the first light of dawn had discovered his mistake. Hurry had rejoined him, and Hurry's
cavalry were soon hot on the trail of the man who had
so befooled them. Montrose got the alarm in time, but
his sleepy soldiers would not stir. It looked as if the three
miles which still intervened before the hills were won might
be three miles too many, and the labours of that marvellous
night rendered vain. But the officers, at the point of the
sword, managed to beat up sufficient troops to make some
sort of stand, and Hurry's horse were checked.[1] Then,

---

[1] Baillie, in his " Vindication," complains bitterly of Hurry's
jealousy and treachery, " which did appear clear enough by his not
charging the rebels with our whole horse at their retreat from Dundee; nor yet would bring them up to me, from whence the rebels
might have been charged in flank, notwithstanding I did require him
to it several times by the laird of Brodie and Mr. Patrick Pitcairne,
as they witnessed thereafter unto the Parliament at Stirling." Robert
Baillie, *Letters and Journals*, II., 418.

with a last desperate effort, the exhausted royalists managed to struggle the last miles into a country of heath and bog, where cavalry could not follow them. Hurry fell back, and by midday Montrose was safe among the wilds of the North Esk.

The retreat from Dundee, however we look at it, remains an astonishing feat of arms. Hurry's cavalry were the troops which had done brilliant service under Leven, and Baillie's foot contained some of the best first-line regiments that Scotland could show. Man for man the Gordon horse, sulky and mutinous as they already were, could not compare with them. The Irish were, of course, tried veterans, and superior to any of the Covenant infantry. But Montrose's men were at the best bone-weary, and at the worst half-drunk and laden with their precious plunder. The general who could stop the sack of a town in a few minutes was a superb leader of men, and he who could execute such a flight was a consummate strategist. " Which," wrote Wishart, " whether foreign nations or after times will believe I cannot tell, but I am sure I deliver nothing but what is most certain of my own knowledge. And truly, among expert soldiers and those of eminent note, both in England, Germany, and France, I have not seldom heard this expedition of his preferred before Montrose's greatest victories."[1]

[1] Ch. ix. The translation is from the first English edition of 1647. In Gardiner's map (*Civil War*, II., 217), the position of Careston castle is not quite accurate, and the route up Glen Esk is wrongly given.

CHAPTER XI

AULDEARN AND ALFORD

(April-July, 1645)

> *King.* And is this not an honourable spoil?
> A gallant prize? ha, cousin, is it not?
> *Westmoreland.* In faith
> It is a conquest for a prince to boast of.
> *First Part of King Henry IV.*

I

THE LETTER WRITTEN BY THE KING IN MARCH, PROMISING A body of horse and holding out hope of his own coming to Scotland, was carried by a gentleman of the name of Small, and found Montrose somewhere among the Grampians. On his way back to the royal headquarters the messenger, disguised as a common beggar, was seized by the Covenanters on the south shore of the Firth of Forth, taken to Edinburgh on 28th April, tried and condemned, and hanged on 1st May. Small had been captured by the Estates the year before, and banished the kingdom under pain of death, so his fate was strictly in accordance with law.[1] From the documents in his possession his captors had their first news of the king's intention, and it deeply disquieted them. They disseminated wild reports of the flight from Dundee, declaring, in order to allay popular fears, that only a few royalists had escaped to the mountains. But Argyll could not deceive himself, and he knew that the coming north of the king, with Montrose unbeaten in the field, meant that he and his ambitions would be caught between two fires. He communicated his anxiety to the generals, and Covenanting strategy acquired a new vigour. The credit probably belongs to Hurry, for Baillie, though a competent soldier, never displayed any strategic ability. The Covenant army was divided. Instead of pursuing the elusive enemy in one cumbrous whole, it was resolved to try to hold him between two separate forces operating from different bases. The Estates ordered a levy of 8,800 infantry and 485 cavalry from the counties south of the Tay, and many cadets of Lothian and Border houses joined the Covenant standard. It was believed that north of the

[1] *Register of the Committee of Estates,* Sept. 20, 1644. Guthry, 186.

Grampians large forces could be raised, so Hurry, borrowing from Baillie 1,200 foot—the regiments of Loudoun and Lothian[1]—and keeping 160 of his horse, hastened north to pick up these levies and to form the upper millstone for the projected grinding of Montrose. Baillie, with 2,000 foot and 500 horse, settled himself in the neighbourhood of Perth.

For Montrose there was once more the weary task of finding an army. Lord Gordon was dispatched to Strathbogie to try to raise Gordon troopers in place of those who had gone off with his petulant brother. Alasdair went west into the Macdonald country to whip up those of his clan who had departed after Inverlochy.[2] Black Pate of Inchbrakie went into Atholl to organize the Robertsons and Stewarts. Montrose himself had to await the result of these missions before he could again take the field. But for him waiting was never inaction. He resolved to investigate the state of affairs on the Highland Line, and to keep Baillie out of mischief. He also wished to gather to his standard one or two gentlemen of his kin who had been hiding in Menteith, and he may have had hopes of pushing south to get some news from the royalists across the Border. He wrote to the king from Doune on 20th April;[3] in that letter he spoke no longer of leading an army into England, for he had no army to lead. The most he could do was to keep the Covenant busy in Scotland.

Already with 500 foot and 50 horse he had swept down upon the Perthshire lowlands, halting for the night at the village of Crieff, twelve miles from Baillie's camp. The Covenant general, as soon as he got the news, set off in the night to surprise him, and at dawn on the 17th found the little army drawn up for battle. A glance convinced Montrose that the odds were too great even for him, so, with his horse fighting a rearguard action, he retreated up the Earn past Comrie, and by the evening was safe from pursuit at the head of Loch Earn. Next day he turned south by Balquhidder, into the heart of the Trossachs. Here he fell in with a welcome ally—no less than Aboyne, Huntly's second son, who had escaped with sixteen horsemen from beleaguered Carlisle, and had a dislocated shoulder, which did not affect him as did Argyll's at

---

[1] Spalding, II., 311.
[2] The Irish were terrible stragglers, and Montrose had to issue severe orders for dealing with them. See his letter to the Captain of Blair, Napier, II., 520. [3] *Mercurius Aulicus*, May 10, 1645.

Inverlochy. He found other friends, too, for by Loch
Katrine side he met his nephew the Master of Napier, and
a son of the Earl of Stirling, who had eluded the Covenant's vigilance.[1] Montrose had more than his share of
family affection, and the kinsmen, says Spalding, " were all
joyful of each other."

Here he had news which put an end to his southern
wanderings. Baillie was busy burning in Atholl, and
Hurry, now north of the Grampians, was bidding fair to
destroy Lord Gordon and his slender forces. Hurry had
failed to raise dragoons on Deeside, had had trouble with
a mutiny in Lothian's regiment, and the day before had
marched out of Aberdeen for the west. Montrose retraced
his steps by one of those lightning marches which were
the despair of his opponents and a confusion to the
chroniclers of his day. He could not fight Baillie as he
was, and to meet Hurry he must first find his Gordons.
Some time on the 20th he was at Doune; by Strathyre he
reached Lochearnhead, and thence sped by Glen Ogle to
Loch Tay, and across the shoulder of Schiehallion into
Atholl. Then by one of the Angus glens he reached Glen
Muick, forded Dee, and by the last day of April was at
Skene on lower Deeside.[2] Somewhere on the road Alasdair joined him, and at Skene he found Lord Gordon with
1,000 foot and 200 horse.[3] His army was badly off for
ammunition, so Aboyne undertook an expedition to Aberdeen for the purpose of supplies. With eighty troopers
the young soldier seized the town, found twenty barrels
of gunpowder in two vessels lying in the harbour, and
brought back the loot to headquarters the same evening.
Whatever the faults of the Gordon blood, it had no lack
of fire and speed.

Montrose's force was now a little over 2,000 foot and
some 250 horse. Hurry meantime had not been idle. The

[1] Spalding, who is followed by Napier, makes a younger Stirling
of Keir join Montrose in Menteith, but there does not appear to
have been any such person, since Sir George Stirling of Keir had
no family.
[2] There is some difference of opinion as to the details of Montrose's march after crossing the Dee at Ballater. Gardiner's map
sends him to Speyside; he may have misunderstood Wishart.
Napier, following Spalding, takes him to Skene, about ten miles from
Aberdeen. Aboyne's raid on Aberdeen (Spalding, II., 315) would
have been possible only from such a base as Skene.
[3] The figures are from Wishart (ch. x.). I suspect the numbers
given for the infantry, for Montrose at Auldearn only allows himself 1,400 horse *and* foot

Covenanters of Moray and Elgin had risen at his call.
Seaforth had recanted his lately professed loyalty and
brought the Mackenzies to his side. Sutherland was
hastening to his support with his clansmen, Lovat rallied
the glens of Beauly, and Findlater was bringing the men
of Easter Ross. The local gentry, who hated the Gordon
name—Frasers, Forbeses, Roses, Inneses, Crichtons—
carried their swords to his standard. He had under him
four regular regiments, all first-line, and two of them among
the best in the kingdom.[1] Altogether he had in being and
in immediate expectation a force of perhaps 4,000 foot and
not less than 400 horse.[2] While Montrose lay on the Dee,
Hurry was on Speyside with the road to Strathbogie open
before him. It was a vital matter for Montrose to keep
the Gordons in good humour, and for this purpose their
lands must be protected. So he hastened from Skene, by
way of the upper Don, the Avon, and the Spey, to give
battle with all speed to the enemy.

Hurry was something of a strategist, and retired for two
reasons. First, he wanted to draw Montrose out of the
friendly hills and the Gordon country; and secondly, he
had still to receive some of the promised forces of Seaforth
and Sutherland. From Elgin to Forres he drew the
royalists on, keeping only a little way ahead, but far enough
to prevent Montrose doing him harm. The ruse succeeded.
By the evening of the 8th of May Montrose had reached
the little village of Auldearn, on the ridge of high treeless
ground between the valleys of the Findhorn and the Nairn.
He believed Hurry to be retreating on Inverness, and meant
to follow him thither the next day. It was a drizzling
evening, and the neighbourhood was Covenanting to a
man, loving not the Gordons nor the Highlanders, and
least of all Alasdair's Irish, whom it remembered after
Inverlochy. No news of the enemy was likely to be got
from the country-folk. Montrose pitched his camp, posted
his pickets carefully, as was his custom, and settled down
for the night.

The position needs exact understanding if we are to
appreciate the events that followed. The hamlet of strag-

[1] Montrose's dispatch of 17th May (*Mercurius Aulicus*, June 2,
1645) gives the four as Buchanan, Lawers, Loudoun, and Lothian.
[2] The figures, as usual, differ in the contemporary accounts.
Spalding gives Hurry 4,000 foot and 500 horse, and Montrose 3,000
foot and horse; Gordon of Ruthven gives Hurry 3,000 foot and 700
horse; Montrose estimated the enemy at between 4,000 and 5,000,
and his own force at about 1,400.

gling cottages ran south from the parish kirk of St. Colm
on the line of the present Boath road. East of the village
curved a low ridge of upland. Below the houses to the
west were the gardens and pig-styes of the villagers, and
beyond them lay a flattish piece of ground covered with
wildwood and sloping gently to the bog of a sluggish burn.
North of this bog was the eminence of the Castle Hill, and
beyond the burn the ground was hard. South of it, and
nearly west of the hamlet of Auldearn, stood a bare hillock,
now called Deadman's Wood and planted with trees. The
burn, which caused the bog, bent round to the south in
a ravine, and so protected the south part of the ridge which
curved behind the village. The position was therefore in
the shape of a horse-shoe, if we take the firmer and higher
ground to the east as the rim. In the middle lay the
village, and enclosed between the points were the bog and
the rough land which sloped from the gardens and pig-
styes. The wet weather had swollen the stream and filled
the marshes, and made even the higher ground heavy
going.[1]

II

Some time before midnight on the 8th Hurry turned to
strike. It was a moonless night with drenching rain, and
the royalist patrols were not inclined to go too far into the
darkness. But Hurry gave notice of his approach, for his
men, finding the powder in their muskets damp, fired them
off to clear them. They were then five or six miles distant, but the quick ear of Alasdair's sentinels caught the
sound, and Montrose guessed at once what was afoot. A
wet, misty dawn was breaking when he drew up his line
of battle. He placed Alasdair with a portion of the Irish
and some of the Gordon foot at the north end of the ridge,
between the village and the Castle Hill, and into his keeping he gave the royal standard, in order that Hurry might
believe the king's lieutenant to be there in person and
deliver there his chief attack. He boldly denied himself a
centre, and instead scattered a few men in front of the
cottages, with instructions to keep up a continuous firing
so that the enemy might think the village strongly held.
This—and the Castle Hill—was the place for his cannon
if he had had any, but during the rapid marches of the past
eight months he had not had time to recover the guns which
he had buried after Aberdeen. The rest of his infantry

[1] See Bain, *History of Auldearn*, 14.

he kept to the south of the village, concealed behind the crown of the ridge, with the cavalry under Lord Gordon in a hollow on his left wing. It was a brilliant disposition,

Boath House

Castle Hill
MACDONALD
Church
HURRY
Boggy Ground
2 2
2 2 2
Auldearn
2 2 2
A
MONTROSE
N

THE
BATTLE OF AULDEARN
Montrose..... ▨▨
Hurry...... ...▭
Scattered Troops ·····
Hill marked A now covered with wood
and known as Deadman's Wood

0   ⅛   ¼   ½
Scale of Half a Mile

made at the shortest notice in the half-light of morning. If Hurry attacked Alasdair under the impression that he was Montrose, he would have difficulty with his cavalry among the village gardens, while Montrose, at the right moment, would be free to swing round his horse from their cover and take him unprepared on his right flank.

Three-quarters of a mile off, at Kinnudie, Hurry put his column into line of battle. The front of advance, between the Castle Hill and the bog, was narrow, so a single regiment, that of Lawers, formed the van, with the three other regular regiments in support. On his left wing, a little withdrawn, were the northern levies, while his right wing was composed of a detachment of Moray horse under Major Drummond. The main body of cavalry, under his personal command, he held in reserve. His problem was more difficult than he realized. On that narrow front he could not properly deploy his men and reap the advantage of his superior strength. Montrose had calculated right.

But there was one mistake in his calculations. Alasdair was undermanned. He had no more than 500 men, all infantry, to oppose the attack of at least six times their number, aided by a strong cavalry contingent. If we remember that the musketeer of those days was held to be unable to face cavalry unless drawn up behind hedges or palisades, we get some notion of the desperate odds. They were increased by Alasdair's own impetuous conduct. He was never the man to await an onset, and while Hurry's army was struggling through the marshy burn he sacrificed the advantages of his higher and drier ground and rushed to meet them. Eight to one is odds reserved to the champions of fairy tales. " Why, how the devil," asks Major Bellenden in *Old Mortality*, " can you believe that Artamines, or what d'ye call him, fought single-handed with a whole battalion? One to three is as great odds as ever fought and won, and I never knew any one who cared to take that, except old Corporal Raddlebanes." But Alasdair's deeds were worthy of the Fianna, and it is not hard to understand how in Gaelic legend his fame is made to outshine Montrose's. He and his Irish conducted themselves like the fierce warriors of the sagas. They were forced back, fighting desperately, into the nest of enclosures in front of the village. Like Ajax by the ships, he himself was the last to retreat. His targe was full of pikes, but he swung his great broadsword round and cut off their heads like cabbage-stalks. He broke his blade, but got another from a dying comrade. Again and again he rushed out to help the stragglers to enter. One of his men, Ranald Mackinnon of Mull, fought swordless against a dozen pikemen, with an arrow through both cheeks and no weapon but his shield. So raged the Thermopylæ among the pig-styes, and every moment Alasdair's case grew more desperate.[1]

Montrose, on the crest of the hill, learned from a galloper what was happening, and decided that the moment had come for that stroke on which the success of his tactics depended. The Gordon horse, in the hollow on his left flank, could see nothing of the fight in the village. They were not seasoned troops, and it was essential that they should go into action in high heart. So Montrose cried to Lord Gordon, their leader: " Macdonald drives all before him. Is his clan to have all the honours this day? Are there to be no laurels for the house of Huntly? " It was the word to fire their spirit. Moreover, they had a grim wrong to avenge. They had not forgotten the death of Donald Farquharson in Aberdeen at Hurry's hands; and a few days before, young Gordon of Rynie, a mere boy, who had been wounded and left behind in a cottage, had been brutally murdered by two of Hurry's lieutenants. With the cry on their lips, " Remember Donald Farquharson and James of Rynie! " the chivalry of Strathbogie wheeled to the charge.

It was the first time that Montrose had used shock tactics. Hitherto his horse had been so few that he had been compelled to employ them after the old fashion of the Thirty Years' War, more like mounted infantry, trusting largely to their pistol fire. But he had not forgotten the new tactics which Rupert had introduced at Edgehill, and which in Cromwell's hands had given the Ironsides the victory at Marston Moor.[2] Now was the time for the *arme blanche* —for cold steel and the weight of thundering horses. Montrose had that high gift in war which can adapt its methods not only to its ends but to its material. He could make his cavalry play a defensive part, with musketeers interspersed, when he was too weak to do otherwise; but when the chance came he could use it as cavalry should be used, with all the dash and fury of a Murat; and he could inspire bonnet-lairds on cart-horses with the spirit of the Maison du Roi.

[1] The *Clanranald MSS.* give a Homeric account of this part of the battle. Its author is not disposed to allow much merit to the Gordon foot with Alasdair. Auldearn is to him a clan battle, Macdonalds against the Lawers Campbells.

[2] The tactics were those of Gustavus Adolphus, and their first use in Britain has been generally ascribed to Cromwell. See, however, as to Rupert's claims, Bulstrode, *Memoirs*, 81; Fortescue, *History of the British Army*, I., 200; and Firth, *Cromwell's Army*, 133.

Hurry, happy in his belief that he was driving Montrose to his death in the village, was suddenly assailed by the cry of " Strathbogie! " as the Gordons, skirting Deadman's Wood, came down on his right flank. His flank guard, Drummond's horse, having had a difficult time crossing the bog, were in no case to withstand that assault of fresh cavalry with the impetus of the slope in their favour. Moreover, in this crisis Drummond gave the wrong word of command, and wheeled his horse to the left instead of to the right, so that he overrode some of his own infantry, and offered a naked rear to the Gordon assault.[1] Presently his troopers were flying, and many a saddle was empty. Lord Gordon, with half his force, followed in pursuit, and Aboyne, with the rest, attacked the now defenceless flank of Hurry's regular infantry. At the same time Montrose unleashed his reserves, hitherto concealed behind the eastern ridge, and the whole line swept down upon the doomed four regiments. Meanwhile, among the pig-styes, Alasdair collected his men for a last effort. He had lost seventeen of his best officers, but the royal standard was safe, and with his bloodstained remnant he charged Hurry's reeling centre. It was the last straw needed to turn the balance. The Covenant army became a mob, and the mob a shambles. The four regiments died gallantly, but the northern levies on their left rear, and the cavalry in reserve, fled without striking a blow. The blood of Ulster and the Isles that day had recovered its ancient berserk fury, and the Gordons were in no mood to spare their foes. Donald Farquharson and James of Rynie did not go unattended to the shades.

For fourteen miles the pursuit continued. Of the Ulstermen who had held the village many must have fallen, and almost all the rest were wounded, but otherwise the royalists had suffered little. It was very different with the Covenanters. The estimates of their dead vary, but the number cannot have been less than 2,000. Sir Mungo Campbell of Lawers, who fought in the centre against Alasdair, perished with most of his fine regiment.[2] There fell, too, the flower of the Lowland officers with Lothian's

[1] I see no reason to assume treachery, for this kind of mistake has often been made in the history of war. Drummond was court-martialled and shot in Inverness.

[2] It was reckoned one of the two " stoutest regiments in the Scots army." *Memorie of the Somervilles*, II., 315. The regiment cannot have been entirely destroyed, for it was present at Alford. *A. P. S.*, VI., i., 469.

Border regiment—a Murray of Philiphaugh,[1] two Gledstanes of Whitelaw, nine nephews of Douglas of Cavers.[2]
It was on the four regular regiments and a portion of the
cavalry that the brunt fell. The northern earls, with their
dishonoured levies, fled to Inverness, and Seaforth, in the
wilds of Kintail, had leisure to reflect on the rewards of
the forsworn. Hurry himself, with a remnant of 100 horse,
escaped to Baillie. He was no coward, and was one of the
last to quit the field.[3]

Auldearn is the most interesting, as it is tactically the
most brilliant, of Montrose's battles. It was the first time
that he had commanded a reasonable force of cavalry, and
the first time that he had been the attacked instead of the
attacker. Hurry had shown considerable strategic ability,
and had attempted with no little art to meet him with his
own methods of surprise. It is rare in the history of war
that a man who can devise lightning raids shows an equal
coolness and skill when he stands on the defence. But the
dispositions made within a few minutes on that wet May
morning could not have been bettered though they had
been the result of days of preparation. Genius for war,
working as it does within certain inexorable limits, repeats
with variations the same methods in every age. The reserv-
ing of fire till close quarters was followed by Dundee at
Killiecrankie,[4] and became a famous usage in the British
army, as witness Fontenoy. The device of a weak right,
dedicated to a desperate holding battle, and forming the
hinge on which the rest of the army swings to break the
enemy's centre, was used on a majestic scale amid the snow
of Austerlitz.

III

The news of Auldearn had its influence on the war in
England. Leven, already aware of the king's plan of
coming north to join Montrose, was summoned by Fairfax
to support Brereton at Manchester, who had been driven
out of Cheshire by Charles's advance from Droitwich. He

---

[1] Wishart mentions also a Sir Gideon Murray, who cannot have
been of the Elibank family, though he bore their favourite Christian
name, for the Elibanks of the time were staunch loyalists. *Cf.* J. W.
Buchan, *History of Peeblesshire*, II., 483.
[2] Entry in Gledstanes Bible in Hawick Museum.
[3] The battle of Auldearn has been brilliantly reconstructed by Mr.
Gardiner (*Civil War*, II., 223-227). The contemporary accounts in
Wishart (ch. x.), Gordon of Ruthven (123, etc.), the *Clanranald
MSS.*, Spalding (II., 319), and the *Wardlaw MS.* (S.H.S.), 295, are
far from clear.   [4] *Memoirs of Locheill*, 267.

announced his coming, but added that he meant to travel
by way of Westmoreland, as that route was easiest for his
guns. His reasons for this circuit are plain. He wished
his army to cover the road to Scotland, for he feared that
at any moment the king might come north and Montrose
come south, and he knew that their meeting in the Lowlands would mean the end of his Covenanting masters.
The same fear kept him long in Westmoreland when he
was urgently needed in Yorkshire. He was beginning, like
most of the Scots, to be very weary of his Parliamentary
colleagues, and had already told an English colonel that,
if he did not do his will about a certain fort at Carlisle, he
" desired no better occasion to cut them all in pieces."[1]
The Estates in Edinburgh were no less concerned, and their
first step was revenge. Lord Napier, now a man of
seventy, whose only offence was that he was Montrose's
brother-in-law, was heavily fined and kept in close confinement. The young Master had escaped and was with his
uncle; but his wife, his sisters, and his brother-in-law,
Stirling of Keir, shared the old lord's fate. Montrose succeeded in making an exchange of certain lesser prisoners
with Argyll, and he used the fact that he held a Campbell
of Crinan at Blair to prevent further reprisals upon the
Napier family. But Lord Graham was also imprisoned,
and his younger brother, Lord Robert, a boy of seven, by
an order of the Estates, was committed to the charge of
Montrose's wife. It is one of the few glimpses we get of
this lady. Apparently she had made her peace with the
Covenant through her own family, for Southesk and his
son Carnegie were of the type that value property and a
quiet life above scruples of honour and a barren renown.

Montrose had now won four notable battles, but it was
still as difficult as ever, in Bishop Burnet's phrase, to " fix
his conquests." Hurry's army was gone, but Baillie's
remained, and Baillie blocked the way to the Lowlands.
He had 2,000 foot and several hundred horse, and, burning
his way through Atholl, had by the beginning of May
crossed the Dee and entered Strathbogie. As a reserve to
this force, Montrose's college friend, Lord Lindsay of the
Byres, who had been granted by the Parliament the forfeited earldom of Crawford, was commanding a newly
raised army on the borders of Perth and Angus. Lindsay
fancied himself a military genius, and, having trenchantly
criticized the performances of Argyll and Baillie, had per-

[1] *Cal. S. P., Dom.* (1644-45), 558.

suaded the Committee to try him in high command. He seems to have had the ear of Parliament, for on their order Baillie, as we shall see, was soon compelled to lend him more than a thousand of his veterans, and accept in exchange 400 of Lindsay's raw Lowland levies.[1]

After Auldearn Montrose went first to Elgin, where he halted for a time to rest his weary troops and look after

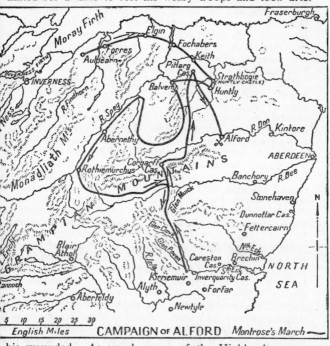

CAMPAIGN OF ALFORD   Montrose's March ——

English Miles

his wounded. As usual, many of the Highlanders went home, and Aboyne departed on sick leave, but he still kept his Irish and the Gordon horse. He marched into Strathbogie to draw Baillie, and proceeded to outmanœuvre him

[1] Wishart (ch. xi., 393) says that Baillie gave up 1,000 men and got only " tirones et rudes." Baillie, the general, says he gave up 1,500 and got 400. Robert Baillie, *Letters and Journals*, II., 419. He got from Lindsay Cassilis' regiment (Kyle and Carrick), and gave him the regiments of Hume (which had come from Ireland), Lindsay (Fife), and Lauderdale (Midlothian).

up and down the valley of the Spey. He had no desire to
fight until he had recruited his strength, for after such a
battle as Auldearn there was need of a breathing-space.
From Strathbogie he moved to Balveny and thence to Glen-
livat, where Baillie lost all trace of his quarry. He found
him again at Abernethy-on-Spey, and presently Montrose
was on the outskirts of Badenoch—" a very strait county,"
says Baillie, and one by no means pleasant to campaign in.
Here the two opponents halted and looked at each other.
Montrose with his Highlanders could draw supplies from
the countryside, but Baillie could only starve. The thing
was soon past bearing, so the Covenanters withdrew to
Inverness to lay in provisions.

The road was now open to deal with Lindsay, who was
waiting in Atholl to prove his boasted generalship. The
news of Montrose's coming sent him back in hot haste to
Newtyle, in Angus, to be nearer his base. Montrose sped
down the upper glens of Dee, through Glen Muick, and
down the headwaters of the South Esk. But when he was
on the Isla, within seven miles of Lindsay, and that general
was already repenting his bold words, a message arrived
from the north to spoil all his plans. Huntly had summoned his clan back to Strathbogie. The reason of his
conduct we do not know. The natural explanation is that
the chief of the Gordons took this opportunity of showing
his jealousy of Montrose and of paying back old scores.
So Lord Gordon interpreted it, and was with difficulty
restrained from dealing summarily with those of his clan
who proposed to obey his father's commands. But it is at
least as probable that Huntly, with Baillie in the neighbourhood, was merely anxious for the safety of his own possessions. Montrose had no other course but to turn back
and begin recruiting again. He might have fought Lindsay
without cavalry and with a much inferior force—he had
taken risks as great before; but on this occasion there was
a strong reason for retiring. To defeat Lindsay would not
advance by one step the main strategy of his campaign.
He would still have to go back and settle with Baillie, and
he would still have to collect an army for the Lowland
war. It seemed wiser to do these necessary things first, and
to leave Lindsay to be dealt with later—or, more likely, to
fall a victim to the endless Covenanting bickerings.

Montrose went back the road he had come, crossed the
Dee, and settled himself at Corgarff castle, at the head of
Strathdon. Here he was in a strong position, whether to

retreat, if necessary, to the high hills, or to sweep down upon the Aberdeenshire lowlands. Once more he sent off Alasdair to collect the Clan Donald, while Lord Gordon and Nathaniel Gordon departed to recruit the men of their name. In this way the time passed till the last days of June. Baillie was thoroughly sick of the business, and begged in vain to be allowed to resign his command. Some of his veteran regiments showed ugly symptoms of mutiny.[1] He was in receipt of the daily and most vexatious instructions of the warlike Committee of Estates, which, with tried warriors like Argyll, Elcho, and Burleigh among its members, was resolved to confide nothing to Baillie's unaided judgment. They were represented at the front by a branch committee, who interpreted their resolutions, and must have driven the unfortunate commander to the verge of madness. One of their performances, as we have seen, was the transfer of the flower of Baillie's foot, first to Argyll, who refused the command, and then to Lindsay, who employed them in futile raidings in Atholl.[2] The Providence which does not suffer fools gladly was preparing for them their reward.

In the last days of June, Baillie, having ravaged the Gordon lands, prepared to lay siege to Huntly's castle of Bog of Gight. The great keep, well defended by Gordon of Buckie, was in no real danger, but the position seemed to call for Montrose's intervention, especially as Lord Gordon had now returned with some 250 troopers. As he advanced he heard of the transfer which Baillie had been compelled to make to Lindsay, and he may have guessed at the tyranny of the peripatetic committee. He found the Covenanters at Keith, on the Deveron, drawn up on high ground, with a gap in front of them strongly held by horse and commanded by artillery. The royalists skirmished before the gap, and endeavoured to draw the enemy, but Baillie was too wise to move. Next morning Montrose sent him a challenge by a trumpeter, inviting the honour of an encounter in the levels, but Baillie replied that he was not in the habit of taking his marching orders from the enemy. Montrose accordingly broke up his camp and retired southward to Strathdon. He argued that Baillie

---

[1] Gordon of Ruthven, 128.
[2] "Vindication," Robert Baillie, *Letters and Journals*, II., 418-419. It is possible that Hume's regiment from Ireland (the Redcoats) may have been transferred because they were mutinous and half-hearted. See Gordon of Ruthven, *loc. cit.*

might be induced to follow if he saw his enemy marching away from the Gordon country in the direction of the Lowlands.

He was right in his guess, for Baillie had heard further news which cheered his spirit. Alasdair and most of the Irish were absent from the royal standard. Auldearn had put the fear of Ulster into the hearts of the Lowland foot, and, as the word sped through the ranks that the terrible Alasdair had gone, the courage of the Covenanters rose. With all speed they hastened south after the enemy, and early on the morning of the 2nd of July came up with him at Alford on the Don.

IV

Montrose had marched from Deveronside by the ancient Suie Road, which forded the Don at the village of Forbes, and was continued to Deeside by a path which, after the " Forty-five," became one of the specially constructed military highways. It was the straight route to Angus and the Lowlands, and Baillie believed that his enemy was in full retreat. South-west of the ford lay the Muir of Alford, with the kirk and smithy and ale-house which then constituted the hamlet of that name, two miles west of the present village.[1] Directly south of the ford stood an eminence called the Gallows Hill, sloping gently towards the north. On this hill Montrose stationed his army, concealing, as at Auldearn, the greater number behind the crest, so that to an enemy beyond the river it seemed an inconsiderable force. It was a strong position, for it was protected on the left rear by the marshy ravine of the Leochel burn. The upper Don, which in these days of surface draining is a shallow and easily crossed stream in the month of July, was then a far more formidable river, with long stretches of bog along its banks. The only good ford was the Boat of Forbes, and it was Montrose's intention that Baillie should cross there. His own position on Gallows Hill was a little to the south-west, and he calculated that Baillie, believing him to be weak in numbers, but not caring to face the direct ascent of the hill, would try to outflank him on the right. If he did, he had some marshy levels to traverse before he reached the *glacis* of Montrose's position, and a defeat would put his army in grave jeopardy, with a bog and a river behind it.

Baillie walked into the trap. But as soon as he crossed

[1] This dates only from 1859, when the railway was constructed.

the Don he observed that his adversary had altered his
alignment, and was now facing not north but north-east,
which would prevent the turning movement he had
designed. It is not easy to be certain of the numbers on
both sides. Lindsay's drafts had reduced Baillie to 1,200

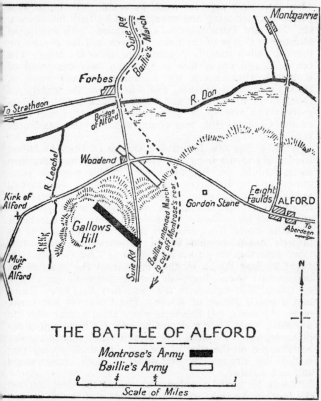

To Strathdon

To Aberdeen

Montgarrie

Forbes

Baillie's March

Suie Rd

R. Don

Bridge of Alford

R. Leochel

Woodend

Kirk of Alford

Gallows Hill

Suie Rd

Baillie's intended March to cut off Montrose's rear

Gordon Stane

Feight Faulds

ALFORD

Muir of Alford

N

THE BATTLE OF ALFORD

Montrose's Army
Baillie's Army

0   ¼   ½   1

Scale of Miles

foot, but that number must have been increased by levies
among the northern counties. We know that of first-line
material he had what remained of the regiments of Cassilis,
Lanark, and Glencairn.[1] Montrose's infantry after Alasdair's departure must have fallen well below 2,000, so it **is**

[1] *A. P. S.*, VI., i., 469.

probable that in foot the two forces were nearly equal.
The Gordon cavalry numbered about 250, and Baillie cannot have had less than from 400 to 500. One advantage
Montrose possessed; he had early notice of the enemy's
coming, and was able to make his dispositions at his leisure.
They were very different from Auldearn. The horse were
placed on each wing and strengthened by Irish musketeers.
On the right Lord Gordon commanded, with Nathaniel
Gordon in charge of the foot. Aboyne had the cavalry on
the left, with a small Irish contingent under O'Cahan. The
centre, drawn up in files of six deep, was composed of
Badenoch Highlanders, the Farquharsons, and some of
Huntly's lowland tenants, and was under the charge of
Drummond of Balloch and Angus Macdonald of Glen-
garry. The reserve of foot, concealed behind the ridge
of the Gallows Hill, was commanded by the Master of
Napier.

When Baillie saw Montrose's change of front he halted
irresolutely in the bog. He would probably have declined
battle had he not been overruled by his precious committee, and by Balcarres, his master of horse, who trusted
to the superiority of his cavalry. The latter was about to
charge under the committee's instructions, when Montrose
anticipated him. Baillie had brought along with him herds
of cattle looted from Huntly's lands, and the sight of his
father's beasts penned up in an enclosure behind the
Covenanters' camp infuriated the young Lord Gordon. He
swore to drag Baillie by the throat from the midst of his
bodyguard. Accordingly he led his horse to the charge
on the royalist right with the same fury that at Auldearn
had avenged James of Rynie. The Covenant left broke
under the onset, but Balcarres was a stout soldier who did
not easily yield. He managed to rally his three squadrons
of horse, and for a little a fierce and well-matched cavalry
battle raged on the edge of the bog. It would appear that
during this struggle the remainder of both armies stood
still and watched.

It was Nathaniel Gordon who turned the tide. He led
the foot on the right wing to the support of the horse, and
he conceived a better way of support than by firing into
the mass, where they were in great danger of wounding
their own side. He cried to his men to fling down their
muskets, draw their swords, and stab and hough Balcarres's
horses. The cruel device succeeded. The Covenant
troopers broke and fled, and the Gordons turned their

swords, as at Auldearn, against the unprotected left flank of Baillie's infantry. Meanwhile Aboyne, with his horse, had at length charged on Montrose's left, and O'Cahan's Irish followed. The two royalist wings closed in on the Covenant centre, and against it also Glengarry led the Gordon foot. The turn of the battle had arrived. Baillie's veteran regiments, having reduced their files to three to prevent outflanking, were utterly overborne. It needed only the advance of the Master of Napier with his reserve to turn the defeat of the Covenant into a rout. The very camp-boys in the royalist army mounted the baggage ponies and took their share in the confusion. Baillie and Balcarres, with their surviving cavalry, escaped by the skin of their teeth. Argyll, on his third horse, just evaded Glengarry's sword.[1] The Lowland foot remained to die on the field. All day the pursuit continued through the Howe of Alford and far down the Don.[2]

On the Covenant side the slaughter fell little short of Auldearn. The royalists, considering how desperate was the cavalry battle, lost curiously few officers and men, but they sustained one loss which made the victory little better than a defeat. Lord Gordon, determined to avenge the theft of his father's cattle, charged the retreating horse once too often. His aim was to capture Baillie, and he was actually seizing that general by the sword-belt when he was shot dead from behind—whether by accident or design will never be known. His death threw the royalist army, more especially Montrose and the Gordons, into the uttermost grief. He had been the young Marcellus of the cause, the one hope of the North. Aboyne stopped his pursuit of Balcarres, and—in Wishart's words—" forgetting their victory and the spoil, they fixed their eyes upon the lifeless body, kissed his face and hands, commended the singular beauty of the corpse, compared the nobility of his descent and the plentifulness of his fortune with the hopefulness of his parts, and counted that an unfortunate victory that had stood them in so much." It

[1] *Clanranald MSS.*
[2] The contemporary authorities for the battle are Wishart (ch. xi.), Gordon of Ruthven (128, etc.), and the *Clanranald MSS.* Mr. Gardiner's ingenious reconstruction (*Civil War*, II., 280-283) is vitiated by his assumption that the village of Alford was the modern village, which puts all his topography awry. The account of Wishart, which he rejects, seems to be literally accurate. I am greatly indebted to a convincing article on the subject by the librarian of Aberdeen University, Dr. W. Douglas Simpson, in the *Aberdeen University Review* for June 1919.

was a sorrowful band that, led by Montrose, took its way
slowly to Aberdeen, where the young lord was laid in the
Gordon aisle of the old church of St. Machar. He was
only twenty-eight years of age, and had spent his short
span of life cleanly and chivalrously in the service of his
country. To Montrose the loss was irreparable, for Lord
Gordon was the one man who in temper and attainments
was fitted to be his companion. Patrick of Ruthven, a
clansman, has described that noble friendship in arms:

" Never two of so slight acquaintance did ever love more dearly.
There seemed to be a harmonious sympathy in their natural dispositions, so much were they delighted in a mutual conversation. And
in this the Lord Gordon seemed to go beyond the limits which
Nature had allowed for his carriage in civil conversation. So real
was his affection, and so great the estimation he had of the other
that, when they fell into any familiar discourse, it was often remarked that the ordinary air of his countenance was changed from
a serious listening to a certain ravishment or admiration of the
other's witty expressions. And he was often heard in public to speak
sincerely, and confirm it with oaths, that if the fortune of the present
war should prove at any time so dismal that Montrose, for safety,
should be forced to fly into the mountains without any army or any
one to assist him, he would live with him as an outlaw, and would
prove as faithful a consort to drive away his malour, as he was then
a helper to the advancement of his fortunes."[1]

V

The armies of Baillie and Hurry had ceased to exist.
To be sure there was still Lindsay, but he was hardly to
be taken seriously. The news of Alford, when it reached
the south-west of England, roused the drooping spirits of
Charles. " It is certain," Digby wrote, " that the king's
enemies have not any man in the field now in Scotland."[2]
Charles had need of heartening, for his cause, whether he
realized it or not, had received its deathblow. Shortly
after Alford, Montrose had news—perhaps from his friend
Thomas Saintserf, who, disguised as a packman, travelled
between his camp and the Border[3]—of a cataclysmic
disaster in the English midlands. On the 14th of June, at
Naseby, Cromwell's " company of poor ignorant men "[4]

[1] Gordon of Ruthven, 138. The character of the dead boy on
pp. 131-132 is one of the great passages of seventeenth-century prose.
[2] Digby to Rupert, July 28, 1645, cited by Gardiner, Civil War,
II., 283.
[3] Saintserf seems to have travelled as a theological colporteur. See
The Covent Garden Drollery, 1672:

" When to the great Montrose under pretence
Of godly books thou broughtst intelligence."

[4] Letters and Speeches (ed. Lomas), III., 247.

had scattered Rupert's chivalry and annihilated the royal foot. The battle had two vital consequences for Scotland. It was Cromwell's first clear personal triumph, and it enabled him to press on with his policy of religious toleration which must sooner or later destroy the tyranny of the Covenant.[1] On the other hand, it put an end to the danger of Charles's advance to the north, and Leven was able to withdraw his army from Westmoreland and march south in his leisurely way to the siege of Hereford, very anxious lest the slaughter of the Irish women after Naseby should be made a precedent by malignants for reprisals on the immense female concourse which accompanied the Scots.[2] Moreover, on the 28th of June Carlisle, after a heroic defence, capitulated to David Leslie, and thereby released for service elsewhere a veteran force of horse and foot, and a general who had none of Leven's timidity. If the royal standard was still to fly in Britain, it was high time that Montrose crossed the Border.

CHAPTER XII

KILSYTH

(*July-August* 1645)

When we look back upon the great things which God hath done for us, and our former deliverances out of dangers and difficulties, which to us appeared insurmountable, experience breeds hope; and when we consider how, in the midst of all our sorrows and troubles, the Lord our God hath lightened our eyes with the desirable and beautiful sight of His own glory in His temple, we take it for an argument that He hath yet thoughts of peace and a purpose of mercy towards us. Though for a small moment He hath forsaken us, yet with great mercies He will gather us. He hath lifted up our enemies that their fall may be the greater, and that He may cast them down into desolation for ever. Arise! and let us be doing. The Lord of Hosts is with us, the God of Jacob is our refuge!

Proclamation of the General Assembly, 1645.

THE COVENANT MADE ONE LAST EFFORT TO RIDE THE STORM. The plague had broken out in Edinburgh, so Parliament was compelled to move to Stirling on the 8th of July.

[1] Cromwell to Lenthall. *Letters and Speeches* (ed. Lomas), I., 206.
[2] He was said to have had a following of 4,000 women and children. Nicholas to Rupert, July 11, 1645, cited by Gardiner, *Civil War*, II., 264 *n.*

H

Stirling, however, proved no refuge, and the seat of government was transferred to Perth.[1] Fresh orders were sent to the nobles and gentry of the Lowlands, and an Act was passed to levy a new army of 10,000 foot and 500 horse, a considerable part of which was appointed to assemble at Perth on the 24th of July. Baillie had brought back no infantry from his last campaign, but he had saved a respectable cavalry contingent, probably at least 400 strong. He had returned in a sullen temper, and had resigned his office; but Parliament passed a vote of thanks to him for his services, and insisted on his taking command of the new levies. For his comfort it appointed the usual committee " to advise," a phrase which, as Baillie well knew, meant to dictate. Among the sixteen members were Argyll, Tullibardine, and Burleigh—experts in their way, for all had already suffered at Montrose's hands.[2]

Alford was fought on the royalist side lacking Alasdair and most of his Irish, the western clans, and the Atholl men. For the final assault on the Lowlands it was necessary to collect all available forces. This meant some weeks of waiting at the shortest, and Aboyne was dispatched to Strathbogie to enlist troopers. He made little speed, either because the Gordons were disinclined to fight south of the Highland Line, or because he was a poor recruiting sergeant, and Montrose had to send him back to try again. Aboyne is a difficult figure to decipher on the page of history. He was devoutly loyal to the king's service; his gallantry was beyond question; but he had much of the intractable and suspicious temper of his brother Lewis and his father Huntly. The fine flower of the Gordon race had gone with the young lord. Montrose waited for a few days at Craigton,[3] on the south side of the Hill of Fare (where is a spot still called Montrose's Trench), till the news of the muster and the session at Perth decided him to go south. It was a sovran chance to strike at the heart of the opposition.

[1] The plague soon reached Perth, as it did nearly every Lowland town. The beautiful ballad of *Bessie Bell and Mary Gray* refers to this summer.   [2] Balfour, III., 294.

[3] Wishart (ch. xii.) gives " Craigston," and Napier, who is followed by Mr. Gardiner, assumes that he marched north to Craigston castle in Buchan, a detour of thirty miles, which would have been impossible in the time. Montrose, in his letter of 6th July, calls it " Craigtoune." *Mem. of M.*, II., 214. Murdoch and Simpson identify the place with Craigton on Dee, seven miles from Aberdeen, but the Hill of Fare site is confirmed by the kirk session records of the neighbouring parish of Echt. See Mr. George Duncan's paper in *Scottish Notes and Queries* for March 1903.

He forded Dee, and marched through the hills to Fordoun in the Mearns, where he waited to receive his expected allies. They arrived in good force. Alasdair

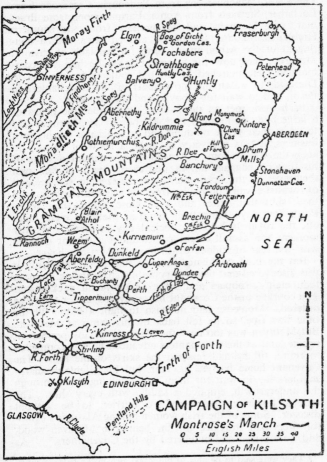

CAMPAIGN OF KILSYTH

Montrose's March

0 5 10 15 20 25 30 35 40

English Miles

brought the rest of his Irish, and a body of Highlanders some 1,500 strong. Among them came the ever-faithful Macdonalds of Clanranald and Glengarry, and not less

than 700 Macleans from Mull, under their chiefs Lachlan
of Duart and Murdoch of Lochbuie. This warrior clan
as a fighting force was second only to the Ulstermen.[1]
There were Macphersons from Badenoch, Camerons from
Lochaber, Stewarts from Appin, Farquharsons from Brae-
mar, and Macnabs and Macgregors from the southern
Highlands. Young Inchbrakie arrived later with a con-
tingent of the Atholl men. Save for his lack of cavalry,
Montrose had now the strongest force he had yet com-
manded. He marched by his old route down the Isla to
Dunkeld, to watch the movements of the Covenanters in
Perth, and to wait for Aboyne and the Gordons.

Parliament met on the 24th of July under the guard of
a large body of infantry and 400 horse. If Montrose was
to upset their peace of mind and have leisure for his own
business, it was necessary to make a show of cavalry to
keep the 400 at home. Accordingly he mounted some of
his foot on baggage horses, and as the Perth citizens cast
their eyes to the north they were amazed to see a cloud
of royalist cavalry on the horizon. It was sufficient to make
them shut their gates and keep close within their walls.
For a few days, from their camp at Methven eight miles
off, the royalists held the ancient city in terror. At any
moment the assault might come, and Parliament debated
with the fear of sudden death in each debater's heart.

But the bluff could not be long sustained. Presently it
was discovered that the cavalry were a sham, being no more
than eighty troopers and some amateurs on pack-horses.
The courage of the Covenant horse revived, and a sally was
ordered. Montrose had no wish to fight a battle till the
time was ripe, so he fell back on his camp at Methven.
But Methven was too near the plains to be any permanent
refuge, and as the Covenanters advanced he was compelled
to retire, till he had reached the skirts of the hills. The
Covenant horse harried his rear, but his Highland sharp-
shooters lay in wait for them, and, stalking them through
the undergrowth, emptied a saddle with every shot. The
retreat, however, had been too hurried to be without
disaster. Some of the Irish women among Alasdair's camp-
followers had straggled too far behind in Methven wood,
and were seized and butchered by the Covenanters.[2] " As

[1] They were said to be able to put 2,000 men in the field. Napier,
II., 654 *n*.
[2] Wishart (ch. xii.) is the only authority for the massacre, but,
except when he tries to expound a battle which he does not quite

at Naseby," says Mr. Gardiner, " the notion of avenging injured morality probably covered from the eyes of the murderers the inherent brutality of their act."[1]   But these poor creatures were no painted madams of the court, but the womenfolk of humble soldiers, who followed their fathers, husbands, and lovers for the same motive that had attracted Scotswomen in hundreds to the tail of Leven's army in England.

For a week Montrose waited at Dunkeld till Aboyne arrived with 200 Gordon cavalry and 120 musketeers mounted on baggage ponies. These latter were the equivalent of the dragoons of the New Model Army, and acted both as light cavalry and as mounted infantry.[2]   Not the least welcome was old Lord Airlie, now recovered from his sickness, who rode in with 80 of his Ogilvys, including his son, Sir David Ogilvy of Baldovie, and young Alexander of Inverquharity.   Montrose now commanded a force of at least 4,400 foot and 500 cavalry,[3] a seasoned force, for all were tough fighting men, and the thousand Irish were probably the best infantry at the time in Britain. Most of the troops had, under his leadership, been present at more than one victory, and all had wrongs to avenge on some section or another of the Covenanters. It was the first time, with the exception of Alford, that he had commanded an army comparable in the strength of all arms to its opponents.

Meanwhile Baillie at Perth was in a sombre and distrustful mood. He thought little of his new levies, and he was distracted by his committee of advice. He considered that he could have cut off Montrose from the hills in his sally from Perth but for the negligence of Hurry and his cavalry. Once again he resigned, and once again he was induced to withdraw his resignation. Montrose marched by way of Logiealmond to have a look at the enemy, and the

understand, he is an accurate chronicler. He may well have had the account of it from the Irish after Kilsyth, and, as Murdoch and Simpson point out, the latter showed great exasperation afterwards in their march past the Ochils.   [1] *Civil War*, II., 292-293.

[2] Fortescue, *Hist. of the British Army*, I., 216.

[3] Wishart makes the Gordon contingent 200 horse and 120 mounted musketeers. Gordon of Ruthven, who generally overstates the Gordon strength, gives them 400 horse. Montrose had nearly 100 horse before they joined (Wishart), and Ogilvy brought 80. Gordon probably included the musketeers among the Gordon cavalry. Five hundred seems a reasonable estimate for the total mounted strength of the royalists. Hope, the Lord Advocate, gives them 3,500 foot and 600 horse. *Miscellany* (S.H.S.), I., 128.

Covenanters promptly retired to their fortified camp of Kilgraston on the Earn. As Montrose followed at his leisure by way of the field of Tippermuir, he had news which determined his strategy. The Covenant was making a desperate bid for success. Cassilis, nicknamed the "Solemn," a zealot of the old rock; Eglinton, called "Grey Steel," one of the chief promoters of the Solemn League; Glencairn, the eternal Laodicean whose actions no man could forecast—were raising the Covenanting westlands. Lanark had collected the Hamilton tenantry, and with 1,000 foot and 500 horse was hastening from Clydesdale. Baillie's army was already superior in numbers to his own, and Montrose did not wish the odds to be too great, for he realized as well as did the Covenant that on the coming fight must depend the future of the king's cause in Scotland. He resolved, therefore, to fling himself between Baillie and Lanark. Baillie was lying at Kilgraston waiting on the Fife regiments. If he fought him now, he would still have the men of Fife to deal with, not to speak of Lanark. If he cut off the Fife men, he would still have Baillie, and during these manœuvres Lanark would have arrived. The wiser plan was to let Baillie get his Fife recruits, and then cut him off from the west. Besides, the farther he could draw the Fife levies from their own country, the less stomach would those home-keeping souls have for fighting.[1] Lanark he knew of old, and he may well have argued that, if he routed Baillie, he could have little to fear from the Hamiltons.

On or about the 10th of August Montrose, having crossed the Earn between Dupplin and Forteviot, swept down Glenfarg to the neighbourhood of Kinross. Baillie must have guessed that he had gone to cut off the Fife recruits, but the arrival of these levies presently in his camp convinced him that this was not Montrose's aim. Then came the news that the grim tower of Castle Campbell, above Dollar, an Argyll possession, had been sacked and burned.[2] While the Covenanters lay at the north-east end of the Ochils, Montrose was turning the southern flank.

[1] The poor fighting quality of the Fife levies was a byword at the time. Some of them had already given Baillie trouble in the advance to Methven. Robert Baillie, *Letters and Journals*, II., 419. Wishart calls them "minus bellicosi." If we are to trust the *Clanranald MSS.*, Baillie had a number of sailors in his command, "who never fought on land before that time," and these could only have come from Fife.

[2] Young Ewen Cameron of Lochiel was in the castle at the time.

He could only have one object—to get to the west of
Baillie and frustrate his junction with Lanark. Further
tidings of him came from the lands of Lord Mar, who was
the father-in-law of the Master of Napier. In so large a
force Montrose could not exercise the personal supervision
which is possible in a small army, and the Irish seem to
have got out of hand, for they plundered the little town
of Alloa and some of the Mar holdings. Mar, however,
bore no grudge, for, while Alasdair led on the foot in
advance, he invited Montrose and his staff to dine with
him at Alloa House.

By this time Baillie had made up his mind. As Montrose
was at dinner he received the intelligence that the Covenanters were marching with all speed along the north side of
the Ochils to cut him off. It was vital to his strategy that
he should keep ahead of them, so, hastily catching up his
foot, he led his army that night across the Forth by the
Fords of Frew, a few miles above Stirling. Next day he
continued his march in the direction of Glasgow, passing
over the field of Bannockburn, and by the evening of the
14th of August was encamped in an upland meadow on the
Colzium burn, one of the affluents of the river Kelvin,
about a mile north-east of the town of Kilsyth. He argued
that it was now Baillie's business to find him and fight him,
for the Covenanters must pass beneath him before they
could join Lanark, who was marching from Glasgow.

Baillie, making the best possible speed past Dunblane
and down the Allan Water, was compelled by Argyll to
waste time in burning Lord Stirling's castle of Menstrie,
and the Graham house of Airth.[1] He found, as he expected, that the presence of the committee made discipline
almost impossible. That band of heroes was now enlarged,
and included Argyll, Lindsay, Burleigh, Tullibardine, Balcarres, and Elcho; Montrose had beaten them all except
Lindsay, whom as yet he had only scared. The Fife levies,
too, grew more out of humour and spirit with every mile
that increased the distance from their homes. On the evening of the 14th he was encamped at Hollinbush, on the

[1] Argyll denied this at his trial in 1661, but he also denied the
similar case of Forthar, which is proved from his own letter of
instructions. See p. 100, *supra*. Baillie seems to confirm the story.
" Did they (the Committee of Advice) not in that capacity sometimes
commend . . . such acts of hostility as I, without a special warrant
from the Estates (though I had been in charge by commission), could
not now have answered but at the rate of my head? " Robert
Baillie, II., 424.

road from Stirling, only two and a half miles from where Montrose lay. His scouts—for he was in a friendly country —had kept him well informed of the enemy's whereabouts, and a great dispute arose in the committee. Baillie, realizing the gravity of the coming engagement, was for taking no risks, and waiting till Lanark, now only twelve miles distant, brought up his reinforcements. But Argyll and his colleagues would brook no delay. They had 6,000 foot and 800 horse. They were in the Lowlands at last; Lanark, at the latest, would be with them in a few hours; Montrose had the Forth behind him to cut off his retreat to the Highlands; he lay in a hollow, and had left the higher ground unoccupied. Let them strike home at once, and Lanark, when he arrived, would help to take order with the fugitives.

It had been a hot summer, the weather that breeds pestilence, and the bent on the hills was as yellow as grain. The dawn of the 15th was windless and cloudless, giving promise of a scorching August day. With the first light the Covenanters were on the move. They left the road and made straight across country in the direction of Montrose's camp, wading through fields of ripening bear and oats, and scrambling up the slopes of the Campsie Hills. Soon they reached the rim of the basin where the royalists lay, and Baillie, believing his men to be tired by the rough journey, would have preferred to halt in what seemed an impregnable position. He held the high ground, and below him the hill fell steeply to the little burn, beyond which lay Montrose. But the military genius of the committee conceived a plan. A quarter of a mile to the right the glen closed in, and the burn descended through a narrow ravine. They believed that Montrose was doomed to defeat, and their only fear was lest he should escape to the north, for there was still a way open to the Highlands through Menteith. If they could outflank him and take up a position on the ridge due north from his left, he would be pinned inexorably between them and the Lowlands.

As Montrose watched the enemy's doings he was content with the ground he had chosen. He had left the higher ridge unoccupied as a bait to draw his opponents into action. He did not believe that Baillie would charge down the steep; if he did, the use of horse on such ground was impossible, and he could guess the condition in which the heavily accoutred Lowland infantry would arrive at the bottom. He believed that the Covenanters would simply

wait for Lanark, and he had made up his mind to charge
their position, since the slopes of the Campsies were nothing
to men who knew Glencoe and the Rough Bounds. He
asked his army whether they were for retreat or fight, and
the fierce cry for battle assured him of their spirit. Fore-
seeing the heat of the day, he bade his Highlanders cast
their plaids and fight in their coarse saffron shirts, knotting
up the long tails of the latter between their legs to give
them freedom of action.[1] His horse he ordered to wear
their shirts above their buff jerkins in order that they might
be easily distinguishable from the enemy. It was a necessary precaution in an army of many different levies, where
the separate parts were scarcely known to each other.
Alasdair's men in the heat of battle must have some clear
mark to distinguish friend from foe, or regrettable incidents
might occur. Near the head of the glen, and on the hill
where the Covenanters stood, were several cottages and
little gardens walled with dry-stone dykes.[2] It was a sort
of Hougoumont, a place which any prudent commander
must seize, so he ordered its occupation by an advance
guard of Alasdair's centre, which happened to be a body
of a hundred Macleans, under Ewen of Treshnish.

But as Montrose watched the crest of the hill he observed
the Covenanters in motion. He could scarcely believe his
eyes when he perceived that they were about to attempt a
flank march across his front. It is never a safe or an easy
manœuvre, more especially when the foe is almost within
musket shot, and in mobility and speed is the superior of
the side attempting it. Baillie bitterly protested, and he
was supported by Balcarres, but the committee would have
their way, and for the rest of the day he was carrying out
orders not his own. To reach the hill directly above
Montrose's left it was necessary to make the circuit of the
glen and cross the ravine of the burn. The movement was
led by Balcarres and the horse, and Baillie, accompanied
by Lindsay and Burleigh, followed close behind with the
foot. His three field-pieces, which might have been of
incalculable value in covering the movement, were apparently forgotten.

On one condition alone might such a course have succeeded. If the Covenanters had kept behind the ridge in
their march, leaving a small force to occupy their old

---

[1] *Clanranald MSS.* For the Highland costume in battle, see
Gardiner, II., 296, and M. & S., 213.
[2] On the present farms of Auchinrivoch and Auchinvally.

position on the crest of the hill, they might have safely reached their goal; and once there, with a gradual slope before them on which horse could be used, they would have seriously embarrassed Montrose. But such tactics

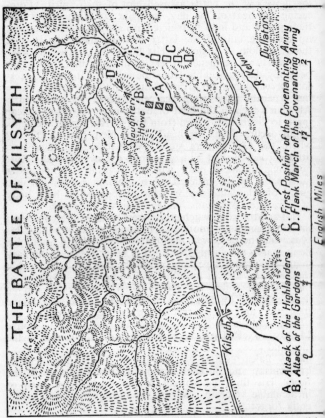

needed a speed and a precision which the Covenanters did not possess. Almost at once they were visible to the royalists below, owing to a grave breach of discipline. A certain Major Haldane, observing the cottages which Tresh-nish had occupied, decided, on his own authority, that he must attack the position. Accordingly, with a handful of

musketeers, he broke off from the main march and started
down the hill. He was soon driven back, but it was never
the Highland way to repel without a counterstroke. Alasdair launched the whole body of Macleans against the
assailants, and they were at once followed by their old
rivals, the Macdonalds of Clanranald, who vied with them
in the race for the ridge. Young Donald of Moidart won,
but Lachlan of Duart was little behind. On surged the
billow of Celtic war till it struck the Covenant line in the
middle. Colonel Hume, who commanded there, drew four
foot regiments—his own, Argyll's, Cassilis', and Glencairn's
—behind some dykes on the hill-top, and attempted a
stand. But the Highlanders leapt the walls with their
targes high and their heads down, and in a few minutes the
Covenant centre was in flight. Alasdair's breach of orders
had succeeded beyond its deserts, and Baillie's army was
cut in two.

Meanwhile the Covenant van had crossed the burn and
rounded the head of the glen. Montrose, who at first can
only have guessed at the aim of the flank movement, now
saw clearly its motive. It was impossible to let the enemy
occupy the height on his left, so he dispatched a body of
Gordon foot, under their adjutant, to forestall them. The
bulk of Balcarres's horse must have been still behind the
ridge, for if Montrose had seen their full force he would
have attempted to hold the hill in greater strength. The
Gordons found the task beyond their power. They were
driven back, and to the eyes of Aboyne—whom Montrose,
remembering Lord Gordon's fate at Alford, had kept at
the rear with a strong bodyguard—seemed to be caught in
a death-trap. He broke away with the Gordon horse to
the assistance of his kinsmen.[1] But he, too, was surrounded, so Montrose called upon Airlie and his Ogilvys
to redeem the day. The gallant old man, for all his sixty
years, led his troopers to the charge, and the tide of battle
on the hill began to turn. Then Montrose dispatched
Nathaniel Gordon with the remainder of the cavalry, seeing
that Alasdair was having his own way in the rest of the
field. Balcarres's cuirassiers were driven off the ridge, the
advance foot were routed, and the Covenant van shared
the fate of the Covenant centre.

Baillie was soon aware that the day was lost. Haldane's
escapade brought him racing back from Balcarres's side,

[1] Wishart seems to imply some hesitation in the Gordon cavalry,
but he is not an unprejudiced witness.

but the mischief had been done. He endeavoured in vain to rally the foot at the ravine of the burn, and then in despair galloped to the rear for the Fife reserves. But the men of Fife had early despaired of the issue, and were in full flight for their homes. About the same time Montrose's trumpets sounded the general advance. The whole royalist army swept up the hill, but no foe awaited them on the crest. The semicircle of the little amphitheatre was empty, and the outside rim was strewn with fleeing horse and foot. Of the 6,000 men who had set out that morning to fight under the Covenant's banner only a few hundreds escaped. The murder of their women in Methven wood had not disposed Ulsterman or Highlander to a mercy which they knew would never be extended to themselves. Many of the horse, too, perished, caught in the mires of Dullatur. The leaders escaped, as commonly happened in the Covenant's battles. The lairds and nobles had better horses, and they had no scruple of honour in saving their own necks and leaving the plain folk, who had trusted them, to die on the field. Well for themselves that the western Covenanters were too late for the fight and had ample time to escape. Lanark fled to Berwick, Glencairn and Cassilis to Ireland. Baillie and Holbourn sought sanctuary in Stirling castle, where they were joined by Balcarres, Burleigh, and Tullibardine. Loudoun and Lindsay posted to England. Argyll galloped twenty miles to Queensferry on the Forth, where he found a boat which landed him in Berwick in the safe keeping of the Scots garrison. As at Inverary and at Inverlochy, he escaped by water from Montrose's swords.[1]

The decisive battle had at last been fought. So far as Scotland was concerned, the forces of the Covenant were annihilated, and its leaders were in exile. Scarcely a year had passed since that August evening when, with two companions, Montrose had alighted at the door of Tullibelton —without men, money, or prospects, and with no resources for his wild mission save the gallantry of his heart. Since then he had scourged the Covenant from Lorn to Buchan, and from Lochaber to Angus. With halting allies and few troops, with poor weapons and scanty ammunition, amid

[1] The contemporary authorities for the battle are Wishart (ch. xiii.), Gordon of Ruthven (137, etc.), the *Clanranald MSS.*, and Baillie's own account (*Letters and Journals*, II., 420, etc.). Mr. Gardiner, from a careful inspection of the ground, has produced what must be taken as the final account of the tactics (*Civil War*, II., 295-300).

broken promises and private sorrows and endless dis-
appointments, he had sought out his enemies and had
beaten them wherever he found them. He had excelled
them in strategy and in tactics, in cavalry and in infantry
movements, in the offensive and the defensive. He had
shown himself able to adapt his slender resources to any
emergency, and to rise superior to any misfortune. His
reward had come. For the moment he was the undisputed
master of all Scotland.

CHAPTER XIII

THE WAR ON THE BORDER

(*August-September* 1645)

Had one seen him returning from a victory, he would by his silence
have suspected that he had lost the day; and had he beheld him in
retreat, he would have collected him a conqueror by the cheerfulness
of his spirit.   THOMAS FULLER.

I

" I PROFESS TO YOU," WROTE DIGBY TO JERMYN ON THE 21ST
of September, a month after Kilsyth, " I never did look
upon our business with that assurance that I do now, of
God's carrying us through with His own immediate hand,
for all this work of Montrose is above what can be attributed to mankind."[1] To Charles, uneasily moving about
the Welsh marches, the star that had arisen in the north
seemed to herald a better dawn. Even at that late hour
it is clear that, if there had been any other royalist leader
with a tithe of Montrose's genius, the king's crown need not
have fallen. But from England he received only empty
praise. What had become of Sir Philip Musgrave's 500
horse, what of the 1,500 men whom Digby had promised?
Montrose had been true to his word; he had scattered the
Covenant in Scotland, and deprived Leven and Leslie of
a base. But to " fix his conquests " was beyond the power
of mortal man unless help came from the south. He himself thought otherwise. He hoped still to lead a great army
across the Border, and redress the sinking balance in

[1] Digby to Jermyn, *Bankes MSS.*, cit. by Gardiner *Civil War*, II.,
344 *n.*

Charles's favour. He had no fear of his antagonists;
" though God should rain Leslies from Heaven, he would
fight them."[1] But his courage outran the possibilities.
Scotland was subdued, not converted, and, unless the king
came north as a conqueror, Montrose would have to wrestle
daily and desperately to hold her to her unwilling allegiance. Never in history have Highlands dominated Lowlands for long.

But at first the prospect had a delusive brightness. After
waiting two days at Kilsyth, during which he sent a message
of assurance to the city of Glasgow, the victorious general
entered the capital of the west. Here, seven years before,
had been held the General Assembly at which episcopacy
in Scotland had been abolished, and Montrose, in his
Presbyterian zeal, had shown himself the foremost in the
baiting of Hamilton. The place had never evinced the
fanatic virulence of Edinburgh. Pride in their great church,
happily saved from the iconoclasts, had kept its citizens on
the side of decency and temperance in religious affairs. A
deputation from the town council met the king's lieutenant
outside the walls, offering the value of £500 in English
money as a largesse to the soldiers, and praying that the
city might be left unmolested. To this request Montrose
readily agreed. He issued stringent orders against theft
and violence, and his entry was welcomed with a popular
enthusiasm hardly to be looked for in the Lowlands.
Zachary Boyd, that erratic singer of Israel, wrote Latin
verses in his honour. Unfortunately the sight of the well-
stocked booths and the prosperous dwellings of the Salt-
market and the Gallowgate was too much for some of his
followers, who had not believed that so much wealth existed
in the world, and could not readily forget their Highland
creed that spoil should follow victory. Looting began, and
Montrose, true to his word, promptly hanged several of the
malefactors. But he saw that Glasgow would prove too
severe a trial to his army, so two days after his arrival,
about the 20th of August, he marched six miles up the river
to Bothwell.

Here he took measures for the government of Scotland,
which the fortunes of war had entrusted to his hands. The
first business was to stamp out the embers of disaffection.
Some of Eglinton's levies were still threatening in the west,
and Alasdair was dispatched to bring them to reason. He
met with no opposition, and to his surprise was welcomed

[1] Row, *Life of Blair*, 176.

cordially at Loudoun castle by the wife of the Covenanting chancellor. The shires and burghs of Renfrew and Ayr sent in their submission and petitioned for favour.[1] Other towns and counties followed suit, and presently arrived the nobles and gentry to greet the rising sun. The midlands of Scotland were naturally foremost. Loyalists like Seton[2] and Fleming and Erskine, cautious men like Linlithgow and Carnegie and Maderty, declared opponents like Drummond, who had commanded the Covenant horse at Tippermuir, hastened to Bothwell. More important were the recruits from the south, the nobles whom Montrose had solicited in vain at Dumfries the year before. Annandale and Hartfell swore allegiance, as did powerful lairds like Charteris of Amisfield, and those Border earls, Roxburgh and Home, who for the past four years had coquetted with both king and Covenant. Traquair, another waverer, sent his son, Lord Linton, with the promise of a troop of horse. Carnwath's brother, Sir John Dalziel, brought the wildest blood in the Lowlands to the standard. And to crown all came the Marquis of Douglas, who, as Lord Angus, had been the travelling companion of Montrose's youth. The prestige of the Bloody Heart had not wholly died even in an age which had tried to bolt the door on the past, and the vast Douglas lands in Clydesdale and Dumfries promised a rich recruiting ground.

There were other allies to be gathered. At the earliest opportunity the Master of Napier and Nathaniel Gordon were dispatched Edinburghwards on a gaol delivery. From the prison of Linlithgow they released Lord Napier and Stirling of Keir, and the ladies of the Napier and Stirling families. Arrived within four miles of Edinburgh, they summoned the city in the king's name, and received the humble submission of a deputation from the town council. A money fine was offered, and it was explained that the city had been driven into rebellion against its will by the craft of a few seditious men. The plague, which was still raging, had sapped all civic valour, and Edinburgh was ready to promise anything for peace. The Tolbooth was full of royalists, and during the year death and sickness had raged in that noisome place. Crawford, Ogilvy, Reay, Irvine of Drum, Ogilvy of Powrie, and Wishart the chap-

---

[1] Guthry, 195. Metcalfe, *History of Renfrew* (1905).

[2] The house of Winton was always loyal and always on the losing side, and came to final disaster in 1715. The Eglintons (paternally Setons) were more worldly-wise.

lain were among those set free, and the released captives, white and gaunt as a bone, stumbled out into the sunlight. Wishart never forgot the experience. It made him, as he said, " a friend of prisoners for ever "; in later years he could not enjoy a good meal at his episcopal table till he had sent part of it to the Tolbooth; and he bore the marks of the rats' teeth to his grave. One captive they did not recover. The young Lord Graham was in the castle, and the castle was still in Covenant hands. The gallant boy refused an exchange, declaring that it would ill become one so young and useless to deprive his father of a single prisoner.[1]

Napier and Gordon had another mission to execute in the east. They carried a letter from Montrose to Drummond of Hawthornden, begging for a copy of his *Irene*, the pamphlet written in 1638 during Montrose's Covenanting days, that it might be printed and published " to the contentment of all His Majesty's good subjects."[2] He had already granted him a special protection for his house and property. The old poet promised to transcribe and send the paper, " since, by the mercy of God on your Excellency's victorious arms, the Golden Age is returned "; but before it arrived Scotland was back in the age of iron.[3]

By the 1st of September Napier and Gordon, with their released prisoners, were in the camp at Bothwell. On that day Sir Robert Spottiswoode, the king's secretary for Scotland, arrived with letters from Charles. He brought with him a patent, dated at Hereford on the 25th of June, creating Montrose lieutenant-governor and captain-general of Scotland.[4] The royal instructions were to join the Border earls and march with all haste to Tweed. As these had been issued before Alford and Kilsyth, they seemed to Montrose to have redoubled force, now that he was master of all Scotland. Besides, Home and Roxburgh had written pleading with him to come to Tweedside and add their spears to his standard. Every prospect seemed rosy, and Montrose dispatched a post to the king, announcing that he hoped speedily to cross the Border with 20,000 men. On the 3rd of September he held a great review of

[1] Thomas Saintserf, in his dedication to the second marquis of his translation of the *Entertainments of the Course* (London, 1658). See Napier, II., 563.

[2] It was not published till it appeared in the folio edition of Drummond's works in 1711.

[3] Masson, *Drummond of Hawthornden*, 405.

[4] *Hist. MSS. Comm.*, 2nd Report, 173.

his troops in Bothwell haugh, when the royal commission
was presented to the viceroy and handed for proclamation
to Sir Archibald Primrose, the founder of the family of
Rosebery. Montrose's first act under his new patent was
to confer upon Alasdair the honour of knighthood. He
had nobly earned it. The next four months of blundering
in Argyll were to show how little of a general the Ulsterman was on his own account. Two years later he was to
disappear from history, stabbed in the back in an obscure
Irish fray. But as Montrose's chief brigadier he was
worth an army, and his stand at Auldearn will live as long
as feats of valour can stir the hearts of men.

As soon as the king's commission was received, Montrose, as viceroy of Scotland, took steps for the administration of the government. He had already in the king's name
assured loyalists in the possession of lands which Argyll
or the Estates had threatened.[1] He now issued proclamation to the chief towns, summoning a Parliament to be
held in Glasgow on the 20th of October following, " for
settling religion and peace, and freeing the oppressed
subjects of those insupportable burdens they have groaned
under this time bygone." He prepared also a statement
which he probably intended to present to Parliament when
it assembled.[2] It is on the lines of his Dumfries manifesto,
but a fuller and clearer confession of faith. He repeats
the justification of the National Covenant—the evils of an
unnatural and enforced prelacy, under which ecclesiastics
intermeddled with civil government, and " the life of the
Gospel was stolen away by enforcing on the Kirk a dead
service book." To every line of that Covenant he still
adhered, but long ago its mission was accomplished. First
at Berwick and then at Ripon the king had granted all their
demands. Further no true Covenanter could go, for the
cause of the Covenant was also the cause of king and
country. All that had been done since had been alien to
the true Covenant spirit, and every honest man must needs
part company with its perverters. " We were constrained
to suffer them to deviate without us, with the multitude
misled by them, whose eyes they seal in what concerns
religion, and whose hearts they steal away in what concerns

---

[1] e.g., he issued letters of assurance to Alan Maclean of Ardgour.
Highland Papers (S.H.S.), I., 333-334.
[2] The document is printed in *Mem. of M.*, I., 215, and Napier,
I., App. III. It is in the elder Lord Napier's handwriting, but the
context makes it clear that Montrose is speaking. Mr. Gardiner
agrees with Mark Napier in assigning it to this period.

loyalty." He expounds his own difficulties—"wrestling betwixt extremities"—till facts decided for him. The nobles had tasted the "sweetness of government," and they would not be content till they had destroyed "lawful authority and the liberty of the subject." The Kirk had coerced men into a blind obedience, a tyranny worse than papacy. He took up arms, he says, first, for national religion, "the restoration of that which our first reformers had"; second, for the maintenance of the central authority, the king's; and, third, for the "vindication of our nation from the base servitude of subjects who, like the Israelites, have their burdens doubled, but are not sensible of them." He answers his critics, especially those timorous souls who are "so stuffed with infidelity that they can believe nothing but what they see, and can commit nothing to God." If he had used the services of Alasdair Macdonald, a "professed Papist," had not his opponents employed in Ireland, under Monro, the selfsame people? He repudiated the charge of blood-guiltiness. He had never "shed the blood of any but of such as were sent forth by them to shed our blood and take our lives," adding with a touch of the Covenanters' own idiom, "and what is done in the land it may sensibly seem to be the Lord's doing, in making a handful to overthrow multitudes." Freedom and toleration in religion, a strong central government, and a lighter taxation for the burdened people of Scotland—for these he had drawn the sword.

It was the appeal to his countrymen on which he hoped to build a civil authority to correspond to that which he had won in war. As an ideal of statescraft it was profound; as tactics, as a step in the political game, it was bound to fail. The appeal was unintelligible to all save a few, and the defence did not convince. The people of the Lowlands had lost friends and kinsmen in the Highland wars, their ears had been horrified with endless tales of pillage and violence, and at the back of every Lowland heart lay a jealousy and dislike of the Celt, whether Ulster or Scottish, as of a race they did not understand. To say that Monro had used similar troops in Ireland was no more convincing to most people than to urge that the clans had once fought bravely at Bannockburn for Scottish independence. To point to Argyll's barbarities in the Highlands as worse than any of Alasdair's doings was to miss the point of the grievance. To a Lowlander the victims in the first case were savages and aliens, and in the latter they were

" kindly Scots." As for the king, there was still some loyal sentiment for him in Scotland, a clannish feeling, for had she not given to England the royal house? But the feeling was only sentimental, while Montrose's royalism was a seasoned appeal for a central authority, whatever name it might be given—an appeal which nobody, except perhaps Napier, understood. As for the Kirk, no doubt its encroachments were becoming a burden, but it had the terrible mastery over its people which is given by the possession of the keys of heaven and hell. Before that tyranny could be broken there were to be long years of struggle and much shedding of innocent blood. Besides, the Lowlands had no other voice or ear than the ministers. They were the sole interpreters, teachers, and guides. No mere proclamation could break through that plate-armour of defence to the starved and puzzled souls behind it. The one argument of practical value was the promise to reduce the grievous weight of taxation. But a Lowland burgher or peasant might well have been pardoned for doubting whether Montrose, with an army of hungry kerns to keep, would prove an easier tax-collector. The remonstrance, while of the highest value as a clue to Montrose's philosophy, shows that he wholly misread the immediate political situation. He could look for recruits only to those who were tired of the domineering Kirk and jealous of the Covenant leaders. Such were to be found among the nobles and gentry alone,[1] and these, and the tenantry they could command, were all that appeared in his camp at Bothwell.

Meanwhile that army which had fought under him in so many battles was beginning to melt away. The Highlanders wanted to get back to their homes. It was their duty, for the families left behind had rarely food for more than a week or two, and would starve if the husbands and fathers did not return often to replenish the pot. Miserably poor, war was a business to them, and they had to deposit their winnings. They had stayed on after Kilsyth, in the hope of the plunder of Glasgow, but Glasgow was inviolate, and one or two of them, who had tried to use the rich town as they considered it should be used, were now

---

[1] Here and there a minister may have been covertly or overtly on his side. In the *Assembly Commission Records*, and in presbytery and burgh records, we meet cases of ministers suspended or deposed for alleged sympathy with Montrose. Most of them were no doubt unlucky time-servers, but there may have been one or two sincere disciples.

swinging from Glasgow gibbets for their pains. Further,
the £500 which the citizens had offered was not to be paid.
The town council, fearing lest the meeting of Parliament
would cost the city large sums, had begged to be let off
the contribution, and Montrose had consented. The clans
were disgusted, and began to trickle away. There were
other reasons. The Macleans must look after their homes
in Mull, or the Campbells would be avenging Kilsyth.
Clan Donald had still grudges to avenge on Clan Diarmaid,
which not even Inverlochy had satisfied. There is no
reason to blame the Highlanders unduly. Organized Lowland warfare, such as Montrose now proposed, was a thing
which they did not understand, and which upset the whole
system and tradition of their lives. Alasdair alone deserves
censure. He was an experienced soldier, and knew something of the difficulties that lay before his chief. But his
knighthood and his new post of captain-general of the clans
under Montrose seem to have turned his head. He proposed to himself a campaign in Argyll which should root
the Campbells out of the peninsula.[1] He promised to
return, and no doubt honestly meant it, but from the
moment when he marched off with half his Irishry and all
the Highlanders, Montrose never saw his old lieutenant
again. Five hundred Ulstermen, under the gallant O'Cahan,
refused, to their eternal honour, to leave the royal standard.

Douglas and Ogilvy had been already dispatched to the
Border to recruit, and on the 4th of September Montrose
broke up his camp at Bothwell and began his advance
towards Tweed. His plan was to march through the
Lothians, and then descend by one of the passes of the
Lammermoors to the country of Home and Roxburgh.
But at the end of the first day he had to face a defection
more serious than Alasdair's. Aboyne had been rapidly
getting out of humour, and his ill-temper was zealously
fomented by Huntly, his father. He was insulted because
Crawford, instead of himself, had been given the command
of the cavalry. The return of Lord Ogilvy had restored
to Montrose his oldest comrade, and to the Gordon it
seemed that an Ogilvy was preferred before him. A
narrative of the campaign by Sir William Rollo, which he
had seen, was, in his view, insufficiently laudatory of his
own doings, and Montrose refused to suppress it. Last and
most important there was old Huntly, whose every letter
upbraided his heir for alliance with an enemy of his house.

[1] The Macdonnells of Antrim had always laid claim to Kintyre.

The untamable perverseness of the Gordon blood triumphed over his loyalty to his king and his duty to his general. In spite of Ogilvy's appeals he marched off with all the Gordon horse and foot. Nathaniel Gordon alone re-

CAMPAIGN OF PHILIPHAUGH

Montrose's March ——
Leslie's March......

5 10 15 20 25 30
English Miles

mained; for him the comradeship in arms begun after Tippermuir was to end only with death.

II

Montrose traversed the moorland country of the Lothians, avoiding plague-stricken Edinburgh, to Cran-

stoun, south-east of Dalkeith. It was now Saturday, the
6th of September, and on the following day it was intended
that Wishart should preach to the army. But news was
received from Lord Erskine which changed the situation.
David Leslie,[1] the future Lord Newark, and a soldier far
abler than either Leven or Baillie, had, after the fall of
Carlisle, taken his horse to the assistance of Leven at Hereford. He was then sent into the midlands in pursuit of the
king, but the news of Kilsyth altered his plans. His men
refused to continue the war in England while Scotland was
defenceless, and, though his first intention was to take only
half his force, he was soon compelled to take the whole
4,000. On 1st September the siege of Hereford was raised
—it was the one direct result of Kilsyth in the king's favour
—while Leslie was hastening with all speed to the north.
Had the king's army been better handled he would never
have reached the Border. There was one moment at
Rotherham, as he himself admitted, when, if the adjacent
royal forces had struck, he would have been destroyed.[2]
But he passed unchallenged, and, collecting reinforcements
of foot from the garrisons of Newcastle and Berwick, he
crossed Tweed on the 6th of September. John Middleton
of Caldhame commanded his advance guard; he had served
under Montrose at Aberdeen in the Bishops' War, and was
to live to receive an earldom and misgovern Scotland after
the Restoration. Leslie followed the coast road to the
Lothians, his aim being to cut off Montrose from the Highlands, and his plan to take up position somewhere on the
neck of land between Forth and Clyde.

He had under him not less than 6,000 men. Of these
more than 5,000 were mounted troops—his own regiment,
the regiments of Dalhousie, Eglinton, Middleton, and
Leven, Fraser's Dragoons,[3] Kirkcudbright's Dragoons, and
Sir David Barclay's independent troop of horse. He had
picked up 800 foot on the way from the regiments of
Clydesdale, Tweeddale, Galloway, Montgomery, Strathearn, and Kenmure.[4] He had also acquired at Berwick a

---

[1] He was not, as some historians have stated, a relative of Leven,
but a Fife man, the son of Leslie of Pitcairly.

[2] Clarendon, IX., 86.

[3] " Known, with Lawers' regiment of foot, to be the stoutest regiment in the Scots army." *Memorie of the Somervilles*, II., 315.

[4] *A. P. S.*, Balfour's *Annales, The Army of the Covenant* (S.H.S.),
I., Introd. Sir Walter Scott's great-great-grandfather, Sir William
Scott of Harden, was lieutenant-colonel of the Tweeddale regiment.
Letters, I., 391. Rushworth (VI., 231) gives Leslie nine regiments of
horse and two of dragoons.

more doubtful increment, no less than ten members of the Committee of Estates, most of them fugitives after Kilsyth, like Argyll, Lindsay, and Lanark.[1] But he did not suffer the committee to interfere with the conduct of his operations as it had done at Kilsyth and was to do later at Dunbar. The crisis was too sharp for a peripatetic debating society.

Lord Erskine advised a retreat beyond the Highland Line while yet there was time, but Montrose refused. He was bound by his duty to the king to carry relief to England, and that at once. His problem was the old one of how to raise an army, but to go north among the clans again would mean an intolerable delay, and he believed that he could achieve the same result on the Border. Cavalry was his first need, for Aboyne's defection had left him with scarcely a hundred troopers, most of them Lord Airlie's Ogilvys. He hoped for large levies as a consequence of Douglas's recruiting, and still more from Home and Roxburgh. His further plans we do not know—whether he intended to seek out and test the quality of David Leslie or to march boldly southward to the king. His immediate business was to get an army, so on the Saturday afternoon the royalists turned to their right and marched down Gala Water towards Tweedside. Next day, at Torwoodlee, Douglas and Ogilvy joined them with a large body of horse from Nithsdale and upper Clydesdale. The recruits were all lairds or lairds' sons, and their immediate retainers—a half-hearted and unstable crew, who had none of the old moss-trooping fire. Somewhere, too, on Gala Water, Linton arrived with his Peeblesshire troop, and his father, Traquair, rode over to visit the viceroy. He came in all likelihood to spy out the nakedness of the land, with results which we shall see.

Marching slowly down Tweed, Montrose reached Kelso on the 8th or 9th. It was the appointed rendezvous, but he found no sign of Home or Roxburgh. He waited for a day, and then he heard ominous news. The Border earls were with Leslie—prisoners, so ran their own story, captured by Middleton and his advance guard. It was a tale which common opinion scouted, and indeed it is inconceivable that two powerful nobles, in their own countryside, twenty miles from Leslie's line of march, and with complete knowledge of his coming, should not have been able to

[1] *Account of the Routing of the Scottish Rebels at Philiphaugh,* etc. London, Sept. 18, 1645.

escape if they had wished it. It is far more probable that, knowing Leslie's strength and Montrose's predicament, they sought security by putting themselves in the enemy's power.[1]

To tarry at Kelso was mere folly, so Montrose turned wearily up Tweed. The spring he had most counted on was dry. Douglas held out hopes of raising the westlands —vain hopes, for in no quarter of Scotland was the power of the ministers so great; he rated the prestige of the Douglas name higher than was warranted by facts. Montrose accepted the plan, for in any case it would lead him back to the hills to which he had always turned his eyes for help. He marched to Jedburgh, but there was nothing to be looked for from the Kerrs, whose chief, Lothian, was a Covenanting general. Then he entered the Scott country, but Buccleuch was with Leslie, and the old raiding spirit was dying in the glens. The successors of Wat of Harden and Dickie of Dryhope were a peaceable folk, and brawls at a fair or a clipping were their only form of war. He would have fared better among the Armstrongs and Elliots farther south, who, as Cromwell was to discover, were still good men of their hands.[2] There was another reason for his failure in the presence of his Irish contingent, for Border memories are long, and a hundred years before Hertford, in his invasion of Scotland, had used Irish in his work of destruction, and these Irish had taken no prisoners.[3]

During the march Sir Robert Spottiswoode wrote a letter[4]—never posted—to Digby, who was still nursing his vain dreams. He told him of Montrose's desperate plight, and upbraided him for not detaining Leslie in England. He asked what had become of the promised cavalry. "You little imagine the difficulties my lord marquis hath here to wrestle with. The overcoming of the enemy is the least of them; he hath more to do with his unseeing friends. . . . All these were great disheartenings to any other but to him, whom nothing of this kind can amaze. With the small forces he hath presently with him he is resolved to

---

[1] Wishart, ch. xv. See Gardiner, *Civil War*, II., 352.

[2] *Scotland and the Commonwealth* (S.H.S.), xix. *Scotland and the Protectorate* (S.H.S.), xxxiv., etc.

[3] Hertford wrote to Henry VIII.: "For the better execution thereof I sent with them 100 Irishmen, for the Borderers will not now willingly burn their neighbours." *Hamilton Papers*, II., 406; *Cal. S. P., Dom.* (Henry VIII.), V., 523; *The Border Elliots*, 67.

[4] The letter is in Napier, II., 572-573, and *Mem. of M.*, II., 233-234.

pursue David Leslie, and not suffer him to grow stronger."
Digby at the moment, and for a fortnight later, was full of
hope and confidence, which even the disaster of Rowton
Heath could not shake. Stories were reaching him of a
mysterious fight in Westmoreland, in which Crawford and
Ogilvy were said to have annihilated Leslie. Soon he was
to hear from Byron that the soldiers in Poyntz's army were
celebrating a great victory which had shattered Montrose's
power.[1] The first tale was false, the second only too true.

On the afternoon of the 12th of September Montrose
arrived at the gate of the hill country, the flat of Philiphaugh, under the little burgh of Selkirk, where the two glens
of Yarrow and Ettrick meet. Just below the junction of
the streams, on the left bank of Ettrick, is a level meadow
a quarter of a mile wide, with the water on one side and
a rugged hill on the other. Here he fixed his camp, and
placed the few guns which had been part of the booty of
Kilsyth. It was protected on the south and east by the
Ettrick, on the north by the hills, and on the west by
Yarrow and the steep wood called the Hareheadshaw. The
position was a strong one, but as the army did not expect
a battle it was very loosely held. There was no premoni-
tion of immediate danger. Leslie was believed to be far
away on the Forth, and, in Sir Robert Spottiswoode's letter
to Digby, Montrose was said to be resolute to chase him.
He did not know that the pursued had become the pursuer.

At Gladsmuir, in East Lothian, late on the 11th of
September, Leslie had received a letter revealing the whereabouts and the weakness of the royalist force. Popular
tradition made Traquair the sender, and there is no reason
to disbelieve a tale so consistent with the character of a
family which, during the Covenant, as during the later
Jacobite wars, was uniformly treacherous. Traquair had
also shown his hand by sending a message to his son, Lord
Linton, to withdraw him and his troops from Montrose's
camp.[2] Leslie, when he got the news, at once changed his
plans. He marched straight down Gala Water, crossed the
ridge at Rink by the old Edinburgh-Selkirk road, and
forded Tweed below the Rae Weil.[3] Late on the night of

[1] Gardiner, *Civil War*, II., 347.
[2] For the conduct of the Jacobite Traquair, see *Memoirs of John
Murray of Broughton* (S.H.S., 1898). Patrick Gordon says that
Traquair recalled his son four days before the battle; Wishart, with
whom Guthry agrees, says " on the very night."
[3] Sir Walter Scott, in his *Minstrelsy of the Scottish Border* (II.,
21), apparently following local tradition, makes Leslie encamp on

the 12th he reached the hamlet of Sunderland, which stood on the peninsula formed by the junction of Tweed and Ettrick. There to his relief he had news of the enemy. Some pickets, under Charteris of Amisfield, were in the village, and these were driven out with a few casualties. Leslie was now less than three miles from the royalist camp. He had caught his quarry, but only by the skin of his teeth, for another day would have seen Montrose safe in the hills.

A little trenching was done on the eastern and western flanks before Montrose's small army settled down for the night. A mounted patrol was sent out under Ogilvy of Powrie, and returned to report that all was quiet; they were probably impressed local men, maybe Traquair's tenants, and they may have taken their commander where nothing

the night of the 12th at Melrose, and he is followed by Mr. Mowbray Morris (*Montrose*, 1892). For several reasons I find it difficult to accept this view. (1) Leslie was at Gladsmuir when he received the news from Traquair, or whoever sent it. He knew his enemy, and his object was to cut off his retreat into the hills; therefore he must have chosen the shortest route to the opening of the hills at Selkirk. He left Gladsmuir the day that Montrose left Jedburgh, so he had no time to lose. If he had crossed by Soutra, and marched down Leader Water, he would have passed Melrose; but we know that he came by Gala (Wishart, ch. xvi.). To follow Gala to its foot below Galashiels, and then ford Tweed and encamp at Melrose, would have been a perfectly aimless detour. Further, it seems certain that Montrose arrived at Selkirk early on the afternoon of the 12th, and his presence there would be known in Galashiels, and communicated to Leslie on his arrival. The easiest way from Galashiels was over the Rink hill to Sunderland. (2) Gordon of Ruthven says definitely that Leslie was at Sunderland on the night of the 12th, and if so he could not have been at Melrose unless he had left Melrose early in the afternoon and forded Ettrick. But in that case Montrose would have got word of him. Wishart does not mention Sunderland; he says that the Covenanters spent the night five miles from Selkirk, which is not decisive. But, in describing the turning movement executed by Leslie's 2,000, he writes " quos adversa amnis ripa hostes transmiserant." Now they would not have crossed Ettrick, if they had been coming from Melrose, till just at the battle-field, and Wishart's words indicate a crossing at the beginning of the morning's march. One Covenant account (*A More Perfect and Particular Relation*, etc., Haddington, Sept. 16, 1645, cited by Lang) says that Leslie encamped within three miles of the enemy. (3) Local tradition seems also to point to the Galashiels-Sunderland route. In the preposterous ballad of the " Bat'le of Philiphaugh " (Scott's *Minstrelsy*, II., 26-30), Leslie is said to have sent his right wing round Linglie Hill, the height between Ettrick and Yair on Tweed. Such a movement, absurd as it is, would have been impossible to a force coming from Melrose, and shows the popular notion of the Covenant march. The subject has been fully discussed by Lieut.-Colonel the Hon. Fitzwilliam Elliot in his *The Trustworthiness of Border Ballads* (1906), where the conclusion arrived at is that of my text.

could be seen or heard. The king's captain-general left the
posting of the pickets to his officers, and retired himself
with his cavalry leaders to a lodging in the West Port of
Selkirk.[1] Here for most of the night he busied himself
with dispatches to the king. He had many heavy matters
on his mind, and was suffering from one of those fits of
bodily and mental languor which come at times upon the
greatest commanders. No doubt he had given instructions
that, except for the most urgent business, he was not to be
disturbed. The night had fallen moonless and dark as
pitch. Some time before midnight Charteris of Amisfield
arrived with his story of having been driven out of Sunderland village. His account must have been confused, and
the incident was apparently regarded by the headquarters
staff as a drunken brawl among Charteris' troopers or a
brush with hostile country-folk[2]—at any rate not of sufficient moment to break in upon the privacy of the captain-
general.

The morning of the 13th dawned with one of those thick
autumnal fogs, which in the valley bottoms in the early
hours prevent a man seeing three yards before him. Scouts
were sent out again at the first light, and reported that the
country was clear. So it was to north, south, and west, on
all sides except the east, the direction of Sunderland, and
Amisfield's report from that quarter had already been dis-
counted. The army in the haugh cooked a leisurely meal,
and Montrose, in his Selkirk lodging, with only an hour or
two of sleep behind him, sat down to breakfast.

Meantime Leslie had launched his thunderbolt. He had
divided his forces into two parts, and with one marched
swiftly up the left bank of Ettrick. The other, 2,000 strong,
which included Kirkcudbright's Dragoons, under the command of James Agnew of Lochnaw,[3] had crossed that
water, and by way of Will's Nick had reached the Selkirk
road. The royalists, having finished their meal, were
assembling for parade, when through the thinning mist
came the rush of Leslie's horse.

[1] Craig Brown, *Hist. of Selkirkshire*, I., 185, etc. As a proof of
the attitude of the local peasantry towards Montrose, it is said that
the woman of the house was busy putting a sheep's head into a pot
when the general passed the kitchen door, and was heard to exclaim
that she wished it was Montrose's head, for in that case she would
be careful to hold down the lid.
[2] Selkirk was notoriously hostile to Montrose, Pringle of Blindlee
being almost the only recorded royalist in the shire.
[3] *Hereditary Sheriffs of Galloway*, II., 26.

To Montrose in the West Port arrived his scoutmaster, Captain Blackadder, with the shattering news. He flung himself on his horse, and with Airlie, Crawford, and Napier, galloped to his army. He found the field in confusion. Douglas's bonnet-lairds, in spite of their gallant leader, had fled at the first shot. The 500 Ulstermen, however, were fighting a desperate fight in their shallow trenches. Montrose collected a hundred troopers, and charged Leslie so madly that for a moment he drove back the whole Covenant horse. But 600 men taken by surprise, and with no advantage of position, cannot for long do battle with 6,000. Leslie's other division harassed the royalist right flank with musketry fire from beyond the stream, and presently had forded Ettrick and were attacking it from behind. The Irish were beaten out of their trenches into a second position, the folds of Philiphaugh farm.[1] Again and again the Covenant troopers charged, only to be driven back by the heroic Ulstermen; again and again Montrose's hundred cut their way deep into the enemy's ranks. Philiphaugh was less a battle than a surprise and a massacre. Soon only fifty horse were left, and of the Irish more than 400 were dead. The remnant under their adjutant, Stewart, were induced to surrender on a promise of quarter.[2]

Montrose fought with a gallantry and a desperation worthy of Alasdair, and but for his friends would have died on the field. Lord Douglas and Sir John Dalziel pled

[1] Guthrie, 203. Leslie to Leven in *The Great Victories*, London (1645) (Bodleian).

[2] The authorities for Philiphaugh are Wishart (ch. xvi.), who was probably an eyewitness, Gordon of Ruthven (156, etc.), and Guthry (201, etc.). The various Covenanting newsletters (*A More Perfect and Particular Relation*, etc., *Montrose Routed in Tividale*, *The Great Victories*, etc.), exaggerate the numbers on the royalist side; these were probably as stated in the text, except that it is difficult to believe that Douglas had the 1,200 with which Gordon of Ruthven credits him. Leslie's own account to Leven puts the royalist force at 2,000, and adds: " I never fought with better horsemen and against more resolute foot." He referred, after Dunbar, to Philiphaugh as an easy victory (*Ancrum and Lothian Correspondence*, II., 297). For some of the country stories about it see Russell, *Reminiscences of Yarrow*, and Craig Brown, *History of Selkirkshire*. The ballad on the subject is probably an eighteenth-century production, and of no use as evidence. The ancient father who guided Leslie must have been at least 116 at the time, for he boasted of having been at Solway Moss, which was fought a century before. He was a prophet as well as an ancient, for he added that he had been at " curst Dunbar," which was not fought till five years later. The ballad was written to glorify Buccleuch's regiment—" The Scotts out o'er the Graemes they ran "—which they certainly did not, for very few of Leslie's foot can have come into action.

with him to take the chance of flight, urging that so long as he lived the king's cause need not go down. He allowed himself to be constrained. With about thirty others, including the two Napiers, Lord Erskine, and Lord Fleming, as well as Dalziel and Douglas, he cut a road to the west and repulsed a feeble attempt at pursuit. The little party galloped up Yarrow vale, and at Broadmeadows took the drove-road across Minchmoor to Tweeddale. As they disappeared into the green hills, with them disappeared the dream of a new and happier Scotland. Montrose's cycle of victories had proved like the fairy gold which vanishes in a man's hand. The year of miracles was ended.

CHAPTER XIV

AFTER PHILIPHAUGH

(*September* 1645-*September* 1646)

> O truth of Christ,
> O most dear rarity,
> O most rare Charity,
> Where dwell'st thou now?
> In the Valley of Vision?
> On Pharaoh's throne?
> On high with Nero?
> With Timon alone?
>
> CARMINA BURANA
> (*Miss Helen Waddell's translation*).

I

MONTROSE DID NOT DRAW REIN TILL HE REACHED THE OLD house of Traquair, whose grey and haunted walls still stand among the meadows where the Quair burn flows to Tweed. Its lord shut his door on the fugitive; his welcome was reserved for the conquering Leslie, when, with Argyll and Lothian, he arrived later in pursuit. He did not cross Tweed at the bridge of Peebles, but rode up the right bank by the Sware to Manor, and thus to Stobo by the Glack.[1]

---

[1] Wishart makes him halt for the night at Peebles, but as that ancient burgh is only sixteen miles from the battlefield, and as the fighting was over by twelve o'clock, it is difficult to believe that the fugitives stayed more than a short space to rest. They probably rode on fifteen miles to Biggar before halting for the night. *Cf.* J. W. Buchan, *History of Peeblesshire*, III., 472. Tweeddale as a shire was far more royalist than Selkirk. Peebles had some of its burgesses

Thence the company pushed on to Biggar in Clydesdale,
where they spent the night, and long before the next daybreak were in the saddle and heading for the north, guided
by Dalziel, who was now in his own countryside. Fugitives
were picked up by the way, including an Ulsterman, who
had wrapped the colours of the foot round his breast, and,
having found a horse, caught up Montrose and restored
to him one of the standards. The other, the cavalry
colours, was carried by Kinnoull's brother, William Hay,
into England, and months afterwards was brought to Montrose in the north. At a ford of Clyde they met, to their
joy, old Airlie and Crawford, who had probably taken the
route by Megget and upper Tweed, and had collected on
the road some of Douglas's fleeing troopers. Somehow the
party made their way through the midlands, and by the
19th were safe in the Perthshire hills.

The Scots troops in Newcastle entertained the mayor and
aldermen to a dinner to celebrate the victory of Philiphaugh.[1] Elsewhere the celebrations were of a grimmer
kind, for now came the harvest of the triumphant Covenant. It began on the day of the battle, when 300 Irish-
women, with their children, were butchered on the field.
Those who wish to sup deep on horrors can find the details
in Patrick Gordon. The cooks and horseboys also perished
to the number of some 200. The remnant of the Irish
under Stewart had surrendered on terms, but the ministers
who accompanied Leslie remonstrated against the Lord's
work being hindered by a foolish clemency. They argued
that quarter had been granted to Stewart alone, and not
to his men; Leslie professed being himself convinced by
this shameless quibble, and the unarmed Irish were cut
down as they stood, or shot next morning in the courtyard
of Newark castle.[2] O'Cahan and another officer, Lachlan,

serving with Montrose, and many of the gentry, like Tait of the Pirn,
Porteous of Hawkshaw, Veitch of Dawyck, and Murray of Elibank
were on his side. The county furnished the prototype of Sir William
Worthy in Allan Ramsay's *Gentle Shepherd*. Pennecuik, *Tweeddale*, 99.   [1] *Army of the Covenant* (S.H.S.), I., 285.
    [2] The authorities for the slaughter of the Irish are Wishart (ch.
xvi.), Gordon of Ruthven (160), and Guthry (203). These are, of
course, hostile sources, but Leslie in his letter to Leven says that
" all Montrose's forces that were Irish or Highlanders (were) killed
upon the place (*The Great Victories*, etc., 1645). The reader will
find the little that can be said in extenuation in Dr. Mitchell's introduction to the *Commission of the General Assembly Records*
(S.H.S.), I. Leslie does not appear to have been a man of scrupulous
honour. A similar case at the surrender of Dunavertie, in Kintyre
(Guthry, 243), is denied by Sir James Turner, who was present

were spared for the moment, only to be hanged later in Edinburgh without a trial. Stewart was also destined for death, but was fortunate enough to escape to Montrose.

The zeal of the Covenant against the daughters of Heth was not satiated by the butchery of Philiphaugh. Many had escaped, and were slaughtered singly as they wandered among the moors of Tweed and Clyde. In most county histories the slaying is ascribed to the infuriated country people, but for this there is no evidence. The Lowland peasantry have never had a taste for such brutalities, and the murders were probably the work of the soldiers of the Covenant, who beat the hills for royalists, as Lag's dragoons were to beat them forty years later for Covenanters.[1] One large party of the poor creatures was brought to Leslie's camp at Linlithgow. They were flung over the bridge of Avon, and were either drowned in the river or stabbed with the pikes of the soldiers who lined the banks.[2] The records of the Irish rebellion hold no more horrid cruelties. The inspiration was not Leslie's; it came from the fierce bigots who accompanied him. Sometimes the soldiers sickened of the work, and asked their clerical advisers, as Leslie asked Nevoy at Dunavertie, " Mr. John, have you not once gotten your fill of blood? "[3]

For these barbarities, sanctioned and inspired by the Kirk, there can be no defence. It is hard to understand the view taken by some apologists that the Irish were name-

(*Memoirs*, 238). Turner was naturally anxious to defend his general, but on the other side there is the evidence in the action raised after the Restoration against Argyll by the Macdougals of Dunolly (*A. P. S.*, VII., 337), and Turner himself records an instance of Leslie's bad faith towards Alasdair's father at the siege of Dunyveg in Islay (*Memoirs*, 48). *Cf.* also Montereul (Montreuil), *Correspondence* (S.H.S.), II., 103. The dishonouring of paroles and promises of quarter seems to have been the official creed of the Covenant. In the " Interloquitur of Parliament " of January 10, 1646, occurs this startling sentence : " If this defence of quarter be sustained, then the whole nation, especially the Estates of Parliament, does violate the oath of the Covenant, and the oath of the Parliament anent the prosecuting and censuring of malignants, opposers of the Covenant " (*A. P. S.*, VI., i., 249).

[1] The Deid Wife, a hill near Stobo, in Tweeddale, commemorates one such slaying.

[2] Gordon of Ruthven, 160. Sir George Mackenzie, *Vindication of the Government in Scotland* (1691), 20. Wishart, ch. xvii. (he gives the story without mentioning the place).

[3] Guthry, 243. Nevoy, a nephew of Mr. Andrew Cant, was the minister of Newmilns, and Loudoun's chaplain. He was in the affair at Mauchline in June 1648, and after the Restoration was banished to Holland. He had a part in revising the Scots metrical version of the Psalms, and turned the Song of Solomon into Latin verse.

less savages, who by their crimes had forfeited all consideration from mankind. It is a royalist historian who has
left the most hostile account of them. " The Irish in particular were too cruel; for it was everywhere observed they
did ordinarily kill all they could be master of, without any
motion of pity, or any consideration of humanity. Nay,
it seemed to them there were no distinctions between a man
and a beast, for they killed men ordinarily with no more
feeling of compassion, and with the same careless neglect
that they kill a hare or capon for their supper. And they
were also without all shame, most brutally given to un-
cleanness and filthy lust; as for excessive drinking, when
they came where it might be had there were no limits to
their beastly appetites, as for godless avarice and merciless
oppression and plundering of the poor labourer. Of these
two crying sins the Scots were as guilty as they."[1] It is a
grave indictment, but it could be written of most armies
of the time, and Patrick Gordon, who, as a decent Aber-
donian, disliked the rude western clans, was a stern critic.
No doubt it was brutal warfare, and in an army of
volunteers discipline must have been hard to enforce. The
Irish, who were mainly Scottish Macdonalds, slew fiercely
in battle, but so did the Covenant troops at Philiphaugh
and Carbisdale, so did the Campbells when Argyll carried
fire and sword through the north, and so would have the
Covenanters in the first Bishops' War if Montrose had not
restrained them. On at least two occasions, Aberdeen and
Inverlochy, they gave little or no quarter, but there is no
evidence that they murdered in cold blood prisoners who
surrendered after an action. Nor is there any record,
except for the sack of Aberdeen, of the slaughter of women
which stains the fair fame of their opponents, both
Covenanters and Cromwellians. Our evidence shows that
they were cheerful ruffians, who loved fighting for fighting's
sake, and cracked jokes in the thick of a battle. As for
the women, no doubt they were often concubines rather
than wives, and no doubt they stole; but marriage lines were
not universal in the Covenant's armies, and Leven's female
followers thieved like daws.[2] Nor can we place the two
sets of outrages in different moral categories, because the
Covenanters were inspired by a religious creed. It makes
small difference in the guilt of murder whether the murderer

[1] Gordon of Ruthven, 161.
[2] Nicholas to Rupert, July 11, 1645, cited by Gardiner, *Civil War*,
II., 263 *n*.

slays because his blood is hot in battle and he likes it, or whether he massacres at leisure because he is playing at being an early Israelite. The motive of both clergy and laity—and their only defence—was naked fear, and there is no such begetter of cruelty. Legends, born partly of the Irish rebellion and partly of rumours from the north, had magnified the Irish into monsters of terror; the same rumours were to be rife later about Cromwell's English soldiers[1]—with more reason, perhaps, for some of them had been at Wexford and Drogheda. Also the theocracy knew that it was fighting for its life.

The roll of captives was long. Some of Montrose's closest friends, like Lord Ogilvy, Sir Robert Spottiswoode, Sir William Rollo, and Nathaniel Gordon, were in enemy hands, having surrendered on promise of quarter. Leslie marched slowly through the Lothians towards Glasgow, where a provisional committee dealt with the prisoners. Meantime the two Irish officers, O'Cahan and Lachlan, had been hanged on the castle hill of Edinburgh—the last we shall hear of two very gallant gentlemen. The royalist leaders were all reserved for death, though the lay members of the court were disposed to be merciful. On the 20th of October, on the date and in the place which Montrose had appointed for the Parliament, the Committee of the Estates sat in judgment. The first to be dealt with was Sir William Rollo, whose brother had married Argyll's sister. For all his lameness he had never left Montrose's side, and he had been one of his most trusted brigadiers. He was beheaded at the Mercat Cross on the 28th. On the following day there died Sir Philip Nisbet, who had fought with Rupert and with Montrose on the English Borders, and young Ogilvy of Inverquharity, a boy in his teens, a " lovely young youth," said the Glasgow bailie who presided at his execution.[2] The lay Covenanters had their scruples over these executions, and Mr. Robert Baillie remembered with disquiet that " to this day no man in England has been executed for bearing arms against the Parliament."[3] But the ministers were inexorable. " The work gangs bonnily on," was their comment.[4] Only by blood could the wrath of the strange deity they worshipped be appeased.

[1] Douglas, *Cromwell's Scotch Campaigns*, 33. Whitelocke, *Memorials*, III., 224, etc.
[2] Wishart, ch. xviii. Gordon of Ruthven, 167. Guthry, 208. Napier, II., 589.   [3] *Letters and Journals*, II., 322.
[4] Guthry attributes the saying to Mr. David Dickson, but one would fain believe him mistaken. The minister of Irvine, philosopher

I

Owing to a raid threatened by Montrose the rest of the executions were postponed. They began again in St. Andrews after Christmas. The Kirk was in terror lest Parliament should be too merciful, and appeals flowed in from synods and presbyteries. Galloway prayed that the " sword of justice may be impartially drawn against those persons now in bonds who have lifted up their hands against the Lord, the sworn Covenant, and this afflicted Kirk." " We need not lay before your honours," said the voice of Dumfries, " what the Lord calls for at your hands in the point of justice, nor what you owe unto the many thousands of His people." " We are confident," wrote the gentle ministers of the Merse, " that your hearts will not faint nor your hands fail until you have cut off the horns of the wicked." Wariston excelled himself, for he proved to his own satisfaction that past lukewarmness in bringing malefactors to justice " had provoked God's two great servants against them, the sword and the pestilence, which has ploughed up the land with deep furrows."[1] The delay, according to the Commission of the General Assembly, was " displeasing unto the supreme judge of the world, and grievous unto the hearts of the Lord's people."

The Lord's people were soon to be comforted, for the Estates set to work in earnest. But meantime one of their chief victims escaped. Lord Ogilvy could look for no mercy, for his family were the pet aversion of Argyll, and during his short three weeks of liberty he had been the right hand of the king's captain-general. But he was a cousin of Lindsay and akin, on the maternal side, to the Hamiltons, so he was permitted the last consolation of a visit from his mother, his wife, and his sister. He was sick in bed when the ladies were admitted in the dusk of a December evening. Adopting Lady Nithsdale's device of a later day, his sister put on his nightcap and got into his bed, while he dressed himself in her clothes. When the guards entered, they found three tearful women taking farewell of the doomed prisoner, and conducted them to the prison gate. Horses were waiting close at hand, and Ogilvy galloped across Fife to join Inchbrakie in Menteith. Argyll would have visited his wrath on the heroic lady, but the Hamilton influence was strong enough to save her from punishment.

and poet, and professor of divinity first at Glasgow and then at Edinburgh, was not of Nevoy's school. His politics were more of the stamp of Mr. Robert Baillie's.

[1] Balfour, III., 324, etc. *Mem. of M.*, 245, etc. *Hist. MSS. Comm.*, 2nd Report, 175.

There was no hope for the others. They were tried, not as the law enjoined by their peers or by the whole Parliament, but by a self-appointed committee. Some of the judges voted with qualifications, but the verdict was certain. Hartfell indeed was pardoned. He was disliked by the Hamiltons, and Argyll owed them a tit-for-tat for their clemency towards the Ogilvys. On January 20, 1646, the " Maiden," which had been brought from Dundee, was set up at the cross of St. Andrews, and the ancient city saw again " the auld rusty lass linking at a bluidy hairst."[1] That day Nathaniel Gordon, Andrew Guthrie—a son of the Bishop of Moray—and Sir Robert Spottiswoode paid the last penalty. Three days later died William Murray, a boy of nineteen, whom the half-hearted pleas of his Covenanting brother, Tullibardine, could not save.[2] Mr. Andrew Cant and Mr. Robert Blair attended the prisoners in their last hours, and found a penitent in Nathaniel Gordon, who was accordingly released on the scaffold from an old sentence of excommunication; for that stout adventurer had a good many dark patches in his career.[3] But. with the others the ministers did not succeed. Andrew Guthrie declared that he could not conceive a greater honour than to meet an honourable death in so just a cause. The boy, William Murray, confessed his private sins, but denied that he was a traitor; his death, he said, was a new distinction for the house of Tullibardine.

The case of Sir Robert Spottiswoode had given qualms to many of his judges. He was an old man; he was a learned lawyer and a ripe scholar; he had been Lord President of the Court of Session; he was a non-combatant, and had surrendered on a promise of quarter to Lanark, whom he had succeeded as the king's secretary for Scotland. There was nothing in his life which his enemies could

---

[1] *Rob Roy*, ch. xxix.

[2] Murray was charged, among other things, with the murder of the minister of Kirkton, near Hawick, after Philiphaugh (*A. P. S.*, VI., i., 526). How he found time, while a fugitive from the battlefield, to kill a minister is one of the minor mysteries of the period.

[3] A pamphlet, *Treason and Rebellion*, etc. (London: Bostock, 1646), gives, in two letters from St. Andrews, an account of Nathaniel Gordon's edifying end and the impenitence of the others. It makes Gordon repent of his politics, but Wishart (ch. xix.) says that, in signing his confession, he declared that " if there was anything in that document derogatory to the king and his authority, he utterly disowned it." On a matter like this Wishart could scarcely be mistaken; if the truth had been otherwise he would not have dared to suppress it. The process against Gordon is in *Hist. MSS. Comm.*, 2nd Report, 174.

cavil at. While the Covenant still kept up a pretence of royalism and legality, his execution was plain murder. He was not permitted to read an address from the scaffold,[1] and replied to the importunities of Mr. Robert Blair that his blasphemous outpourings were abominable to God. His last words were: " Merciful Jesus, gather my soul unto Thy saints and martyrs, who have run before me in this race."

The night before his death Sir Robert wrote a letter of farewell to Montrose,[2] which breathes a spirit of Christian forbearance unhappily lacking in those who had the name of religion always on their lips. He commends to the viceroy's care his orphan children and nephews, and hopes to do more for the king's cause by his death than by his life. " One thing I most humbly recommend to your Excellence that, as you have always done hitherto, so you will continue by fair and gentle carriage to win the people's affection for their prince, rather than to imitate the barbarous inhumanity of your adversaries." The advice was nobly followed. There were no reprisals on the Covenant prisoners confined in the castle of Blair. " Never," ran Montrose's address to his troops, " shall they induce us to rival their crimes, or seek to outdo them except in valour and renown." In a great civil struggle neither side has a monopoly of the virtues. There were many in the Covenant ranks in whom the fire of religious faith had burned up all human fears, and who were to give honourable proof of the manhood which was in them. It was a time of darkness and suffering, when men's minds were turning from the bleak world of sense to the dream of a better world beyond the grave, and in such seasons the homely virtues on which depends the conduct of our mortal life are apt to be forgotten. This forgetfulness was most marked in those who lived most constantly in the contemplation of a promised immortality; and in the matter of human charity and mercy there can be little comparison for the unbiased historian between the two parties. Montrose's army was guilty of acts of cruelty in hot blood, but never at its worst did it approach the consistent, deadly barbarity of the Kirk and the Estates. Twenty years later, when the Covenant

[1] The address is printed in his grandson's edition of his *Practicks of the Laws of Scotland*, and as an appendix to the 1819 edition of Wishart.
[2] The letter, from the *Spottiswoode Papers*, is reprinted in *Mem. of M.*, II., 254. Ewen Cameron of Lochiel visited Spottiswoode in prison, and that visit was the turning-point of his life (*Memoirs of Locheill*, 76-82).

was the losing side, and the fanatics who now ruled in Scotland had been driven to the mosses, there must have been many quiet, old-fashioned folk in the land, who, casting back their memories to the days after Philiphaugh, saw in the change the slow grinding of the mills of God. In one respect the later persecution, bad and indefensible as it was, fell short in grossness of the earlier, for its perpetrators in their evil work did not profane the name of the meek gospel of Christ.

II

For Montrose defeat was only a spur to fresh effort. The flexible steel of his courage could not be bent or broken. From his refuge in Atholl he sent Erskine to recruit in Mar, and Douglas and Airlie to raise the royalists of Angus. He made a further effort to get into touch with Alasdair, and wrote again to Digby, begging for horse. In Atholl the country-folk were busy with the late harvest, but the name of the viceroy was a spell, and 400 followed him. But his principal aim, as ever, was the Gordon cavalry. He hastened over the Grampians, and early in October was at Drumminor castle, near Strathbogie, where Aboyne, his late grievances apparently forgotten, joined him with 1,500 foot and 300 horse. A less welcome recruit appeared in the person of the mischievous Lord Lewis. There followed news of the father. After Kilsyth Huntly had removed himself from the Strathnaver bogs, and was now at his castle of Gight. He sent Montrose a tepid message of good wishes, and spoke nobly of what he and his clan would still do for the king. For the moment it looked as if the chief of the Gordons had learned wisdom in exile.

Meanwhile Middleton, with 800 of Leslie's horse, had marched north to the Aberdeenshire lowlands, and was now lying at Turriff. Montrose had two alternatives before him. He could attack Middleton with his new army and settle with him before turning to Leslie. Such a course would protect the Gordon lands, and might keep Huntly in good humour. On the other hand, his friends were prisoners in Glasgow, and unless he rescued them forthwith they would perish. Leslie, too, was the more formidable foe, and it was always Montrose's habit to take the greater danger first. Besides, Leslie lay between him and the Border, and on the Border he still cherished vain dreams of meeting the king. Accordingly he gave marching orders for the south.

Lewis Gordon, with such of his clan as he could induce to follow him, deserted on the second morning. Aboyne

remained for another day's march, but peremptory letters
arrived from his father to recall him. Huntly's insane
jealousy had revived, and he would neither fight himself
nor permit his men to fight under another leader. Montrose
sent Lord Reay and young Irvine of Drum to reason with
him, but they were unable to shake his purpose. The
precious days were slipping past in this barren diplomacy,
and on the 22nd of October Montrose, then at the Castleton
of Braemar, decided to advance without the Gordons.
That night he lay in Glenshee, and on the 23rd was on
Lochearnside, where he may have heard that the first executions of his friends had taken place. He was momentarily
cheered by a message from Aboyne that he hoped soon
to join him, and, as he waited for the Gordons, Ogilvy of
Powrie appeared with other news. The king had at last
made a desperate effort to fulfil his promise, and on the
14th of October Digby and Langdale had set out from
Welbeck with 1,500 horse. Montrose was summoned to
join hands with them on the Border, and he at once sent
off word to Huntly and Aboyne. But, as he waited, there
presently arrived melancholy tidings. On the 15th Digby
and Langdale had scattered Poyntz's infantry at Sherburn,
but were in turn surprised and driven north in confusion
to Skipton. Digby himself, with Nithsdale and Carnwath,
resolved to make a wild dash for the Border, and, in spite
of a defeat at Carlisle, pushed on across Esk with a small
party of horse. On the 22nd or 23rd he was as far north
as Dumfries, but he could not stay. He had no news of
Montrose, and far too much news of Leslie; he began his
retreat, his men deserted into the Cumberland hills, and he
himself was compelled to flee to the Isle of Man. On the
day that Montrose left Braemar, Digby's raid had come to
an inglorious end.

Montrose's one object was now to prevent further executions, so he marched south into the Lennox, where lay his
own lands of Mugdock, now transferred by Parliament to
Argyll. He had a force of some 1,500, mostly Atholl men
and Farquharsons, including 300 horse raised by Erskine
and Ogilvy, and his appearance so near Glasgow did indeed
procure a postponement of the bloody work at the Mercat
Cross. He took up his quarters at Buchanan on Lochlomondside—then the seat of the Covenanting Sir George
Buchanan,[1] but now the home of Montrose's descendants
—and for a week or so threatened Glasgow. Leslie had

---

[1] The *A. P. S.* calls him George; Wishart calls him John.

3,000 troops in or about the city, and Montrose, with his raw levies, did not dare to meet that veteran horse in open battle. It was a hopeless form of war, as he soon realized, and early in November he passed into Menteith. Presently he made a journey into Angus, from which he was hunted back by Middleton's dragoons. Historians have assumed that he went to attend his wife's funeral, but, since Lady Montrose lived till 1648, that explanation must be abandoned.[1]

He returned to Atholl to find that his brother-in-law and most trusted adviser, the old Lord Napier, had died at Fincastle in his absence. Napier was over seventy years of age, and had spent his long and blameless life in the pursuit of the liberal arts and the service of his fellow-men. He was the wisest head in the Scotland of his day, a staunch Presbyterian, an upholder of popular liberties, an exponent of the unpopular doctrine of toleration—the type of what the Covenanters might have been in happier circumstances. About the same time Montrose received a letter from Charles, written from Newark on 3rd November, which may have done something to sweeten his memory of Digby's failure. " As it hath been none of my least afflictions and misfortunes," the king wrote, " that you have had hitherto no assistance from me, so I conjure you to believe that nothing but impossibility hath been the cause of it. . . . Be assured that your less prosperous fortune is so far from lowering my estimation of you, that it will rather cause my affection to kythe (show) the clearlier to you. . . . Upon all occasions, and in all fortunes, you shall ever find me your most assured, faithful, constant friend."[2]

From his old friend's grave Montrose turned again to the weary business of chaffering with Huntly. He sent Sir John Dalziel to him to ask for a conference; but Huntly, as shy as he was vain, seemed to fear to meet his rival and declined. Montrose resolved to see him at all costs, and early in December set off again from Atholl across the hills. It was now midwinter—a worse cold, says Wishart, than his generation had ever known.[3] A bitter frost coated

---

[1] Napier took the story from Burns's diary in Maidment's *Historical Fragments*, and it has been generally accepted. But in the disposition of the Montrose lands by the Committee of Estates to Sir William Graham of Claverhouse on February 21, 1648, provision is made for her liferent. She seems to have died shortly afterwards. See Balfour Paul, *The Scots Peerage*, VI., 253. Her life was so retired that a story like Burns's passed without contradiction.

[2] Napier, II., 613-614.

[3] It was as bad in England. See Turner, *Memoirs*, 41.

everything with ice, but did not make the streams the easier
to cross, and that December passage of the barrier mountains of Esk and Dee lived in the memory of men who were
no strangers to hardships. The feet of the infantry were
clogged with snow, the horses floundered in half-frozen
bogs, or crashed through the ice of mountain pools.
Christmas that year, which saw the death sentences of his
friends at St. Andrews, found Montrose pursuing the
evasive Huntly from one refuge to another. He looked for
him in Strathbogie, but Huntly fled to the Bog of Gight.
Thither Montrose followed, and the Gordon, at bay, was
obliged to receive him. Under the spell of the viceroy's
grace and courtesy the cloud of suspicion seemed to lift.
Huntly was roused to interest. He had 1,400 foot and 600
horse. These, combined with Montrose's 800 foot and 200
horse, would make a formidable army. He promised his
support in the northern war, and offered to lead his men
through the lowlands of Moray to the siege of Inverness,
while Montrose marched down Strathspey. The capture
of that town might fix Seaforth's loyalty, which once more
was up for auction. Aboyne and Lord Lewis wished, in
Wishart's phrase, " damnation to themselves " if they failed
the king in the future. They were to do their best to
earn it.

The operations of the year 1646 began, therefore, with
good promise of success. The promise was not fulfilled.
The next few months must have been among the most
wretched in Montrose's life. With a heart aching from the
loss of his comrades, with a drenched and starving following, and with no news save the gloomiest from the south,
he conducted an ineffective guerilla war up and down Speyside. Huntly had nearly twice his number of foot and
thrice his number of horse, but he refused to co-operate.
The splendid fighting force of the Gordons was frittered
away, and their chief declined to undertake any operation
of war except the siege of some little castles in Moray to
gratify private animosities. Montrose's patient letters to
him are the only clues we have as to the movements of the
royal army.[1] It was at Advie and Castle Grant in the end
of December 1645, moving about Strathspey in January
1646, at Kylochy on the Findhorn in February, and at Petty
on the coast in March.[2]

[1] See the letters in *Mem. of M.*, II., 260, etc., and the itinerary in
M. & S., 164 *n.*
[2] Boswell found at Coll two letters from Montrose to Maclean

Elsewhere there were bold deeds to record. Twelve hundred of Argyll's clan, under Campbell of Ardkinglass, finding commons short in Lorn, had come raiding to the Menteith lands of Napier and other royalists, where they were joined by oddments of various clans, like the Menzieses and the Stewarts of Balquhidder. Inchbrakie and young Drummond of Balloch, having been sent to recruit in Atholl, heard of these doings, and, with some 700 of the Atholl men, came up with the raiders on the 13th of February, near Callander, and thoroughly routed them. The remnant was found by Argyll huddling under the walls of Stirling; he dispatched them into Renfrewshire, where the local Covenanters would have none of these strange allies of the Covenant, and finally—Inchbrakie and his men having gone north—sent them back into the Lennox to live on the country.[1] Another fine performance was the defence of Kincardine castle by the young Lord Napier. With fifty men he held the place against Middleton for fourteen days, and then, when capitulation was imminent, escaped by night with Drummond of Balloch to Montrose. Middleton, on the 16th of March, burned the house where Montrose had spent his youth, and left the viceroy landless and homeless.[2]

There were no such exploits to redeem the futile campaign in the north. The vital objective was Inverness, the capture of which would not only give control of a large piece of territory and important communications, but would recruit trimmers like Seaforth and the Mackenzies, the Grants, Macleod of Skye, and Macdonald of Sleat. Accordingly, early in April Montrose sat down before Inverness, and on the 29th of that month drew his lines close and fixed his guns on the top of the old Castle Hill. The Ness was unusually low, and the invading army lived largely on the Fraser country to the west of it.[3] The garrison was strong and well-supplied, and it ruthlessly destroyed all outlying buildings of the town which might give shelter to the enemy; but Montrose, strengthened by

of Coll, one written from his camp at Petty, urging him to make efforts with " those slack people that are about you " (*Tour to the Hebrides*, ch. xi.). Much of Montrose's time was always spent in the work of a recruiting sergeant.
[1] Wishart, ch. xix. Guthry, 213-214. Willcock, *The Great Marquess*, 188-189.   [2] Guthry, 215.
[3] " Betwixt the bridge end of Inverness and Guisachan, twenty-six miles, there was not left in my country a sheep to bleat, or a cock to crow day, nor a house unruffled." *Wardlaw MS.*, 315.

some of Seaforth's Mackenzies and by Macdonalds from
the west, would beyond doubt have captured it had it not
been for Huntly. Middleton had come north again, Leslie
having departed for England to look after arrears of pay,
and the 1,400 men he brought with him, joined to the
Aberdeen garrison he had left behind, made a formidable
army on the royalist flank. The Gordons lay between
Middleton and Montrose, and it was their business to
watch the former and prevent him from crossing the Spey.
But Huntly was busy with private vendettas, and sent only
insulting replies to his colleague's appeals. Montrose was,
therefore, compelled to detach three troops of horse, which
he could ill spare, to watch the Spey crossings. Lord
Lewis, who held the castle of Rothes, whether out of
treachery or a misplaced sense of humour, sent a false
message to the troops, decoyed them to Rothes, and
detained them there till Middleton was across the river.[1]

The first news Montrose had of Middleton was the
sounding of his trumpets on the 5th of May, two miles from
Inverness. He had nothing to withstand so strong a cavalry
force, so he was compelled to raise the siege. With Crawford commanding his rearguard, he crossed the Ness above
the town, marched north-west by way of the Caiplich, and
put the Beauly between him and his pursuer. In the hurry
of his retreat he was compelled to leave behind him all his
stores and ammunition and his two brass field-pieces.
Middleton followed at his leisure, but on 8th May Montrose gave him the slip, doubled back by Strathglass and
Stratherrick, and presently was again on Speyside.[2]

Matters had now reached a crisis. Huntly was not only
no friend, but was becoming an active enemy, and Montrose resolved to treat him as such. He had just, with considerable losses, taken and plundered Aberdeen, and was
clearly determined to play for his own hand. But first
Montrose made one final effort to see him and bring him
to reason. On the 27th of May he rode twenty miles to
the Bog of Gight, but Huntly saw him coming and fled.

[1] This is Wishart's account (ch. xx.). Gordon of Ruthven (184,
etc.) loyally attempts to defend Lord Lewis, but his apology does
not convince, and he has no real excuse to offer for Huntly's
supineness.
[2] For the siege of Inverness see Wishart, ch. xx.; Gordon of Ruthven, 177-187; the *Wardlaw MS.*, 314-316. The town of Inverness
had a heavy bill of damages to present to the Estates, largely for
destruction caused by its own garrison. See the details in *More
Culloden Papers* (ed. Warrand, 1923), I., 31, etc.

It was the last straw. The viceroy decided to write off the Gordons from the royal strength in Scotland, and to let Middleton make of them what he pleased. He would form a light flying squadron and ride through the northern Highlands to beat up recruits for the king. If Alasdair was gone beyond reach, he had some hopes of Seaforth and Sleat, he had Reay on his side, and he was certain of the Macleans, of Clanranald, and of Glengarry. It was a course which his wisest counsellors advised, and, with such allies, it would be strange if he could not bring to the field as stout a force as that which had scattered the Covenant in a year of battles.

III

But on the 31st of May a fateful message arrived from the king. This is not the place to describe the alternations of hope and despondency through which Charles passed, between Digby's fiasco in the north and that day in April when he slipped out of beleaguered Oxford to cast himself upon the mercy of the Scots. Negotiations had been for long in progress with Montreuil, the French ambassador, as intermediary, but Leven and his friends, while hinting at much, would commit nothing to writing. The Scots had lost all love for their English allies. The ministers had begun to realize that their conception of Presbytery was very different from that held by the English Parliament and the City of London. "The Pope and the King," wrote Baillie, " were never more earnest for the headship of the Church than the plurality of this Parliament;" and again, " The leaders of the people seemed to be inclined to have no shadow of a king; to have liberty for all religions; to have but a lame Erastian Presbytery; to be so injurious to us as to chase us home by the sword."[1] The Scottish laity were now less high-flying in their demands. They wished to see Presbyterianism entrenched in England as a protection to their own liberties, for they realized the growing military power of Independency; they wished the neighbouring government to be in the hands of their friends; and they could not mistake the meaning of the clause in the capitulation of Exeter which exempted the besieged from taking the Covenant.[2] The Independents were rapidly becoming the national English party, hostile alike to the French, the Irish, and the Scots. Argyll saw this clearly, and his speech in the House of Lords on 25th June is

[1] II., 360, 362.
[2] By this clause Thomas Fuller was enabled to continue preaching.

perhaps his chief claim to statesmanship, for he proposed an elastic and tolerant form of Presbytery and combined it with some admirable good sense on the subject of a constitutional kingship.[1]

But the time was past for such moderation. Antagonisms and suspicions had been created which must battle together till they destroyed each other. The mood of the nation was too feverish to permit of compromise. The future lay with Hyde and men like him, who would make no concession to what they regarded as sectional tyrannies. " He represented . . . the only living force with which Cromwell had seriously to count. The English Presbyterian members of Parliament, the Scottish Presbyterian lords—nay, even the king himself—were but the weavers of one vast intrigue with many faces. Hyde stood firmly upon the ground of a sentiment which would one day, through the errors of his antagonists, gain a hold upon the nation, and he knew how to bide his time till the nation had declared in his favour. It was not Puritanism, but the very opposite of Puritanism —the expansion of the reasoning intelligence—which held the main current of the thought of the seventeenth century. Cromwell, mighty as he was, could but dam back the current for a time, and when he had done his utmost he would have toiled only that Hyde might step into his place."[2]

Even had there been a chance of agreement, it would have been wrecked on the personality of the king. He could not realize that the establishment of Presbytery in England was a bed-rock claim for the Scots; they could not realize that their sovereign could be blind to this constant article of their faith. Hence all talk about the king being secured in conscience and honour if he entrusted himself to them was idle; by these words the two parties did not mean the same thing. Charles did not realize that, though the breach between the Scots and the Independents was widening, there remained between him and them an impassable gulf. No doubt there was on the Scottish side a grave lack of candour and honesty, but there was an equal disingenuousness on the part of the man who could write, as Charles did from Oxford in March, that he was " not without hope that I shall be able so to draw either the Presbyterians or the Independents to side with me for extirpating one another, that I shall really be a king again."[3]

[1] Lords' Journals, VIII., 392.　[2] Gardiner, Civil War, III., 119-120.
[3] Charles to Digby, March 26, 1646. Carte, Ormonde Papers, III., 452.

It is not safe to take refuge with an army if it is your settled purpose to betray it; the deceiver is apt in turn to become the deceived.

On 25th April Charles, disguised as a servant, rode out of Oxford over Magdalen bridge, and about seven in the morning of 5th May he arrived in the Scots camp at Southwell. For what happened in Montreuil's lodgings at the Saracen's Head we have the evidence of an eyewitness, Sir James Turner.[1] Before the king had eaten or drunk, Lothian hurried to his presence and formulated his demands. The royalist garrison must surrender Newark, the king must sign the Covenant, and establish Presbytery in England and Wales, and must order " James Graham " to lay down his arms. To this imperious speech Charles replied with the dignity that never failed him : " He that made thee an earl made James Graham a marquis."

Then began a pathetic correspondence between the king who had done so little and his captain-general who had done so much. The esteem of Charles for his great servant had ripened into a warm affection. " From henceforth," he had said a few months earlier, " I place Montrose among my children, and mean to live with him as a friend, and not as a king."[2] On 18th April he wrote to him from Oxford, telling him of his intention to go to the Scots army, and suggesting that Montrose, if he found that Leven had declared for the king, should join forces with him; the letter was sent in cypher through Nicholas to Montreuil to be delivered at the latter's discretion, and naturally was not forwarded.[3] On the 19th of May he wrote to Montrose from Newcastle :

" I am in such a condition as is much fitter for relation than for writing. Wherefore, I refer you to this trusty bearer, Robin Ker, for the reasons and manner of my coming to this army; as also, what my treatment hath been since I came, and my resolutions upon my whole business. This shall therefore only give you positive commands, and tell you real truths, leaving the why of all to this bearer. You must disband your forces and go into France, where you shall receive my further direction. This at first may justly startle you; but I assure you that, if for the present I should offer to do more for you, I could not do so much."

Montrose received this letter on Speyside on the last day of May. He called a council of his officers and laid it before them; he invited Huntly, who replied haughtily that he knew all about the matter, having himself had letters

[1] Memoirs, 41.   [2] Gardiner, Civil War, III., 23.
[3] It is printed in Mem. of M., II., 274, and Clarendon State Papers, II., 224.

from the king. In his reply on 2nd June Montrose declared himself at his Majesty's commands, but asked that some protection should be secured for those who had risked all in the royal cause.

" For, when all is done that we can, I am much afraid that it shall trouble both those with your Majesty, and all your servants here, to quit these parts. And as for my own leaving this kingdom, I shall in all humility and obedience endeavour to perform your Majesty's command, wishing (rather nor any one should make pretext of me) never to see it again with mine eyes; willing, as well by passion as action, to witness myself your Majesty's most humble and most faithful subject and servant."

He also wrote privately to the king, asking if his surrender to the Scots had been by his own will or by compulsion; if the latter, he would keep his army in being.[1] Then he broke up his camp and marched to Glenshee to await the king's answer.

Charles replied on the 15th of June, repeating his commands, and promising protection for Montrose's followers.

" I assure you that I no less esteem your willingness to lay down arms at my command for a gallant and real expression of your zeal and affection to my service than any of your former actions. But I hope that you cannot have so mean an opinion of me that, for any particular or worldly respects, I could suffer you to be ruined. No. I avow that it is one of the greatest and truest marks of my present miseries that I cannot recompense you according to your deserts, but, on the contrary, must yet suffer a cloud of the misfortunes of the times to hang over you. . . . For there is no man, who ever heard me speak of you, that is ignorant that the reason that makes me at this time send you out of the country is that you may return home with the greater glory; and in the meantime to have as honourable employment as I can put upon you. This trusty bearer, Robin Ker, will tell you the care I have had of all your friends and mine; to whom, albeit I cannot furnish such conditions as I would, yet they will be such as, all things considered, are most fit for them to accept. Wherefore, I renew my former directions of laying down arms unto you, desiring you to let Huntly, Crawford, Airlie, Seaforth, and Ogilvy know that want of time hath made me now omit to reiterate my former command to them, intending that this shall serve for all, assuring them and all the rest of my friends that, whensoever God shall enable me, they shall reap the fruits of their loyalty and affection to my service."

On the 16th of July the king wrote again :

" The most sensible part of my many misfortunes is to see my friends in distress and not to be able to help them, and of this kind you are the chief. Wherefore, according to that real freedom and friendship which is between us, as I cannot absolutely command you to accept of unhandsome conditions, so I must tell you that I believe your refusal will put you in a far worse estate than your compliance will. This is the reason that I have told this bearer, Robin Ker, and

---

[1] Guthry, 219. Montrose must have received a private assurance on this point

the Commissioners here, that I have commanded you to accept of Middleton's conditions, which really I judge to be your best course according to this present time; for, if this opportunity be let slip, you must not expect any more treaties; in which case you must either conquer all Scotland or be inevitably ruined. . . . Wherefore if you find it fit to accept, you may justly say I have commanded you, and if you take another course you cannot expect that I can publicly avow you in it until I shall be able (which God knows how soon that will be) to stand upon my own feet; but, on the contrary, seem to be not well satisfied with your refusal, which I find clearly will bring all this army upon you—and then I shall be in a very sad condition, such as I shall rather leave to your judgment than seek to express."[1]

The command admitted of no refusal. Seaforth and Huntly were making their own terms; moreover, the futile Antrim had arrived in Scotland to assist Alasdair in a private war in Argyll, and was summoning the Highlanders to follow his own standard.[2] Accordingly, towards the end of July Montrose met Middleton on the banks of the Isla to arrange terms. Middleton was to stain his later record with many crimes, but he had some of the instincts of a soldier. He granted better conditions than might have been looked for. A free pardon was given to all the royalists except the viceroy, Crawford, and Sir John Hurry, who, since Kilsyth, had been with Montrose. These three were to leave the country before the first day of September, the Estates providing a vessel. All forfeited lands were to be restored, except in the case of the three excepted, and of Graham of Gorthie, whose estate was already in the hands of Balcarres. Montrose accepted the conditions, and, assembling his army on 30th July at Rattray, near Blairgowrie, bade his men farewell. He told them that what he did was for the king's sake and by the king's command. It was a melancholy parting with those Highlanders of Atholl who had never failed him, and with comrades such as Airlie and Ogilvy and the young Napier, who, in good and evil report, had been true to their salt. For such men " passion " was a harder service than " action."[3]

[1] The correspondence will be found in *Mem. of M.*, II., 277-284, and *Hist. MSS. Comm.*, 2nd Report, 170.

[2] He claimed to be the king's general of the Isles and the Highlands. See note on p. 138.

[3] Wishart, ch. xxi. Gordon of Ruthven, 194, etc. Guthry, 219, etc Burnet (*Mem. of the Hamiltons*, 280) has a story that the mildness of the terms was due to the intervention of Hamilton, now released from prison; but the terms to be offered by Middleton were settled before Hamilton reached Newcastle. *Cf.* Napier, II., 638-639. Hamilton and Lanark may, however, have helped, as Burnet alleges, in the ratification of the terms by the Estates. It was to their interest to get Montrose out of Scotland.

The Committee of Estates did not accept with any graciousness the terms which Middleton had agreed. They dared not repudiate their general, for Middleton was not a man to brook insults, and his forces, added to Montrose's, might soon be hammering at the Edinburgh gates. But they did their best to defeat the bargain by delay. Montrose had received a private letter from the king at Newcastle, dated the 21st of August, of which the postscript bade him defer his going beyond seas " as long as you may, without breaking your word."[1] It was a dangerous instruction, but Montrose accepted it. As the last days of the month approached he grew suspicious of the Covenant's good faith. There was no sign of the promised vessel till, on the 31st, a ship put into Montrose harbour with a sullen master and a more sullen crew. English men-of-war, too, had appeared off the coast. When Montrose proposed to embark at once, the skipper declared that he must have time to caulk his vessel and attend to the rigging.[2] This meant that the days of grace would be exceeded, and the viceroy left stranded, an outlaw at the mercy of his enemies.

Happily a small Norwegian sloop was in the harbour of Stonehaven, and its master, one Jens Gunnersen, agreed to sail with the exiles. Hurry, Wishart, and Drummond of Balloch; Harry Graham, Montrose's half-brother; John Spottiswoode, one of the nephews whom old Sir Robert had entrusted to the viceroy's charge; three soldiers, John Lisle or Lillie, whom we shall meet later at Carbisdale, Patrick Melvin, and David Guthrie; a Frenchman Lasound, who had been Lord Gordon's valet; and a young German called Rudolf made up the little party. The sloop sailed down to Montrose roads on the 3rd of September,[3] and that evening Mr. James Wood, a minister, and his servant put off in a wherry from the shore, and were taken aboard. The servant was Montrose. " This," says Wishart, " was in the year of our Lord, 1646, and the thirty-fourth of his age."

[1] *Mem. of M.*, II., 284. This letter may have been in reply to a private letter from Montrose telling him that Seaforth, who had now declared for the king, could raise 8,000 men, and that there was an offer of 7,000 from the Irish royalists. So Gardiner (III., 152) reads an undated message in the *Archives des Affaires Etrangères*, LIII., 517. [2] Wishart, ch. xxi. Monteith, 245.
[3] So Wishart; Monteith says the 5th. " His friends put out to sea on the 5th of September, having run the risk of being murdered by the country people, who cut the cable while the ship was at anchor, and put them in danger of splitting upon the rocks." *Op. cit.*, 245.

BOOK III

PASSION

CHAPTER XV

THE YEARS OF EXILE

(*September* 1646-*March* 1650)

Byrhtwold spoke and grasped his shield—he was an old companion
—he shook his ashen spear, and taught courage to them that fought:
" Thought shall be the harder, heart the keener, mood shall be the
more, as our might lessens. Here our prince lies low, they have
hewn him to death! Grief and sorrow for ever on the man that
leaves this war-play! "

Song of Maldon
(**W. P. Ker's translation**).

I

FOR OVER TWO YEARS MONTROSE **HAD BEEN LIVING THE LIFE**
of the camp, his mind concentrated upon the immediate
purpose of winning battles.[1] His main strategical plan of
joining hands with the king on the Border and severing the
alliance of the Scots and the English Parliament had failed
through no fault of his, and the lack of this larger co-
operation had nullified his local victories. But he had not
given up hope, even though Charles was a prisoner. Before
he left Scotland he had sent Crawford to the queen in Paris
with a proposal to raise the clans and rescue the king from
his captors.[2] He regarded himself as still a serving soldier,
and his survey was narrowed to the field of arms. No more

[1] It was a life of the sternest kind. " During a winter of exceptional severity he lived for the most part in the open air, without
quarters, without even tents. He endured all war's hardships, with
nothing to appease his thirst and hunger but icy water or melted
snow, without bread and salt, and with only a scanty supply of lean
and starveling cattle " (Wishart, *Dedication*).

[2] *Clarendon Papers*, cited by Napier, II., 653. With Irish and
Lowland support Crawford estimated that he could raise over 23,000
men. He included Macleods (1,000), Grants (1,000), and Mackenzies
(2,000).

for him those speculations on the theory of the State, which had been his earlier interest. The time had gone by for reason and philosophy; unreason, armed and mailed, had seized the reins of power, and the philosopher must now be the warrior and appeal to a harsher arbitrament than dialectic. Some such narrowing of vision was inevitable. The king was no longer the king of his discourse on "Sovereign Power," but the master who commanded his sword, and the kaleidoscopic changes of events and parties in England he regarded with an eye only to their military reaction. His life and thought were restricted to a single purpose.

After a week's tossing in the North Sea Montrose reached the Norwegian port of Bergen, where he found a Scot, one Thomas Gray, in command of the castle. His immediate purpose was to visit Denmark to meet Christian IV., with whom, as the uncle of Charles, he might confer on the next step. He had talked for months with none but rough-handed Scots nobles, and he needed some one with a wider survey to advise him on the complications of his task. He had sheathed his sword at his master's bidding, but his life was dedicated to the cause, and from that devotion there could be no release but death. So on 15th September the exiles started on the overland route to Christiania, probably sailing up the Sognefiord to Leardalsören, and then traversing the backbone of mountains by the Leardal valley and Valders. From the little port of Marstrand they crossed into Denmark, only to find that King Christian was in Germany. Montrose passed on to Hamburg, where he spent the winter waiting for instructions.

But no instructions came—not even his credentials as ambassador-extraordinary to France which Charles had promised him. One letter he had from the king, dated from Newcastle on January 21, 1647, in which he was referred for orders to the queen; and one from Henrietta Maria, written from Paris on 5th February, promising further dispatches, and subscribing herself his " very good and affectionate cousin and friend."[1] The parasites and adventurers who surrounded the queen were resolute that Montrose should not break in upon their follies with his untimely zeal. When, tired of waiting on orders that did not arrive, he left Hamburg in March, he was met in Flanders by John Ashburnham with a second letter from Henrietta, and a suggestion from Jermyn that he should

[1] *Mem. of M.*, II., 299-302. *Hist. MSS. Comm.*, 2nd Report, 170.

return to Scotland and renew the war. As no reference was made to his own proposals sent through Crawford, Montrose naturally refused to engage in an enterprise for which he had no resources and no warrant from his master. Ashburnham then hinted that he might make his peace with the Covenanters, following the royal precedent. The proposal was indignantly rejected. " Not even the king," he said, " should command his obedience in what was dishonourable, unjust, and destructive to his Majesty himself."[1]

In Paris the queen received him graciously, but, when he preached the immediate necessity of armed intervention in her husband's behalf, she made it very clear that his counsels were not those most grateful to the royal ears. Jermyn and the rest gave him tepid smiles and the cold shoulder. To one of his temper the mingled silliness and vice of Henrietta's court must have been in the extreme repulsive. The king was a captive, the flower of English and Scottish chivalry had died for his sake, and these mountebanks were turning life into a thing of backstairs gossip and idle laughter. There appears to have been a suggestion that his niece, Lilias Napier, a spirited girl in her teens, should become a maid of honour, but Montrose sternly forbade it. " There is neither Scots man nor Scots woman welcome that way; neither would any of honour and virtue, chiefly a woman, suffer themselves to live in so lewd and worthless a place."[2]

But if the tawdry court-in-exile had little to say to him, Paris made amends. His fame had gone abroad throughout Europe, and the most distinguished men in France came to pay him their respects. He was given precedence before the regular ambassadors. De Retz, who had followed his campaigns with admiration, welcomed him as a Roman hero reborn in a degenerate world. The great Mazarin offered him the command of the Scots in France, and a lieutenant-generalship in the French army; then the captaincy of the Gens d'Armes, with a large pension; and, last, the captaincy of the king's own guard and the rank of Marshal of France. The young Napier, who had now joined him, was eager that he should accept. A dazzling career opened before him, for with his talents in the field he might look to be a second Condé, rich, idolized, the head of a great army, and not the impoverished captain of a few ragged exiles.

---

[1] Wishart, Part II., ch. i.
[2] Napier, II., 661. I agree with Napier's interpretation of this letter. *Cf.* the letter from Lilias, ibid., 647.

But to enter the French service meant, in common decency, to give up thoughts of any other, and his sword had been dedicated and was not his own to sell.[1]

Meanwhile strange things were happening in the country which he had left. On January 30, 1647, the Scots army, as Montrose had always anticipated, had handed over the king to the English Parliament. The carts, laden with the deferred pay of Leven's soldiers, were soon rumbling over the Border, while the women of Newcastle were with difficulty prevented from stoning the retiring troops, and ribald songs were beginning to be sung everywhere in England and France.[2] It is difficult to read the dispatches of Montreuil and Bellièvre, and not believe that the Scots had guaranteed to Charles personal security; their very Covenants bound them to this, and beyond doubt, when Charles committed himself to their charge, he believed that with them, even if he did not find support for his doctrine of government, he would at any rate be assured of safety. He believed it, and they knew that he believed it; they seem to have believed it themselves, for there is on record a declaration of a Commission of the General Assembly that the Scots did not deliver up the king " until sufficient surety was given by both Houses of Parliament ensuring the safety and the preservation of his Majesty's person." Such a guarantee, implied and explicit, was broken by his transference to other hands. But it is no less certain that the consideration for the bargain was not the money. Had Charles complied with their conditions about Presbytery, they would gladly have forfeited the arrears of the English payments and defied English Parliament and English army. They sold their king indeed, but it was for a different price, and one which was never paid—the enforcement, urged by some on prudential and by others on mystical grounds, of an alien church polity which was rapidly becoming anathema to the English nation.

The transference of the king was the defeat of Presbyterianism south of the Border; thenceforth the struggle was of Royalist and Independent. The division between Scotland and England became sharper; monarchy and intolerance were arrayed against republicanism and toleration. In June Charles passed from the Parliament into the charge of Cromwell's army, and on his way south he wrote to

---

[1] Lord Napier to his wife, June 14, 1647. Napier, II., 665, etc.
[2] " Traitor Scot, 　　　　　　 " L'Ecosse, parjure à sa foi,
　 Sold his king for a groat." 　 Pour un denier vendit son roi."

Montrose from Newmarket, bidding him again take instructions from Henrietta, and thanking him for the present of a sword.[1] It was a strange gift to one whose career in the field was closed for ever. But the doings of Cornet Joyce had alarmed the more moderate of the Covenanters, and that party began to reveal the characteristic of all factions, and split in two. There had been much divided opinion about the transactions of the preceding January; there was now no dominant party in England to which the Covenanters as a body could adhere; English dislike of them was returned with interest; they regarded the sectaries and their gospel of toleration with scarcely more love than they regarded episcopacy and royalism. Hamilton was back in Scotland, and was busy making a party of those who favoured the Covenant but did not favour Cromwell, and professed devotion to the principle of monarchy. In November Charles escaped to Carisbrooke castle, in the Isle of Wight—a mere change of prison; and there, on 27th December, he entered into a secret engagement, with Lanark, Loudoun, and Lauderdale as signatories. The scheme was doomed from the start, both by its terms and the character of its promoters. They combined these incompatibles, the king and the Solemn League; their royalism offended the Independents, their Covenant alienated the royalists, and they had nothing wherewith to attract any substantial English following. They had not even a creed to unite Scotland. They strove for nothing which had any real meaning. There was no half-way house between Montrose and Argyll.

Nevertheless, the Estates, when they assembled in March 1648, gave the Engagers a large majority, and sanctioned the raising of an army to rescue the king from that captivity into which a year before they had sold him. Argyll went into opposition, as well he might. Apart from his dislike of the Hamiltons, who sponsored the Engagement, a man of his acumen realized that out of such a medley of half-hearted blunderers there could only come disaster. Robert Baillie, who was against the Engagement, yet deplored the intransigence of the leaders of the Kirk and his own party, was moved to write almost in Montrose's words: "I am more and more in the mind that it were for the good of the world that churchmen did meddle with ecclesiastical affairs only; that, were they never so able otherwise, they are unhappy statesmen; that, as Erastian Cæsaro-Papism

[1] *Mem. of M.*, II., 303.

is hurtful to the Church, so an Episcopal Papa-Cæsarism is unfortunate for the State. If no man were wiser than I am, we should not make so many scruples to settle the throne and pull down the sectaries."[1]

One of the first steps which the Engagers took was to communicate with Henrietta and the Prince of Wales in Paris. The queen did not inform Montrose of their proposals till she had made up her mind to accept them and had already committed herself. He knew too much of Hamilton to look for great things in that quarter, but he offered to do all in his power to save the situation by enlisting under his own banner those royalists who would enlist under no other, and by supporting the Engagers in the field. Hamilton's envoys, however, had warned the queen that Montrose must have no share in the business, and his offer was coldly declined. In despair he looked elsewhere for a sphere of action where he could further his master's interests and raise troops for his service. Mazarin and his colleagues were half-hearted in Charles's cause, and too cordial in their treatment of the English Parliament. So at the end of March 1648 he slipped away from Paris with some of his friends, and travelled by Geneva and Tyrol to the Emperor's court at Vienna.[2]

Wishart's account in Latin of the *annus mirabilis* of 1644-45 had been published in Holland towards the close of 1647, and had leaped at once into a wide popularity.[3] The doings of the Scottish soldier were the talk of every

---

[1] III., 38-39.

[2] Clarendon's explanation of his departure is wounded vanity (XII., 15). Burnet's gossip, given on the authority of Hamilton's daughter, that Montrose left Paris in disgrace with the queen because " he had talked very indecently of her favours to him," is sufficiently refuted by Montrose's character. See Napier, II., 698.

[3] The Latin text of Part I., *De Rebus Auspiciis Serenissimi et Potentissimi Caroli, etc., sub imperio illustrissimi Jacobi Montisrosarum marchionis, etc., Commentarius interprete, A. S.* (Agricola Sophocardius, *i.e.* George Wishart), was issued in 1647 at the Hague or Amsterdam. A second edition, superbly printed, appeared in Paris in 1648, a third at Amsterdam in the same year, and (if we are to believe the preface to the 1756 translation) a fourth in 1649. The first English translation was published by Samuel Browne at the Hague, probably in 1647 (I have in my collection the copy of this edition specially bound for presentation to Prince Charles). It was reprinted in 1648 in a beautiful small quarto, and in 1649 in a barbarous duodecimo, with various passages differently rendered. In 1652 the same translation, with additions consisting of a continuation of Wishart's Part I. by a different hand, and an account of Montrose's trial and death, was issued in London under the title of *Montrose Redivivus*. Another edition, with additional matter, ap-

camp and city in Europe, and at the imperial court Montrose found himself welcomed as a hero. The Emperor Ferdinand IV., whom he found at Prague, gave him the crimson baton of a Marshal of the Empire, and empowered him to raise troops in any quarter of his dominions. The Emperor's brother and successor, the Archduke Leopold, was Governor of the Spanish Netherlands, and Montrose was advised that the western border of the empire was the place for his purpose. It had the further merit of being nearer Britain in case of a summons from home. Germany was too much harassed by war to make easy travelling, so Montrose returned by Cracow and Dantzig to Denmark, and thence by way of Groningen to Brussels. He found the archduke at Tournai, but it was his fate to look for help from those who at the moment had none to give. As he had met Rupert on the morrow of Marston Moor, so he found Leopold on the morrow of Lens, where, on the 20th of August, the genius of Condé had scattered the imperial troops.

He accordingly returned to Brussels, where he received startling news from Scotland. To the bulk of the English royalists the Engagement made no appeal, since it contained " so many monstrous concessions that, except the whole Kingdom of England had been likewise imprisoned in Carisbrooke Castle with the king, it could not be imagined that it was possible to be performed."[1] Scotland was wildly divided. The great bulk of the ministers were

peared in 1660. A new translation, with various letters and additional notes, was published in 1720 and reprinted in 1724, and a revised version was issued by Ruddiman in Edinburgh in 1756. This was reprinted, with some further notes, by Constable in 1819. Meantime there had appeared in Paris in 1767 a French translation in two volumes. In 1893 Canon Murdoch and Dr. Morland Simpson issued, under the title *Deeds of Montrose*, a complete edition of both parts of Wishart's Latin narrative, with a new English version, and three chapters on Montrose's last expedition, largely based on the Danish and Swedish archives. This must rank as the definitive edition, and the editors' learned and ample notes cannot be overpraised. For the bibliography of Wishart see their Critical Introduction. Wishart prefaces his text with a long dedication to the Prince of Wales. This was printed in the Latin edition, and in the first English translation of 1647, but omitted in the subsequent translations. The reason appears in Burnet, *Mem. of the Hamiltons*, 344: " To oblige the Duke (of Hamilton) the more, a book being dedicated to his Highness containing some passages much to the Duke's dishonour, he refused to accept of it, and ordered it to be called in." The letter on the subject from the prince to Montrose is in Bodleian MSS., 895. This may account for the rarity of the first English edition.

[1] Clarendon, *Hist.*, X., 167.

opposed to it, for though they liked the English sectaries
little they liked the king less; the pulpits rang with denunciations, and in May there was an armed rising at
Mauchline, in Ayrshire, which was with difficulty suppressed by Middleton and Callander. Argyll, Eglinton,
Balmerino, Elcho, Cassilis, and Balcarres, the leaders of
the opposition, were joined by Loudoun the Chancellor,
who suddenly turned his coat. The Engagers were in
desperate straits for money, and in still more desperate
straits for leaders, for David Leslie belonged to the other
faction. Hamilton, who had not a vestige of military
talent, was their commander-in-chief, with Callander, who
was no more than a disciplinarian, as his second-in-command; Middleton, his master of horse, was the only able
soldier.

Leaving their enemies mustering behind them, the
Engagers crossed the Border on 8th July, with Sir Marma-
duke Langdale as their solitary English ally, and their only
appeal to the English people their proposals to free the
king, disband the Parliament army, and restore the Covenant. Lanark would have liked to take order with Argyll
and the ministers before leaving Scotland[1]—the wiser plan;
but indeed the wisdom of any plan signified little under
such generalship as Hamilton's. He had 10,500 men, Langdale had nearly 3,000, and Sir George Monro joined him
at Kendal with part of the Scots army from Ireland. The
history of the disastrous march may be read in Clarendon
and Burnet and the memoirs of Sir James Turner. The
Scottish forces were under no central command, and their
division was their undoing. Lambert was waiting for them
in Yorkshire, and Cromwell joined him on 13th August.
On the 17th Callander and Middleton, with the cavalry,
were as far south as Wigan; Hamilton was at Preston,
about to cross the Ribble, with Langdale behind him, while
Monro was far behind with Musgrave in the north. Cromwell, having made, in Montrose's fashion, a swift flank
march over the Lancashire hills, fell upon the centre at
Preston—it was " St. Covenant's Day," the anniversary of
the signing of the Solemn League—routed it and cut the
army in two. The dismembered van dribbled south, Baillie
with 4,000 foot surrendering at Warrington bridge, and
Hamilton with the cavalry at Uttoxeter.

During the next weeks Scotland was in dire confusion.
Eglinton and Loudoun organized the Whigamore Raid of

[1] Burnet, *Mem. of the Hamiltons*, 351.

west-country peasants, which occupied Edinburgh. Monro almost captured Argyll at Stirling, and Lanark, with Monro's aid, could no doubt have destroyed the Whigamores, had not his colleagues over-ruled him. The Estates capitulated on shameful terms to the Kirk. On 21st September Cromwell crossed the Tweed and met Argyll, and on 4th October was in Edinburgh. He stayed in Lord Moray's house in the Canongate, dined with Argyll and Wariston, and met the leading ministers like Blair, Dickson, and Guthrie. Of the nobles he wrote that " he found nothing in them other than what became Christians and men of honour."[1] Mr. Blair thought him " an egregious dissembler, a great liar . . . and a greeting deevil."[2] Argyll, as usual, was right in his diagnosis. With his keen eye for political values he had attached himself to the strongest force of the day. But he cannot have thought hopefully of the future, for the extremists of the Kirk, to whom both by conviction and policy he was bound, held no single article of Cromwell's creed except his distrust of the king, and they had rejected the only help which could enable them to stand against him. He must have felt the foundations cracking under his feet. He had begun that half-hearted alliance with Oliver which was to bring him to the scaffold.

The news from home revived in Montrose the old eagerness to strike another blow for the king. He had appealed in vain to the queen and her circle; he was excluded from the dreary and futile schemes of the Engagers; he had failed with middle age, and during the winter of 1648, in Brussels, he tried an appeal to youth. He wrote to the Prince of Wales, to the Duke of York, and to Prince Rupert—repeatedly to the last, whose temper resembled his own in so far as its besetting sin was not supineness. Rupert was now at Helvoetsluys in charge of the small royalist fleet, much beset by the Parliamentary ships of war under Lord Warwick, and in constant difficulty from mutinous crews and short supplies.[3] On 7th September Montrose wrote to him:

" When your Highness shall be pleased to know that I was ever a silent admirer of you, and a passionate affecter of your person and all your ways, you will be pleased to allow me recourse to your goodness and generosity. And the rather that your Highness sees

    [1] Carlyle, *Cromwell's Letters* (ed. Lomas), I., 369.
    [2] Row, *Life of Blair*, 210.
    [3] Scott, *Rupert, Prince Palatine*, ch. xiii.

I am for the present at such distance with all interests, as no end but naked respect can now prompt me to it; which, if your Highness shall do me the honour to take in good part, and command me to continue, I shall hope it will not wrong the king your uncle's service, nor what may touch your Highness both in relation to those and these parts, in either of which I should presume to be able to do you some small services."

Rupert replied affectionately, and the stately and involved correspondence continued till January 1649. A meeting was constantly discussed, but Rupert could not leave the fleet and come to Brussels, and Montrose could hardly venture to that nest of spies, the Hague. The latter's purpose is clear. He wanted Rupert to take the fleet to Scotland, and he did not want him to involve himself in Lauderdale's toils.

" Since there be so handsome and probable grounds for a clear and gallant design if the measures be rightly taken, I should be infinitely sorry that your Highness should be induced to hazard your own person, or these little rests (remnants) upon any desperate thrust."

It does not appear that a meeting ever took place, and in January 1649, after refitting by the sale of his sister's jewels, Rupert took the fleet to join Ormonde in Ireland.[1]

Hitherto there had been no word from the Prince of Wales; he and his mother had still hopes of the Engagers, and feared to offend them by any intercourse with their deadly enemy. Presently, however, the young Charles emancipated himself from the queen and her set, and took up his residence with Hyde at the Hague. Montrose had friends who had the prince's ear, and in January 1649 he received a message from him, bidding him arrange with Hyde for a secret interview. The prince had entered upon the policy of keeping two strings to his bow. While holding the Engagers in play, he wished to have Montrose as a last resort; but, as the insistence upon secrecy shows, he was anxious to make the former believe that he looked only to them. Montrose replied that he would joyfully obey the summons, but implored the prince to distinguish true loyalty from false. " If your Highness shall but vouchsafe a little faith unto your loyal servants, and stand at guard with others, your affairs can soon be whole."[2]

---

[1] The correspondence between Rupert and Montrose is printed in *Mem. of M.*, II., 353-363. *Hist. MSS. Comm.*, 2nd Report, 173. Among the Montrose papers is preserved the key to the cypher used by Montrose at this time. Montrose himself is " Venture Fair "; Hamilton, " Captain Luckless "; Argyll, " Ruling Elder "; Callander, " Almanach "; Lindsay, " Judas "; the General Assembly " the Goodwife that wears the breeches."   [2] *Mem. of M.*, II., 364-365.

He wrote also: "I never had passion upon earth so strong as to do the king, your father, service." This was on the 28th of January. Two days later, on a snowy afternoon, on a scaffold in Whitehall, that king " not cowardly " put off his armour.

II

From the day when he heard from Hyde the news of the tragedy, almost to the close of his life, a strange oppression settled upon Montrose. A sense of dark and menacing fate hung like a cloud about him. He had. been no sentimental cavalier; he did not believe in Divine Right; to him the Lord's Anointed had never had the sanctity which he possessed for many royalists. But out of his inner soul he had created the image of an ideal monarch, wise with a wisdom to which no earthly king has attained, a personification of the dreams which had always haunted him. He had, too, the devotion of a loyal soldier to the master for whom he had risked so much. But, more than all, he saw in the tragedy the darkening of the skies over his own unhappy land. The savage and stupid barbarism of the Covenant, which had revelled in blood in the Lord's name, now seemed at last to have reached omnipotence, for it had destroyed the centre of all civil order. Henceforth there could be no compromise. He knew nothing of the folly and duplicity which preceded Charles's ultimate heroism; his rejection of compromises which would have secured to him all that was worthy in his cause; his futile search for allies who were alike perjured and impotent, and his double-dealing towards those who had on their side both honesty and power. He saw only the shedding of innocent blood, which must make a breach for all time between those who loved righteousness and those who pursued iniquity. When he heard the news he fainted among his friends. For two days he kept his chamber, and when Wishart entered he found on the table these lines :

> " Great, good, and just, could I but rate
> My grief, and thy too rigid fate,
> I'd weep the world in such a strain
> As it should deluge once again.
> But since thy loud-tongued blood demands supplies
> More from Briareus' hands than Argus' eyes,
> I'll sing thine obsequies with trumpet sounds,
> And write thine epitaph in blood and wounds."

From this moment there is an uncanniness about him, as of one who lives half his time in another world. He

has himself painted in coal-black armour; his eyes have
a fire which changes their cool greyness into something
wilder and fiercer; all youthful weaknesses seem purged
away—his pride, his intolerance, his condescension—for his
patience becomes unearthly, and his gentleness unhuman.
He has the air of a " fey " man, for whom the barriers
between the seen and the unseen are breaking down.

In the middle of February he met Hyde at Sevenbergen.
Hyde never liked him as Nicholas and Hopton and Digby
did, and in the writings of the future Lord Clarendon
admiration is always tinged with acid. But he was a loyal
servant of the new king, and he recognized capacity when
he saw it; to him Montrose was the man of the " clearest
spirit and honour " among the king's advisers, and to be
preferred " before any other of that nation."[1] Montrose
proposed an immediate expedition to Scotland, but Hyde
urged delay, and begged him not to show himself as yet
publicly at the king's court. But when the former heard
that the commissioners from Scotland were at the Hague,
he insisted on presenting himself at once to the king.[2] He
found the young Charles already in the thick of Scottish
intrigues, for the immediate result of the king's death had
been to send a wave of loyalty over that distracted land.
On the 4th of February Charles the Second was proclaimed
at the market-cross of Edinburgh by Loudoun the Chancellor. As we have seen, there had always been an odd
royalism flickering through the nation, often in the most
unlikely places; the king was a poor thing, but their own,
like the misguided Covenant; it might be well for his own
people, the Scots, to take order with him, but it was high
treason in those who hated Scotland as much as they hated
Charles. The feeling was of a piece with the later Jacobit-
ism, an assertion of nationality on the part of a small,
proud, bitterly poor country, jealous of her rich neighbour,
not yet confident in herself. It was sentimental, not
reasoned, and was found even among the extreme Covenanters. Mr. Robert Blair of St. Andrews was anxious to
attend Charles on the scaffold. " He made his account to
die with the king, and would as willingly have laid down
his head to the hatchet as ever he laid his head to a pillow."[3]

[1] *Hist.*, XII., 15.
[2] His arrival scared away that whimsical worthy, Thomas Cunningham, the Scottish Conservator at Campvere, and the fabricator of
the " Thrissels-Banner." See Cunningham, *Journal* (S.H.S.), 188-189.
[3] Row, *Life of Blair*, 215.

In November 1650 we find Mr. Robert Baillie writing to Mr. David Dickson: " If my lord Argyll at this strait should desert the king . . . I think, and many more with me of the best I speak with, that it would be a fearful sin in him, which God will revenge."[1] No doubt in ministerial breasts loyalty was intertwined with the Covenant, but it was loyalty of a kind. Hamilton's death on the scaffold in March[2] intensified the feeling of national resentment which Preston had kindled. The luckless duke was not a brilliant figure. His epitaph has been spoken by Alison Wilson in *Old Mortality*: " That was him that lost his head at London. Folks said that it wasna a very guid ane, but it was aye a sair loss to him, puir gentleman." It had been prophesied—and the prophecy had hag-ridden his mind— that he would succeed the king; but he fell heir not to a throne, but to a scaffold.

Montrose, watching Scotland from a distance, may well have believed that the aspect of affairs was more promising than ever before. There were, indeed, no Gordons to appeal to. Huntly had at last fallen into his enemy's hands, and his " bustling in the north," as Sir James Turner called his vagrant activity, was over for ever. On 23rd March he was beheaded in Edinburgh, lamenting pathetically that he had done so little for the cause he died for, and stoutly refusing to be released from the excommunication of the Kirk, which could not affect him where he was going.[3] Aboyne was in exile, dying of a broken heart, and the Gordon lands were in the power of Lord Lewis, who was soon to make his peace with his uncle. But the great northern clan of Mackenzie was hopeful. Its chief, Seaforth, had arrived at the exiled court, and his brother, Mackenzie of Pluscardine, had raised his clan in March, and along with Reay and Ogilvy had taken Inverness and given much trouble to David Leslie. They were soon to be scattered, but the hope of the Mackenzies remained. Moreover, the Covenanters could not long maintain peace with the English Parliament, or Argyll continue his pact with

[1] Baillie, III., 109. For other examples of clerical royal'st see *ibid*. III., 34, and *Commission of the General Assembly Records*, I., 427.

[2] Burnet gives a long account of his last hours, and prints his beautiful letter to his children. *Mem. of the Hamiltons*, 397. His speech on the scaffold, as well as those of Lord Holland and Lord Capel, was published in a pamphlet by Peter Cole, London, 1649. For the English royalists' view of Hamilton see the pamphlet, *Digitus Dei—God's Justice upon Treachery*. London, 1649.

[3] Balfour, III., 393.

Cromwell, since they stood for monarchy and the Covenant, while Cromwell would have none of either. In such a quarrel honesty might come by its own.

During the next few months the Hague was the battlefield of contending factions. There were three parties in Scottish politics: the rigid Covenanters with Argyll at their head, who were prepared to accept Charles if he would accept the Solemn League and Covenant and agree to the imposition of Presbytery on England; the Engagers, whose emissaries in Holland were Lanark and Lauderdale, and who had similar principles, but proposed to apply them more laxly;[1] and the royalists *sans phrase*, like Montrose, Kinnoull, Sinclair, and Napier, who were wholly against a Covenant which would make co-operation with the English loyalists impossible. In March the envoys of the Estates arrived, among them Cassilis and Mr. Robert Baillie, who, with many protestations of loyalty, demanded as the price of kingship the Covenant in all its rigidity and the repudiation of all excommunicated persons, " especially James Graham, a man most justly . . . cast out of the Church of God . . . upon whose head lies more innocent blood than for many years hath done on the head of any one, the most bloody murtherer in our nation."[2]

It is not easy to see exactly what Argyll would have been at. He was a realist in politics, and not a dreamer, but it would appear that he was losing his sense of reality. The king's execution had broken his alliance with Cromwell; his desire was for the establishment of Presbytery in both nations, but his speech in the House of Lords on June 25, 1646,[3] showed that he was prepared to advocate an elastic Presbytery with toleration for other sects; on such a programme he might have secured most of the Engagers, and considerable English support. But to return to the extreme Presbyterian claims, to demand a subscription from the king which must involve the sin of perjury, to refuse all alliance except with those of the same narrow creed, was to make Cromwell's triumph as certain as the rising of the sun. He was opposed to a great soldier with a powerful army, and he began by depriving himself of the best natural fighting material in Scotland—the clans—and the only generalship of the first order—Montrose's. Moreover, a united England and Scotland had always been one of his worthiest policies, and this intransigence was to make the

---

[1] Montrose suspected some collusion between Lanark and Argyll. See Lang, III., 200 *n*.   [2] Baillie, III., 512.   [3] See page 267, *supra*.

fissure a gulf. The conditions which he would impose on the king brought on him the hostility of most loyalists; his fidelity to monarchy set him in opposition to Cromwell and the Independents; his insistence upon the most intolerant Scots type of Presbytery marshalled against him the whole of England. It is impossible to resist the conclusion that from henceforth this adroit politician is losing his grip. He ceased to be a realist, and fell back upon the deepest strain in his nature—the religious enthusiasm which he had acquired long before at the Glasgow Assembly; and this, shot with flickering lights of irrelevant worldly wisdom, remained his mood till his death. " My thought," he wrote of this period to his son, " became distracted, and myself encountered so many difficulties in the way, that all remedies that were applied had the quite contrary operation. Whatever, therefore, hath been said by me or others in this matter, you must refute and accept them as from a distracted man of a distracted subject in the distracted time wherein I lived."[1]

The Engagers were more politic, and pressed their demands more modestly, but in substance they asked for the same thing. Lanark, indeed, in his first zeal after Preston, was prepared to " join with the lord Marquis of Montrose and all the king's party," and was " so far from contesting about command, that he would be a serjeant under Montrose."[2] But as Duke of Hamilton in his brother's stead, he fell into timider courses; if Charles was to become king it was necessary to unite Scotland, and Montrose was a perilous bone of contention. As for Lauderdale, his pure soul had been shocked (so he said) by Montrose's barbarities, though, on cross-examination by Hyde, he was unable to give an instance of any slaughter " but what was done in the field." The man whose foul table-talk was the byword of the Restoration court, and sickened even the king, was an odd censor of morals. There is a picture by Cornelius Janssen in which Hamilton and Lauderdale are portrayed side by side, a scroll passing between them, and in the dark, uncertain features of the one and the gross, gobbling mouth and cunning eyes of the other may be read all the weakness of the Engagement.

It was Montrose who was now the realist. He desired a policy which would attract the maximum support in the two kingdoms—the restoration of monarchy on constitu-

---

[1] " Instructions to a Son," cited by Willcock, *The Great Marquess*, 223. [2] *Clarendon State Papers*, II., 460.

tional lines, with freedom secured to each country for the kind of church it favoured. Charles demanded an opinion from both the royalists and the Engagers as to the conditions of the Estates. Montrose's reply is still extant, and differs from the other remonstrances and declarations through which he had already published his faith to the world only in that it is directed to a narrower issue.[1] It traced the history of the Covenant movement from its justifiable beginnings to its impossible end; it pointed out that the Covenanters required from the king a renunciation of his own private form of worship, " and yet they made it a ground of rebellion against your royal father that they but imagined he intended to meddle with them after the like kind." The document was read in Charles's council on the 21st of May, the terms of the Estates were refused, and Montrose was confirmed in his viceroyalty and appointed admiral of the Scottish seas.

Apparently the king had made up his mind. He had rejected Argyll and, having accepted Montrose, had also rejected the Engagers. He stood committed now to some such bold attempt as his captain-general had always urged. He wrote to Montrose from Breda on 22nd June that he would come to no decision touching the affairs of Scotland without consulting him, and the Duke of York a month later wrote to congratulate him on his new " occasion of employment."[2] At that time the plan was for the king to go to Ireland and establish there his principal base, but Cromwell's expedition in August caused its relinquishment.[3] Scotland remained, and in Cromwell's absence in Ireland during the whole of the winter 1649-50 there lay a sovran chance of organizing the former country for the king. Montrose had wished the king to join him there, but he had acquiesced in the Irish alternative, for his one fear was that Charles should go to Scotland in bond to the Covenant. But already Charles had begun to regard the Scottish expedition with uncertain eyes. He favoured it chiefly that he might have another asset in bargaining with the Estates. In the wars of the Middle Ages both sides on the eve of peace endeavoured to take as many fortresses as possible in order to have something to give up when the day of renunciation came; and so it was with Charles now. The intrigues with Covenanters and Engagers still went on, though the scene was moved to Paris and the court of Hen-

[1] *Mem. of M.*, II., 376, etc.   [2] Napier, II., 206.
[3] M. & S., 223, *n.* 13.

rietta. Jermyn seems to have patched up a friendship with the new Hamilton, and attempted to get Montrose's commission as viceroy annulled in his favour. "They are all mad, or worse," was the judgment of Elizabeth of Bohemia on that nest of futile and selfish schemers.

III

Montrose, at the Hague, made a new friend, and while following Charles that summer to Breda and Brussels, and when, later in the autumn, he was recruiting among the countries of northern Europe, he had a correspondent who kept a jealous eye on his interests. In his youth sentimental girls had written him love-letters; his marriage had been a love-match; but since he had been compelled to serve a new mistress, "the first foe in the field," no woman had played a part in his life. The lady who now entered it was the most celebrated in Europe. Elizabeth of the Palatine, for some brief winter months Queen of Bohemia, had the strange compelling power of her grandmother, Mary of Scots, over the hearts of men. As a girl she had been the idol of her country, for she had the fire and brilliance and endearing simplicity of her brother Henry. Her wedding to the Prince Palatine had set all England junketing for weeks. Then came the disastrous episode of the Bohemian throne, the beginning of the Thirty Years' War, the loss of both Bohemia and the Palatine, her husband's death, and the squalor of a court in exile, dependent upon foreign bounty. But misfortune, no more than age, could dim her charm. When Montrose first met her she was in her early fifties, as we see her in the portraits by Honthorst and Miereveldt—a woman who had left youth behind her, one who had known the whole range of mortal joys and sorrows, with a mouth a little narrowed by pain and disappointment, but with great brown eyes still full of the hunger of life. Few crossed her path but were beguiled, and either became her devotees and the sharers in her broken fortunes, or to their dying day cherished the memory of her as if in a shrine. Zachary Boyd, in far-off Glasgow, came under a spell which is patent even in his halting verses. Donne sent her his sermons and his prayers. To the staid Sir Henry Wotton she was "the eclipse and glory of her kind," and he wrote in anguish, "Shall I die without seeing again my royal mistress?"

> "You meaner beauties of the night,
> That poorly satisfy our eyes

K

> More by your number than your light,
> You common people of the skies,
> What are you when the moon shall rise? "

Was ever woman praised more nobly? But the glamour
fell on others than the poets. " I see it is not good to be
my friend," she once wrote, and indeed a following so loyal
could not but suffer in a cause so calamitous. But for
Elizabeth's sake men forgot worldly wisdom, and were
back in the high days of chivalry. There were the young
gentlemen of the Middle Temple, who kissed a sword and
swore a solemn oath to live and die in her service. There
was Sir Ralph Hopton, who, fresh from Oxford, accompanied her in the flight from Prague; and Conway, and
Lord Carlisle, and Sir Dudley Carleton, and Lord Cromwell, and Sir Thomas Roe, and Christian of Brunswick.
Soldiers, courtiers, ambassadors, bravos, each subscribed
himself, like Christian, " your most humblest, most constant, most faithful, most affectionate, and most obedient
slave, who loves you and will love you, infinitely and
incessantly to death." And there was Lord Craven, who
laid his great fortune at her feet, and lived only to serve
her.

What was there in Elizabeth to draw forth this wealth
of love? Reckless, extravagant, exacting, perhaps a little
heartless, there was about her a kind of stellar greatness,
a spirit that could not be soiled or subdued by fate. Like
Constance, she had " instructed her sorrows to be proud,"
but it was a laughing pride which endeared as well as awed.
" Though I have cause enough to be sad," she wrote to Sir
Thomas Roe, " yet I am still of my wild humour to be as
merry as I can in spite of fortune." She was a better friend
than a mother, for her daughter Sophia declared that her
monkeys and her dogs came before her children. The
buffets of the world had a little calloused her. But her
flawless courage remained, her winning humour, her
subtlety, her abounding zest for life.

Montrose was a soldier after her own heart, and to him
the mother of Rupert and Maurice was a joy in that rabble
of half-hearted casuists. Her little sheaf of letters to him
during these months shows how gracious an interlude their
friendship was. She rallies the grave cavalier, and gives
him the news of the court from the point of view of an
ardent well-wisher. The Prince of Orange is against him,
the Princess for him. " For God's sake leave not the king
so long as he is at Breda, for without question there is

nothing that will be omitted to ruin you and your friends."
It was at her request that he sat for the splendid Honthorst
portrait, which she hung in her cabinet that it might
" frighten away the Brethren." She is full of nicknames:
Seaforth is " my Highlander," Montrose himself, " Jamie
Graham." She commends recruits for his service, she
invites him to Rhenen, her country house, to shoot at the
butts with Kinnoull and exhibit his old undergraduate
prowess; she sends him gossip to amuse him, and wild
rumours from England. She tells him that " old Brain-
ford " (Lord Brentford, who had once been Patrick Ruthven) was constant to him—" he says he is now too old to
be a knave, having been honest ever "; no doubt he was
honest, but he was rarely sober. And in every letter she
sends fervent prayers for his success, and in the last for his
" safety in Scotland."[1]

The bankrupt Palatines, men and women, were for a
while the most dazzling things in Europe. Of the four
daughters, Elizabeth, the handsome bluestocking and friend
of Leibniz, died a spinster; the pink and white Henrietta
married the Prince of Transylvania; Sophia espoused the
Elector of Hanover, and became the ancestress of the royal
house of Britain; Louise, charming, kind, ill-dressed,
artistic, turned Catholic and died in extreme old age as
abbess of Maubuisson. In the lively pages of Sophia's
memoirs there is a story of a projected marriage between
Montrose and the last princess, but it may be dismissed
as an idle tale.[2] That chapter in his life had long ago been
closed.

IV

The preparations for the Scottish campaign began in
June. Charles had promised that he would do nothing in
any of his negotiations to prejudice Montrose's commission
as viceroy, and he had further nominated him his ambassador to the northern courts. Recruits there were in
plenty, so far as officers were concerned—Scots mercenaries
who had fought in the German wars and were only too
anxious to find new employment; Scots patriots, such as
Gustavus's old colonel, John Gordon, who were eager to
strike a blow for their country.[3] Some of the said Scots
were compromising allies, and the murder of the Commonwealth envoy, Dr. Dorislaus, at the Hague on 3rd May,

[1] The letters are in *Mem. of M.*, II., 384, etc.
[2] *Memoirs of Sophia, Electress of Hanover* (Eng. trans., 1888), 22
[3] See Gordon's letter in M. & S., 283.

did not lessen the difficulties of the king and his captain-general.[1]   But foreign troops and foreign money were also necessary, and to secure these Montrose sent his emissaries far and wide.   His half-brother, Harry Graham, was dispatched to the Elector of Brandenburg, and got the promise of a large sum, which was never paid.   In August Kinnoull, with 80 officers and 100 Danish recruits, set sail for the Orkneys in an ancient patched-up vessel, and after much trouble with tempests and Parliamentary frigates, arrived at Kirkwall in September.[2]   The reason for the choice of such a base is clear.   The islanders were strangers to the religious strife of the mainland, and Lord Morton, their feudal superior, was Kinnoull's uncle, and well disposed to the royalist cause.   The Commonwealth navy, occupied with preventing Rupert's escape from Ireland, was less likely to interfere with the transports if their route lay so far to the north.   Further, the parts of Scotland adjoining were close to the Mackay and Mackenzie country, and Montrose looked for support from both clans.   If he could command the northern apex of Scotland, then Leslie, to meet him, would have to march through the hostile hill country, and in the event of a royalist victory the central Highlands would rise to a man.

Montrose himself arrived at Hamburg early in September.   Here he negotiated for supplies with the Duke of Courland, and presently set off to Schleswig to meet Frederick, the new King of Denmark.   He lingered for some time at Copenhagen, for this diplomacy was a slow business, and thence he dispatched letters to Rupert and Ormonde in Ireland, and to his friends in Scotland, which latter epistles were captured by the Estates.   There, too, he had news of Kinnoull's successful landing.   Morton had welcomed him with open arms, and all was going well for the cause.   The common people of Scotland, so Kinnoull reported, were on the eve of revolt against their masters.   " Your lordship is gaped after with that expectation that the Jews had for their Messiah, and certainly your presence will restore your groaning country to its

---

[1] Clarendon (XII., 24) ascribes the murder to Scotsmen, " servants or dependents upon the Marquis of Montrose."   A certain Colonel Whiteford, taken at Dunbeath after Carbisdale, was pardoned by the Estates because of his share in this murder.   Clarendon, XII., 141. Balfour, IV., 60.   *A. P. S.*, VI., 594.   The Covenanters seem to have considered it a justifiable vengeance upon a regicide.
[2] See the account of the voyage in Gwynne, *Military Memoirs*, 83-85.

liberties and the king to his rights."[1] But he had other
news less pleasing. Charles wrote from St. Germains on
19th September :

> " I entreat you to go on vigorously, and with your wonted courage
> and care, in the preservation of those trusts I have committed to
> you, and not to be startled with any reports you may hear, as if I
> were otherwise inclined to the Presbyterians than when I left you.
> I assure you I am upon the same principles I was, and depend as
> much as ever upon your undertakings and endeavours for my service,
> being fully resolved to assist and support you therein to the utter-
> most of my power."[2]

This was ominous. Henrietta was at St. Germains, and
Montrose knew too well her notion of policy.

Early in November, finding it impossible to do much
with Frederick, he passed over to Gothenburg in Sweden.
The port was full of long-settled Scots merchants, and one,
John Maclear, put his house and his wealth at his disposal.
Montrose's chief fear was that the reports of a treaty with
the Covenant, at which Charles had hinted in his letter,
would utterly dishearten the Scottish loyalists, and to
counteract such a danger he issued what he had prepared
some months before, the last and most famous of his
declarations.[3] The document is inspired by his old un-
hesitating courage. Montrose is as confident of the sacred-
ness of his mission as any Covenant minister. He begins
with a pertinent quotation from Tacitus; he indicts the
Covenanters alike on their past and present policy; he
offers in the king's name pardon to all except proven

---

[1] M. & S., 256. The original is in the *Wodrow MSS.*, in the
National Library of Scotland   [2] M. & S., 263.
[3] The copy in " Civil War Tracts " in the British Museum is dated
Copenhagen, July 9, 1649, but the copy in my collection has the imprint of " Gothenberge." I possess another declaration, also dated
July 9, 1649, from " Hassuia in the Kingdom of Denmark," and
apparently published in London, to which I can find no reference
elsewhere. In it Montrose defends himself against " that harsh and
uncharitable censure which the Parliament and Kirk of Scotland are
pleased to pass against me," and undertakes to do nothing prejudicial
to " the well-being and present government of that Kirk and kingdom." He undertakes also to " leave the continuance or alteration
of government either in Church or State in his Majesty's other
dominions to the judgment and discretion of his Majesty and the
Parliaments thereof." He then enumerates the crimes of his opponents, culminating in Charles's death. All this is in Montrose's
authentic manner. But the declaration concludes with the astonishing announcement that he is coming presently to Scotland, an
invitation to loyalists to meet him at Inverness, and a summons to
all rebels to lay down their arms before 1st November, otherwise
they will receive no mercy. " I will with all violence and fury pursue and kill them as vagabond rogues and regicides, not sparing one

regicides, and in a noble ending he summons all true
Scottish hearts to make a last effort for freedom:

" Resolving, with Joab, to play the man for their people and the
cities of their God, and let the Lord do whatever seemeth Him good;
wherein, whatsomever shall behappen, they may at least be assured
of Crastinus's recompense that, dead or alive, the world will give
them thanks."

The declaration was circulated in Edinburgh in December,
and, on the second day of the new year, Wariston issued
the reply of the Estates, in which it was ordered to be
burned by the hangman and its author denounced as " that
viperous brood of Satan, whom the Estates of Parliament
have long since declared traitor, the Church hath delivered
into the hands of the devil, and the nation doth generally
abhor."

Christina of Sweden, Gustavus's daughter and Descartes's
erratic disciple, was no more inclined than her neighbour
of Denmark to support publicly the royalist cause. She
could not afford to risk the displeasure of a great sea-power
like England. It was from northern Europe that the
Commonwealth looked for the expected invasion, and
every port was full of its spies.[1] The most she could do
was to wink at his presence in Gothenburg and permit him
to buy war stores. This was his chief task during December, and it is one of history's ironies that certain
supplies of powder and shot, which he did not take with
him to Scotland, were afterwards used by the Covenanters

that had any hand in that horrible and barbarous murder, committed
upon the sacred person of our late dead sovereign, but utterly
extirpate and eradicate them, their wives, children, and families, and
leaving none of their cursed race (if possible) breathing upon the
face of the earth." This peroration is such manifest folly as a pre-
liminary to the kind of campaign which Montrose projected, and so
out of keeping with his general attitude, that one must consider the
declaration an unauthorized publication by some hot-headed royalist
who perhaps had got hold of one of Montrose's drafts. Though it
bears a London imprint the style of printing is not English. Montrose is referred to as captain-general of his Majesty's forces in
" Great Britain," not in Scotland only.

The Gothenburg declaration was printed in London in 1650 by
Matthew Simmons, together with the reply of the General Assembly
and extracts from the reply of the Estates, and a cynical postscript
by some Englishman who did not love the Scots. The replies of the
Estates and the Assembly were printed at Edinburgh by Evan Tyler
in 1650 in English and Latin. They will be found also in an
appendix to the 1819 edition of Wishart.
[1] In a pamphlet, *The Great Plot Discovered, etc.* (London,
G. Cotter), Montrose was believed to be about to descend upon Nor-
folk from Denmark as early as February 8, 1647.

against Cromwell.[1] Early in that month a ship arrived from the Orkneys with melancholy news. David Leslie had marched north to Caithness in the end of October, and had written to Kinnoull advising him to depart while there was yet time. The letter was ordered to be burned by the hangman, and Leslie went south without crossing the Pentland Firth.[2] But on the 12th of November the loyal Morton died, and a few days later Kinnoull fell sick of pleurisy and followed him to the grave. The loss of his friend and " passionate servant " was a heavy blow to Montrose. But Sir James Douglas, Morton's brother, who arrived in the Orkney sloop, brought good news of the general feeling in Scotland. He implored the viceroy to sail at once, for " his own presence was able to do the business, and would undoubtedly bring 20,000 men together for the king's service, all men being weary and impatient to live any longer under that bondage, pressing down their estates, their persons, and their consciences."[3] Montrose may well have believed a report so consonant with his desires. His ardour was always prone to make light of difficulties, and he had no wise old Napier to remind him that the feelings of Sir James Douglas and his friends were scarcely an index to the temper of burgesses and peasants, wearied out with poverty and the terrors of an Old Testament God.

In December he made an effort to leave. Transports were indeed dispatched with Danish troops and Scottish officers, as well as ammunition and stands of arms, and the wild weather they encountered gave rise to tales of shipwreck which gladdened the heart of the Estates. He wrote to Seaforth on the 15th of December saying that he meant to sail for Scotland next day. But the winds were contrary, and floating ice blocked the harbour, and it was not till January 10, 1650, that he actually embarked in the *Herderinnen* (" Shepherdess "), a frigate which Maclear had bought for him from the Swedish Admiralty. Still he did not start, and on the 18th we find him living in Maclear's house on shore. We know now the reason of that delay which so puzzled the Swedish statesmen and the spies of the Commonwealth. He had received word that a dispatch was coming to him from the king in Jersey. For such a message he could not choose but wait.

[1] Douglas, *Cromwell's Scotch Campaigns*, 237 *n*.
[2] Gwynne, 86-87.
[3] Nicholas to Ormonde; Carte, *Ormonde Papers*, I., 345, etc.

But at that season of the year, in those northern waters, communications were uncertain, and Montrose had to leave Gothenburg without the royal letter. The *Herderinnen*, with stores and guns, sailed at the beginning of March, and he crossed the snowy backbone of mountain that separates Sweden from Norway, and joined her at Bergen. The Commonwealth agents reported him there on 14th March, waiting to collect various officers, who were immobilized by lack of passage money at Hamburg or Bremen.[1] Harry May, the king's messenger, had to follow the viceroy to Kirkwall in the Orkneys, where he delivered the king's letter on the 23rd of March. It was dated from Jersey on 12th January, and with it came the George and the blue riband of the Garter. There were two letters, one to be shown to his friends, and the other a private note for Montrose's own eye, and enclosed in the packet were copies of the recent correspondence with the commissioners of the Estates. In the first letter the king informed his viceroy of the negotiations with the Scots Parliament and the chance of a treaty. Montrose, however, is assured that " we will not, before or during the treaty, do anything contrary to that power and authority which we have given you by our commission, nor consent to anything that may bring the least degree of diminution to it; and if the said treaty should produce an agreement, we will, with our uttermost care, so provide for the honour and interest of yourself, and of all that shall engage with you, as shall let the whole world see the high esteem we have for you." It ends with an exhortation to " proceed vigorously and effectively in your undertaking "; and then, with an excess of candour, makes clear the reason. " We doubt not but all our loyal and well-affected subjects of Scotland will cordially and effectually join with you, and by that addition of strength either dispose those who are otherwise minded to make reasonable demands to us in a treaty, or be able to force them to it by arms, in case of their obstinate refusal." He desires an asset to bargain with, a second string to his bow. The private note merely assured the recipient that Charles would never consent to anything to his prejudice, and bade him " not to take alarm at any reports or messages from others."[2]

It was a clear instruction to proceed with the invasion of Scotland, but it had an ugly air of double-dealing. The

[1] *A Brief Relation* (April 9-16, 1650), 472-473.
[2] *Mem. of M.*, II., 410. etc.

warning against reports argued that something had been
done or said to give good cause for reports. Montrose,
regardless of self, thought only of the danger to the king—
the risk that by trusting his enemies he might walk into the
same trap as his father. In his reply, on the 26th of March,
he repeats that " it is not your fortune in you, but your
Majesty in whatsomever fortune, that I make sacred to
serve "; but he beseeches his master " to have a serious eye
(now at last) upon the too open crafts are used against you,
chiefly in this conjunction, and that it would please your
Majesty to be so just to yourself as, ere you make a resolve
upon your affairs or your person, your Majesty may be
wisely pleased to hear the zealous opinions of your faithful
servants, who have nothing in their hearts, nor before their
eyes, but the joy of your Majesty's prosperity and greatness,
which shall be ever the only passion and study of your most
sacred Majesty's most humble, faithful, and most passionate
subject and servant! "[1]

There can be no doubt that when he wrote the letters of
January Charles was loyal to Montrose, and that he counted
more on Montrose's success in the field than on the prospect of a treaty. This was the opinion of the shrewd
Commonwealth agent, with an admirable gift of phrase,
who contributed to the official gazette of the Council of
State, *A Brief Relation*. It was proved by the royal warrants, dated as late as 29th March, appointing the veteran
Lord Eythin to be Montrose's second-in-command. The
king was no doubt determined to secure honourable terms
for his captain-general in any treaty. But he hankered after
a union of all Scotland on his side, which would be linked
to a royalist rising in England, and he believed that incompatibles might be harmonized by an adroit negotiator, the
more if there were a triumphant army in the background.
The plan was an idle dream; Montrose was the true realist
when he held that Charles's only chance lay in a policy of
Scottish ways for Scotland, English ways for England, and
the king for both—a policy which meant good-bye to
Argyll and the theocrats of the Solemn League. Charles
had no intention of bringing Montrose to catastrophe, but
he made it certain by the treaty which he pursued, nay, by
the very fact of negotiating at all at such a juncture. Moreover, when Montrose received the king's message that had
happened which, had he known it, might have added

---

[1] This tragic letter was printed for the first time by Mr. Gardiner
in his *Charles II. and Scotland in 1650* (S.H.S.), 43.

K*

another protest to his reply. As early as 19th January the first letter had been published in Paris, and a précis was in the hands of the Commonwealth Government. It may have got out by a clerical blunder, for the royal secretariat was not over-competent.[1] It may have been published by the Montrose faction in Paris to defeat the projected treaty, or the issue may have been authorized by Charles to help the treaty's fortunes. There is evidence for each of the three explanations.[2] But, whether we account for the publicity given to it by accident, maladroit diplomacy, or blundering psychology, the result was disastrous. Already the letter had been broadcast over Scotland. Had Montrose been accompanied by a large and well-equipped foreign army no harm would have been done, but he had still his army to find, and it was in Scotland that he sought it. It is one thing to fight in a crusade; it is another to share in a campaign whose avowed purpose is no more than to create an object to bargain with. On such mercantile terms you cannot conjure the spirit that wins battles. The half-hearted would wait upon the result of the chaffering. Well might Mr. Secretary Nicholas write to Ormonde: " Some (not without reason) apprehend that the report of the now approaching treaty will make those of a better sort forbear to appear for him, until they shall see the issue of this treaty."[3] The dice had been loaded against the venture before it was begun. The king had sent Montrose to his death.

CHAPTER XVI

THE LAST CAMPAIGN

(*March-May*, 1650)

When my affaires goe wrong, I remember that saying of Loucan.
Tam mala Pompeii quam prospera mundus adoret.
                                        Claverhouse to Menteith, July 1680.

IT HAS BEEN THE FASHION AMONG HISTORIANS TO DESCRIBE the last campaign as doomed from the start. So in a sense it was, but its hopelessness did not lie in the actual military

---

[1] Long to Ormonde, March 2, 1650. *Ormonde Papers*, I., 367.
[2] See *A Brief Relation* (Feb. 12-19, 1650), 337, (March 12-19) 411, 416; and the letter of Abraham Cowley to Ormonde. March 3, 1650, quoted by Gardiner, *Charles II. and Scotland in 1650*, xix.
[3] *Ormonde Papers*, I., 363.

and political situation in Scotland at the moment. That had never been more favourable. Montrose was, indeed, as far off as ever from commending himself and his faith to that Covenanting *bourgeoisie* which he never lost the hope of converting. But the arm of the Covenant was shortened. The disaster at Preston had depleted the fighting strength of the Lowlands, and had driven a wedge into the Estates. Many of the nobles who had once obeyed Argyll were now prepared to follow him only in so far as he allied himself with the king. A real bitterness against England had surged up in the nation, and this meant popularity for Charles, and a fall in esteem for those who had dallied with Charles's enemies. The Estates had no war-chest; every burgh had been bled white by taxation, and all sections of the people were out of humour with the Edinburgh junta. The government of the Covenanters, now an undisguised theocracy, was as incompetent as it was oppressive. In January of the preceding year the famous Act of Classes had been passed,[1] which excluded from every office—from a ministry of state to a burgh deaconate of crafts—all who were not of one narrow type in political and religious opinions and conduct, and which gave the Kirk an absolute veto on all public appointments. It was as if the theocracy had set out to caricature itself, and it was fast disillusioning every sympathizer who had the smallest share of practical wisdom.

The military situation was not less promising. Of the former Covenant generals, Leven was too old, Baillie had been an Engager, and Hurry was now one of Montrose's companions. Middleton was waiting to be persuaded.[2] Only David Leslie remained, with his lieutenants Holbourn and Strachan; of these, Holbourn had been handsomely beaten at Kilsyth, and Strachan, an extreme sectary, was not trusted by his commanding officers. At the most they had 3,000 foot and 1,500 horse, strung out over a wide front in the northern Highlands. The estimate of what forces might be raised for the king in Scotland, which Montrose had sent to Henrietta by Crawford in the autumn of 1646, had exceeded 20,000.[3] There were uncertain items, like the 1,000 who had been credited to Lord Nithsdale, the 2,000 to Macdonald of Sleat, the 1,500 to Huntly, and the 2,000 to Seaforth; but, putting all doubtful elements aside, it looked as if in the Highlands alone he could count on

10,000 men. Things had improved since the date of that
estimate. The clan of Mackenzie had risen with Pluscardine, and might rise again, for their chief, the Queen of
Bohemia's " Highlander," was apparently at last on the
royalist side. There is no equivocal figure of that time but
has found its defender—Huntly in Patrick Gordon, Hamilton in Burnet—and we have Seaforth's defence in the simple
pages of his clansman, Mackenzie of Applecross; but the
best that the author can say is that Seaforth " in the beginning of the king's troubles had not the light that was afterwards given him."[1] It might reasonably be assumed that
now that light had been vouchsafed. The Engagers, at least
the fighting element in them, were losing some of their
hostility to Montrose. The new Hamilton was again declaring his willingness " to trail a pike or ride a private trooper
under him."[2] The new Huntly, too, whom we have known
as Lord Lewis Gordon, was reported to be waiting obedi-
ently on the king's commands,[3] though a little annoyed at
not receiving the Garter. Again, if Montrose got one-half
of the levies and supplies promised from the Continent, if
he got one-quarter of the help hinted at from Ireland, he
would be able to put into the field from 4,000 to 5,000
regular troops as well.

Leslie was in a poor position both for attack and defence,
and defeat to him would mean annihilation. For Montrose
to succeed, all that seemed essential was that he should have
sufficient troops in the far north to win the first round. If
that happened, he might count on the Macleods and the
Mackenzies; probably, too, on the Gordons; and then the
safety of his route to the south would be assured. Once
in Badenoch, he had all the loyal levies of the west and
of Atholl to draw upon, and with the Lowlands divided it
was hard to see what could prevent him from dominating
Scotland. Then he could cross the Border and appeal to
the royalists and the English moderates, not like the luckless Hamilton with an insolent dogma of Presbyterian
ascendancy, but with a wise recognition of national rights,
a generous policy of toleration, and that constitutional
creed of his which John Hampden would not have scrupled
to subscribe. We know to-day how little hold the army
of the Commonwealth had upon the affection of the
English people. Of the two leaders, Montrose was not the

---

[1] *Highland Papers* (S.H.S.), II., 65.
[2] *A Brief Relation* (March 12-19, 1650), 401.
[3] *Charles II and Scotland in 1650*, 49.

inferior in military genius, and if, with 20,000 Highland
and foreign foot and Lowland horse, and with England's
goodwill, he had met Cromwell on his return from Ireland
somewhere south of Trent, the odds are that the Restoration would have been antedated by ten years.

Dis aliter visum; rightly, perhaps, for Cromwell had still
much to give to the world. As it chanced, every condition
of success was to fail. Montrose had far too few foreign
troops. The local clans did not rise in his support, and
there was no sign of movement in the Lowlands. The
king's letter, and the news that negotiations were on foot
between him and the Estates, had done their work. Men
were weary of fighting, and half-hearted in any cause. The
satiety which attended the Restoration was beginning. Let
them be shown a way of peace and they would acclaim it,
but meantime it was the duty of wise folk to stay at home.
The Covenanting régime was becoming so intolerable to
every class that, had there been no alternative, many might
have grasped at Montrose's way of deliverance; but, since
an alternative was openly held before the nation by the
king his master, the cautious man let his sword sleep in the
thatch and hoped for a quiet life.

The king might handicap him and stultify his mission,
but Montrose was true to himself. For him there could be
no turning back on this side the grave, for he had been to
the edge of the world and looked over the other side. The
" waft of death " had gone out against him, and all his
doings have a touch of the unearthly. He devised strange
standards, like those which, in Bunyan's *Holy War*, Em-
manuel and Diabolus used in their battle for Mansoul. His
foot bore on a black ground the bleeding head of the dead
king, with the words *Deo et Victricibus Armis.* The cavalry
colours, too, were black, with three pairs of clasped hands
holding three drawn swords, and the legend *Quos Pietas
Virtus et Honor fecit Amicos.* His own flag was of white
damask, with two steep rocks and a river between, and a
lion about to leap from one to the other. His motto was
Nil Medium.[1] He was putting it to the touch, as he had

[1] *A Brief Relation* (Feb. 19-26, 1650), 360; Balfour, III., 439.
Fantastic standards were the fashion of the age, on both royalist and
Parliament side. One of the former had a lion couchant with a cur
biting its tail, and the motto *Pym, Pym, Pym! Quousque tandem
abutere patientia nostra?*—one of the latter, an armed soldier,
threatening a kneeling bishop, and the words *Visne episcopari?
Nolo, Nolo.* Firth, 45.

sung, " to win or lose it all." There is an air of doom and
desperation in everything, as of some dark saga of the
north.

The early days of April were spent at Kirkwall in
marshalling his little forces. There were four or five
hundred Danish troops already there.[1] The Orcadians,
then very far from being a warlike people, were strong on
the king's side, and raised 1,000 men. With Montrose were
a number of cavaliers and soldiers of fortune: Lord Frendraught, Sutherland's nephew and his old opponent at
Aberdeen; veterans of the German wars like Sir William
Johnston and Colonel Thomas Gray;[2] his half-brother,
Harry Graham; Sir John Hurry, now twice a turncoat; Sir
James Douglas, a brother of Morton; William Hay, the new
Kinnoull; Sir Francis Hay of Dalgetty, Drummond of
Balloch, Ogilvy of Powrie, and Menzies of Pitfoddels; and
one or two English royalists, like that Major Lisle who had
left Scotland with him in September 1646. These gentlemen were mounted and made up the whole cavalry of the
force, probably some 40 or 50 in all. Hurry was dispatched
in advance with a picked band of 500 men, to look into the
chances of a landing on the mainland. He found no
difficulty, and, hastening on past Wick and Dunbeath,
secured the Ord of Caithness—the narrow pass on the shore
through which ran the road to the south.

Montrose, with the rest of his army, crossed the Pentland
Firth in fishing-boats about the 12th of April. There was
little chance of recruiting in Caithness, but some of the
gentry, who were partisans of the Reay interest, joined his
standard. It was his business, seeing that his forces were
so inadequate, to push on with the greatest possible speed,
so as to pass the low coastlands and reach the shelter of
the hills, where the Covenant horse could do him no harm
and reinforcements could be awaited. Leslie held the
castles of Brahan, Chanonry, Eilandonan, and Cromarty;
and the Earl of Sutherland, who was hot for the Covenant,
garrisoned Dunrobin, Skibo, and Dornoch—all key-points
on the coast road. But Montrose had not hitherto been
wont to trouble about fortresses in his rear. If he marched
with his old speed, another week should find him in
Badenoch.

[1] Almost our only authority for the Orkney part of the campaign
is Gwynne. He was left stranded in those parts, and finally escaped
in a fishing-smack to Amsterdam, where he was found fainting in
the streets from starvation.
[2] Was this the ex-governor of Bergen? See page 274, *supra*.

At first his movements were swift enough. Landing near John o' Groats, he dashed upon Thurso, and the local lairds, except the Sinclairs, took the oath of allegiance.[1] Leaving Harry Graham with 200 men to keep them to their word, he marched south over the Caithness moors to Sir John Sinclair's castle of Dunbeath, took it after a few days' siege, and left a garrison. He had something less than 800 men when he joined Hurry at the Ord of Caithness. Two days later he reached Sutherland's castle of Dunrobin, which he summoned; admission was denied, and the place was too strong to take, but another day was wasted, and some of his men, who had incautiously ventured between the castle and the sea, were made prisoners.[2]

Now began the fatal delay. There was no need to diminish his tiny army by leaving garrisons behind him. Orkney was not a base the communications with which it was necessary to guard; he had still to reach his true base, which was the central Highlands. His business was not to waste an hour in getting to Badenoch. But he may have felt himself too weak to face the garrisons of the Dornoch lowlands, and he was in strong hopes of reinforcements from the north-west. So he turned in'and up the glen of the Fleet—the route taken to-day by the railway—and moved past Rhaoine to Lairg, at the foot of Loch Shin. It was now the 23rd of April. To reach the south he must cross or turn the long inlet known as the Kyle of Suther-land; the shortest way was down the Shin, but the winter had been severe and the fords were bad, so he preferred to cross the hills to Rosehall in Strath Oykell. Thence he moved down the right bank of the Oykell, reaching the Kyle early on the 25th.[3] He was expecting hourly a great acces-sion of Mackenzies from the west, and he hoped for recruits from the Monroes and Rosses[4] south of the

---

[1] So, apparently, did the ministers. One, Mr. William Smith, refused; and Wodrow (*Analecta*, I., 268) has a story that Montrose had him dragged a mile behind a boat, whereupon Mr. Smith prophesied of his tormentor's coming death. This legend has been exploded by Mark Napier in his *Graham of Claverhouse*, I., 98-102. Gordon of Sallagh, a witness hostile to Montrose, mentions the case of the recalcitrant Mr. Smith, but merely says that " he was sent to the ships to be put in irons," but was " afterwards released " (*Earldom of Sutherland*, 552).   [2] Gordon of Sallagh, 552-553.
[3] I have followed throughout this book the old style of chronology, which was eleven days behind the sun. It was now the first week of a bleak northern May.
[4] Monteith, 511 Both Ross of Balnagowan and Monro of Lemlair had been in Pluscardine's rising.

Dornoch Firth. He believed that he need fear no immediate opposition, and that there was in all Ross but one troop of enemy horse.[1]

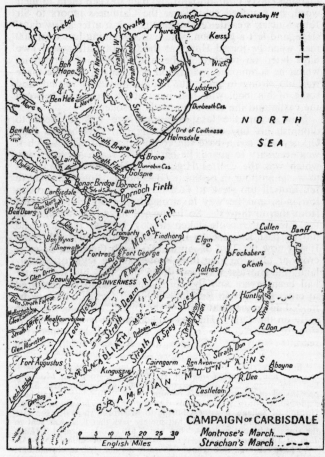

CAMPAIGN of CARBISDALE

Montrose's March _____
Strachan's March _ _ _ _ _

0   5   10   15   20   25   30
English Miles

Meantime Leslie was hurrying north to a rendezvous at Brechin, which he had appointed for the 25th of April. He had instructed Strachan and Halket, who commanded the

[1] Gordon of Sallagh, 553.

Covenant troops in Moray, to do their best to delay Montrose's advance; so Strachan, with the garrisons of Brahan and Chanonry, went north to Tain, where he was joined by other Covenant posts. He had five troops of horse—220 men in all;[1] 36 musketeers of Lawers's regiment, and a reserve of 400 Monroes and Rosses whom Montrose had vainly hoped to attach to his standard. Lord Sutherland was sent north of the Kyle to oppose Harry Graham, and cut off the way of retreat in that direction.

On Saturday, the 27th of April, Strachan marched west from Tain to a place called Wester Fearn, on the southern shore of the Kyle, a few miles south-east of Bonar Bridge and the mouth of the river Carron. Leslie only left Brechin the same day. Montrose had meantime encamped at a spot about five miles off near the head of the Kyle, under the lee of the steep hill of Craigcoinichean. It was covered with a light undergrowth, and in front was a piece of more or less level ground, with the tarn of Carbisdale at the north end, and to the south-east the deep-cut channel of the Culvain burn. He had the hill to guard his rear, the Culvain burn on one flank and the Kyle on the other, and to defend his front towards the Carron mouth a line of trenches and breastworks had been erected. Already Montrose had occupied the position for two days, waiting for the local clans, notably the Mackenzies. Had he pushed on, he might have crossed by the hill road to Alness, and have easily given Strachan the slip. After that, in another two days he could have passed Beauly and been on his old secret road to the Spey. As it was, he had found a strong position, if he chose to stay by it, for no cavalry could force the pass of Craigcoinichean, and he commanded the shore road down the Kyle by which his own scouts could bring him early intelligence of any enemy advance. He had found that, but nothing more, and meantime the precious hours were flying.

Strachan reached Wester Fearn about three in the afternoon of the 27th. He knew from his scouts where the royalists lay, and he knew their weakness in numbers. It was his business to draw them down from the hill to the flat ground, where his cavalry could act. Accordingly he concealed most of his horse among the long broom which covered the slopes about Wester Fearn. The contingent of Monroes and Rosses made a circuit up Strath Carron to a point on the heights above Carbisdale, where they

[1] Balfour, IV., 9.

awaited the issue. Like Rob Roy at Sheriffmuir, their heart was not in the fight, and they waited to see how the day went before sharing in it. Strachan then advanced a single troop up the coast till he had passed the Carron.

Major Lisle, who commanded Montrose's 40 horse, was sent to reconnoitre, and returned with information of the single troop. One of the gentleman volunteers, Monro of Achnes, repeated the assurance which Montrose had already received—that there was but one troop of horse in all the shire, and that he saw it before him. Montrose ordered Lisle to halt, and gave the word to the foot to advance. Meantime Strachan was bringing up the rest of his force from Wester Fearn. As soon as the royalists were on the low ground they could see nothing of his movements, and in the cover of the broom and the wildwood the whole Covenant cavalry crossed the Carron.

Suddenly upon Lisle's 40 horse Strachan dashed with 100 of his dragoons. Instantly there appeared a second troop under Halket, and then the reserves and the musketeers. Lisle was driven backward upon the foot, who were not deployed for battle and were easily cast into confusion. They cannot have been more than 1,200 in all—400 Danes and Germans, and the rest the raw Orkney levies. The foreigners were not accustomed to receive a cavalry charge unsupported, and the Orcadians had probably never seen a dragoon in their lives. They fell back in disorder, and Montrose saw that his one chance was to regain the safety of the Craigcoinichean entrenchments. At Dundee, once before, he had done the same thing under greater difficulties; but then his force had been of a different quality. Had he had his 500 gallant Irish the day would have been saved, but they had long been below the turf of Slain-Man's-Lee. The mercenaries retreated in some order, but the hapless islanders, farm-boys and fisherfolk unused to war, fled without a blow. Upon the fugitives came Strachan's reserves, and Lisle's handful of cavalry, in attempting to cover their retreat, was cut to pieces. There fell Lisle himself, Menzies of Pitfoddels, who bore the royal standard, Douglas and Guthrie and Ogilvy of Powrie. Soon the broken remnant of the royalists, a few hundreds at the most, was making its last stand on the wooded slopes of Craigcoinichean.

Down from the hills came the Monroes and the Rosses, convinced at last, to take their share of the victory. The Orkney men were drowned in hundreds trying to cross the Kyle, or were cut down in the haugh. Not a family in the islands but lost a son or a brother. Presently the fire from the woods slackened, and the royalists, making for the higher slopes across the open, were shot or stabbed by the horse. Hurry was captured, and with him 58 officers and nearly 400 men. Montrose had his horse shot under him. It was Philiphaugh repeated, and once more he was prevented from finding the death which he desired in battle. Frendraught, himself spent with wounds, forced him upon his own horse, and bade him remember his duty to the king's cause. In the late spring gloaming the viceroy of Scotland, accompanied by two of the Sinclair gentry, turned his face from the lost field toward the trackless wildernesses of the west.[1]

He flung away his sword-belt and coat with the star of the Garter that he might escape recognition, and on Frendraught's horse swam the tidal waters of the Oykell. Then he discarded the horse and managed to buy or borrow some rough Highland clothes. Strath Oykell was no place for a mounted man. There were two courses before him: to get into Strathnaver, and so reach Harry Graham at Thurso, and finally pass into Orkney; or to make for the friendly Reay country in the north-west. For the first he must reach Loch Shin and travel by Glen Tirry; for the second his route lay by Loch Shin or by Glen Cassley, and then by Loch More and the Laxford. But he had no knowledge of the country, nor had either of the Sinclairs, one of whom was an Orcadian and the other of Brims in Caithness; and they missed their way among the darkening hills. Instead of going north they wandered due west up the Oykell.

For two days and two nights they were without food and shelter. There were few houses in that land, and no roads; it had been a backward year, and the snow was still far down on the slopes, the bogs were full, and every stream was an icy torrent. With starving and hunted men the sense of direction soon disappears, one stretch of sodden bent is like another, and presently the hills lose their features and become a mere blur to the wearied eye. Somehow the three struggled over the watershed, where the

---

[1] The authorities for the Carbisdale campaign are Gordon of Sallagh, Balfour and Monteith. Murdoch and Simpson (289-321) have provided an admirable reconstruction, in which they have used also local tradition and Taylor's MS. account of the parish of Assynt from the Dunrobin papers.

streams began to flow to the Atlantic. It is possible that they believed that they were twenty miles farther north and beginning the descent towards Scourie. But they were now in desperate case for food, and they resolved to separate and take different roads on the chance of stumbling on help. Sir Edward Sinclair, the Orcadian, was never heard of again; somewhere in the wilderness he died of famine, and only the foxes and the eagles could tell of his end.[1] On the third day Montrose was given bread and milk at the shieling of Glaschyle. His enemies were already beating the glens, and a party reached the hut while Montrose was indoors, but he was hidden by the shepherd under a trough. On departing, he regretted that he had put his host in danger, and " determined never to do the like again to avoid death, of which, he thanked God, he was not afraid."[2] He was now some thirty miles from the scene of the battle.

But the hue-and-cry was out against him. The laird of Assynt was a certain Neil Macleod, a young man of twenty-two and a member of a sept, the " seed of John the Grizzled," with a dark record for deeds of blood. He had married a daughter of Monro of Lemlair, whom Montrose had hitherto looked upon as an ally, and he had himself been protected by Seaforth, and seems to have passed for something of a royalist. His brother-in-law sent him a letter bidding him search his country for fugitives, and " chiefly James Graham,"[3] and Neil was no laggard in the business. One of his men found the famished wanderer on the confines of Assynt, and Montrose, when he heard his master's name, probably asked to be taken to him. He thought that he had much to hope for from a Macleod and a son-in-law of Lemlair. On the evening of the 30th of April he was brought to the castle of Ardvreck, which still stands on the northern shore of Loch Assynt. There he found Neil, and there he met, too, the surviving Sinclair, who had been brought in by Neil's gillies. But from Assynt he got no kindness. The head of the viceroy was worth

[1] Gordon of Sallagh makes Kinnoull accompany Montrose and perish with Sinclair. Now George, the third earl, had died in Orkney three months before, and William, the fourth earl, did not die, but lived to escape from Edinburgh castle in 1654 and for more than twenty years after. So, unless we interpolate a fourth earl of whom nothing else is known, we must reject Sallagh's story. It is probable that he did not know about the death of the third earl in Orkney, and, observing that after Carbisdale William received the title, assumed that his predecessor had died in the flight to Assynt. For the other view, see S. R. Gardiner, *Athenæum*, Nov. 11, 1893.

[2] *Miscellany* (S.H.S.), I., 223.   [3] Gordon of Sallagh, 555.

sufficient gold to set up for good his impoverished family. Montrose asked to be sent to Orkney, and offered him money, but Neil was resolute, knowing well that the Estates would outbid the fugitive. He dispatched an express with the happy news to Leslie, who had now arrived at Tain, and confined the prisoners in the cellars of his castle. A few days later, on the 4th of May, Holbourn arrived at Ardvreck, and Montrose was committed to his hands.

Carbisdale, like Philiphaugh, was a surprise and a rout rather than a battle. It was the first action which Montrose ever fought with a superiority in numbers, for he had 1,200 men as against Strachan's 660; but the only contest was between the 220 Covenant troopers and Montrose's 40 horse and 400 foreigners. Further, infantry in those days, unless of exceptional quality or magnificently posted, had little chance against even a weak body of cavalry; so for the purpose of the battle we may rule out all the foot who were struggling in the flats, and say that the contest lay between Lisle's 40 gentlemen volunteers and Strachan's horse. There could never have been any doubt as to the issue, and, though Strachan deserves all credit for a bold feat of arms, yet his task was easy. Montrose was doomed when he left the heights of Craigcoinichean, and he left them, as we have seen, because of the defective information of his local scoutmaster. But indeed he was lost long before, during the days when he waited for the Mackenzies who never came. He failed because, instead of pushing on with all speed to Badenoch, he wasted time on a half-hearted clan. If Neil Macleod was the immediate cause of Montrose's fate, his patron, Seaforth, was the ruin of the campaign; and Seaforth's indecision was due beyond doubt to the two-faced tactics of Charles. On the 2nd of May, the day on which Montrose's doom was sealed, the king signed with the Covenanters the draft of the Treaty of Breda.

The name of the laird of Assynt lives in Scottish history with that of Sir John Menteith, who sold Wallace. It is remembered as the solitary case of a Gael who betrayed a suppliant for gold. Ian Lom, the bard of Keppoch, has left bitter verses on the " stripped tree of the false apples, Neil's son of woeful Assynt." He made little of his infamy. His lands were raided by Glengarry, the Macleods, and the penitent Mackenzies. After the Restoration he was a good deal in gaol, and was twice tried for his life. His castle was burned, and no children survived to bear his name. He was awarded 25,000 pounds Scots for his services, of which 20,000 were to be paid in coin and the rest in oatmeal. It does not appear that he ever got the money, but the receipts for the meal were long extant, and Highland tradition is positive that two-thirds of it were sour.[1]

[1] The question of Assynt's guilt is exhaustively examined by Murdoch and Simpson (App. XIII.) who decide against him on every count. There can be no question about his surrender of the fugitives, but I cannot find it proved that he had ever served under Montrose, though Montrose probably assumed him to be friendly from his knowledge of his connection with Seaforth and Lemlair. For his later fate see M. & S. *loc. cit.*, and for a defence see *Trans. of the Gaelic Society of Inverness*, xxiv., 374, etc. Ian Lom's verses are worth quoting (*Cumha Mhontroise* in Mackenzie's *Beauties of Gaelic Poetry* (1841), 50; the translation is by Sheriff Nicolson:

" I'll not go to Dunedin
Since the Graham's blood was shed,
The manly, mighty lion
Tortured on the gallows.

That was the true gentleman,
Who came of line not humble.
Good was the flushing of his cheek
When drawing up to combat.

His chalk-white teeth well closing,
His slender brow not gloomy!—
Though oft my love awakes me,
This night I will not bear it.

Neil's son of woeful Assynt,
If I in net could take thee,
My sentence would condemn thee,
Nor would I spare the gibbet.

If you and I encountered
On the marshes of Ben Etive,
The black waters and the clods
Would there be mixed together.

If thou and thy wife's father,
The householder of Leime (Lemlair?)
Were hanged both together,
'Twould not atone my loss.

Stript tree of the false apples,
Without esteem, or fame, or grace,
Ever murdering each other
'Mid dregs of wounds and knives!

Death-wrapping to thee, base one
Ill didst thou sell the righteous,
For the meal of Leith,
And two-thirds of it sour! "

CHAPTER XVII

THE CURTAIN FALLS

(*May* 1650)

No man kills his enemy, therefore, that his enemy might have a
better life in heaven; that is not his end in killing him: it is God's
end. Therefore he brings us to death, that by that gate he might
lead us into life everlasting. And he hath not discovered, but made,
that Northern passage, to passe by the frozen Sea of calamity and
tribulation to Paradise, to the heavenly Jerusalem.

JOHN DONNE.

I

NOW THAT THE LAST BLOW HAD BEEN STRUCK, AND ONLY
death remained, the oppression was lifted from Montrose's
soul. The "fey" mood had passed, and his spirit was
enlarged. The touch of haughtiness, which his contemporaries remarked in him, the self-assurance necessary for
one whose daily bread was peril, had gone from him;
courtesy he had never lost, but he recovered the modest
simplicity which Clarendon had approved long ago in
Oxford. Once more he is the clear-sighted and constant
patriot, the great gentleman who, in the hour of deepest
degradation, can meet the taunts of his enemies with a
smiling face, the Christian who has compassion upon the
frailty of mankind. For six years his name had terrified
his opponents, and as their hold upon the nation had
declined, so had their nerve and courage. The news of his
landing in the north had shaken the Estates to their
foundation. The crowning mercy of Carbisdale was at first
scarcely believed, and when Strachan himself arrived post-
haste to claim his reward, their exultation of relief knew
no bounds. Mixed with it was the zest of coming revenge.
Their tormentor had been marvellously delivered into their
hands, and we can judge of their past trepidation by the
punishment they devised. The measure of their vengeance
is the measure of their fear.

It is not easy to judge Charles with either patience or
fairness, the master was so immeasurably smaller than the
servant. In the compost of graces and infirmities which
made up his character, a fine sense of honour had no part,
since for that some spiritual discipline is required. He was
an engaging creature of impulse, with a tolerant humour
which could laugh at himself as well as at others, with the

courage which comes from a good constitution and a high
vitality, and which could face misfortunes with equanimity
—both his own and his friends'. But it is almost certain
that, before signing the Treaty of Breda, this " gentle,
innocent, well-inclined prince " (so he seemed to Baillie)[1]
had convinced himself, with his ready optimism, that he
had made provision for the safety of his captain-general.
On the 5th of May he wrote to Montrose, bidding him
lay down his arms and disband his men. He seems to have
received assurances from the Scottish commissioners of an
indemnity for the royalist army. On the 8th of May he
wrote to the Estates asking that Montrose and his forces
should be allowed to leave the country in safety. A private
letter was also written to the viceroy, telling him that 12,000
rix-dollars were at his call in Sir Patrick Drummond's
hands. Sir William Fleming, a cousin of Montrose's, had
further orders, dated the 12th of May, written apparently
after some rumour of Carbisdale had reached the king.
These latest instructions were not to deliver the letter of
the 8th of May to Parliament unless Montrose was still
unbeaten and at the head of a reasonable force; if he had
been defeated, the letter was to be concealed. Apparently
Charles did not want to ask for grace for his captain-
general from the Estates if he was a fugitive; he trusted to
his private arrangement with the Scottish commissioners.
It is a tangled story, but it is inconceivable that the king
hoped to conceal or disavow his complicity in the invasion.
This was already clear from the published letter of the 12th
of January, which every one in Scotland knew of, and from
his personal letter of the 5th of May to Montrose, which
was delivered and read to the Estates. Still another letter,
dated the 12th of May, was also read to Parliament, in
which Charles disclaimed all responsibility for Montrose's
doings.[2] But it is impossible to believe that the king, who
was no fool, and had the rest of the correspondence in his
memory, could have been guilty of so futile and purpose-
less a piece of treachery by which no one could be deceived.
It is more likely that this was a fabrication of Will Murray,
Argyll's emissary, with the view of alienating from the now
Covenanted king the last remnants of royalist respect in
Scotland and Cavalier support in England. Base and

---

[1] III., 88.

[2] Balfour, IV. It is to be noted that the king's letter of this date,
printed in *Charles II. and Scotland in 1650*, 103, has an altogether
different tenor.

heartless as was Charles's conduct, it is incredible that it reached the height of perfidy which Argyll and Loudoun would have had the world believe.[1]

To Montrose royal duplicity and Covenanting intrigues had become matters of little moment. For him the long day's task was nearly done, and the hour of unarming had struck. He was led in triumphant progress by his captors through the length of Scotland, but the triumph was not theirs. On the 5th of May Holbourn hurried him from Ardvreck by way of Invershin to Skibo, on the north side of the Kyle. A night was spent there, and the lady of the castle, finding that the rank of the prisoner was not sufficiently recognized, is said to have beaten Holbourn about the head with a leg of mutton and had Montrose given the seat of honour.[2] He was ferried over the Kyle, and on the 8th delivered to David Leslie at Tain. Thence next morning he was carried by way of Dingwall to Brahan castle. On the following day he was at Beauly, and we have the record of Mr. James Fraser, afterwards Lovat's chaplain, and then a boy of sixteen, who now joined the march. The viceroy sat " upon a little shelty horse, without a saddle, but a quilt of rags and straw, and pieces of rope for stirrups, his feet fastened under the horse's belly, with a tether and a bit halter for a bridle."[3] It was a mode of progress which was later endured by many saints of the Covenant, notably Mr. Donald Cargill. He still wore peasant's clothes, on his head was a montero cap, and around his shoulders a ragged, old, reddish plaid. The fatigue and privations of the past week had induced a high fever. At Muirtown, near Inverness, he begged for water, and there the crowd from the town came out to gaze on him. The two ministers of Inverness also appeared, and showed in their behaviour a decency unusual in their profession; one of them, Mr. John Annand, had been a former acquaintance of the prisoner. At the bridge-end an old woman railed at him and reminded him of the houses which had been burned when he besieged the town. " Yet he never altered his countenance, but with a majesty and state beseeming him kept his countenance high."[4]

[1] This paragraph embodies the impression left on my mind by reading the letters, which are in the *Wigton Papers* (Maitland Club). The whole of the complicated question has been exhaustively examined by Lang (III., 221-226). Gardiner (*Commonwealth and Protectorate*, I., 190, etc.) takes the view set out above.

[2] Taylor's " Assynt " in *Dunrobin MSS.*

[3] *Wardlaw MS.*, 353.   [4] *Ibid.*, 354.

The magistrates met him at the cross, where they had
set up a table of refreshments. He was offered wine, and
mixed it with water. Fraser saw the other prisoners drinking heartily under a forestair, and remarked among them
Sir John Hurry, " a robust, tall, stately fellow, with a long
cut in his cheek." Hurry was the true soldier of fortune,
own brother to Dugald Dalgetty, and throughout his varied
career and many changes of side he preserved a certain
disarming audacity and humour. As was said of a more
famous Sir John, the world could have better spared a
better man. The provost, Duncan Forbes of Culloden, a
courteous member of an honourable house, said on taking
leave: " My lord, I am sorry for your circumstances."
That night the company were lodged at Castle Stewart, on
the road to Nairn.

On the way through Moray many friends came to greet
him, college companions at St. Andrews, and loyalists such
as Pluscardine, whose clan had so grievously failed him.
At Elgin he was greatly cheered by the sight of an old
college friend, Mr. Alexander Somers, the minister of
Duffus. His well-wishers conveyed him over Spey, and on
the 11th he halted at Keith, where he lay on straw in a
tent set up in the fields. The next day was the Sabbath,
and he attended the ministrations of Mr. William Kinanmond, who preached from the favourite Covenanting text
of the hewing of Agag and the Amalekites. He violently
abused the prisoner, till he disgusted even his Covenanting
hearers. " Rail on, Rabshakeh," was his victim's only
reply. " All honest men," says Fraser, " hated Kinanmond
for this ever after."[1]

On the 13th the prisoner reached Pitcaple castle, the
home of an Engager, John Leslie, whose wife was a kins-
woman of Montrose.[2] The quicker road to the south
through Mar was not taken, probably through fear of a
rescue by the Farquharsons, and the route chosen was one
by which Montrose had often led his swift armies. Now
he traversed the scene of his victories with a herald pacing
before him, proclaiming: " Here comes James Graham,
a traitor to his country." He was probably at Fordoun
on the 14th, and on the 15th he reached Southesk's castle
of Kinnaird. There he saw his two younger children,
Robert and Jean. When he left them he left the last slender
ties which still bound him to earth. His wife and his eldest
son were gone; his best friends had perished on the scaffold;

---

[1] *Wardlaw MS.*, 355.   [2] M. & S., 318 *n*.

the great comradeship was broken, and its members dead or on their way to death; his cause, the clean and sane ideals he had championed, was undone; death had no terrors for one who had nothing to live for, and who had faced it so often with a lover's gaiety. His words might have been those of Kent in *Lear*:

> " I have a journey, sir, shortly to go;
> My master calls me, I must not say no."

On the night of the 15th he halted at the house of Grange, a property of the Durhams, five miles from Dundee. Here there seems to have been an attempt as at Pitcaple, to assist him to escape. The lady of the house plied the guards with strong ale and brandy, and they, being Highlanders of Lawers's regiment, willingly succumbed. But the outer guards had not been tampered with, and the fugitive was discovered by a trooper of Strachan's horse.[1] Next day he entered Dundee, and to the eternal credit of that staunchly Covenanting town, which, moreover, had suffered more than most at Montrose's hands, he was received with sympathy and respect. " The whole town expressed a great deal of sorrow for his condition, and presented him with clothes and all other things suited to his place, birth, and person."[2] We have no record of the two days' march across Fife. No doubt the ministers flocked to upbraid him, and the heroes who had returned from Tippermuir and Kilsyth came to stare at one who had given them little cause to love him. From Dysart or Kirkcaldy the company took ship for Leith, and reached it about four o'clock on the afternoon of Saturday the 18th. On the same day and at the same port arrived Sir William Fleming, with the king's letter of disbandment.

The Covenanters had made ample preparation to receive the prisoner. They knew that what they had to do must be done quickly. The viceroy must be dead before the king's coming to Scotland, or trouble would follow; a party, now royalist in policy, could not put to death one who carried the royal commission. Further, the Commonwealth had never shown any bitterness against the great captain, and might interdict those of the Estates who favoured Cromwell from the kind of vengeance which Cromwell as a rule preferred to leave to his Maker. There were magnanimous men, too, in all parties in Scotland, who resented the unsoldierly treatment of a soldier, and there were his many friends in foreign courts, especially

[1] *Memorie of the Somervilles.*   [2] *Wardlaw MS.,* 355.

in the court of France, who would be certain to plead for him if time were allowed. Such an appeal was actually sent at the instigation of Cardinal de Retz, signed by the young king, Louis the Fourteenth,[1] in which it was eloquently urged that Montrose had always acted within the terms of his royal commission, and therefore could not be condemned by those who now acknowledged the royal authority. But the appeal arrived after the deed had been done. Argyll and Loudoun were not the men to tarry when it was a matter of getting rid of a rival so formidable and so feared.

Immediately upon the news of Carbisdale, the Estates had met to consider the question of punishment. In a time of civil confusion nice questions of legality are out of place, and the condemnation of Montrose was as legal as any other act of the Parliament then sitting in Scotland. He had been attainted and outlawed in 1644, and there had been no reversal of the sentence.[2] A commission was appointed to decide on the details of the penalty, and on the 17th of May it made its report.[3] The captive was to be met at the gates by the officers of justice and the hangman, and conducted with every circumstance of ignominy to the Tolbooth. Thereafter he was to be hanged on a gibbet—not beheaded, as was the custom with State prisoners—with Wishart's book and a copy of his own last declaration tied around his neck. Thus would be fulfilled the words of the prophet Rothes, and he would be " lifted up above the rest in three fathoms of a rope." After death the head was to be struck off and placed on a spike on the Tolbooth; the body dismembered, and the limbs fixed in public places in Stirling, Glasgow, Perth, and Aberdeen. If he repented of his misdeeds, the ban of excommunication would be removed, and the body buried in Greyfriars churchyard; if not, it would go to the felons' pit on the Boroughmuir. It was piously hoped that the common folk of Edinburgh, who had lost kith and kin in his wars, would await his entrance and show their hatred with filth and stones. For this purpose his hands were to be pinioned behind his back.

The afternoon was clear and chilly, such as is common on the shores of the Firth in late May. The magistrates of Edinburgh met him at Leith, and the procession was

[1] Monteith, 517. M. & S., App. XII., 1.
[2] The Earl of Argyll, in 1685, was in the same position.
[3] Balfour, IV., 12.

formed, the other prisoners on foot, and Montrose himself
mounted on a cart-horse. His face was drawn and wasted
with fever, and his grey eyes burned with an unnatural
brilliance. The good folk of Dundee had given him clothes
more suited to his condition than those he had worn when
captured, and he bore himself among the hostile crowd
with a gentle dignity. A smile, it is said, flickered about
his mouth, not of scorn but of peace. When he passed
the Watergait, where the *faubourg* of the Canongate began,
in which stood the houses of the nobility, he found awaiting him the officers of justice, the hangman, and a hangman's cart drawn by four horses. He was shown the
sentence of the Estates and read it carefully, saying that he
was sorry that the king, whose commission he bore, should
be so dishonoured. Then he entered the cart, and was
tied to a high seat with cords across his breast and arms.
The hangman wore his red bonnet, but Montrose, according
to his sentence, must ride uncovered.

Slowly, in the bright evening, the procession moved up
the ancient Via Dolorosa of Scottish history.[1] The street
was lined by a great crowd—the dregs of the Edinburgh
slums, the retainers of the Covenanting lords, ministers from
far and near—all the elements most bitterly hostile to the
prisoner. But to the amazement of the organizers of the
spectacle there was no sign of popular wrath. Rather there
was silence, a tense air of sympathy and pity and startled
admiration. The high pale countenance set up in that place
of public scorn awed the mob into stillness. " In all the
way, there appeared in him such majesty, courage, modesty,
and even somewhat more than natural, that these common
women who had lost their husbands and children in his
wars, and who were hired to stone him, were, upon the
sight of him, so astonished and moved that their intended
curses turned into tears and prayers."[2] In the strained
quiet, broken only by excited sobs, there was one jarring
note. Lady Jean Gordon, Lord Haddington's widow, Argyll's
niece and Huntly's daughter, is said to have laughed shrilly
and shouted a word of insult from the balcony where she
sat. A voice cried out of the crowd that the right place
for her was in the hangman's cart to expiate her sins.[3]

[1] We have three accounts of Montrose's entry into Edinburgh:
that of James Fraser in the *Wardlaw MS.*; that of the *Wigton
Papers*; and the report to Mazarin of a French resident in Edinburgh, M. de Graymond, Napier, II., 781 and App. IV.
[2] *Wigton Papers.*
[3] There seems to be no contemporary evidence for the vices with

In the lodgings along the Canongate the Covenant chiefs
were assembled to witness the degradation of their enemy.
In the balcony of Lord Moray's house Lord Lorn sat with
his young bride, Lady Mary Stewart, the same man who,
thirty-five years later, was himself to go to a not inglorious
scaffold. Inside the house, with the shutters half-closed,
stood Argyll with Loudoun and Wariston. Montrose, as
he passed, caught a glimpse of the anxious, unhappy face
which he knew so well, and for the first time for long the
two men looked into each other's eyes. . . . The shutters
were closed and the faces disappeared. There was an
English soldier in the crowd who observed the incident and
cried: " It was no wonder they started aside at his look,
for they durst not look him in the face these seven years
bygone."[1]

It is the last we shall see of Argyll. What he thought
in that moment we can only guess. In his letter to Lothian,
written on the day of the execution, he reflects that Montrose had " got some resolution how to go out of this world,
but nothing at all how to enter into another."[2] But there
must have been more in that subtle mind than this pious
platitude, for in Montrose he looked upon his stark
opposite, and in his enemy's downfall he could read the
presage of his own. If Montrose had failed, so had he, and
with a far more complete failure. Of all that he had built
nothing had any hope of permanence. The theocracy on
which his power was founded was crumbling beneath him.
A mind of his calibre cannot have been bemused by the
ministerial dreams of Presbyterian dominance in Britain;
he had fleeting visions of political moderation and religious
tolerance which were denied to his colleagues. But, playing
with the skill of the adroit politician for immediate gains,
he had been too successful; he had won in the short game
only to find that his victory made the larger purpose for
ever impossible. The Solemn League hung round his neck
like a millstone. He had summoned spirits from the deep
which he could not control. He had allied himself with
the English Parliament, and discovered too late that he was
being ground between rival fanaticisms. That very year
he was to call his associates " madmen,"[3] and for the rest

which the writer in the *Wigton Papers* charges the lady. See Willcock, *The Great Marquess*, 232 *n*.
  [1] *Wigton Papers*. Graymond to Mazarin, Napier, II., 839.
  [2] Kirkton, *Hist. of the Church of Scotland*, 124 *n*.
  [3] *Cal. S. P.*, *Dom*. (Aug. 28, 1650), 310.

of his life, in his intrigues with Charles and his intrigues with Cromwell, he was to be no more than a distracted politician, without creed or comfort. Nothing remained to him but the sombre religion which he had acquired long before at the Glasgow Assembly, and which at any rate taught him how to die.

As Montrose passed the cross he saw the new gallows standing ready to receive him—that gallows which was to earn the name of the " Ministers' Altar." About seven o'clock he reached the Tolbooth. His bonds were cut, and as he descended from the cart he gave the hangman the customary drink-money. Scarcely was he inside the prison when a deputation from the Estates, with its retinue of ministers, arrived to interrogate him. He refused to answer, for indeed he was very weary with travel and sickness, and at last his tormentors withdrew. His parting words to them were a jest. " The compliments they had put upon him that day," he said, " had proved something tedious." He was still young—not yet thirty-eight.[1]

II

Next day, being the Sabbath, there was a great preaching. From every pulpit in the city the clergy thundered against the excommunicate, James Graham, and no less against the mob which had refused to stone him. The prisoner was visited by a deputation of ministers and members of Parliament, among them Sir James Stewart of Coltness, the Provost of Edinburgh, who was responsible for the details of the execution, and who, though a staunch Covenanter, had protested against its barbarity—" so much butchery and dismembering."[2] They got no satisfaction. He told them that " if they thought they had affronted him the day before by carrying him in a cart they were much mistaken, for he thought it the most honourable and joyful journey ever he made; God having all the while most comfortably manifested Himself to him, and furnished him with resolution to overlook the reproaches of men, and to behold Him for whose cause he suffered."[3]

He was given no peace. At eight o'clock on the Monday morning his persecutors returned to the attack. Mr. James Guthrie, Mr. Mungo Law, Mr. Robert Traill, and others were no doubt bound in duty to visit an erring member

---

[1] *Wardlaw MS.*; *Wigton Papers*; Wishart, Part II.; *Montrose Redivivus*; Balfour, IV.
[2] *Coltness Papers*, 30. Napier, II., 797.   [3] *Wigton Papers.*

of their own communion, and they hoped to extract some confession from him which could be used to efface the profound impression that his appearance had made on the people of Edinburgh. They charged him at a venture with imaginary personal vices, of which he had none. Then they accused him of taking up arms against his country, of using Irish troops, and of shedding Scottish blood. He replied, as Wodrow's informant told him, in a manner " too airy and *volage*, not so much suiting the gravity of a nobleman."[1] Using their own armoury, he reminded them that David, in the cave of Adullam, had gathered together an odd fighting force; and as for bloodshed, he declared " if it could have been thereby prevented, he would rather it had all come out of his own veins." Lastly, they charged him with a breach of the Covenant, and his answer was ready. " The Covenant which I took I own it and adhere to it. Bishops, I care not for them. I never intended to advance their interests. But when the king had granted you all your desires, and you were every one sitting under his vine and his fig tree—that then you should have taken a party in England by the hand, and entered into a League and Covenant with them against the king, was the thing I judged my duty to oppose to the yondmost." Mr. James Guthrie then touched on the excommunication, and said that since the prisoner showed himself obdurate it must remain. With the strange arrogance of his kind, he had the " fearful apprehension that what is bound on earth God will bind in heaven." Montrose replied gently that he would gladly be reconciled to the Church of Scotland, but that he could not call that his sin which he accounted to have been his duty.

When the ministers left him he was given a little bread dipped in ale for his breakfast, but he was not allowed a barber to shave him. At ten o'clock he was taken before the bar of Parliament to hear his sentence. It was common knowledge that he had acted under the king's credentials, and therefore nothing in the nature of a trial could be allowed on the question of the Carbisdale campaign, since it was difficult for Loudoun and Argyll to deny a mandate for which they had the royal evidence. The Chancellor

[1] *Wodrow MSS.* in the National Library of Scotland. Napier, II., 785, etc. The informant was a Mr. Patrick Simson, for whom see Warrick, *Moderators of the Church of Scotland, 1690-1740* (Edinburgh, 1913). He had been for some time chaplain at Inveraray, and had formed his notions of deportment on Argyll. His *Spiritual Songs* are almost the worst religious verse in the language.

seems to have harped on the incidents of the Highland wars, mingled with violent denunciations of the viceroy's person. Since his arrival in Edinburgh Montrose had been provided, probably by the Napier ladies, with clothes worthy of his rank. When he stood up before his accusers in Parliament, he wore a suit of fine black cloth, with a richly laced scarlet cloak to his knee; on his head was a black beaver hat with a silver band; and on his legs stockings of carnation silk.[1] His bearing was modest but " unmoved and undaunted "; his face was haggard, unshaven, and very pale,[2] and he often sighed. He replied to his accusers in a speech, happily preserved,[3] in which he repeated the substance of his many declarations—his loyalty to the true Covenant, his abhorrence of the Solemn League. " How far religion has been advanced by it this poor distressed kingdom can witness." War could not be waged without the shedding of blood, but he had repressed all disorders as soon as they were discovered. " Never was any man's blood spilt but in battle; and even then, many thousand lives have I preserved. And I dare here avow, in the presence of God, that never a hair of Scotsman's head that I could save fell to the ground." His last campaign had been " by his Majesty's just commands, in order to accelerate the treaty betwixt him and you: his Majesty knowing that, whenever he had ended with you, I was ready to retire upon his call." He asked to be judged " by the laws of God, the laws of Nature and nations, and the laws of this land." But he knew that the plea was vain, so he appealed to a higher tribunal—" to the righteous Judge of the world, who one day must be your Judge and mine, and who always gives out righteous judgments." He had said his say; he had fulfilled the proud boast which he had made to Parliament nine years before: " My resolution is to carry along fidelity and honour to the grave." His judges had no answer. Loudoun replied with abuse, and Wariston read the sentence, which Montrose heard on his knees. We are told that he lifted up his head as the grim words were uttered, and looked Wariston calmly in the face.

He was taken back to the Tolbooth, where all day he was

---

[1] Relics of these garments belonged to the Napier family till 1912. They are now, along with his George and his Garter riband, in the possession of the Duke of Montrose.   [2] Balfour, IV., 16.
[3] Summaries of the speech are in the *Wardlaw MS.*, Wishart, and Balfour; but the simplicity of the *Wigton Papers* seems to embody the actual words of Montrose.

tormented by ministers. According to one account, he had
a talk apart with Mr. Robert Baillie;[1] if so, that honest and
perplexed soul can scarcely have been happy about the
business, and it is remarkable that in his voluminous
writings he never mentions this final scene. To the
magistrates who visited him he said: " I think it a greater
honour to have my head standing on the ports of this town
for this quarrel, than to have my picture in the king's bedchamber. I am beholden to you that, lest my loyalty
should be forgotten, you have appointed five of the most
eminent towns to bear witness of it to posterity."[2] The
captain of the town guard was the famous Major Weir,[3]
the warlock of Edinburgh legend, who afterwards expiated
his many crimes at the stake. By his orders the guard were
always in the prisoner's room, and filled it with tobacco
smoke, which Montrose, unlike his father, could not abide.
None of his friends were allowed to come near him.
Nevertheless, we are told, in spite of fever and pain and
the imminence of death, he continued his devotions un-
perturbed, and slept as peacefully as a child. That last
night, like Sir Walter Raleigh, and much in the same strain,
he, who had so long forsaken the Muse, returned to his
old love. These lines were written amid the smoke and
wrangling of the guards :

> " Let them bestow on every airth a limb,
>   Then open all my veins, that I may swim
> To Thee, my Maker, in that crimson lake ;
>   Then place my parboiled head upon a stake,
>   Scatter my ashes, strew them in the air.—
>   Lord! Since Thou knowest where all these atoms are,
>   I'm hopeful Thou'lt recover once my dust,
>   And confident Thou'lt raise me with the just."[4]

On Tuesday morning, the 21st of May, he rose for the
last time. Like the Spartans before Thermopylæ, he
combed his long locks for death. The usual concourse of
ministers and politicians was in his cell, and Wariston
reproved him for his care of the body. " My head is still
my own," was his answer. "To-night, when it will be

[1] Mr. Robert Traill's *Diary*, Napier, II., 789-790.
[2] *Wigton Papers.*
[3] He had served in the Covenanting army against Montrose in
1644-45 as a major in Lanark's regiment. See Roughead, *Twelve
Scots Trials*, 43, 45.
[4] Voltaire refers to these lines in his *Essai sur l'Histoire générale*,
and adds: " C'était un des plus agréables esprits qui cultivassent
alors les lettres, et l'âme la plus héroïque qui fût dans les trois
Royaumes."

yours, treat it as you please." Presently he heard the drums beating to arms, and was told that the troops were assembling to prevent any attempt at a rescue. He laughed and cried: "What, am I still a terror to them? Let them look to themselves; my ghost will haunt them."

He was taken about two in the afternoon by the bailies down the High Street to the Mercat Cross, which stood between the Tolbooth and the Tron Kirk—that dolorous road which Argyll and Wariston and James Guthrie were themselves to travel. He still wore the brave clothes in which he had confronted Parliament; nay, more, he had ribbons on his shoes and fine white gloves on his hands. James Fraser, who saw him, wrote: "He stept along the streets with so great state, and there appeared in his countenance so much beauty, majesty, and gravity as amazed the beholder, and many of his enemies did acknowledge him to be the bravest subject in the world, and in him a gallantry that braced all that crowd." Another eyewitness, John Nicoll, the notary public, thought him more like a bridegroom than a criminal.[1] An Englishman among the spectators, a Commonwealth agent, wrote an account to his masters. "It is absolutely certain that he hath overcome more men by his death, in Scotland, than he would have done if he had lived. For I never saw a more sweeter carriage in a man in all my life."[2]

The scaffold was a great four-square platform, breast-high, and on it a 30-foot gallows had been erected. On the platform stood the ministers, Mr. Robert Traill and Mr. Mungo Law, still bent on getting a word of confession or penitence. They were disappointed, for Montrose did not look at them. He was not allowed to address the mob, which surged up against the edge of the scaffold—a privilege hitherto granted to the meanest criminals; but he spoke apart to the magistrates and to a few of the nearer spectators. A boy called Robert Gordon[3] sat by and took down his words in some kind of shorthand, and the crowd, with that decency which belongs to all simple folk, kept a reverent silence. The Estates were afraid lest he should attack the king and spoil their game, but he spoke no word of bitterness or reproach; rather—*splendide mendax*—he praised Charles's justice. It was the testament of a man

[1] Nicoll, *Diary of Public Transactions, etc., 1650-67* (Bannatyne Club), 12, etc.　　　　　　　　[2] Napier, II., 805.
[3] Son of Sir Robert Gordon of Gordonstoun, the author of the *History of the Earldom of Sutherland*.

conscious of his mortal frailty, but confident in the purity of his purpose and the mercy of his God.

" I am sorry if this manner of my end be scandalous to any good Christian here. Doth it not often happen to the righteous according to the way of the unrighteous? Doth not sometimes a just man perish in his righteousness, and a wicked man prosper in his wickedness and malice? They who know me should not disesteem me for this. Many greater than I have been dealt with in this kind. But I must not say but that all God's judgments are just, and this measure, for my private sins, I acknowledge to be just with God, and wholly submit myself to Him.

" But, in regard of man, I may say they are but instruments. God forgive them, and I forgive them. They have oppressed the poor and violently perverted judgment and justice, but He that is higher than they will reward them.

" What I did in this kingdom was in obedience to the most just commands of my sovereign, and in his defence, in the day of his distress, against those who rose up against him. I acknowledge nothing, but fear God and honour the king, according to the commandments of God and the just laws of Nature and nations. I have not sinned against man, but against God; and with Him there is mercy, which is the ground of my drawing near unto Him.

" It is objected against me by many, even good people, that I am under the censure of the Church. This is not my fault, seeing it is only for doing my duty, by obeying my prince's most just commands, for religion, his sacred person, and authority. Yet I am sorry they did excommunicate me; and in that which is according to God's laws, without wronging my conscience or allegiance, I desire to be relaxed. If they will not do it, I appeal to God, who is the righteous Judge of the world, and will, I hope, be my Judge and Saviour.

" It is spoken of me that I should blame the king. God forbid! For the late king, he lived a saint and died a martyr. I pray God I may end as he did. If ever I would wish my soul in another man's stead, it should be in his. For his Majesty now living, never any people, I believe, might be more happy in a king. His commandments to me were most just, and I obeyed them. He deals justly with all men. I pray God he be so dealt withal that he be not betrayed under trust, as his father was.

" I desire not to be mistaken, as if my carriage at this time, in relation to your ways, were stubborn. I do but follow the light of my conscience, my rule; which is seconded by the working of the Spirit of God that is within me. I thank Him I go to heaven with joy the way He paved for me. If He enable me against the fear of death, and furnish me with courage and confidence to embrace it even in its most ugly shape, let God be glorified in my end, though it were in my damnation. Yet I say not this out of any fear or mistrust, but out of my duty to God, and love to His people.

" I have no more to say, but that I desire your charity and prayers. I shall pray for you all. I leave my soul to God, my service to my prince, my goodwill to my friends, my love and charity to you all. And thus briefly I have exonerated my conscience."[1]

There is a tradition that during the morning there had been lowering thunder-clouds and flashes of lightning, but

[1] *Wardlaw MS.*, 359-362. There are versions of the speech in Wishart, and in the *Wigton Papers*.

that as Montrose stood on the scaffold a burst of sunlight flooded the street. When he had finished speaking, he gave money to his executioner, and prayed silently for a little. His arms were pinioned, and he ascended the ladder with that stately carriage which had always marked him. His last words were: " God have mercy on this afflicted land! " Tears ran down the hangman's face as he pushed him off, and we are told that a great sob broke from the crowd. They had cause to sob, for that day there was done to death such a man as his country has not seen again.

According to the sentence, the body was cut down after three hours and the limbs distributed among the chief towns. The remains in Aberdeen must have caught the eye of Charles when he arrived a few weeks later. The trunk was buried beside the public gallows on the Boroughmuir.[1] The head was placed on a spike on the west face of the Tolbooth, and eleven years later was taken down to make room for the head of Argyll.[2]

III

There was to be another funeral besides that melancholy scene by lantern light among the marshes of the Borough-muir. After the Restoration, one of Charles's first acts was to give public burial to the remains of his great captain. On January 4, 1661, the Scots Parliament resolved on " an honourable reparation for that horrid and monstrous barbarity in the person of the great Marquis of Montrose."[3] The trunk was solemnly taken up from the Boroughmuir,[4] and the limbs gathered from the several

---

[1] On the spot now occupied by the factory of Thomas Nelson and Sons, where this volume was first printed in its original form.

[2] On account of rumours that the head was to be stolen by Montrose's friends, " a new cross prick of iron to cross the former prick " was added six days after the execution (Nicoll, *Diary*). Cromwell had the limbs taken down in Glasgow, Stirling, Perth, and Aberdeen. The Aberdeen " member " was laid in Huntly's vault till 1661, when it was moved to Edinburgh for the second funeral (M. & S., App. XIV.). There was a story recorded by Sir Edward Walker that after Dunbar Cromwell caused the head to be removed from the Tolbooth (Douglas, *Cromwell's Scotch Campaigns*, 121 *n*.), but it remained till 1661, when James Fraser saw it taken down. One Thomas Binning, mariner, serving as a gunner at the Castle, who had a regard for Montrose's memory, tried to have it shot down, but the ball only knocked off part of the stone support of the spike, which in its fall " killed a drummer and a soldier or two." " Providence," Captain Binning piously reflected, " had ordered that head to be taken down with more honour." See Binning, *A Light to the Art of Gunnery*, 1675.   [3] *Mercurius Caledonicus*, ed. by Saintserf. Jan. 4, 1661.

[4] Nicoll, *Diary*, 316.

towns, a ceremony attended by " the honest people's loud
and joyful acclamations." The remains, wrapped in fine
linen in a noble coffin, lay in state in the Abbey Kirk of
Holyrood from the 7th of January to the 11th of May. On
the latter date took place the great procession to St. Giles's.[1]
First rode Sir Harry Graham, Montrose's half-brother,
carrying the arms of his house. Then followed the Graham
kinsmen with their different standards—Duntroon, Morphie,
Cairnie, Monzie, Balgowan, Drums, Gorthie; and Black
Pate of Inchbrakie, who had been with Montrose on the
August afternoon in Atholl when the curtain rose upon his
campaign, bore his insignia of the Garter. The body was
carried by fourteen earls, including the men, or the sons
of the men, who had betrayed him—such as Seaforth, and
Home, and Roxburgh, as well as old opponents like Eglinton and Callander. Twelve viscounts and barons bore the
pall, among them Strathnaver, the son of the Sutherland
who had locked the gates of the north after Carbisdale.
The young Montrose and his brother, Lord Robert,
followed the coffin, and in the procession were representatives of almost every Scottish house. Argyll's friend and
Montrose's brother-in-law, Rollo, was there, and Marischal,
who had held Dunnottar against him, and Tweeddale, who
had voted for his death. There, too, were the faithful
friends who had not failed him—Maderty and Frendraught
and the Marquis of Douglas, and old Napier's grandson.
The morning had been stormy, but as the procession moved
from Holyrood the sun shone out brightly, as it had done
at his end. The streets were lined with the trainbands, who
fired their volleys, while the cannon thundered in reply
from the castle, wherein lay Argyll under sentence of death.
The nobles of Scotland, according to their wont, had
moved over to the winning side. The pageant was an act
of tardy justice, and it pleases by its dramatic contrasts,
but it had small relevance to Montrose's true achievement.
He was as little kin to the rabble of the Restoration as to
the rabble of the Covenant. The noble monument which
now marks his grave in the ancient High Kirk of Scotland
is a more fitting testimony, for it has been left to modern
days to recognize the greatness of one who had no place
in his generation.

The fate of his heart is a curious romance, like the tale
of that ring which Marie Antoinette gave to Axel Fersen.
Shortly after the execution young Lady Napier sent her

[1] *A Relation of the True Funeralls*, 1661, Napier, II., App. III.

servants by night to the grave on the Boroughmuir, and had the heart taken from the body. It was skilfully embalmed, and placed in a little egg-shaped case of steel made from the blade of his sword.[1] This in turn was enclosed in a gold filigree box, which had been given to her husband's grandfather by a Doge of Venice. She sent the box to the young Marquis of Montrose on the Continent, who duly restored the heart to the body in 1661 at the second funeral.[2] The casket after a time passed out of the possession of the family. It was recognized in a Dutch collection by a friend of the fifth Lord Napier, who procured it for him. Napier bequeathed it on his death to his daughter, who had married a Johnston of Cairnsalloch, an officer of the East India Company. It was carried to India, and on the way out was struck by a shot in a battle with a French squadron off Cape Verd Islands, and the gold filigree box was shattered. But the adventures of the case were not ended. It remained for some time in the Johnstons' house at Madura, where the natives came to reverence it as a talisman. It was stolen, and was purchased by a tributary chief of the Nawab of Arcot, in whose treasury it long lay. The young Johnston in a hunting expedition happened to save his life, and the chief in gratitude restored the relic to his family.[3] It was brought home to Europe by the elder Johnstons in 1792, and, as they travelled overland through France, they heard of the edict of the Revolution Government requiring the surrender of all gold and silver trinkets. Mrs. Johnston entrusted it to an Englishwoman at Boulogne till it could be sent to England, but the lady died soon afterwards, and in the troubled days that followed the relic disappeared. Since then it has been lost to the world. Some day, perhaps, an antiquary, rummaging in some back street in a French town, may come on a casket of Indian work, and opening it find the little egg-shaped case. It would be a precious discovery, for it once held the dust of the bravest of Scottish hearts.

[1] The heart of Lord Capel was treated in the same way and presented to Charles II. after the Restoration.

[2] This is clear from the Lord Lyon's accounts (see Mr. J. C. Robbie's paper in the *Book of the Old Edinburgh Club*, I.). The heart was embalmed by a chirurgeon on May 11, 1661. On this point Napier's story (II., App. I.) must be amended.

[3] See Mr. Stephen Wheeler's articles in the Allahabad *Pioneer*, May 13 and August 9. 1920

CHAPTER XVIII

"A CANDIDATE FOR IMMORTALITY"[1]

Truly I know not whether to mervaile more, either that he in that mistie time could see so clearly, or that wee in this cleare age walke so stumblingly after him.

SIR PHILIP SIDNEY.

I

MONTROSE FOUNDED NO SCHOOL AND LEFT NO SUCCESSOR. He was a lonely figure in his day, and for almost two centuries his bequest remained unnoted and unshared. Cromwell, indeed, came north into Scotland the same year, and enforced one part of his message. Dunbar was the avenging of Philiphaugh and Carbisdale, and the heavy hand of the greatest of Englishmen was laid on the strange edifice which had been built out of the rubble of the Middle Ages. The nine years of the English occupation saw the plain man raising his head once more. Sir Alexander Irvine of Drum was moved to tell the Moderator of the Assembly that his wild charges were " but undigested rhapsodies of confused nonsense,"[2] and none could gainsay him. Monk bade the ministers of Perth leave politics alone and " preach the gospel of Jesus Christ," which, the chronicler adds, " it seems is not their business."[3] Wariston had the "strange thought " that, like Hamilton and Montrose, Cromwell would ere long be brought to public justice in Edinburgh,[4] but no such fate befell the great iconoclast. He enforced his views on religious toleration, and did his best to curb the appetite of the Kirk for witch-finding. He made an attempt at uniting Scotland and England, reduced taxation, established free trade with the south, took the sting out of excommunication by preventing any civil penalties attending it, and finally, to the infinite comfort of the lieges, suppressed the General Assembly. For the first time for generations even-handed justice was done between all classes. And, as we know from Mr. Robert Law, the spiritual life of the country, long bound under the desolate frosts of faction, began to put forth hopeful shoots.

Cromwell passed, and the king who had so cheerfully betrayed his servant came to his own again. The old strife

[1] The phrase is Wishart's, from the last sentence of his book.
[2] *Scotland and the Commonwealth* (S.H.S.), 354.
[3] *Ibid.*, 7.
[4] *Diary*, II., 24.

was renewed of nobles and king and Kirk, and again the commons of Scotland were the victims. One thing had indeed been gained—the impossible theocracy had perished. The Kirk, as always happens, having asked too much, was to get less than her due, and the spiritual liberty which she had denied to others in her heyday was now to be denied to herself. The later Covenanters, whose sufferings have left so dark a memory among their countrymen, fought for a cause similar only in name to that of their predecessors before 1660. They resisted a despotic " bond " imposed on them by the Government to the outraging of their consciences, as Montrose had resisted the " bond " of Guthrie and Wariston. The men who suffered on the western moorlands, though his name was anathema to them and they revered his executioners, yet stood confusedly on the principles for which he died. The best of them asked for that spiritual liberty he had pled for, and resisted that constraining of men's consciences he had warred against. But the evil had been wrought. Fanaticism had raised a counter-fanaticism, and the struggle had to continue till both were dead of their wounds. The way was prepared for the long lack-lustre régime of eighteenth-century Scotland, when the Kirk was ossified into a thing of forms and dogmas, and civil government sank to a dull and corrupt servitude to the powers of the moment. The spiritual fires of the Covenant had burned too murkily to be allowed to last, and the clear flame of Montrose had gone from a world that was not worthy of it. We can look back upon that tangled era and judge both parties without bitterness. Argyll's monument stands close to Montrose's in St. Giles's, and the most fervent admirer of the latter can admit the value of the tradition bequeathed by the founders of the Kirk. But it must not be forgotten that that tradition, which has at once educated and ennobled their countrymen, was a by-product, and was never the chief aim of the pre-1660 Covenanters. For that enduring work, the liberty of the Church and the elevation of the lowliest citizen to the dignity of an immortal soul, Montrose laboured as zealously as they. In their declared and paramount objects, which were the establishment of a theocracy above any civil power and an inquisition over every man's conscience, they failed utterly, and in their failure brought their land to the last misery and degradation.

The history of Scotland was written first by the divines and then by the Whigs, so it is small wonder that Montrose

L*

has fared badly. A kind of literary convention arose, according to which the most pagan of Edinburgh lawyers, when he took pen in hand, thought it his duty to pay tribute to the Solemn League and its abettors. It is only within recent generations that the balance has been redressed.[1] Hagiology is not an exact science, and that of the Covenant, born in frenzy and confusion, and nurtured in bitterness, has not withstood the slow sapping of a fuller knowledge and a more critical temper; yet it was able for the better part of two centuries to hide from his countrymen the rarity and majesty of Montrose's character. But popular tradition was more just. The fame of the great marquis in the Lowlands seems always to have been attended by a kind of respect. Stories of his humanity, his beauty, and his tragic fate were handed down—a curious interlude in a memory of blood and suffering. Lowland legend never gave him the name of " persecutor," and he never sat at that grim tavern-board in hell with the " fierce Middleton, and the dissolute Rothes, and the crafty Lauderdale."[2] It would be strange if he had, for these were the men who brought him to his death. To royalist and Jacobite Scotland he became an almost mythical figure, little understood, and valued chiefly, perhaps, as the legendary victor over the Campbells. " The banes of a loyal and a gallant Grahame hae long rattled in their coffin for vengeance on thae Dukes of Guile and Lords for Lorn."[3] As for Celtic Scotland, she has taken him to her heart. Sir Ewen Cameron of Lochiel " had Montrose always in his mouth." In the account of the proceedings of the Estates on December 3, 1689, it is recorded: " That which gave the late Viscount of Dundee so much credit with, and authority over them,

[1] Burnet, as the Hamilton champion, was of course hostile (cf. Hist. of his Own Time (1724), I., 38). Later writers, like Laing, Brodie, and Hill Burton, have been uniformly unfavourable, and Hallam repeats baseless charges without examination. Even Hume Brown, for so just a writer, is curiously carping in his references. To Charles Knight, Montrose was only a skilful actor " playing his heroic rôle to perfection "; Godwin considered that " he possessed the temper of the commander of a gang of pirates "; to Mackenzie he was a " vain-glorious butcher "; to Dr. Burns, the editor of Wodrow, he is " that infamous ruffian but eminent loyalist." The reaction began with Lingard and Lord Stanhope, and the most recent historians, such as Gardiner and Lang and Mathieson, have done ample justice to " the most sympathetic figure in Scottish history."

[2] " Wandering Willie's Tale " in Redgauntlet.

[3] Garschattachin in Rob Roy. Sir Walter took the phrase from some satirical verses of Alexander Craig, quoted in Scotstarvet's Staggering State of Scots Statesmen.

though he understood not their language nor was of their country, was his name and relation to the great Marquis of Montrose, for whose memory these Highlanders have all imaginable respect and veneration, and believe that fortune and success was entailed on that name of Graham."[1] To the Highlands he was their chosen knight, the only Lowlander who has ever entered the sacred circle of Gaelic folk-tale and song. Under him the Celt reached his apotheosis, and for one short year held the Saxon in the hollow of his hand. Clan rivalries have been forgotten in the homage to a racial hero. Said an old gillie on the Beauly: " My name is Campbell, but my heart is with the great Montrose."[2]

On the political side Montrose was a modern man, as modern as Burke and Canning, and speaking a language far more intelligible to our ears than that of the Butes and Dundases of a later Scotland. The seventeenth century produced two curiously premature characters in the great Marquis and Sir George Mackenzie;[3] but Mackenzie, lawyer-like, made a sharp distinction between theory and practice, and while his theory was modern his practice was of the Dark Ages; whereas Montrose knew no cleavage between thoughts and deeds. Most great men have been in advance of their day. Some have had the insight to see several stages ahead and have tried to expedite the wheel of change; some have thrown out ideas which were to fructify afterwards in a form of which they did not dream. Montrose was before his time, not from paradox or from hurry, but because almost alone in his age he looked clearly at the conditions of all government, and, having formed his conclusions, was not deterred by prudence or self-interest from acting upon them. As we have seen, he was notably free from contemporary prejudices. He had none of the current belief in Divine Right; he had no excessive reverence for a king as such, and very little for a nobility; he would not have shrunk from the views of Cromwell's Ironsides as to the historical origin of the peerage, which so scandalized the decorous soul of Richard Baxter.[4] He was willing to accept any form of government, provided it fulfilled the requirements which are indispensable in all

---

[1] Terry, *John Graham of Claverhouse*, 12 *n.*
[2] Lang, III., 117 *n.*
[3] For an acute study of Mackenzie's modernism, see Andrew Lang, *Sir George Mackenzie: His Life and Times* (1909).
[4] *Reliquiæ Baxterianæ* (1696), 51.

governments; and these he defined with an acumen and a precision which cannot be challenged.

Statesmanship demands two gifts—the conception of wise ends and the perception of adequate means. The first Montrose possessed in the highest degree, the second scarcely at all. He was a most fallible politician, and he was without skill in the game of parliamentary intrigue. He did not read the temper of the people with the accuracy of Argyll, or the possibilities of the moment with the profound sagacity of Cromwell. He was an optimist about his dreams; he saw the Lowland peasantry looking for a deliverer, when they regarded him as a destroyer; he did not understand the depths of the antipathy of Saxon to Celt, or how fatally the use of Alasdair's men prejudiced his cause; he looked for loyalty in quarters which knew only self-interest, and courage among those who had it not. Practical statesmanship works essentially by compromises, accepting the second or third best as an instalment, and by slow degrees leading the people to acquiesce in an ideal which they have come to regard as their own creation. It must judge shrewdly the situation of the moment, and know precisely what elements therein are capable of providing the first stage in the great advance. It must have infinite patience, and infinite confidence in the slow processes of time.

Such a gift Montrose did not possess—indeed it may be questioned whether the problem before his age permitted of such evolutionary methods. There was no material to his hand in the shape of a nation at least partially instructed or a group of like-minded colleagues. But he was a statesman, if it be the part of statesmanship to see far ahead and to stand for the hope of the future. He stood for the Scottish democracy against those who would have crushed it and those who betrayed it with a kiss. In views and temperament it is not easy to find his parallel. He had Marlborough's contemptuous superiority to parties, but he lacked his passionless Olympian calm. With his kinsman Claverhouse—*Montrosio novus exoritur de pulvere phœnix*[1]—he had little in common except the power of leadership. There is some resemblance to Ireton in political creed, in his scorn of abstractions, and his belief in the need of a strong central government, monarchical, parliamentary, or both;[2] he shared the same view with Strafford, but, unlike

[1] *Grameid* (S.H.S.), 40.
[2] For Ireton's opinions, see the *Clarke Papers, passim.*

him, he did not come to regard monarchical and parliamentary authority as mutually exclusive. He never relinquished his doctrine of a just balance, and if in his last years he was compelled to put the emphasis on the royal power, it was for the same reason as Sir Thomas More was forced into opposition to Henry VIII.—because the balance had been unduly depressed.

The truest kinship is perhaps with the troubled humanity of Cromwell. The Lord Protector fought for " the poor godly people "; Montrose for the plain folk without any qualification. Both were tolerant, both were idealists, striving for something which their age could not give them. Montrose had one obstacle in his way above all others, and that was Scotland. Her jealous nationalism was not ripe, even had the century been ripe, for his far-sighted good sense. She was still hugging to her breast her own fantastic creations, her covenants, her barren survivals, her peculiar royalism, still prepared to sacrifice peace and fortune to her pride. If Cromwell shipwrecked upon the genial materialism of England, Montrose split upon the rock of the sterile conservatism of his own land. Scotland was not ready for civic ideals or luminous reason. She had not found the self-confidence which was to give her a far truer and deeper national pride. She had still to tread for long years the path of coarse and earthy compromises, lit by flashes of crazy quixotry, till through suffering and poverty she came at last to find her own soul. Montrose was in advance of his age, he was in advance of England at her best, but he was utterly and eternally beyond the ken of seventeenth-century Scotland. Yet of the two great idealists he has had the happier destiny. Cromwell, brilliantly successful for the moment, built nothing which lasted. Except for his doctrine of toleration, he left no heritage of political thought which the world has used. The ideals of Montrose, on the other hand, are in the warp and woof of the constitutional fabric of to-day.

The moderate man is slow to appeal to arms. He sees too clearly the values on both sides to commit himself readily to that desperate hazard. But in a revolution it may be the only way. If men's passions are deeply stirred there must be recourse to the last and sternest arbitrament. In such a crisis it is the soldier who turns the scale, whether it be Cæsar's army of Gaul, or the Puritan New Model, or Washington's militia, or Napoleon's Grande Armée, or Garibaldi's Thousand, or Lincoln's citizen levies. A Holles or a Vane may dream his dreams, but it is Cromwell who brings his into being. Montrose both courted and warred against revolution. He desired to preserve the monarchy as against its anarchical assailants, but he was as ardent a revolutionary as Lilburne in his crusade against the existing régime in Scotland, with its dull tyranny of kirk and nobles. For there is a moderation which is in itself a fire, where enthusiasm burns as fiercely for the whole truth as it commonly does for half-truths, where toleration becomes not a policy but an act of religion. Such inspired moderation is usually found in an age of violent contraries. Henri IV. of France possessed it, as did William the Silent. Montrose, like Henri, was the supreme moderate of his age; and, like Henri, he realized that it needs a fiery soul to enforce moderation in a rabble of fanatics and debauchees. In such a strife, the ultimate word can only be spoken by one who is willing to make the ultimate sacrifice. To enter into the kingdom of the spirit a man must take his life in his hands, as martyr or as soldier.

II

As a soldier Montrose ranks by common consent with the greatest of his age, with Cromwell and Condé. The historian of the British army has described him as " perhaps the most brilliant natural military genius disclosed by the Civil War."[1] Like Cromwell, he seems to have learned his art rather by intuition than by experience, for, till his great campaign, his only training was the inglorious Bishops' War. He had never, like Leven or David Leslie, served under eminent foreign generals; he was as unprofessional as Rupert, and, like him, he had that natural eye for country and dispositions, that power of quick resolution and that magnetism of leadership, which discomfited the more prosaic commanders who found themselves his opponents. He had learned the lesson of which his friend, the Cardinal de Retz, has given a famous epitome : " Il n'y a rien dans le monde qui n'ait son moment décisif; et le chef-d'œuvre de la bonne conduite est de connaître et de prendre ce moment."

It has been sometimes urged that it is easy to overpraise Montrose's military capacity, since he usually fought against inferior troops and incompetent generals, and that

[1] Fortescue, *Hist. of the British Army*, I., 228. Sir John Fortescue's other comment, " a woman in emotion and instability," is hardly appropriate to one of the most patient and resolute of military commanders.

on the only occasion on which he met a commander of ability and a seasoned army he was defeated. But the argument does not bear examination. The men he scattered at Tippermuir and Aberdeen were, it is true, raw levies, though present in great numerical superiority; but they were precisely the men with whom he had been victorious in his first campaign, and his conquering Highlanders were of the race which he had routed in 1639, when they fought under Aboyne. At Inverlochy he had against him the best disciplined of the Highland clans, and Auchinbreck had ten times his own experience of war. At Dundee and Auldearn and Alford he faced regular cavalry and foot, the pick of the men who had won renown under Leven in England; and Hurry and Baillie had a high repute among the commanders of the day. Philiphaugh and Carbisdale are too much unlike normal battles to be made the basis for any judgment of one side or the other. No doubt Montrose's Highland and Irish troops, nourished on beef and game, were of a more stalwart physical type than the Lowland second line. But the regular Covenant foot were stout fellows, and they had the priceless advantage of a strict discipline and freedom from the endless clan jealousies. So far as equipment went, Montrose won his victories in the face of crushing odds. His army was always a fluid thing; after every success a large part of it departed with their booty to their homes; more than half his time was spent in the work of shepherding back to his standard the volatile clans.[1] Under such conditions it is hard to make a plan of campaign, and harder still to execute it.

As a strategist he showed an extraordinary eye for country. The tangled passes of the Grampians, little known except in patches to the different clans, were grasped by him as a geographical whole, and he arranged his marches accordingly. He had a boldness, too, which staggered even those inured to mountain warfare, and his flank march before Inverlochy seemed both to friends and foes outside the limits of human power. His incredible speed was a further strategical advantage, for he could march over twenty miles in a single night among snowy mountains, as in his pursuit of Argyll in December 1644; or in thirty-six hours cover sixty miles, with fighting between, as at Dun-

---

[1] Claverhouse had the same trouble up to the eve of Killiecrankie (*Memoirs of Locheill*, 237, etc.). So had Stonewall Jackson with Ashby's horse in the Valley Campaign of 1862 (Henderson, *Stonewall Jackson*, I., 333).

dee. This swiftness, indeed, was apt to be a snare to him. He despised his slower antagonists, and was twice almost caught—at Fyvie and Dundee—before the final surprise came at Philiphaugh. For strategy in the widest sense he was given no scope. He could not plan a campaign to correspond with the king's in England, for his hands were tied by the composition of his army; his Highlanders would not fight south of the Highland Line, and deserted in droves after each victory. In such circumstances there could be no continuity of purpose, and the marvel is that Kilsyth was ever fought. But it is clear that Montrose was fully alive to the need of the larger strategical intention, and that it was only the lack of response from the English side that confined him to mountain warfare. With a force such as Charles repeatedly frittered away, he would have swept these islands from Sutherland to Devon.

In tactics he had in a supreme degree the gift of suiting his scheme of battle to his material, using his horse now as mounted infantry and now as cavalry, and getting full value from the impetuous Highland charge. His power of rapid decision never failed him, and in the stress of fight he could keep his head and alter his arrangements at the shortest notice. As proofs, we have the sudden strengthening of the left wing at Aberdeen, and his rapid dispositions in the hurry of the surprise before Auldearn, as well as the marvellous retreat from Dundee. At leisure he could dispose a battle with great skill, as at Alford, and could defy the ordinary rules of war with success, as at Kilsyth. Kilsyth is, indeed, an interesting case, for there is every reason to believe that Montrose deliberately chose what seemed to be the worse position. He was probably convinced that the Covenanters, finding themselves with the hill in their favour, would take some foolish risk and so play into his hands, and he counted on the power of his Highlanders to charge up a slope and arrive unwearied at the top. He knew, too, the value of the sudden word in the strain of battle to turn the tide, and his insight into the hearts of fighting men was at least as great a factor in his success as his tactical skill.

More notable than even his gifts for strategy and tactics was his unique power of leadership. He discerned the fighting value of the clans, and welded into an army the most heterogeneous materials on earth. Hitherto it had seemed impossible to band two minor septs together for one purpose for more than a week; Montrose united the whole central Highlands in a campaign of a year's duration. Nor did he win this strange authority by any pandering to the vices of savage warfare. Except for the sack of Aberdeen, there is no stain on his record. He refused to turn the captured cannon on the fugitives of Tippermuir; he tried to check the slaughter after Inverlochy; he punished looting severely, as at Glasgow; he observed scrupulously the etiquette of war; he never put a prisoner to death, not even when his dearest friends were being murdered by the Estates. He did not stoop, as his opponents did, to the methods of the dirk and the ambuscade. It should be remembered that he was no fire-eating giant like Alasdair, but a slim young man of middle height, somewhat grave and courtly in his manner, and fonder of a book than a drinking-bout. Yet no iron-fisted Hercules ever kept a wilder force in a sterner discipline. The man who, at Dundee, could draw off half-tipsy troops in the middle of a sack in the face of a superior enemy, and lead them, weary as they were, for thirty miles in the thick of night to the safety of the hills, had miraculous gifts as a leader. We may search for long in the annals of war to find an equal achievement.

Cromwell also had that moral authority which fused the forces under him into a single weapon for his hand to direct. But Cromwell, except at Dunbar, fought with numbers on his side, and he had the supreme advantage that his men were largely bound already by the tie of a strong religious faith. For Montrose there was no such aid to discipline. It was personal authority, and personal authority alone, that kept Gordon and Macdonald in the same firing line. The two great captains were fated never to meet, and their relative prowess must remain in the realm of hypothesis. The chief historian of the epoch rates Montrose the higher. " On the battlefield Montrose had all Cromwell's promptness of seizing the chances of the strife, together with a versatility in varying his tactics according to the varying resources of the enemy, to which Cromwell could lay no claim, while his skill as a strategist was certainly superior to that of his English contemporary."[1] Probably the judgment is just. At any rate, we can say that Montrose performed feats not inferior to Cromwell's best, with weaker resources and against greater odds.

Scale must not be confused with kind. Since Montrose's day the technical equipment of the soldier has been incon-

[1] Gardiner, *Civil War*, II., 351.

ceivably enlarged, armies have grown into armed nations,
the advance in the variety and precision of weapons has
made every problem more intricate. But modern inventions, which make levies of millions possible, have provided
in an equal ratio the facilities for leading them. Military
genius remains in its essentials the same, and it is still
possible in this respect to compare the soldiers of all ages,
and to rank one who commanded a few thousands in a
moorland war among the masters of the art. In virtue of
his achievement, Montrose must stand as the foremost
Scottish man of action—perhaps the only Scot who
approaches the confines of that small inner circle of the
profession of arms, which, among men of our own blood,
contains no other names than Marlborough, Wellington, and
Lee.

III

Few careers have such romantic unity. In one aspect
he is the complete paladin, full of courtesy and grace, a
Volcker of Alsace with his sword-fiddlebow, whose every
stroke is a note of music. He wins fights against odds, and
scribbles immortal songs in his leisure, and dies in the end
like some antique hero, with the lights burning low in the
skies and the stage darkened. In another he is the thinker,
who read, as no one else did, the riddle of his times, and
preached a doctrine of government which had to wait for
nearly two hundred years till it found an audience. In
that fierce seventeenth century, when men died for half-
truths or less, when the great forces of the State were apt
to be selfish competitors for material gain, and the idealists
were driven into the wilds or overseas—in that gross and
turbid age he lit the lamp of pure duty and pure reason.
There were those who followed duty, but it was too often
blindly. There were those who loved reason, but they
either retired from the struggle or, like Falkland, fought
with the air of martyrs rather than of soldiers. Montrose
was armed and mailed Reason, Philosophy with its sword
unsheathed. He is a far rarer type than the quietist who
has fascinated historians, or than the grim Ironside, " the
most formidable of combinations, the practical mystic."
He had all the grave lucidity of a Falkland, but he had
none of his sad despair, for he went out joyfully to do
battle for his faith. He was as stubborn and passionate
in his cause as any Ironside, but he was no fanatic; he was
not even any kind of mystic. He saw life clearly and
calmly, and his spiritual force did not come, as it often

comes, from a hectic imagination or a fevered brain. The springs of his being were a pellucid reasonableness of soul, joined to a power of absorption in duty which is commonly found only in the ranks of fanaticism.

It is a figure which must always haunt those who travel the rough roads of Scottish history. We see him in the brave clothes which still dazzle us in his portraits, the long, north-country face, the broad brow, the inscrutable grey eyes. He is thinking, wondering, brooding on the needs of his land, while others are preying on them. Then he reaches his conclusions, and, with something between the certainty of the thinker and the enthusiasm of the boy, he sets out on his desperate errand. We see him in battle, a flush on his cheek, a youthful ardour in his eye, but his mouth set like iron. We see him among his friends, conquering all hearts with his wit and grace. We see him in triumph and in failure, careless of self, his course set unfalteringly towards his dreams, carrying, in Keats's words, " an awful warmth about his heart like a load of immortality." He is always very human, very much the man, for Alasdair and his kerns would never have followed the ordinary dreamer. And then, when the last blow has been struck, he has neither fears nor reproaches. Clearly and reasonably he states his defence, and when it is flouted and he is condemned to a shameful death, he takes it meekly, knowing something of the fallibility of mankind. The Edinburgh mob is awed into a hush by his appearance; his enemies declared that it was his fine clothes and noble looks; more truly we may read it as that inward vision which is the beatitude of the pure in heart.

No great cause is ever lost or ever won. The battle must always be renewed and the creed restated, and the old formulas, once so potent a revelation, become only dim antiquarian echoes. But some things are universal, catholic, and undying—the souls of which such formulas are the broken gleams. These do not age or pass out of fashion, for they symbolize eternal things. They are the guardians of the freedom of the human spirit, the proof of what our mortal frailty can achieve. Of this happy company Montrose is one. His qualities in the retrospect seem to be drawn to a fine edge of burning light. But, as we wonder and revere, there comes a voice from behind the flame, and awe is changed to wistfulness; for it is a voice of comradeship and joy and youth which " sweetly torments us with invitations to his own inaccessible homes."

INDEX

341